Who's Been Sleeping in Your Head?

Also by Brett Kahr

D. W. Winnicott: A Biographical Portrait (1996)

Forensic Psychotherapy and Psychopathology:
Winnicottian Perspectives (2001)

Exhibitionism (2001)

The Legacy of Winnicott: Essays on Infant and
Child Mental Health (2002)

Who's Been Sleeping in Your Head?

The Secret World of Sexual Fantasies

BRETT KAHR

A MEMBER OF THE
PERSEUS BOOKS GROUP

NEW YORK

Books published by Basic Books are available at special discounts for bulk purchases in the United States by corporations, institutions, and other organizations. For more information, please contact the Special Markets Department at the Perseus Books Group, 2300 Chestnut Street, Suite 200, Philadelphia, PA 19103, or call (800) 255-1514, or e-mail special.markets@perseusbooks.com.

Designed by Timm Bryson
Set in 10.5 point Sabon

Library of Congress Cataloging-in-Publication Data
Kahr, Brett.
  Who's been sleeping in your head? : the secret world of sexual fantasies / Brett Kahr.
      p. cm.
  Rev. ed. of: Sex and the psyche.
  Includes index.
  ISBN 978-0-465-03766-7 (alk. paper)
  1. Sex (Psychology). 2. Sexual fantasies. I. Kahr, Brett. Sex and the psyche. II. Title.

  BF692.K27 2008
  155.3'1—dc22
                                    2007042050

10 9 8 7 6 5 4 3 2 1

Dedicated to Kim

"Half a prayer, half a song"
—*nulli secundus.*

What a man's mind is, that is what he is.
—SAMUEL PEPYS

I guess we all like to know other people's secrets so that
we can live with our own.
—JONATHAN AMES, *WAKE UP, SIR!*

Contents

A Note on Caution
and Confidentiality

He that cannot bear with
other people's passions,
Cannot govern his own.

—BENJAMIN FRANKLIN,
Poor Richard's Almanack

This book contains a great deal of extremely sexually explicit material—literally hundreds and hundreds of sexual fantasies. Some of the intimate fantasies reproduced in these pages may shock you; some may disgust you; some may leave you cold and anesthetized; some may invoke a feeling of pity, contempt, or superiority; but some, if not many, of the fantasies may produce titillation or arousal.

These fantasies derive from the inner recesses of the minds of normal, ordinary British and American adults—men and women, aged eighteen to ninety-plus years old, randomly selected from every British county and every American state, from every social group, from every religious background, and from virtually every profession imaginable, ranging from doctors to dairymen, from bankers to businesswomen, from clerks to clerics, from the overworked to the unemployed. Although a very small proportion of the anonymous respondents in this study will have sought the services of mental health professionals in an outpatient setting from time to time, none suffers from an incapacitating psychotic illness; therefore, these fantasies cannot be readily dismissed as the rantings of the emotionally unwell. Every single one of the men and women whose fantasies appear in this book leads a reasonably healthy life. None of the participants resides in either a prison or a psychiatric institution. All of the authors of these fantasies live, at liberty, in the community.

None of these fantasies has ever appeared before in print. These original creations of the British and American mind have remained safely confined inside the heads of the participants in my large-scale research study up until now. In fact, hitherto, approximately 95 percent of the subjects had never revealed their sexual fantasies to another living soul, even to their long-term partners—marital or otherwise—or to their closest friends.

Some of the participants in this research project submitted their fantasies in writing, while others spoke their fantasies into a mini-disc recording machine; these different methods of data collection account, in large measure, for the wide range of stylistic differences in the fantasies themselves. All of the fantasies appear in their original form; although, in the case of those women and men who submitted their fantasies in writing, I have corrected some spelling errors that might have detracted from the experience of reading; and likewise, I have from time to time inserted some judiciously placed commas and semicolons, merely to facilitate the flow of the sentences. Otherwise, I have endeavored to preserve precisely the language used by the authors themselves.

One notable change has been made to all the texts: I have altered the names and geographical locations of the contributors in the interests of confidentiality. The extremely frank and forthright sexual fantasies in this book appear with the express written permission of the British and American men and women who generated them. Each of the thousands and thousands of research participants signed an agreement, prepared by one or more specialist lawyers, which would allow me to publish their fantasies, providing that I did not reveal any biographical information that could readily or reasonably identify them. For instance, I would not be permitted to write: "This fantasy appears courtesy of Mrs. Jane Doe, a fifty-one-year-old accountant and mother of two who lives at 850 Broadway, Topeka, Kansas." In a great many cases, I never knew the real names of the authors in the first place, particularly of those women and men who responded to a detailed, computer-administered questionnaire that guaranteed anonymity. As for those adults whom I interviewed face-to-face, many of these research participants may well have told me their real names when we first met, and in these instances, I have certainly altered their identities. I remain honor-bound to preserve the confidentiality of those who shared their most intimate thoughts as part of a psychological research project, not only for reasons of clinical confidentiality, but also because at this time, we still treat sexual fantasies—especially private masturbatory fantasies—as a relatively taboo subject in our cultural discourse. Some of the participants in my interview study may have elected to introduce themselves pseudonymously, giving a false name.

As a Registered Psychotherapist practicing in Great Britain, I have spent many years in full-time clinical practice, and during this time, I have worked with a large number of individuals who have entrusted their most private stories to me. Patients or clients undergoing psychotherapy both *demand* and *deserve* complete confidentiality when they seek therapeutic assistance so that they can reveal the full extent of their often troubling histories without fear of reprisal or public exposure. There may be occasions when confidentiality must be breached in order to protect all parties concerned. For instance, if a patient informed me of a well-developed plot to kill the British Sovereign, then my professional Code of Ethics would require me to report this matter to the appropriate authorities. Fortunately, in more than two decades of clinical work, I have not had to do this.

In the spirit of recognizing the importance of privacy, particularly in this era of CCTV footage and Googling, I have refrained from using any *detailed* sexual fantasies of patients and clients with whom I work or have worked in a formal psychotherapeutic capacity. The consulting room has, of course, served as the indispensable laboratory in which I have learned about the manner and the mechanisms of sexual fantasy. Owing to the strictures of clinical confidentiality, however—the very bedrock that allows for secret revelations to emerge in psychoanalytical sessions—the sexual fantasies of my patients must remain a private matter. Thus, apart from brief, unidentifiable vignettes, all of the stories which follow derive not from my clinical work, but from my research work with individuals who offered their informed consent, and who allowed me to conduct intensive psychodiagnostic research consultations with a view to publishing their fantasies, with the understandable proviso that I would refrain from releasing either their names or their addresses.

Introduction: On the Couch at 7:00 A.M.

Careless lust stirs up a desperate courage,
Planting oblivion, beating reason back.
— WILLIAM SHAKESPEARE,
Venus and Adonis

For more than twenty years, I have worked as a psychotherapist. In other words, I am one of the tens of thousands of mental health professionals in Great Britain who devotes his or her daytime life to the treatment of people who struggle with, or suffer from, a wide range of psychological problems. I completed a lengthy training and apprenticeship that included both university-based study in clinical theory and research methods and supervised therapeutic work with patients in psychiatric hospitals and community mental-health settings. As part of that training, I also underwent intensive psychoanalysis myself. All of this helped to prepare me for my profession. Though I have studied and worked predominantly in Great Britain, I also undertook a training fellowship in the United States, and I have worked with a large number of American émigrés in London; I therefore have experience treating the mental health issues of both Britons and Americans.

I have a small, discreet office in London—a consulting room—hidden away in a tiny mews courtyard, complete with a couch and several comfy chairs. I arrive at my office quite early, at 6:45 A.M., in time to open the windows for a blast of fresh air and to plump up the cushions; and then, throughout the day, starting at 7:00 A.M., women and men of all ages, shapes, and complexions come to see me for private appointments to discuss their most intimate psychological concerns.

1

Often, people burst into tears in my room as they reveal their most shame-laden secrets and confront their most heart-wrenching decisions. Some suffer from extreme mental illness, while others function quite well in their *public* lives, maintaining families and jobs, but might, in *private,* be addicted to cocaine, or use prostitutes. Some of these brave individuals harbor aching secrets, kept well hidden from their husbands, wives, or partners. Some have secrets that they keep even from themselves.

Inevitably, the presenting problems involve sexuality in some way. At 7:00 A.M. on one day of the week, I might meet with "Mrs. Smith," who admits that she and her husband have not had sexual contact with one another for the last *thirty* years. This may seem shocking, but in my line of work I hear stories of sexual anesthesia in long-term marriages and partnerships quite often. All of Mrs. Smith's female friends believe that she and "Mr. Smith" have the perfect marriage, but, in fact, she hates him for his many infidelities; and now that the children have finally left home, she wants a divorce. Mrs. Smith wakes up every night in torment because she married Mr. Smith while still a teenager, straight from her parents' house, and so has never lived alone in her entire life. The thought of divorcing her philandering husband fills her not with relief or anticipation, but rather with dread. Clutching clumps of tissues from a box on the bottom shelf of my bookcase, positioned just a few inches away from the patient's chair, Mrs. Smith pleads with me to tell her what she should do. My heart breaks knowing that I cannot offer such direct advice to Mrs. Smith. Nor would I. We both know that we will have to explore her dilemma over a period of time in order to find the right solution, because although she hates her husband and wants to run away, she also still has a deep-seated attachment to him and feels as though she cannot function without him.

Mrs. Smith leaves at 7:50 A.M. In fact, I see all of my individual patients or clients for exactly fifty minutes, following a practice developed by Sigmund Freud, the founder of psychoanalysis, in Vienna in the 1920s. He decided to reduce the length of session times from sixty minutes to fifty in order to accommodate an American psychiatric trainee who had come to Austria specifically to learn his new method for alleviating psychological distress. This practice of the "fifty-minute hour" has sustained itself worldwide since then, and I must confess that fifty minutes seems just about right. This period of time readily allows the patient and psychotherapist to explore and examine important aspects of the patient's story in detail without becoming either overly burdened or exhausted. (In America, many of my colleagues have adopted a forty-five-minute hour, but in Great Britain the fifty-minute hour has remained sacrosanct.)

Between 7:50 A.M. and 7:59 A.M., I have a brief nine-minute break before my next client arrives. At this time I collect my thoughts, check my telephone messages, and perhaps have a sip of water or a piece of an apple. Owing to the early start, I rarely have time for a proper breakfast, but somehow, after many years of this routine, my body seems to have adjusted to this physiological arrangement; in fact, although I always enjoy my food, the thought of a full English breakfast before work leaves me rather queasy. Psychotherapists begin working with patients very early in the morning so that people can come for appointments before the commencement of their own workday. Surprisingly, 7:00 A.M. and 8:00 A.M. prove to be extremely popular times, and although some might balk, I find it completely natural to be seated in my office chair at 6:45 A.M., in preparation for the bell, having already reviewed my notes and turned on the central heating—or, on rare hot British summer days, the electric fan.

At 8:00 A.M. sharp, the buzzer sounds again, and this time the soft-spoken and socially maladroit "Mr. Jones" comes into my consulting room. Unlike Mrs. Smith, who sits across from me in a leather chair, Mr. Jones, who attends several times a week, chooses to lie down on the couch, just as Freud's patients would have done a hundred years ago. He finds that he can talk to me more frankly and with greater concentration if he reclines, facing away from me. I sit behind the couch in a red-leather tub chair, listening. Unlike Mrs. Smith, who has just celebrated her thirty-fifth wedding anniversary, Mr. Jones has never married; in fact, he has never even had a girlfriend, nor, for that matter, a boyfriend. Mr. Jones calls himself "the only fifty-year-old virgin in London"—he has never had sex, not even a kiss or a fumble. Mr. Jones's erotic life revolves exclusively around his daily masturbation. He has often explained to me that he prefers masturbation to sex with a partner, but sometimes, when he feels more vulnerable, he adds, "But of course, as a virgin, I wouldn't really know, would I?" When he masturbates, he will invariably fantasize at the same time, but in spite of gentle attempts on my part to elicit the content of his masturbatory fantasies, Mr. Jones will not tell me anything. I have often wondered whether he has fantasies that, if put into practice, would land him in prison. Instead, Mr. Jones lives in a different sort of prison—a mental prison—tormented, lonely, and full of shame. His difficulties relating to me in an open, relaxed, and engaging manner may well be indicative of his wider interpersonal struggles, as all his office colleagues shun him, and he never receives even a single invitation to any lunches, parties, pub crawls, or other communal gatherings.

Although I have changed the names of "Mrs. Smith" and "Mr. Jones," I have not manufactured their stories; in fact, Mrs. Smith and Mr. Jones would be surprised to realize that I have met many other patients over the years who present with exactly the same sorts of struggles regarding intimacy and sexuality. People often joke that "shrinks" have an obsession with sex—this may be true, perhaps; but if it does prove to be the case that we talk about sex and think about sex more than dental hygienists or traffic wardens do, you cannot blame us, because we hear about sex, *especially sex gone wrong,* in our private offices and clinics on a daily basis.

I try not to listen in an ordinary fashion but rather with my "third ear"—a term introduced by one of Sigmund Freud's most creative disciples, the Viennese psychoanalyst Dr. Theodor Reik, who reasoned that *anyone* can listen with *two* ears, but the psychotherapist must listen with *three,* concentrating not only on what the patient says, but also on what the patient does not say. The psychotherapist must attempt at all times to decipher the secret meanings of the patient's dilemmas, meanings which remain obscure even to the patient.

For instance, let us consider the case of "Mr. Fitch," who invariably spends the first fifteen minutes of his weekly psychotherapy sessions ranting about "that bastard Gunderson," a very successful colleague who has just received a hefty pay raise, a whopping Christmas bonus, and a pat on the back from Mr. Fitch's boss, the redoubtable head of finance. Fitch becomes so embroiled in a repetitive, compulsive rampage against the bastard Gunderson that he cannot recognize his own envy, his own feelings of inadequacy, and his own experience of failure, which, in truth, have little or nothing to do with Gunderson. Poor Mr. Gunderson becomes merely the vehicle through which Mr. Fitch discharges his own undiluted rage. But by spending all his time attacking Gunderson, Mr. Fitch protects both his conscious sense of self-esteem and the fragile parts of his own mind from having to face the painful reality that, for various reasons, he has not achieved what he wishes; nor has he received the adulation that he craves. By listening with the "third ear," I endeavor to help Mr. Fitch hear himself. He spends so much time fuming in an unthoughtful manner that he cannot actually listen to himself at all; and so I become, in part, a mirror to his soul, and together, through gentle, sustained conversation, we try to understand more and more about the way in which the unsuspecting Gunderson becomes a reincarnation of Fitch's older brother, "Howard," another "bastard," who obtained better grades at school, nabbed the pretty girl who lived next door, and now works as a glamorous television director. Eventually, as our weeks and months of psychotherapeutic work unfold, Mr. Fitch discovers that, actually, Gunderson might be "all right—a decent bloke, in fact"—and that through identification with Gunderson's creative capacities, Fitch might learn to internalize some of his archrival's talents instead of experiencing him as Lucifer incarnate. To our mutual joy, Mr. Fitch has gradually begun to demonstrate fledgling creativity; eventually, he too at last received a pat on the back at bonus time for his clever new work initiative.

For most of my career, I have worked principally with individuals, people like Mrs. Smith, Mr. Jones, and Mr. Fitch, on a one-to-one basis, but some time ago I decided to undertake five further years of specialist postgraduate training in "marital psychotherapy." This development grew out of my work with young adult men and women who had suffered brain damage and who needed an enormous amount of care from their aging parents. From time to time, I would meet with the elderly parents, more than 80 percent of whom had extremely strained marriages. The burden of caring for a child with a handicap often takes a toll, and I felt extremely unskilled in knowing how best to support these parents in their marital distress while also helping them with their caretaking capacities. It had become increasingly clear to me how many of my patients without overt handicaps suffered with difficult marriages as well, and I wanted to improve my ability to help.

Although fully employed as a psychotherapist at the time, working exclusively with individuals, I managed to juggle the extensive postgraduate training requirements, and I eventually qualified in marital psychotherapy—a highly specialized branch of mental health work. I thus joined the tiny band of only thirty or so other colleagues in Great Britain who have completed this exhaustive (and sometimes exhausting) training. Although I received my professional registration as a diplomate in "Marital Psychotherapy," any new student graduating in the field will receive licensure in "Couple Psychotherapy." Because we now work with an increasing number of people who cohabit without ever having exchanged wedding rings, my colleagues and I decided that the concept of "Marital Psychotherapy" seemed somewhat outdated. The term "Couple Psychotherapy" better reflected the reality. We also find ourselves working with more gay and lesbian couples—and though many do regard themselves as married, many others prefer to describe themselves as living in a committed couple partnership. So, although I hold official registration as a "Couple Psychotherapist," I often slip and refer to myself by the more antique term of "Marital Psychotherapist," as I have treated most of my couples under this arguably outdated rubric.

Working with couples has made me become even more concerned with sexual matters than before. An individual patient might spend a whole fifty-minute session telling me how much she hates her evil, persecutory boss; or she might launch into a monologue about the horrors of her teenage children. But with couples, one cannot avoid the question of sexuality. I have now seen dozens and dozens of couples in consultation, and I would be hard pressed to recall any couple who presented for marital psychotherapy with a healthy sex life. As we may not fully appreciate, sex might be the most sensitive barometer of the solidity of the relationship between husband and wife or between two lovers; and when the gremlins of infidelity or inattentiveness or other forms of cruelty enter the relationship, then the sexual life will suffer as a consequence. Many partners turn in desperation to skimpy lingerie, scented candles, imported bath oils, and other such paraphernalia in a hopeful effort to reignite passion in the bedchamber, but as any couple psychotherapist will realize, true sexual excitement returns only when both spouses have had an opportunity to talk through the multiple grievances that have accumulated over the months and years. Often, this healing process occurs only with the guidance of a mental health professional. As one of my marital patients exclaimed years ago, "It takes two to break a marriage, and three to mend it."

I have now reached a point in my career where almost nothing that a couple tells me will either surprise or shock me, because I have found that when marriages or relationships do begin to collapse, they tend to do so in quite predictable ways. Consider the following real-life couples, characteristic of the casebook of the workaday couple psychotherapist. In the interests of confidentiality, I have, of course, altered the surnames of the couples.

- "Mr. and Mrs. Aronson" stopped having sex after the birth of their first child. Mrs. Aronson spends so much time breastfeeding little "Alison" that she cannot bear the thought of her husband touching her increasingly sore nipples. Mr. Aronson has reported that he feels jealous of his own daughter, even though he knows that he has had much more intimate, adult access to his wife's body. The closeness that has emerged between Mrs. Aronson and her daughter has served as an unconscious reminder of Mr. Aronson's own feelings of boyhood exclusion following the birth of his baby sister.

- "Mr. and Mrs. Bentley" have stopped having sex because Mr. Bentley has started having an affair with his wife's sister "Berenice." The secret has finally emerged, and Mrs. Bentley has now threatened divorce. During psychotherapy, it became increasingly evident that Mr. Bentley bedded his sister-in-law not because of a primary sexual attraction to Berenice, but, in large measure, as a calculated means of exacting revenge upon his wife. He had come to regard her, in fact, as an increasingly narcissistically preoccupied and castrating woman who no longer lavished love and affection on him as she had done so readily during their courtship.

- "Mr. and Mrs. Cameron" no longer enjoy sexual relations because Mrs. Cameron has recently begun to be haunted by memories of early child sexual abuse at the hands of her father. Now, as a grown woman, she cannot bear the sight of Mr. Cameron's naked body, especially his penis, as she believes that both Mr. Cameron and her father have identical-looking genitalia.

- "Mr. Dean" and "Mr. Drummond," a homosexual couple, have ceased having sex because Mr. Drummond has become obsessed with the films of a certain gay pornography "superstar" and spends all of his free time masturbating to gay videos, so much so that he can no longer bear being touched by Mr. Dean. Mr. Drummond enjoys highly sadomasochistic homosexual pornography, and he fears that his partner would be horrified if he knew the truth. Mr. Dean recently discovered Mr. Drummond's stash of pornography, and this precipitated both a huge marital row and a referral for couple psychotherapy.

These four vignettes represent only a tiny handful of the many ways in which sexual relationships may be attacked by changes and transitions, sometimes by traumas, and sometimes by fantasies, that exert a deleterious impact on the marital or couple situation.

When we complain about our lives to our friends and families, we often find ourselves moaning about our credit card bills, or about our incompetent office colleagues, or about the Republican Party; but when we visit the psychotherapist, the agonies become infinitely more intimate. I spend my working days listening to grown men and women, and also to postpubescent teenagers, who struggle with problems they find so embarrassing that they can barely articulate them. Clients might come to talk about their inability to achieve an erection, or their disgust about fellatio, or their desperate need to have sex at least five times a day to the exclusion of all else, or their fear of vaginal penetration, or their hatred of the hair on their bodies, or what have you—sexual concerns and anxieties that turn their otherwise healthy minds into dungeons of despair.

Not only do my psychotherapy patients talk about their difficulties negotiating the anatomical practicalities of sex (e.g., "I rubbed her clitoris all night, and still she couldn't come," or "He ejaculated all over my face, and I couldn't wait to wash it off"), but some of the more bold patients in my practice will also talk to me about their most private sexual fears and their most hidden sexual fantasies, those scenarios that flash through their heads in an often unbidden and unexpected fashion.

Sexual fears are often quite basic. I shall never forget "Miss Stein," a highly attractive woman, aged twenty-eight years, who carried herself with all the slinkiness of Nicole Kidman. Simply looking at her, one would naturally have assumed that Miss Stein had an enjoyable sex life. But in spite of the fact that large numbers of men made passes at her on a daily basis, this young woman announced to me one day that she could not bear to be touched and found physical contact abhorrent. Miss Stein had no memory of having suffered early childhood sexual abuse; instead, she traced her detestation of even cuddling to her memories of her overbearing mother. She managed to feel psychologically safe as an adult only by avoiding physical intimacy completely.

People's sexual fantasies, like their sex lives, become frequent topics of conversation in my office. Sexual fantasies can serve not only as a source of deep pleasure but also as a cause for great shame. Often, our fantasies will stimulate both excitement and revulsion simultaneously, and this produces a great deal of psychological turmoil. As a psychotherapist, I listen to my clients reporting a goodly number of sexual fantasies that help them to achieve a thundering orgasm, but I also listen to those that cause despair. After nearly a quarter of a century of clinical practice, I sometimes believe that I have heard every possible fantasy imaginable, until of course the next patient comes along and reveals an erotic fantasy that I never knew existed. Throughout my working day, my patients entrust me with a veritable cornucopia of sexual fantasies, generated in the depths of their minds, sometimes stimulating pleasure, but more often creating an acute sense of self-loathing and disgust:

- When "Mrs. Elphinstone" masturbates, she thinks about her elder brother, and also about her seventeen-year-old nephew, "Claude," both of whom have really hirsute chests, which she adores. She cannot bear to think about her husband, the smooth-chested "Mr. Elphinstone," who, as she puts it, has the body of a "skinned chicken." Mrs. Elphinstone, a staunch Catholic, believes that she will go to hell for having these thoughts, but the moment her fingers penetrate her vagina during masturbation, the thoughts of her hairy-chested brother and nephew whoosh into her mind, causing her simultaneous pleasure and pain. According to Mrs. Elphinstone, "I know I should be relaxed about these things—it's the twenty-first century, after all—but I feel really dirty and think I must be perverted. I mean, it wouldn't be so bad if I lusted after a hairy-chested builder, but why my brother and nephew? Do you think I'm mad?"
- When "Mr. Franciosi" penetrates his wife, he thinks about the nineteen-year-old female office assistant at work. Once, when he saw her bending over the photocopy machine, he caught a glimpse of her underwear, and he found himself sporting an instant erection. "It's classic, I know," confessed Mr. Franciosi, "but I got such a stiffy that I had to nip out to the toilet to take care of it then and there." Now, during sex with "Mrs.

Franciosi," he thinks of nothing else but a "good hard-core fuck with this girl, from behind, over the photocopier." Mr. Franciosi, a faithful husband for nineteen years, burst into tears in my office, explaining that, although he has never cheated on his wife, and never would, the young woman from his office has begun to obsess him completely. Often he cannot concentrate on his financial projections. He also believes that he has become "mentally unfaithful" to Mrs. Franciosi, especially as he now relies exclusively on the mental image of his junior colleague in order to obtain an erection when in bed with his wife.

- When "Mr. Grigoriev" leaves his office in Euston, North London, he often makes a detour to a pornography shop in nearby King's Cross in order to check out the latest selection of gay DVDs, videos, and magazines. He always makes his furtive purchases with cash, as he does not want any evidence of his entertainment preferences to appear on his credit card statements, lest his wife, "Mrs. Grigoriev," should discover his passion for films about homosexual bondage and anal penetration. Mr. Grigoriev hates sex with his wife, and now, after eight years of marriage, which has nonetheless produced two beautiful children, he tells me, "I have made my bed, literally speaking, and now I must lie in it. Besides, I would never, never, ever leave my kids." After two or three initial years of relatively good sex with Mrs. Grigoriev, the bloom began to disappear, and his long-standing homosexual urges, present since his mid-adolescence, started to recolonize his mind. Now, whenever he fantasizes, Mr. Grigoriev masturbates to scenes from the videos and magazines that he has purchased at King's Cross in London. He keeps them hidden in a box of gardening supplies and pesticides in the dirty garage of his house, which his wife never enters. When he came to see me for an appointment on Friday, July 8, 2005, only one day after the horrific terrorist explosion near King's Cross station on July 7, Mr. Grigoriev emitted an agonizing wail: "Jesus Christ, I go to King's Cross a couple of times a month to buy this filth . . . this filth which is jeopardizing my marriage. If I had been at King's Cross just a few hours earlier, I could have got myself blown to pieces, and for what? For some disgusting pornography?"

I suspect that the fantasies I learn about may well be very different from the type that we might share with our friends or with our sexual partners. In this era of seeming sexual enlightenment, it costs us little to admit, in public, our passions for film stars or pop stars. In one episode of the television program *Sex and the City*, the young female protagonists compare sexual fantasies. One of the women asks the others to name their greatest sexual fantasy, and the others all respond, simultaneously: "Russell Crowe." Nowadays, admitting to a fantasy about Russell Crowe hardly constitutes a great risk—many women (and perhaps some men as well) would find the Australian actor very attractive. I tend to refer to this sort of confession as "barroom fantasy" or "pub fantasy," the sort that we would not hesitate to share with our contemporaries in a social setting. When I hear about fantasies in the consulting room, I tend to learn about something much more private, much more shameful, much more insidious, such as in the case of the woman who did become aroused by Russell Crowe, but only by the thought of being raped by him to the point of bleeding—something she certainly had not divulged to her girlfriends in *Sex and the City*–style.

Fantasies can provide untold ecstasy, yet many generate pain and despair. The fantasies that I have reported thus far, however, represent only the tip of the iceberg, because although I do hear many different sexual fantasies, the vast majority of my patients, and the vast majority of patients treated by my colleagues, have never reported a sexual fantasy. As one of my patients remarked, "You'll never hear about my masturbatory thoughts, because they are just too awful to share, and you will lose all respect for me."

I have now researched the subject of sexual fantasies for several years. I have collected data on more than 19,000 British sexual fantasies and more than 3,000 American sexual fantasies, much of it through direct, face-to-face interview, and much more through the completion of anonymous, extensive questionnaires, not to mention all of the data that I have accumulated from the clinical consulting room. In the chapters that follow, I explore this terrain, rather like an anthropologist who has stumbled upon a relatively untouched, faraway tribe, in the hope that through an account of my clinical and research journey we will all be able to derive a greater appreciation of what constitutes normal human sexuality, what aspects of human sexuality require professional help and support, and what aspects, if any, demand incarceration. We may find that our fantasies produce suffering at certain times, pleasure at others, may be occasional treats, or may be serious addictions. But we do not yet have a sufficiently clear idea about whether our fantasies may be good for us; they may, in fact, induce the most potent of orgasms, but, if we dwell on Miss Kidman or Mr. Crowe in the process, might this indicate that our relationship at home could be in trouble? These represent only some of the many perplexing questions raised by this study.

It surprises me greatly that I find myself writing a book about the secret psychology of sexual fantasies. I never imagined that this subject would become the focus of my research, but after approximately twenty-five years of clinical work with both healthy and tormented individuals, I could not avoid the subject any longer. It came bounding into my consulting room, most explicitly in my work with long-standing couples. In my London office I have spent many years struggling to understand the secret meaning of our subterranean sexual fantasy world, a world that we tend to keep hidden from our spouses, our partners, our friends, our confessors, and even, from time to time, our very selves. I now wish to bring this hidden world more fully into the open in the hope that doing so will lead to greater understanding of both our sexuality and our humanity.

PART ONE

The Secret Cinema in Our Minds

Once we are destined to live out our lives in the prison of our mind, our one duty is to furnish it well.
— PETER USTINOV, *Photo Finish*

Why We Make Love with the Lights Out

Si dipinge col cervello et non con le mani.
[One paints with the brain, and not the
hands.]

— Michelangelo Buonarotti

Jared and the German DVD

"Jared" leads an extremely enviable life. A twenty-nine-year-old investment banker earning a six-figure salary with equally impressive annual bonuses, he lives in a ritzy penthouse apartment in a fashionable part of town. Dashingly good-looking with a gym-toned six-foot frame, this playboy with an MBA degree has received a great deal of adoration from some truly stunning women throughout his life. After sampling a string of gorgeous girlfriends, several of whom wanted to marry him, Jared finally entered into a very satisfying partnership with twenty-four-year-old "Lucy," a part-time fashion model and actress. Staggeringly beautiful, with a curvaceous figure, Lucy absolutely dotes on Jared, not only because of his satisfying features and winning personality, but also because Jared is the very first man to be able to bring her to orgasm every single time they make love. Lucy's constant praise of Jared, and her effusive appreciation of his sexual techniques, please him enormously, and every morning, after leaving Lucy's apartment en route to his plush office, he revels in his good fortune and his many privileges.

Jared spends most of his evenings with Lucy, enjoying either expensive, romantic suppers à deux or clubbing with their many friends;

however, before he steps out with Lucy for a night of pleasure, Jared always adheres to a very strict and largely predictable routine. At 6:00 P.M., or thereabouts, he tidies the papers on his chrome desk in fastidious fashion, bids good night to his secretary, and then proceeds to work out for forty-five minutes at his local gym—mostly running at very impressive speed on the treadmill. He showers and returns to his home before meeting Lucy at 8:30 P.M.—their usual time for a rendezvous. But though dressed and ready for his evening with Lucy, Jared still has one more activity to perform before he emerges to sample the London nightlife with his enviable girlfriend. In fact, Jared must perform a *secret ritual,* over which he seems to have little control.

After returning from the gym, freshly showered, Jared double-locks the door to his apartment and ensures that he has properly shut the electronically operated metal shutter-curtains surrounding his penthouse picture windows. Next, he pours a very large drink—either a Glenlivet single malt Scotch whisky or some other very expensive brand. Sipping slowly, he dims the lights in his grand reception room with the aid of a remote control. Next, Jared ensures that he has turned down the volume button on his answering machine and that he has switched off his mobile telephone. Having set the atmosphere with immense care and precision, Jared then pops into his kitchen and opens the faux-marble-fronted cupboard containing large canisters of sugar, flour, and other cookery ingredients. From the jar marked "Coffee," Jared removes a plastic bag in which he has secreted three DVDs, which he purchased on a recent business trip to Berlin. Clutching his hidden booty in his hands, he returns to his reception room and perches in front of his overpriced home-entertainment center, a present from some wealthy Japanese clients.

Fortified by his whisky, and confident that he has bolted the doors and drawn the shades, Jared inserts one of his German discs into the machine and begins to unzip the trousers of his black silk designer suit, pushing them down to his ankles, along with his Umbro underpants. As the DVD whirs into starting position, he sinks back into his Chesterfield couch and begins to masturbate. A title card, written in German, appears on the television screen: *Boxen-Frauen* [*Women Who Box*]. Satisfied from the sheer physicality of his earlier workout at the health club, and now slightly buzzed from the booze, Jared can feel all of the stress and tension of his high-powered job begin to seep out of his body as he stares with exquisite concentration at the screen. After the opening credits, underscored with sleazy, synthesized music, two buxom, long-haired women appear on screen, one blonde and one brunette, both in their mid-twenties and dressed in skimpy, shiny, silky boxing outfits, with quite well-worn leather boxing gloves covering their hands. Through the fabric of their tops, Jared can just about make out the contours of their nipples. A male referee blows on a whistle, whereupon the two women begin to dance about, Muhammad Ali–style, hurling well-placed punches at one another's helmeted heads.

The very sight of the boxing gloves immediately causes Jared to become aroused, and as he grips his increasingly erect penis, he pushes away a disturbing thought from his mind: "I never get this hard, this quickly, with Lucy." Soon the film overtakes him, and Jared begins to imagine himself in the front row of the boxing arena, watching beads of perspiration forming on the brows of his boxing Fräuleins, whom he has named, privately, Helga and Ulla, after two physically striking women he met while drinking alone in a hotel bar on his most recent business trip to Germany. As the film progresses, Jared's masturbatory activity reaches fever-pitch, and usually, after ten minutes, he enjoys a climax, which he describes as "the most powerful jerk-off of my life." As Jared remarks: "The explosion is so intense that I can still feel a tingling sensation in the head of my penis for at least twenty minutes afterwards."

After a few more gulps of the Glenlivet malt and a very brisk power-shower—his third of the day—Jared dresses in more casual clothes, and then he meets Lucy in town for supper. He will generally polish off a full bottle of vintage wine with his meal—Lucy does not drink, much to his chagrin—and after supper the couple return to her apartment. Lucy finds herself aroused quite readily, and Jared manages to bring her to orgasm within the first five minutes of lovemaking, simply by massaging her genitals with a lubricant that Lucy keeps on her bedside table. Although Jared finds Lucy's eminently photographable face a delight, he always insists upon turning off the lights in her bedroom, because this helps him to think about Helga and Ulla, the two boxing broads from Berlin. Invoking the mental images of these young women helps Jared to become immediately tumescent, so much so that he speedily dons a condom and starts to penetrate his girlfriend. As Lucy cries out Jared's name, often whispering that she loves him, Jared shushes her gently, because Lucy's vocalizations interfere with the private soundtrack of his secret, inner thoughts. But with the lights turned off, and with Lucy muted, Jared can transport himself to his very own private mental cinema.

As he restages the scenes from the DVD in his mind, Jared imagines himself not in Lucy's bed with the silky sheets, but rather in a noisy, crowded German boxing ring. After much practice, Jared has learned to coordinate his pelvic thrusts with the punches of Helga and Ulla, and in due course he enjoys his second orgasm of the day. However, he sighs internally at the realization that he did not derive as much physical satisfaction from his *coital* orgasm in Lucy's bed as he did from his *masturbatory* orgasm several hours earlier in the sanctity of his very own sitting room. After two sexual climaxes, a tumbler of whisky, and a bottle of wine, Jared lapses into a deep sleep, with Lucy cradling him in her arms. He dozes well for several hours, but he often awakens in the night, covered in perspiration and shouting. Lucy comforts him by stroking his hair, and within a few minutes, Jared drifts back to sleep until the alarm clock wakes him at 6:15 the following morning.

While driving to work in his forest-green sports car, in the midst of rush-hour traffic, Jared reflects on his life. On the whole, he feels pretty smug: perfect health, flashy penthouse, gorgeous girlfriend, high-powered job, friends to spare, and cash to burn. He knows that many of his comrades from college envy him his good fortune. And yet, Jared feels an ache deep inside his stomach—not a physical pain as such, but rather a sense of queasy discomfort that sometimes borders on nausea—the very pain that causes him to wake in a sweat and to cry out in the middle of the night. For in spite of Jared's many external material successes, privately he suffers from a deep sense of shame and guilt about his secret sexual fantasy.

Still en route to the office, Jared pauses to grab a frappuccino from his nearby designer coffee shop, which he drinks in his car. With the radio blaring in the background, the queasiness in his tummy intensifies as he asks himself some very uncomfortable questions regarding his sexual fantasy about the boxing women. Jared wonders: "Am I some kind of a pervert for getting off on women hitting each other?" In his ordinary, waking life, Jared detests violence of any kind. He has never, ever struck any of his girlfriends, and he never would; even as a child he never got into any scrapes or fisticuffs. But in his fantasy, he deeply enjoys the thought of vigorous punching and the infliction of pain. In fact, the more stridently Helga and Ulla punch one another, the more erect Jared becomes.

Jared frets further as he recalls the few occasions when he did try to penetrate Lucy without thinking about the busty boxers. But whenever he abandoned his fantasy, he found himself remaining quite limp. This thought truly terrifies him, and he often wonders whether he might be, at best, moderately perverse, or, at worst, highly insane.

As Jared continues to drive, another disturbing thought pops into his already overcrowded head: "Since I can only get off by thinking of the boxing scenario, does this mean that I don't *really* love Lucy? Am I being cruel to her by thinking of other women? And should I really be thinking about marrying her? Will it all end in disaster?" He also finds himself wondering whether Lucy would leave him if she knew the secret contents of his "Coffee" container, let alone the contents of his mind.

Work proves a great respite from Jared's nagging inner monologue, and although he finds himself eyeing up one or two of his short-skirted colleagues at the office—imagining what they might look like in a boxing ring—the endless round of frantic telephone calls and the flood of e-mails and faxes help Jared to banish complicated sexual thoughts from his consciousness. But at 6:00 P.M., his unwavering ritual begins again, as Jared dashes to the gym for another assault on the treadmill, followed by his furtive session of masturbation at home with the German DVD. As his sense of shame and loathing starts to bubble up in his thoughts, Jared grabs the remote control and switches off the DVD, telling himself that this time, he will think about Lucy and no one else. Although he finds Lucy physically appealing, and he enjoys her touch and her smell, his penis will not become sufficiently firm, in spite of much frantic self-stimulation. At last, with deep relief upon his face, he turns on the DVD once again, and with the desperate thrill of a heroin addict who has just injected the needle after too long a delay, Jared delights in the punches of Helga and Ulla, who facilitate his climax.

Later that evening, after supper with Lucy and a few mutual friends, the couple have sexual intercourse once again. Jared now realizes that his reliance upon the private mental images of his German boxers has reached the proportions of a compulsive illness, for he simply cannot penetrate Lucy without thinking about his "other girls."

As the weeks and months unfold, Jared and Lucy have become increasingly fond of one another, and Lucy has suggested that they move in together, recommending that he sell his flat (apartment), as he lives further away from the center of town than she does. This thought terrifies Jared, for although he enjoys the notion that one day he and Lucy might marry and have children, he immediately begins to worry that if they lived together, he would find it much more difficult to indulge his secret penchant for masturbation. And Jared cannot help but wonder where he would store his collection of pornography if he and Lucy did share a flat or a house.

Once, Lucy telephoned Jared in the middle of his DVD session. On this particular occasion, he had forgotten to silence his answering machine, and so, to his great annoyance, he heard Lucy's voice penetrating through into his reception room: "Jared, darling, are you home? You're not answering your cell phone. I was wondering whether we could meet an hour earlier than usual, as I have a really important photo-shoot tomorrow, and I need an early night." Although he could easily have jumped into his car in order to accommodate his lovely girlfriend's request, Jared remained rooted to the sofa and continued to masturbate. This failure to respond to Lucy's not-unreasonable request caused him the most guilt of all. He finds himself troubled by the fact that he had to reach orgasm with two anonymous, celluloid, German boxing women instead of helping out his extremely devoted girlfriend. Again, Jared suspects that he might have a serious clinical addiction.

Jared's intensely pleasurable sexual fantasies have begun to perplex him with increasing concern. Most of his close male friends enjoy boasting about their ostensible "normal" sexual exploits, penetrating their girlfriends in a straightforward way. Jared feels certain that none of them would have a secret collection of seemingly bizarre pornography. Once, he asked his best friend, "Dominick," whether he ever used pornography, and to Jared's dismay Dominick just sloughed him off, replying, "Only if I'm fuckin' desperate, man." Jared smiled at Dominick's remark, as if to say, "Yeah, of course, me too," but inside, he felt very disturbed, very abnormal.

Jared has also begun to question why on earth he should find the boxing so erotic—after all, "it's not as though my mom was a lady boxer or anything like that." Jared would very much like to talk to somebody about his situation, but he knows that Lucy would be absolutely gutted if she discovered his secret stash of pornography. Although he has many male friends, he simply cannot trust any of them to be sufficiently sensitive to listen to his story without laughing at him or mocking him. In desperation, Jared telephoned me, a psychotherapist, for assistance, convinced that he must be very deviant indeed.

As a practicing mental health professional, it saddens me greatly to know that Jared has endured so much shame and suffering about his internal world, dominated by such a perplexing sexual fantasy. Throughout my career, I have met many Jareds, each convinced that he or she must be the only "perverse" person who has such peculiar, sinister, singular fantasies. I do not wish to imply that Jared's fantasy should readily be diagnosed as "disturbed," but nor do I wish to imply that it might be "healthy," in part because social scientists and psychological professionals alike have not really studied sexual fantasies as thoroughly as one might imagine. Definitive pronouncements about the relative health or illness or our sexual fantasies seem premature.

Penetrating Questions

Jared's situation raises a number of crucial questions:

- What is a sexual fantasy?
- What constitutes a "normal" sexual fantasy?
- Why do we have sexual fantasies in the first place?
- What purpose or purposes do our sexual fantasies serve?
- Does everybody have sexual fantasies?
- Should we be worried if we have *no* fantasies at all?
- Should we ever share our fantasies with our partners?
- Should we ever share our fantasies with our friends?
- Would it be wise to act out our sexual fantasies with our lovers?
- Can our fantasies ever be damaging or dangerous?
- If we fantasize about "ordinary" sex, does this mean that we must be boring?
- If we have very outlandish fantasies, does this mean that we must be mentally unbalanced?
- If we fantasize about our partners during sex or during masturbation, does that mean that we have a good relationship?
- If we fantasize about someone other than our partners during sex or masturbation, does that mean that our relationship might be in trouble?
- If we fantasize about something "illegal," does this mean that we may be at risk for acting it out?

- Do our fantasies represent just a bit of private fun, or do they have more profound implications for how we lead our lives?
- How can we explain the range of fantasies experienced by human beings? In other words, why do some people prefer to be kissed and cradled while others enjoy the infliction of often agonizing physical pain?
- Can we ever change our fantasies?
- How often do we lie about our sexual fantasies?
- Do our sexual fantasies differ from our daydreams or our nighttime dreams?
- Is there a difference between the fantasies that we have during sex with a partner and the fantasies that we indulge in during private masturbation?
- Do we control our fantasies, or do our fantasies control us?

Sexual fantasies—our secret inner thoughts—can provide us with immense pleasure, but they can also gnaw at our minds, causing anxiety, shame, guilt, disgust, or confusion. Many people claim to enjoy their fantasies unrestrictedly. However, on the basis of both my clinical work and my research, I have come to the conclusion that a significant majority of adults maintains a most uncomfortable relationship with their private sexual fantasies, in spite of the fact that most fantasies culminate in orgasm. I refer to this tension in human psychology as the "masturbatory paradox" to reflect the fact that, as a result of our fantasies, we experience pleasure in our genitals and our bodies, but often, simultaneously, and paradoxically, disquiet in our minds.

I suspect that, rather like Jared, many British and American men and women prefer to make love with the lights off not only because the darkness will hide our flabbiness and what many of us regard as our bodily imperfections, but also because a darkened bedroom allows the world of fantasy to come to life. After all, if we visit the cinema or the theater, we expect that the management will have turned down the lights so that we can focus more fully upon the screen or the stage. So too, in the bedroom, many people will prefer to make love without the lights on, so that the "secret cinema" of the mind can unfold in a full, uninterrupted manner.

Not only do many Britons and Americans need to become amateur lighting technicians in the bedroom, but many of us endeavor to become sound engineers as well, controlling the volume of our partner's moans and groans. I once interviewed a middle-aged woman who complained to me that her husband had insisted that she remain completely still during sex, demanding that she keep her mouth firmly shut. If she succeeded in remaining totally quiet, then the husband could obtain an impressive erection and penetrate her fully; but if this lady so much as uttered a peep, even a pre-orgasmic gasp, then the husband would become instantly flaccid. Although this woman enjoyed the sex, she felt frustrated that her husband would not allow her to talk. I never interviewed the husband, so I cannot be certain as to why he insisted that his wife keep her mouth zipped shut. But I strongly suspect that he became tumescent only when he could indulge in a private sexual fantasy that really aroused him—one that may not have involved his wife—and if she dared to speak, she would have interrupted the fantasy, thus putting him off his stride.

Another patient enjoyed placing a rolled-up pair of nylons in his girlfriend's mouth, and then securing duct tape over her lips, in order to silence her during lovemaking. The girlfriend provided consent for this arguably sadomasochistic activity. The male patient explained to me that unless his girlfriend "shut the fuck up" he would not be able to listen to the "soundtrack" in his own head—a cruel soundtrack in which he heard voices exclaiming the many abuses that he wanted to inflict upon his lover—hence his motivation, in part, for seeking psychotherapeutic treatment.

Another patient, although a more gentle and loving man, chided his wife if she spoke during sexual intercourse. Although he loved her devotedly, this gentleman told me that after twenty years of marriage, the sight of his wife's sagging breasts and buttocks had begun to repel him, and he preferred to think about a twenty-something secretary in his office. The fantasy of this younger woman allowed the husband to achieve an erection, which he would then use to penetrate his wife quite successfully, allowing her to reach orgasm; but if the wife spoke at all, her vocalizations would spoil his fantasy.

I certainly do not wish to imply that each time we make love with the lights out, or do something to eliminate background noise, we do so in order to indulge some subversive, private sexual fantasy. But it seems that in many cases we do so for precisely that reason.

These brief vignettes—just a few of several hundred that I have encountered in clinical practice over the years—force us to pose a painful question, namely: *Who has been sleeping in your head?* In most instances, we do know the name of the person in our *bed,* but our partner will be less certain as to the name of the person in our *head.*

In the chapters that follow, I shall explore these vexing problems and questions about sexual fantasy in greater detail, and I hope to provide some answers to these very complicated issues. Welcome to the intriguing and often taboo world of sexual fantasies.

2 The Science of Psychological Fingerprints

*That is the essence of science: ask an
impertinent question, and you are on
the way to the pertinent answer.*
— JACOB BRONOWSKI, *The Ascent of Man*

Alex Rodriguez's Broken Foot and Other Secret Phantasmagoria

Imagine that you have spent the whole of your childhood completely obsessed with baseball and that more than anything else in the world you wish that you could be Babe Ruth or Alex Rodriguez. You practice and you practice until your arms and legs ache, you plaster your bedroom with posters and other memorabilia, and you count the days until your father takes you to see the New York Yankees playing live. In the car, on the way, you begin to drift off into a little reverie, imagining that the stadium announcer starts speaking through a booming sound system: "Ladies and gentlemen, we regret to inform you that Alex Rodriguez has broken his foot. But fear not, in his place, we have ten-year-old Tommy from Seattle, the youngest star baseballer in America." The crowd cheers, and in your fantasy you save the day, hitting home runs galore and grinning in ecstasy as your teammates hoist you onto their shoulders and parade you triumphantly before the crowds. As you tumble into your bed that evening, you relive the fantasy and drift off into a peaceful slumber. Whether imagining ourselves as baseball players, film stars, symphonic conductors, gods of rock and roll, or great lovers, how many of us will not have indulged in such fantasies as young children, or, indeed, as adults?

How might we best define a fantasy? And what might be the difference between an *ordinary* fantasy and a *sexual* fantasy?

Psychoanalysts and developmental psychologists alike have long speculated that the capacity to generate private, internal thoughts begins at least as early as birth, and perhaps even weeks before, during the third trimester of pregnancy. If we study a human baby intently, we can learn a great deal about the newborn's unspoken fantasy life. For example, if a baby begins to howl and then a loving mother places the baby on her breast, calming the child and satisfying the infant's craving for milk, might we reasonably infer that the baby harbored a fantasy for milk, or for some sort of food-like substance, which on previous occasions had magically removed the pain from the baby's stomach? Freudian psychotherapists such as myself would argue that even at this early age our minds contain a great many thoughts and desires, most of which we never share with others, and many of which we do not fully comprehend.

As we progress from infancy to toddlerhood, our fantasies revolve less and less around the actual breast milk or bottles that keep us alive; instead, the fantasies begin to develop into more symbolic transformations of the early love-objects. For example, a little boy may desperately yearn for a certain toy as a birthday or Christmas present, eagerly hoping that his mother or father (or Santa) will know about this strong wish or fantasy and act accordingly. As we become older, we not only yearn for external, concrete objects, such as a teddy bear or a Barbie doll or a toy tank; we crave, additionally, new identities. A little boy who wholeheartedly wishes to become Harry Potter may pretend to fly around on a broomstick, or to perform rudimentary magic tricks, and a little girl may jump up and down with a hairbrush in her hand, pretending to be a pop star, perhaps Beyoncé Knowles.

As we grow older still, our fantasies develop in even more complex ways. A seventeen-year-old boy deeply immersed in the agony of school exams may fantasize that he will achieve sufficiently satisfactory results to gain entrance to a prestigious Ivy League university. His eighteen-year-old sister, fresh from a summer stint at a tennis camp, may ache to become the next Venus Williams. On the eve of a wedding, a young man or woman may fantasize that love will last forever and that the union will produce two healthy children, one boy and one girl.

Others may fantasize about becoming chairman of the board, or a multimillionaire, or simply famous. Whatever the content, every single sentient human being engages in the process of creating fantasies—often, untold millions of fantasies—throughout the course of a lifetime.

I would regard the capacity to fantasize as completely normal. In fact, I would be extremely concerned if I met a patient who could not fantasize, as this might indicate an impoverishment of mental functioning characteristic of the more severe varieties of mental illness. One of the most vivid descriptions of fantasizing can be found in the classic nineteenth-century French novel *Madame Bovary*, written by the observant storyteller Gustave Flaubert. The young heroine, Emma Rouault, later Emma Bovary, grew up on a stultifyingly provincial farm near the French village of Caux, a desolate place from which she yearned to escape. As a schoolgirl, she delighted in the stories that she heard from an old maid who visited her convent, and also from the "long chapters" of the books that she read in secret. According to Flaubert,

> They were about love, lovers, loving, martyred maidens swooning in secluded lodges, postilions slain every other mile, horses ridden to death on every page, dark forests, aching hearts, promising, sobbing, kisses and tears, little boats by moonlight, nightingales in the grove, *gentlemen* brave as lions, tender as lambs, virtuous as a dream, always well dressed, and weeping pints. For six months, at the age of fifteen, Emma dabbled in the remains of old lending libraries. From Walter Scott, subsequently, she conceived a passion for things historical, dreamed about coffers, guard-rooms and minstrels. She would have liked to live in some old manor-house, like those châtelaines in their long corsages, under their trefoiled Gothic arches, spending their days, elbows on the parapet and chin in hand, looking out far across the fields for the white-plumed rider galloping towards her on his black horse.

With no CDs, DVDs, iPods, Palm Pilots, Blackberries, MP3 players, cell phones, e-mails, faxes, broadband, and other such technological paraphernalia to preoccupy her, can one blame Emma Bovary for losing herself in thoughts of historical legends, as though she had become a character in Sir Walter Scott's *Ivanhoe*, indulging what Gustave Flaubert called, so tantalizingly, Emma's "secret phantasmagoria"? Of course, technological distractions will not prevent fantasy; in many cases, DVDs will inflame fantasy, as we have seen in the case of Jared, described in the previous chapter. But the bleak landscape of Emma's life, both external and internal, will certainly have contributed to her penchant for fantasizing.

In the case of Madame Bovary, we see quite clearly the way in which fantasy provides conscious pleasure, escape from the confining strictures of ordinary reality. Whether we may be more like ten-year-old Tommy from Seattle, desperate to be Alex Rodriguez, or fifteen-year-old Emma Rouault, aching to become the heroine of a Gothic adventure story, we all fantasize, and we do so regularly. Sometimes we refer to our fantasies as "daydreams"; and we know from the research of prominent academic psychologists such as Professor Jerome Singer, for many years professor of psychology at Yale University in New Haven, Connecticut, that the average human being will daydream copiously as a normal feature of psychological life. In Professor Singer's original research, he noted how some common daydreams might be summed up in simple statements:

- I plan how to increase my income in the next year.
- I have my own yacht and plan a cruise of the eastern seaboard.
- I suddenly find I can fly, to the amazement of passers-by.
- I see myself in the arms of a warm and loving person who satisfies all my needs.
- I picture an atomic bombing of the town I live in.

Singer's seminal research in this field, based on American research participants, revealed that although most of us do daydream quite frequently, differences among subgroups can nonetheless be detected. For example, those who live in bustling cities reported daydreams more frequently than those who grew up in suburban environments. There may also be cultural differences, as indicated by one of Singer's earlier studies that demonstrated higher rates of daydreaming among African-American people and Jewish people compared to those from an Anglo-Saxon background. One wonders whether people from traditionally oppressed minority groups tend to fantasize about greater freedom and equality, whereas those born into the majority "in-group" already feel that they have arrived. Whatever the individual differences and variations may be, the rich research literature has indicated that most of us daydream quite extensively, indulging in waking fantasies of every conceivable variety.

But not only do we enjoy *conscious* fantasies or daydreams, we also have our *unconscious* fantasies. How can we have a fantasy if it remains unconscious, outside of our awareness? This concept has developed from the work of Freud, who observed over many decades of clinical practice, working with relatively stable as well as highly neurotic and psychotic individuals, that much of mental life remains buried in the unconscious portion of the mind. Freud hypothesized that even though we may not be aware of the secret, underwater depths of our mental functioning, the unconscious mind still exerts an influence. In this way the mind is rather like an iceberg, a small portion of which juts out above the water in full view, but the bulk of which will be hidden leagues beneath the ocean. And yet that unseen portion will nevertheless exert an often devastating impact, as the passengers of the RMS *Titanic* tragically discovered in 1912.

A sixty-one-year-old gentleman called "Mr. Hildebrand" suffers from an unconscious fantasy of self-destruction, but sadly he does not know it. On a conscious level, Mr. Hildebrand bemoans the fact that he has had three wives, each of whom instituted divorce proceedings, that he has lost two small fortunes through careless investments, and that most of his friends, as well as his five children, have stopped speaking to him. Consciously, Mr. Hildebrand craves stability, solidity, and creativity; but unbeknownst to himself, he has somehow found a way to sabotage and ultimately destroy all the goodness in his life. When he first started psychotherapy with me many years ago, he regarded himself simply as "unlucky," as the victim of the treachery of "evil ex-wives," his "fucker" of a boss, and his "ungrateful" children. He could not countenance the possibility that he had contributed to this most unfortunate scenario in any way. Happily, after years of sustained and dedicated therapeutic work on both our parts, Mr. Hildebrand began to function more productively and less savagely in both his private life and his working life. The impact of his earlier years of sadomasochistic self-attack, however, has left him scarred and in far less secure a position in life than virtually all of his contemporaries.

Mr. Hildebrand grew up in a deeply punitive household with a highly competitive mother who undermined him at every turn, insisting that he could do nothing right. When he drew in his coloring book, and could not keep his crayon within the lines of the drawing, his mother made him feel worthless. She screamed whenever any crayon shavings spilled onto the polished wooden table top. When he did not achieve 100 percent on a spelling test, she screamed as well, projecting her own feelings of frustration and inadequacy into her tiny son. In spite of his solid abilities and high degree of intelligence, he eventually developed an idea in his unconscious, what psychoanalysts would describe as an "unconscious" fantasy: "I am a stupid, worthless wreck, and everything I do in life will be nothing but rubbish." Owing to the terrifying nature of this destructive thought, he repressed this mental constellation, and yet, it still exerted a great determining pull on his personality development, albeit at an unconscious level.

So, our fantasies or daydreams may be conscious, or they may be unconscious. They may be unreservedly pleasant, such as that of ten-year-old Tommy from Seattle, who wants to become the new Alex Rodriguez; they may be escapist, as in the case of Emma Rouault, the future Madame Bovary; or they may be destructive, as Mr. Hildebrand has discovered to his great sadness.

But where do our sexual fantasies fit into this picture of the human mind? And how exactly do we define a sexual fantasy, anyway?

For the purposes of this investigation, I wish to define a sexual fantasy as, first and foremost, a conscious thought or set of thoughts that contain a depiction of a sexual act or acts, a sexual scene or scenes, sexual imagery, and often sexual language, which will in many instances produce pleasurable sensations ranging from mental enjoyment to physical stimulation in the genitalia. In many instances, the physiological arousal will provoke a series of bodily changes, ranging from engorgement of the nipples in both women and men to the partial or complete emission of fluids from either the vagina or the penis. In my psychotherapeutic work, I have often encountered cases in which a sexual fantasy will cause someone to become both aroused and horrified at once, turned on and turned off simultaneously, which is illustrative of what I have already termed the masturbatory paradox, since many of our most conflicted attitudes and ambivalent feelings toward our sexual fantasies emerge during solo masturbation.

A sexual fantasy might occur as a very brief, fleeting sexual thought lasting only a matter of seconds or less. For example, we might find ourselves walking down the road, staring at an attractive stranger in the crowd, and imagining: "Gee, I wonder what she looks like naked," or "I wonder what he might be like in bed," or "I'd really like to stick my tongue down this person's throat." But a sexual fantasy may last for a longer period of time—it might be an intricate and complicated narrative, continuing for five minutes, thirty minutes, or even longer, accompanied by masturbation, which quite often results in orgasm. Similarly, a sexual fantasy can occur in our minds during foreplay or during sexual intercourse with another person. In some instances we will have a particular sexual fantasy on only one occasion, but for most adult men and women the same sexual fantasy or fantasy constellations return again and again.

Sexual fantasies may occur at any time of the day or night, in any location, in any state of consciousness, whether fully sober, slightly inebriated after having consumed a bottle of beer, or "high" on marijuana or cocaine. Contrary to a lingering Victorian stereotype, women fantasize just as much as men do.

Our fantasies may be extremely simple, direct, and straightforward, and, if rated by a film censor, might be found to be quite suitable for a general audience; for instance, we might have a fantasy of embracing our long-standing marital partner, sharing a warm and smoldering kiss. Other reasonable, straightforward fantasies might be rather more explicit, such as those of fondling another person's genitals or performing sexual intercourse. By contrast, some people report infinitely more complicated fantasies involving a wide array of characters enacting intricate scenarios that other people might regard as "filthy" or "perverted." For instance, one of the participants in my survey reported a favorite sexual fantasy involving Her Majesty the Queen and former British Prime Minister Margaret Thatcher. In this gentleman's fantasy, he would bind both the Queen and Baroness Thatcher with rope and then make love to each woman in turn.

Sexual fantasies may be described as highly personalized. Some readers may find the aforementioned fantasy about the Queen and the ex–prime minister deeply arousing, some may find it deeply distressing, and others may simply snigger at a fantasy that may differ greatly from their own. The ancient Romans would often intone, "*de gustibus non est disputandum*" (literally, "About tastes, there is no disputing"), a phrase that could also loosely translate as "There's no accounting for taste." As we proceed further into our investigation of the psychology of sexual fantasies, we shall, however, begin to discover that although we may not readily understand another person's desire for Margaret Thatcher—especially if we lust after someone like, say, Jennifer Lopez instead—our erotic preferences may not be as accidental or haphazard as we have assumed. We might, perhaps, after all, now have enough clinical psychological knowledge to account, in full, for our own sexual tendencies.

Many of our sexual fantasies, rather like many of our daydreams, will be conscious. In other words, we know exactly which fantasies we enjoy in the privacy of our bedroom, whether we choose to share them or not. But, unbeknownst to many of us, we also have secret, unconscious sexual fantasies, ideas and thoughts that swirl around in the depths of our mind, and which may not manifest themselves for many years, if ever. Consider the case of "Mr. Illingsworth," a forty-six-year-old stockbroker who came to my office because of his lingering difficulty with alcoholism. During his twenties and thirties, Mr. Illingsworth had a wife with whom he enjoyed "vanilla sex," the colloquial term for straightforward, uncomplicated intercourse. He led an essentially quiet, suburban, conservative life. But as the years unfolded, he became increasingly bored, and then ultimately depressed, a psychological state of being that he attempted to ameliorate, unsuccessfully, through excessive drinking. Eventually, Mr. Illingsworth's wife abandoned the marital home, unable to tolerate his growing verbal abusiveness and his increasingly frequent drunken stupors. Within six months, Mr. Illingsworth had found his way to an "S and M" club, where he observed men and women beating one another with wooden paddles and metal rods. Although he had never practiced any form of sadomasochism before, Mr. Illingsworth told me that he had become instantly erect. Within a matter of weeks, he had become a regular visitor to this club, and soon he became extremely proficient in the art of beating his new sexual partners, enjoying a more explosive quality of orgasm than he had ever experienced in his marital life.

I would argue that Mr. Illingsworth had by this point entered the realm of sexual perversion. Admittedly, the term "perversion" often rankles, and many regard this label as outmoded and judgmental. But in contemporary psychoanalytical discourse, mental health professionals use the diagnosis of "perversion" in a very specific way. We define it as the wish to cause harm to oneself or to another, a wish so strong that it also evokes sexual pleasure in the perpetrator. Mr. Illingsworth had now developed a full-fledged sadomasochistic sexual perversion that he practiced compulsively, endangering both his "partners" and himself, physically, psychologically, and potentially legally.

The intensification of Mr. Illingsworth's sexual perversion surprised him greatly. Indeed, he explained during the course of our interview, "I never knew I had these feelings inside of me. They just came whooshing out. I felt as though I had come home. I found the mother ship!"

I suspect that Mr. Illingsworth had always suffered from a sado-masochistic mental structure, and that he had always had unconscious sadomasochistic sexual fantasies, yet until this point they had remained outside his conscious awareness. Now, in the disinhibiting wake of his wife's departure, they had at last become conscious, and hence more fully available. Sexual fantasies may exist at several different levels of consciousness simultaneously, some of which we know about, and others of which remain more shrouded, often for decades at a time.

Throughout the course of my research on sexual fantasies, I have come to understand that many individuals, if not most, have two different sets of conscious sexual fantasies, namely, those which we reveal to our friends, and those which we share, often with deep reluctance, only with one's confidantes or partners, if that. For instance, in a barroom setting, when comparing notes with our friends, we may discover, perhaps unsurprisingly, that all five of the heterosexual men we are with find Hollywood actress Sharon Stone arousing; or all five of the heterosexual women chatting in a restaurant may confess that they drool over Brad Pitt. At one level, the erotic frisson generated by such iconic film stars indicates that many people may have similar sexual fantasies. But these fantasies represent what I have already referred to as "barroom fantasies" or "pub fantasies"—simple, safe fantasies that anyone might enjoy without revealing anything more intimate about his or her private sexual self. I would wager a large amount of money that when each of the pub-frequenting drinking buddies returns home at night to his or her partner, or to a solo session of masturbation, Sharon Stone might make a fleeting appearance; likewise, Brad Pitt may briefly appear in the women's fantasies. But in my clinical and research experience, when the pub bravado recedes, we find that someone else, and often *something* else, will predominate in our minds. The most elaborate and pleasure-inducing fantasies occur not during bar conversations, but during sexual intercourse, and most especially during masturbation, when we have no partner to distract us from our most private sexual scenarios. Many people believe that these masturbatory sexual fantasies cannot be thought about in the presence of a partner, just as

Mr. Illingsworth would not have dared to indulge his sadomasochistic fantasies with his wife, for fear of sullying the marital bedroom.

Through my research, I have discovered that each of us harbors one or more infinitely more detailed, and sometimes more disturbing, fantasies that we would never reveal in the bar, around the coffee table, or even on the psychotherapist's couch. Psychoanalysts working in the tradition of Anna Freud—the daughter of Sigmund Freud, a clinician in her own right who specialized in the psychological treatment of troubled children—have developed a term for this: the "central masturbation fantasy." This particular fantasy may be defined as a pivotal erotic fantasy to which we return again and again, and which, according to many classical and modern Freudian psychologists and psychoanalysts, provides the very key to our psychological lives. Indeed, some of us do return again and again to the same fantasy, which never varies; others utilize a broader range of fantasies; yet others enjoy the same structure (e.g., domination, submission, humiliation, pain, or whatever) but vary the details, so that one night a particular person might fantasize about being abused by a schoolmistress, and on the next night by an employer at work.

Our fantasy lives can be fixed and rigid, or more fluid and plastic. Most of us will recognize a fantasy life that lies somewhere in between, along a continuum.

Many people will share their sexual fantasies, reporting them to a best friend, or to a wife or husband, or girlfriend or boyfriend, or even to a psychotherapist. Other people, by contrast, will articulate their central masturbation fantasies only to a prostitute, or to an anonymous stranger via an Internet chat room. Still others will go to their graves never having breathed a single word about their secret, subterranean fantasy life. Some individuals restrict their fantasies to the bedroom, reserving them for intercourse with a partner or for a session of masturbation; others go to great lengths to reenact their fantasies with costumes, props, and assorted paraphernalia, often in public or semi-public places such as sex clubs, private parties, street alleys, or cruising grounds.

Our fantasies may be rather predictable—for example, thinking about making love with one's spouse—but in the vast majority of cases our sexual fantasies involve people, or animals, or objects, with whom, or with which, we have no real connection in the external world. Sometimes the fantasies shock even ourselves. One of the participants in my research survey, an elderly Jewish woman whose parents perished in 1942 during the Nazi Holocaust, told me, rather shame-facedly, that whenever she masturbates, she imagines a group of S.S. officers in jackboots and other Nazi regalia forcing her to strip naked before strapping her to Dr. Josef Mengele's medical examination table, where she must submit to probing of the most deadly surgical nature. This fantasy—which we might regard as utterly horrific and completely illogical—also produces the most explosive of orgasms, yet another instance of the compelling nature of the masturbatory paradox. This lady had absolutely no idea why the men who murdered her parents should become the desired objects of her secret sexual fantasy life; and until recently, such seemingly bizarre fantasies have baffled mental health experts and clinical sexologists alike.

Another example of a predictable fantasy would be an archetypal middle-aged man fantasizing about stunning blonde women, such as Marilyn Monroe. Other fantasies will be rather more perplexing and less immediately comprehensible, as in the case of a woman whom I interviewed who has sex only with men, but whose private masturbatory fantasies feature only women. In spite of indulging in copious erotic fantasies about other women, this lady told me emphatically that she would never, *ever* actually sleep with one. Where do such perplexing fantasies come from?

Our fantasies originate from various disparate sources. Many of us create our fantasies within our heads; in other words, we make them up ourselves, drawing upon earlier impressions and experiences. But others among us rely mightily on fantasies that our partners have related to us, or on fantasies we have stumbled upon in a film, in a magazine, on the Internet, or in any of the myriad other types of pornography so readily available, especially if these fantasies resonate with earlier childhood events.

Certain people utilize sexual fantasies as a spicy adjunct to their sex lives, but for others, engaging in fantasy stimulation may well be the sole source of sexual gratification. In due course, I shall discuss one of the findings from my research project, namely, that in Great Britain and America today, literally millions of people have no sexual contact with another human being, and so they rely exclusively upon sexual fantasies during masturbation as their *sole* source of erotic pleasure.

Some men and women do not engage in any sexual activity whatsoever because they cannot find a willing partner; others fear sexual contact because of the increasing risk of contracting a sexually transmitted disease; and still others fear psychological intimacy so much that the search for physical contact becomes the least of their concerns. "Troy," a fifty-one-year-old man whom I interviewed, told me that he had enjoyed a great deal of sex in the carefree days of the 1970s and 1980s, but as soon as AIDS became a deadly presence, he began to refrain from all sexual activity. Since 1987, he has had only two sexual encounters, both very unsatisfactory because he was full of the fear of becoming infected in spite of his use of condoms. In fact, Troy has become so terrified of AIDS that he has developed a deep phobia about psychological intimacy as well. Today he remains single, masturbating three or four times daily in order to achieve sexual release. Thus, for Troy, and for millions of other Britons and Americans, the secret phantasmagoria of sexual fantasy constitutes the vital backbone of their erotic life.

Before concluding this section about the range and scope of sexual fantasies, I wish to remind readers that the vast majority of sexual fantasies, whether sequestered in the privacy of our minds or enacted theatrically in the privacy of our bedrooms, remain reasonably safe and encapsulated, impacting no one other than ourselves and our partners. But sometimes, one's deepest sexual fantasies will erupt in a criminal manner, exerting a deleterious or deadly influence upon any number of victims. Having worked clinically for many years in the branch of mental health work known as "forensic psychotherapy," treating dangerous patients such as pedophiles and rapists, I know that many of these individuals had engaged in extended periods of pedophile pornography usage, for example, before progressing to the perpetration of actual pedophilic crimes. Other people, however, have managed to confine their pedophilic impulses to private masturbation, never having laid a hand upon a child in an inappropriate manner. One might reasonably argue that masturbating to pedophile pornography itself constitutes a criminal activity, in that it fuels the underground industry of child pornography. Thus, some sexual fantasies, if put into practice, would be illegal and highly dangerous; and many sexual fantasies become the launching point of a subsequent "career" as an adult pedophile or rapist. One must stress, however, that a huge difference exists between fantasy and action in most instances. Sexual fantasies can become the greatest private pleasures, and yet, if unmanaged, can in certain instances damage the bodies and minds of innocent victims, sometimes for life.

In summary, I regard our sexual fantasies as completely normative activities that develop from our earliest infantile fantasy capacities and become increasingly sexualized as we progress through the life cycle. Although we may sometimes enjoy the exact same fantasy as someone else, each one of us *transforms* that fantasy, painting it onto our own very private and particular canvases, and each of us will become aroused by the particular features highlighted in our personal versions. Three different grown men, all masturbating about television star Jennifer Aniston, for example, may use the image of Miss Aniston in very different ways. One chap may masturbate as he imagines having genital intercourse with her; another may reach climax at the thought of having prized Miss Aniston away from her former husband, actor Brad Pitt; while the third gentleman may enlist Miss Aniston as a participant in his own private sadomasochistic masturbatory ritual. So the mere claim that "I fantasize about Jennifer Aniston" tells us very little about someone's secret sexual psychology. In order to learn about our truest, most intimate nature, we must research the subject more thoroughly, deriving a deeper picture of our secret phantasmagoria, or what I have come to think of as the particular "psychological fingerprints" that differentiate each mind from every other.

The Sexperts

Before I report some of the findings from my own formal research project on the psychology of sexual fantasies, I wish to put the subject into a historical perspective, paying tribute to the intrepid sexological investigators who have made groundbreaking contributions to the field. It is these researchers who have provided the foundation stones that have underscored my work. The number of truly serious pioneers in the study of sexual fantasy can be counted on the fingers of one or two hands, for in spite of the fact that we live in a sexualized era, we still understand far less about the origins of sexual preferences, the health or pathology of certain sexual activities, and the sources of true sexual pleasure than those of us in positions of "expertise" would dare to admit.

The discipline of sexual fantasy studies emerged rather reluctantly, having remained an extremely taboo subject for many centuries. Dr. Heinrich van Kaan, a mid-nineteenth-century German physician who specialized in the treatment of the "insane," published a book in 1844, entitled *Psychopathia Sexualis,* about the mental pathology of human sexuality. In particular, van Kaan expressed grave concern about the dangers of masturbation, a viewpoint shared by many medical doctors at the time. But unlike other physicians who warned against masturbation because of the lassitude that would supposedly develop as a result of wasting semen, van Kaan regarded masturbation as a dangerous sexual perversion that could lead to degeneration of the mind, especially because it would so often be accompanied by a fantasy, in which the mind might roam wild, or even become completely mad. One wonders how many millions of men and women will have suffered extreme mental anguish as a result of van Kaan's much-respected medical pedagogics. We now know, of course, that sexual fantasies constitute a normal, universal component of human psychology. In van Kaan's repressive, restrictive times, when even the legs of baby grand pianos would be covered with little pantalettes, the idea that our minds might contain vivid sexual thoughts at any time of night or day proved so troublesome that van Kaan and his psychiatric colleagues condemned ordinary sexuality as perverted.

Psychopathia Sexualis seems to have proved a catchy title, because in 1886, some forty-two years after the publication of Heinrich van Kaan's textbook, an Austrian psychiatrist of noble birth, Professor Richard von Krafft-Ebing, produced an even more influential tome of the same name, subtitled *Eine klinisch-forensische Studie (A Clinical-Forensic Study)*. Fortunately, Professor von Krafft-Ebing espoused a somewhat more liberal and tolerant viewpoint about human sexual psychology than van Kaan and his mid-Victorian predecessors had done, and as a result, many tormented Austrian men and women allowed themselves to consult Krafft-Ebing about their private and often agonizing fantasies. In one illustrative case, reported in 1890, Krafft-Ebing discussed the plight of a gentleman from Berlin who would indulge in veritable "orgies of fantasy," generally involving being beaten and humiliated. An articulate patient, the Berliner explained to Krafft-Ebing that he had become aware of his masochistic beating fantasies—especially the wish to be imprisoned, flogged, kicked, and tortured by a woman—as early as childhood. This man also helped Krafft-Ebing and later investigators to understand that when he did indeed act out his beating fantasies with the assistance of a prostitute, he found the experience very dissatisfying. The patient from Berlin explained that he derived more pleasure from the *fantasy* than he did from the *reality,* a phenomenon that contemporary psychotherapists encounter daily in clinical practice. As one of my patients admitted, "Sometimes a mind-fuck is better than the other kind."

Krafft-Ebing referred to sexual fantasies by the quaint term of "psychical onanism." The word "psychical" refers to the mind, and "onanism," the widely sanctioned nineteenth-century medical term, refers to masturbation, a moniker derived from the Old Testament figure of Onan in Genesis 38 who spilled his seed on the ground. By introducing the term "psychical onanism," Krafft-Ebing unwittingly launched the discipline of sexual fantasy studies. He helped us to appreciate that masturbation cannot be described solely as a matter of rubbing one's genitalia, but rather, may take place, and often does take place, within the contours of one's own mind. By 1903, in a later edition of his formidable compendium on sexual perversions, Professor von Krafft-Ebing observed that psychical onanism (masturbatory fantasies) feature prominently in the lives of masochists. He also noted that male homosexuals often used fantasies about other men in order to arouse themselves with women—he was writing, after all, at a time in history when actual sex between men could have resulted in criminal prosecution. Thus, from the pioneering sexological writings of Richard von Krafft-Ebing, physicians and other scientists began to learn more about the widespread existence of sexual fantasies among those deemed mentally ill, or at the very least, highly neurotic. But could these Prussian and Austrian men teach us anything about sexual fantasy among ordinary, "normal" adult individuals?

During Krafft-Ebing's tenure as Vienna's most distinguished psychiatrist, a bright young colleague began to appear at professional conferences in the hope of presenting his burgeoning findings on the origins of neurotic illness. Dr. Sigmund Freud, a Jew, had qualified in medicine at the University of Vienna in 1886, the very year in which Krafft-Ebing had published the first edition of his classic *Psychopathia Sexualis*. Over the years, Freud would come to purchase at least four different editions of Krafft-Ebing's book, one of which still contains Freud's original pencil markings, suggesting that he had read Krafft-Ebing quite carefully. But although Freud acknowledged his indebtedness to the aristocratic Krafft-Ebing, he expanded our understanding of sexuality and sexual fantasies in a radically different way. Krafft-Ebing remained somewhat unappreciative of Freud's views on the relationship between early sexual experiences and neurotic illness. When Freud presented a scientific paper on the genesis of hysterical illness to the Vienna

Society of Psychiatry and Neurology in 1896, Krafft-Ebing, serving as the chairman, condemned the work as "a scientific fairy tale." This observation prompted Freud to reply, in private, "They can all go to hell."

Bruised, but ultimately undaunted, by Krafft-Ebing's rebuff, Freud continued to undertake both his clinical and his sexological researches, and he would ultimately come to deserve our appreciation as the man who did more than anyone else to normalize the contents of the human mind. He argued strenuously that every single person, no matter how "normal" or "abnormal," struggles with both strong erotic impulses and powerful violent urges. In his pioneering work *Three Essays on the Theory of Sexuality,* published in 1905, Freud observed that so-called "perverse" sexuality (whether sucking, licking, or biting) derives from our early infantile experiences at the breast, and that most of us will not confine our sexual activities to heterosexual, genital intercourse designed solely for procreative purposes. In other words, from a scientific point of view, Freud put foreplay on the map as an acceptable, indeed inescapable, feature of erotic life.

Building upon Krafft-Ebing's researches on sexual psychopathology, Freud extended the field even further by exploring the secret origins of sexual fantasies and the role that sexual fantasies play in our broader lives. Krafft-Ebing had attempted to lift the veil of secrecy from the study of sexuality, but he still regarded much of human sexual functioning as degenerate. Freud, by contrast, helped us to appreciate the sheer normality of sexuality, regardless of whether one engaged in procreative or nonprocreative sexual activities.

As he became more immersed in his private sexual research project, Freud made two important discoveries, namely, that sexual fantasies serve as the fulfillment of primitive, unbearable wishes, and that sexual fantasies also protect the mind from often even more uncomfortable thoughts. Sexual fantasies could not be dismissed as the prelude to a "quick jerk-off" or a breathless climax; by contrast, Freud regarded the sexual fantasy as a mental product that performed an important function in the human mind.

In 1895, Freud described the case of a young female singer, known to us by the disguised case-study name of "Frau P.J.," a newlywed whose husband worked as a traveling salesman. One day, after her husband's departure on a business trip, the young opera singer began to warble the famous "Séguidille" from Georges Bizet's opera of 1875,

Carmen. To her great astonishment, she suddenly felt her body overcome by a strange sensation, and during her rehearsal of the lilting
number in triple time she experienced an orgasm. Now, I have asked
many female opera singers whether the score to *Carmen* has ever induced an orgasm for them, and although many would describe the music as luscious, stirring, even orgasmic, none has ever achieved an
actual climax as a result of singing it. In desperation, Frau P.J. visited
Freud's consulting room, undoubtedly distressed by this unusual reaction. Ever the super-sleuth, Freud used his detective skills, and he soon
discovered the reason for the young singer's ill-timed orgasm.

For those unfamiliar with the libretto to *Carmen*'s "Séguidille," the
aria provides the main character Carmen with an opportunity for
reverie as she sings about the joys of being reunited with her lover. In
the bridge, or contrast section to the main melody, Carmen explains:

> *Oui, mais toute seule on s'ennuie,*
> *Et les vrais plaisirs sont à deux;*
> *Donc, pour me tenir compagnie,*
> *J'emmènerai mon amoureux!*
>
> *[But all alone what can one do?*
> *True joy begins when there are two;*
> *And so, to keep me company,*
> *I'll take my lover dear with me!]*

Freud soon realized that the libretto concerns a young woman who
desperately craves being part of a couple. Through her lyrics, she reduces the pain of loss and separation by fantasizing a union with a
lover. In this respect, Carmen's fictional situation mirrored the real-life
predicament of the newly married Viennese *Hausfrau,* a lady whose
traveling husband had deserted her, and with whom she wished to be
reconnected.

Now, of course, many husbands leave their wives to embark on
business trips, but few of the wives will reach orgasm while singing
snippets of nineteenth-century French opera. We must remember, however, that Freud treated Frau P.J. in the 1890s, at the height of Victorian sexual repression. In all likelihood, Frau P.J. entered her marriage
a virgin and would have had her first overtly sexual experiences only
very recently, before her husband disappeared on the business trip.

Thus, she had begun to enjoy marital intercourse only to experience sexual deprivation and loss a mere three months later. Although Freud wrote in a gentlemanly style in his case history, he implied only too clearly that Frau P.J. must be "gagging" for sex with her husband. In her acute frustration, the mere reference to a Spanish cigarette girl such as Carmen longing for a man proved just enough to send her into paroxysms of sexual ecstasy. So, according to Freud, sexual fantasies result at least in part from a lack of sexual fulfillment, with the fantasy serving as a means of satisfying a frustrated wish.

According to Freud, the sexual fantasy of longing, and the consequent orgasm during Carmen's "Séguidille," not only gratified Frau P.J.'s sexual wish but also served a defensive function. It allowed Frau P.J. to enjoy thoughts of blissful reunion with her husband rather than subject her mind to the possibility that her traveling husband might be having an extramarital affair with a young Fräulein in Breslau, Bucharest, or Salzburg, or even fail to return home.

As Freud continued to acquire further clinical psychoanalytical experience with his private patients, he became increasingly aware that our fantasy lives do not always unfold in predictable ways. Through the treatment of Frau P.J., he had already learned that arousal and orgasm might occur in the most seemingly unlikely of places—for instance, seated behind the keyboard of a piano in a bourgeois Viennese parlor. By 1899, Freud had learned so much more about the vicissitudes of human sexual life that he wrote to a trusted medical colleague: "I am accustoming myself to the idea of regarding every sexual act as a process in which four persons are involved." But what does Freud mean by this rather provocative notion that every sexual act might actually involve four people?

Earlier in his letter, Freud had written about bisexuality, a subject that fascinated him greatly; and although he did not elaborate in great detail, I suspect that his observation about sex requiring four people may well be a condensed reference to his idea that when a woman and a man make love, each individual's mind contains both male and female component parts. But Freud may also have begun to hint that when a person performs a sexual act, he or she often has a fantasy image of someone else in mind. When Mr. Smith and Mrs. Smith have coital relations, he may well be thinking of another woman and she may well be thinking of another man; hence the bed becomes crowded with four people instead of two. As a very experienced mental health professional, Freud would have known not only about the extramarital affairs of his patients, but also about what I have termed the "intra-marital affair" as well, namely, those private sexual thoughts that permit us all to cheat on our partners even while making love to them.

As his work progressed, Freud speculated that the content of people's fantasy lives develops from real experiences that have occurred during their earliest developmental years. For Freud, and for modern Freudians such as myself, the choice of one's fantasy-objects derives in large measure from one's earlier "lovers" of infancy and childhood, principally our parents or caretaking figures. Freud also noted that although sexual fantasies become variations of infantile and childhood experiences, they do not always mirror the original childhood experience point for point. For instance, "Kelvin," a participant in my research project, told me that he had learned how to masturbate in a darkened cupboard in his parents' home. He would hide there so that his "authoritarian" parents would not discover him masturbating in his bedroom. Born into a country family who lived near a muddy English moor, Kelvin's mother kept all sorts of rubber boots in the cupboard, and as Kelvin reached orgasm, he would push his body up against the hardened rubber boots to provide himself with some further physical friction. Years later, when Kelvin became a grown man and lived on his own, the thrilling memories of enjoying secret mastur-batory pleasure in the cupboard would return to him, and in his sexual fantasies he would always imagine his lovers wearing rubber wading boots. This vignette provides an indication of Freud's notion that we seize upon a piece of early infantile or childhood experience, then develop it, transform it, or even theatricalize it, so that this experience becomes the very basis of sexual fantasies and sexual arousal in later life. Kelvin's fantasy would not have surprised Sigmund Freud, who recognized as early as 1905 that erotic fantasies can take any form. Freud, in fact, noted that erotic daydreams assume "endless varieties."

After more than twenty years of psychological practice, Freud no longer wrote with the bemused curiosity of a fledgling clinical scientist groping his way through a welter of new and unusual findings. By 1908, Freud offered a rather more harsh assessment of the sexual fantasy. Not only did the fantasy fulfill secret wishes and protect the mind from uncomfortable thoughts, he said, and not only did it develop from early childhood experiences, but now Freud reported that the sexual fantasy indicated the presence of mental turmoil. In his short essay on "Creative Writers and Day-Dreaming," Freud opined, "We may lay it down that a happy person never phantasies, only an unsatisfied one. The motive forces of phantasies are unsatisfied wishes, and every single phantasy is the fulfilment of a wish, a correction of unsatisfying reality." In the same article, Freud also observed that our fantasies not only provide pleasure, but also create distress, noting that: "The adult, on the contrary, is ashamed of his phantasies and hides them from other people. He cherishes his phantasies as his most intimate possessions, and as a rule he would rather confess his misdeeds than tell anyone his phantasies. It may come about that for that reason he believes he is the only person who invents such phantasies and has no idea that creations of this kind are widespread among other people." In this respect, Freud trod an uncomfortable line. He observed, essentially, that sexual fantasies occur in all of our minds, and they cause us shame and anxiety; but even though fantasies may result from frustrations, we all enjoy them. Nevertheless, we often suffer from a sense of isolation because of them, and we frequently believe that no one else has ever had such unusual private sexual thoughts.

Although some people do seem to have a relatively straightforward and uncomplicated sexual fantasy life, dreaming of tender, loving intercourse with their long-term marital partners, the vast majority of women and men seem to have a much more colorful set of fantasies, many of which produce not only pleasure but also pain. Shortly before his death in 1939, Freud wrote a case report, published posthumously, about a male patient who suffered from psychogenic impotency; this individual simply could not achieve an erection during sexual relations. But when he masturbated by himself, the patient invoked a fantasy of having intercourse with both his mother and his father, and this very vivid fantasy facilitated tumescence. I suspect that this male patient must have blushed considerably before revealing this private masturbatory fantasy to Professor Freud; but to his credit, Freud strove to provide a quiet and confidential setting in which just such sexual confessions could occur. Further, when a patient becomes so troubled by a sexual symptom, he or she will often go to great lengths to find a treatment, as many sexual difficulties of this nature can destroy one's marriage or one's relationships with one's nearest and dearest.

Although Freud did not provide many details of this particular case, the fantasy of having intercourse with one's mother and one's father raises many questions. Why would the patient become aroused by the thought of his elderly mom and dad, rather than by his more nubile female partner? Might he simply be an incestuous pervert? Or had this patient allowed his mental censor to lift sufficiently to offer Freud an insight into the origins of our erotic attractions in adult life? Perhaps, as Freud thought, our parents do become our first fantasized lovers, as they will have been the very people who had most access to our young bodies by feeding us, cradling us, bathing us, and changing our diapers. The pleasurable stirrings that we may experience as infants become repressed, but according to Freud, they also remain ever present in the unconscious regions of our mind, and they continue to operate in a powerful, subterranean manner for the rest of our adult lives. A careful study of Freud's clinical observations forces us to confront a crucial question, namely, Do his findings shed light only on the most disturbed members of our population, or do they have relevance for understanding the psychology of reasonably mentally healthy men and women everywhere?

Although the study of sexual fantasy never became a predominant focus in Freud's substantial research career, he has provided all modern psychologists, psychotherapists, psychoanalysts, and sexologists with the essential tools that we have needed to begin our subsequent journey of understanding. Freud occupies the most towering position within the study of human sexuality, not least because he overcame the terrific resistances of his colleagues, most of whom regarded him with suspicion and derision for talking so frankly about sexual matters at a point in history when even physicians regarded sex as not only a completely private but also a shameful topic.

Less than nine years after the death of Sigmund Freud in 1939, another revolution took place in the history of human sexology when Professor Alfred Charles Kinsey, a mild-mannered, bow-tied, Midwestern entomologist and zoologist at Indiana University who had until then devoted most of his professional energies to the scientific study of gall wasps, shocked America with the publication of his overnight sensation *Sexual Behavior in the Human Male*, the most comprehensive and most frank survey of sexual practices ever undertaken. Alfred Kinsey's book, coauthored by his research associates Wardell Pomeroy and Clyde Martin, became such a preoccupation among the chattering classes in the United States that, within five weeks of publication, it topped the nonfiction best-seller list, shifting some 100,000 copies in just over two months. Several months thereafter, in December 1948,

Broadway songwriter Cole Porter would immortalize Kinsey in the lyrics to the song "Too Darn Hot," the Act Two opener of his hit musical *Kiss Me, Kate.*

Kinsey scandalized a nation, still recovering from World War II, not only by conducting the largest, most intimate study of male sexuality in history, but also by revealing that beneath the apple-pie exterior of a nation reared on the saccharine films of box-office sensation Shirley Temple, and beneath the flag-waving for the revered President Franklin Delano Roosevelt, lurked a secret, subterranean sexuality.

Professor Kinsey's original publication, some 804 pages in length, could not be dismissed as the work of a repressed pornographer. He and his research colleagues spent years scouring the nation in order to interview some 12,000 Americans face to face. They recruited their interview subjects from college fraternities, junior high school classes, denizens of roominghouses, groups of conscientious objectors, professional men, delinquents, prisoners, hitchhikers, mental patients, and even the cast of the Broadway production of Tennessee Williams's play *A Streetcar Named Desire*—so somewhere in the data we may have an anonymized sexual history from Marlon Brando, who created the role of Stanley Kowolski. Kinsey spent a lengthy period of time training his interviewers, who then conducted searing, standardized examinations of the research participants, men both "White" and "Negro," "Heterosexual" and "Homosexual," from Michigan to Manhattan and beyond. They asked their subjects on average between 300 and 521 questions each, covering everything from marital status to masturbatory techniques. By the end of the study, Kinsey had elicited full sexual histories from such diverse occupational groups as bootleggers, clergymen, farmers, gamblers, male prostitutes, "ne'er-do-wells," pimps, prison officials, psychiatrists, public-school teachers, thieves, hold-up men, and welfare workers, not to mention clerks, college professors, lawyers, physicians, and police officials.

The findings that proved most startling at the time included the discovery that virtually all men masturbate, though few had ever admitted this fact to anyone before; further, extremely large percentages of men had engaged in premarital sex, homosexual sex, or extramarital sex. While much of this data will not be alarming to a twenty-first-century audience (except perhaps the high rate of homosexual experience or experimentation in otherwise heterosexually orientated men), Kinsey had set off a time bomb. Owing to the sheer size of his research sample, and the rigor with which he both collected and recorded his data, his findings could not be ignored. A companion volume appeared in 1953 entitled *Sexual Behavior in the Human Female*. Coauthored by Kinsey, Pomeroy, and Martin, with the assistance of the anthropologist Paul Gebhard and nine other research workers, it revealed equally explosive material, shattering the myth of the 1950's housewife as the bouffant-haired, taffeta-clad virtual virgin who had only ever had sex two or three times, in the missionary position, and strictly for procreative purposes.

One would require the services of a social historian of American attitudes to explore the full effect of Kinsey's explosive blast upon the development of sexuality in America, in Great Britain, and elsewhere, but all sexologists and mental health practitioners would agree that Kinsey exerted a monumental impact, principally through the removal of the veil of secrecy that had covered so much human sexuality. He thereby reduced the incalculable amount of shame and guilt experienced by most mid-century citizens over sex—masturbation and homosexuality, in particular.

Although Kinsey had made an enormous contribution to the study of human sex, unparalleled, and probably unmatchable, in our lifetime, his study concentrated almost exclusively on actual, external behavior. In other words, he elicited information about *what* we do in bed (i.e., *which* sex acts we enjoy, *how often*, and *with whom*). Though deeply sympathetic to Freudian psychoanalysis, Kinsey had received no formal training in modern psychology, and therefore he treated the human being very much like a gall wasp, a specimen whose behavior could be studied visually. He provided us with very little information about the contents of the human mind during sex, or about the causes of sexual activities or preferences, or about the psychological reactions to various sexual experiences. He left the field of sexual fantasy to his colleagues in the psychotherapeutic and psychoanalytical communities. Indeed, in the whole of his 804-page textbook on male sexuality, one will find only one small paragraph on sexual fantasy, in which he notes that fantasy and behavior may correspond to one another perfectly (e.g., as in the case of a heterosexual man having heterosexual sex while fantasizing about heterosexual sex), or, alternatively, that the behavioral reality and the intrapsychic fantasy may be more disparate (e.g., a heterosexual man having heterosexual sex while fantasizing about farmyard animals). Kinsey also noted, in a throwaway sentence, that although fantasy often accompanies masturbation, the fantasies sometimes do not become conscious until a year or so after the male in question will have begun to practice self-stimulation.

In the wake of this towering achievement by Alfred Kinsey and his research team (many of whom do not receive the proper credit that they deserve as Kinsey's traveling foot soldiers), the explicit landscape of Western sexuality could no longer remain quite so repressed. Indeed, his work ushered in the development of a more frank dialogue around sexuality that reached its apex during the cultural revolution of the 1960s, when sexual interactions could be explored and enjoyed with newfound refreshment, not only for men, but also, perhaps especially, for women, vast swathes of whom had never previously experienced orgasm, or even known that they could.

By the 1970s, the era of Heinrich van Kaan and Richard von Krafft-Ebing had become all but eclipsed, and the more humanist and liberal progressivity of Sigmund Freud and Alfred Kinsey held sway, opening the floodgates for many more serious researchers, such as the American writer Nancy Friday, who, though untrained in psychology, caused one further explosion in 1973 with the publication of her culture-shaping book *My Secret Garden*. This book proved to be not only a great contribution to the study of the female mind, but also a proto-feminist tract that documented in graphic detail that women could be every bit as sexual as their male counterparts. Beneath the suburban housewife, Friday revealed, lay a smoldering, creative, pleasure-seeking, and often guilt-ridden landscape. Her work demonstrated that many American women in the 1970s fantasized uncompromisingly about hard-core sex throughout the day, some about soft wind-swept beaches, and others about being raped by brutish men or by animals. Three further compendia collected by Nancy Friday appeared between 1975 and 1991— *Forbidden Flowers; Men in Love—Men's Sexual Fantasies: The Triumph of Love over Rage;* and *Women on Top*—each more revealing than its predecessor. Friday thereby established the discipline of sexual fantasy studies as a legitimate area of clinical, academic, and cultural inquiry, spawning a growing literature of psychotherapeutic case studies, experimental psychological studies, and published volumes of erotica. As Friday herself has noted with characteristic modesty, perhaps one of the greatest achievements of her work will be the recognition that virtually all adult men and women do have a private sexual fantasy life, and that, although many people may find their own fantasies lewd, dirty, tormenting, or bizarre, other sane and sentient people enjoy the very same fantasies. As Friday reported, she has received copious letters from women on both sides of the Atlantic, many of whom conveyed similar sentiments including this confession from one reader: "I have never heard other women express thoughts like these. I thought I must be some sort of freak or pervert for having such sexually 'wrong' ideas. Now I feel I can accept myself. Thank God, I am not alone."

The Sexual Fantasy Research Project

I began working psychotherapeutically with patients in 1982, as a young trainee under clinical supervision. Since that time I have treated several hundred individuals and couples in short-term, medium-term, and, principally, long-term psychotherapy. Additionally, I have conducted over 3,000 assessment interviews—introductory consultations designed to ascertain a patient's suitability for a particular type of psychological intervention. In such cases, following the assessment interview I refer these patients to colleagues, to psychotherapeutic groups, or to other forms of psychological services. Although I have accumulated a great deal of clinical experience, hearing tales of abuse, bereavement, perversion, even murder, I have had, over the decades, very few psychotherapy patients who would entrust me with the full, intimate details of their sexual fantasy life. This would not be unusual in the casebook of the practicing mental health professional.

My colleagues have reported a similar lacuna in their work with psychotherapy patients. Since embarking on my research project on sexual fantasies, I have begun polling colleagues at mental health conferences and meetings, and I can report that fewer than 5 percent of them have had the experience of hearing patients or clients discussing either masturbatory fantasies or coital fantasies. I suspect that we rarely hear about fantasies in the consulting room because of the lingering shame of the content of our fantasies—content that often violates our very sense of self. In the few cases where I did hear about sexual fantasies during the early years of my working life, I came across the following sorts of problematic situations:

- A member of the medical profession whose masturbatory fantasies involved performing acts of surgical sadism on young women.

- A self-identified heterosexual, married male, who had fathered three children, yet whose fantasy life involved being urinated upon by homosexual men.
- A childcare worker who harbored pedophilic masturbatory fantasies, although he had never acted upon them.
- A successful romantic novelist who would herself fantasize about sex with animals, and not with human beings. She felt fraudulent writing "slushy" novels about fairy-tale romance when her own psychological life revolved around bestiality.

Clearly, one can imagine the internal dilemmas and the personal anxieties with which these individuals had to contend. Can it be any wonder that it took each of these men and women a great deal of time and courage to articulate the very fantasies that threatened to annihilate their sense of identity? How can one live with oneself as a healer of illness who simultaneously derives orgasmic pleasure from the thought of carving up women's bodies with one's own surgical instruments—a veritable Florence Nightingale by day and Sweeney Todd by night?

One of my London-based marital psychotherapy colleagues, Elspeth Morley of the Society of Couple Psychoanalytic Psychotherapists, offered a helpful and cogent explanation as to why psychotherapeutic workers learn about their patients' fantasies—especially the patients' truest, most private masturbatory fantasies, as opposed to the barroom variety—so infrequently. She suggested that unless patients take the plunge and risk sharing a deeply embarrassing and potentially humiliating fantasy in the early stages of therapeutic work, they will be unlikely to do so at all. Many remain too inhibited to reveal such fantasy material at a later stage, especially after the professional relationship between the psychotherapist and the client has become increasingly well established. In other words, many people would find it easier to reveal their fantasies to an anonymous prostitute, or to a fellow subscriber in an Internet chat room, than to someone they meet with on a regular basis, possibly several times weekly over many years. In this respect, we as psychotherapists find ourselves in a position similar to that of a long-term marital partner, being often the last to know.

I have to admit that although much of my psychotherapeutic work in those years could be described as "deep," as I frequently spent months, if not years, with patients reconstructing infantile traumas of abuse, neglect, and other forms of cruelty, the most private sexual core of my clients remained, in most instances, incommunicado. It may be, of course, that many of the patients who attended for sessions had no sexual fantasies, or perhaps no shameful ones that could be readily described. But I did know from speaking to the aforementioned surgeon who fantasized about chopping up women's bodies, and the predominantly heterosexual father-of-three who fantasized about homosexual urination, how very complicated this subject can become and how deeply difficult it may be for people to have even a confidential, professional conversation about these issues.

One would, of course, be well justified to wonder about this material; perhaps, as may be the case with many mental health professionals, my vision had become distorted by listening to the confessions of some very emotionally unwell individuals over too many years. Undoubtedly, psychotherapists do hear about the uglier side of life more frequently than those in other fields. I cannot remember a working day in recent years in which I have *not* heard about child sexual abuse, infidelity, and death, often within the same fifty-minute session. But in spite of this, I wish to confirm that the vast majority of individuals who have come to see me over the years cannot be described as mad. I have, of course, worked with those diagnosed as suffering from schizophrenia, affective disorders, and other psychoses, as well as those struggling with borderline personality disorder, not to mention forensic patients who break the law. But the bulk of my caseload has consisted, and continues to consist, of stable, creative, human, and decent women and men who nevertheless have certain areas of anxiety, inhibition, or torment in their emotional lives, and who have both the courage and the intelligence to come for psychotherapy rather than sitting and stewing unproductively, as so many people do. Therefore, I would be reluctant to dismiss the sexual fantasies that I have heard about over the years as the products of "disturbed" minds, for this does not at all reflect the clinical reality.

In spite of the difficulties of accessing true, deep, honest sexual fantasy, such material continued to seep into my practice, especially over the past decade, owing in part to the increasingly widespread availability and popularization of pornography on the Internet. As someone who divides his time between working one-on-one with individuals and working with couples, I could not escape hearing stories of Internet pornography and Internet sex addiction in my consulting room, especially among couples who had come to see me together with marriages or partnerships in deepest jeopardy.

But even though I had begun to learn about an increasing number of Internet pornography cases in both my clinical practice and the practices of my marital psychotherapy colleagues—a great way to learn about the complexities of hidden sexual fantasies—I still realized, as the 1990s unfolded, that my colleagues and I knew relatively little about fantasies and about the potential dangers of Internet pornography. The husbands would dismiss their Internet usage as "just a bit of fun"; the wives, invariably, would be utterly devastated to learn of their husbands' secret Internet fantasy life. By 2002, I knew that the field of sexual fantasies could not be ignored, and I resolved to examine this neglected aspect of human psychology in greater detail. And so I commenced first the British Sexual Fantasy Research Project, and then a cross-national (Anglo-American) Sexual Fantasy Research Project. Inspired by the psychological insights of Sigmund Freud, by the large-scale methodological rigor of Alfred Kinsey, and by the brave public dissemination of Nancy Friday, I decided that I would attempt my own research, a "Kinsey of the mind," so that I could begin to answer some basic questions.

For instance, I wanted to know something more about the typical Internet pornography user. Did all modern British and American men use the Internet to gratify sexual fantasies, just as during adolescence virtually all boys will snag a copy of *Playboy* or *Penthouse*, for example? Could the behavior of an Internet pornography addict be described as ordinary and "normal," something that partners would just have "to deal with," or did it represent something much more sinister? I saw a growing number of cases of men who enjoyed examining Internet images of violence toward women, images that would cause these men to become sexually aroused. I wondered, should these individuals be *tolerated*, or should they be *treated*? Did these men pose an actual threat to women in real life, and should they therefore be incarcerated? These cases highlighted many moral, ethical, professional, and even criminological questions, and I knew that my colleagues and I all felt hard pressed to generate thoughtful, cogent responses.

Fortified, in particular, by Kinsey's methodology, I proceeded by conducting a number of face-to-face "pilot" interviews with volunteers in order to ascertain whether anyone would actually speak to me in sufficient detail about the content of their sexual fantasies and the role of sexual fantasies in their lives. I decided that I would not, and could not, use any of my psychotherapy patients as interviewees, because conducting a research interview in the middle of ongoing therapeutic treatment would potentially cause an unhelpful interference. The trained psychotherapist never dictates what a patient should discuss on any given occasion, and if I interrupted a session in order to request a formal interview on sexual fantasies, this would have created unwanted difficulties. Therefore, I knew that I would have to find "real" members of the general public, ordinary people who had not necessarily had any experience of psychotherapy, counseling, or other mental health services, who could talk to me about their sexual fantasies, helping me to understand more about the origins, structure, and function of their private masturbatory and coital fantasy life.

But where would I find such people? I had reservations about putting up posters on notice boards, or placing advertisements in newspapers or magazines. After all, I had no idea what sort of people might emerge through such means.

A timely supper party provided the impetus. While dining with some friends and colleagues, I happened to mention my plan to undertake a research study on the psychology of sexual fantasies, but that I had not yet proceeded very far, beyond having studied the relevant published professional literature in great depth, and having discussed the subject with psychotherapeutic colleagues at length, for years. One of the supper guests, Dan Chambers, a television executive who had received an undergraduate degree in experimental psychology from the University of Oxford, and who had commissioned a number of quite serious science documentaries, suggested that he might be able to offer assistance. After a series of meetings, he donated a small amount of funding so that I could offer a token payment to a selection of randomly chosen men and women who might participate in my pilot interview research. Chambers did not offer this support solely out of the goodness of his heart; he very much hoped that such research might ultimately prove sufficiently interesting to serve as the basis of a science television documentary. I knew that as a private practitioner of psychotherapy, I would need the assistance of a team of researchers, and the prospect of collaborating with television documentary makers seemed a potentially creative solution to the administrative burdens of conducting a large-scale study.

In order to find willing research interviewees, I resolved that it would be best if I could enlist the services of a reputable national polling company—an organization that regularly canvases people in order to ascertain their opinions on a host of topics. By selecting a polling bureau, I would thereby ensure that I would be able to access a random sampling of adult men and women throughout Great Britain, in the first instance, and later, abroad, thus obtaining a more representative set of responses.

After interviewing a number of different polling companies, I decided to collaborate with YouGov, an organization founded in 2000 to specialize in eliciting viewpoints from members of the general public about political parties. YouGov typically sends out questionnaires to a random selection of adult Britons in order to gauge, for instance, how many plan to vote Labour, how many Conservative, and how many Liberal Democrat in the next national election—indispensable information for British politicians and their advisers. The company provides extremely reliable data, and in a number of notable instances their final polling predictions have been vindicated on election night. Nadhim Zahawi, the joint chief executive officer of YouGov, immediately grasped the potential import of a research project on sexual fantasy, and he and his colleagues agreed to embark with me upon a multiyear research collaboration.

The technical staff at YouGov sent out an e-mail in 2003 to 3,617 individuals from their large, computer-based panel of approximately 55,000 British men and women, all citizens with voting rights, aged eighteen years and above. The e-mail inquired whether anyone would be willing to come to London to speak to a Registered Psychotherapist, for which a small payment would be offered in addition to travel expenses. I suspect that I could have dispensed with the payment, but I knew that I wanted to conduct very detailed and intense psychodiagnostic interviews, and that this would require many long hours of interviewing. I therefore wanted to reimburse those who participated for their time, as a mark of both respect and appreciation.

Of the potential participants, 22 percent offered their services—some 795 people—many more than I could ever hope to meet in any other way.

I resolved to begin with a small number of pilot interviews—ten in all—evenly divided between men and women, chosen on a first-come, first-served basis. I interviewed my ten pilot subjects, who all lived within a reasonable traveling distance from London, in the order presented in Table 2.1.

A pilot interview in clinical research might be likened to a test drive of a new car. In social science research, the pilot interview serves an important function, allowing the researcher to ascertain whether the data obtained will be sufficiently interesting to justify an even more extended and costly research project at some point in the future. As part of the pilot interview scheme, I met with a small cohort of adult volunteers, and after explaining the nature of my research, I asked these

TABLE 2.1

The Pilot Interview

Interview Number	Sex	Age
01	Male	51
02	Female	26
03	Male	23
04	Male	24
05	Female	54
06	Male	64
07	Male	41
08	Female	62
09	Female	44
10	Female	31

individuals whether they would feel comfortable discussing their sexual histories with me, focusing not only on their actual sexual behaviors but also on their sexual fantasy life. To my surprise, and to my great delight, I found not only that I could pose the potentially awkward questions in a calm and noninvasive manner, but also that the participants themselves could overcome their barriers and inhibitions and successfully relate their sexual biographies to me in considerable detail.

I conducted all the pilot interviews in a neutral office building in Central London—not in my own consulting room. I share a suite of offices with other psychotherapy colleagues, and I did not want to have large numbers of strangers traipsing in and out of our suite, creating more than the usual amount of noise and potential disruption.

I offered each potential interviewee a time, explaining in advance that the interview would last approximately five hours and that it would cover some very sensitive topics, including sexual fantasy. The prospective interviewees also learned that the interview would be conducted by a man rather than a woman, and that the interviewer was an officially Registered Psychotherapist. I also confirmed that a modest payment of £50, plus travel expenses, would be offered as a token of appreciation. When the interviewees arrived for their appointed times, I asked them to read and then sign a written consent form, drafted by a lawyer, in which the interviewees would confirm, in writing, that they understood fully the nature of the interview, that the interview would contain sensitive questions about sexual matters, and that the findings might be published later in confidential, anonymized form. All the ten interviewees read the consent form with care, and each of them signed.

I then ushered each interviewee into the office, which contained two comfortable sofas, one for each of us, as well as a table with a box of tissues, a selection of drinks (ice water, soft drinks, etc.), and an assortment of fresh fruit. After inviting the guest to sit down, I explained that I would be tape-recording the interview, but that each tape would be marked with a special code number, rather than with the interviewee's name, and that apart from myself, only one secretary, experienced in typing sensitive materials and sworn to secrecy, would even hear the contents of the tape. I promised that once the secretary had produced a transcription of the interview, and once I had completed my analysis of the data, the original tape would be destroyed. I then asked each interviewee again whether he or she would still be happy to continue. Once again, all of the prospective interviewees agreed to these terms and conditions.

I began the interview by confirming my name, my credentials, and qualifications, and I stated the name of the national registration and certification body to which I belong: the United Kingdom Council for Psychotherapy. As none of the prospective interviewees knew anything about me, I felt it would be essential to establish my seriousness as a researcher. At this point, I explained the reasoning behind the interview study, noting that as a marital psychotherapist I often meet couples who harbor incompatible sexual fantasies, and that, surprisingly, the mental health profession does not understand as much about the nature of sexual fantasies as we would wish; therefore, an interview study of this type would help us to develop a greater understanding of the psychology of sexuality. I reassured the interviewees that we would have a long conversation that would contain no trick questions, and that he or she would certainly know the answer to each of the questions that I would pose.

In discussion with a team of mental health colleagues, and with the collaboration of a senior academic colleague from the field of sexual health and sexual epidemiology, I had already devised a structure for the interview. I would ask a small number of questions about broad areas within the interviewee's life, conducting what researchers call a "semi-structured interview," as distinct from a loose, free-associative conversation or a tightly structured interview (such as Alfred Kinsey and his associates had undertaken). As a clinician, I know that asking direct questions, paradoxically, can alienate interviewees and even close down a line of thought. By asking a small number of broad questions, one implicitly encourages the other person to roam more freely, offering often unexpectedly edifying material. For instance, if I had asked a close-ended question such as, "Have you ever had sex on a Saturday night between 10:00 P.M. and 11:00 P.M.?" the interviewee would, in all likelihood, respond with a simple yes or no. This would shut down the potential for a richer conversation. But if I asked a more open-ended question—perhaps, "Tell me about your sexual life, if you wouldn't mind?"—it would provide the interviewee with a blank canvas, thus allowing the individual to speak at much greater length.

I divided the semi-structured interview into five sections, each lasting for approximately one hour:

1. Current life
2. Family history
3. Infancy and childhood history
4. Sexual behavioral history
5. Sexual fantasy history

In the first hour, we began very gently. I asked the interviewee to tell me something about his or her current life, encouraging the participant to "paint a picture for me" of what life looks like. With this simple invitation, I soon learned more than I ever imagined I would, ranging from what the person eats for breakfast to his or her living conditions, employment, hobbies and interests, friendship group, pet loves and loathings, and so much more. This first hour of interviewing served two very important functions: First and foremost, it provided me with some basic biographical material; additionally, it served as the ice-breaker for the rest of the interview, which, as I knew, would become infinitely more intimate and revealing as we progressed. By speaking for a full hour about more mundane matters, such as one's favorite films, a more trusting conversational rapport developed between myself and the interviewee, thus creating a foundation upon which we could build as the interview unfolded.

In the second and third hours, the interview became increasingly personal as I asked for as much biography about parents and grandparents as the interviewee could recall. This sort of information proves critical for the psychotherapist, allowing us to learn more about the difficulties and traumas with which the ancestors of the interviewee had to struggle. This data helps us to appreciate more fully the sort of emotional climate in which the interviewee has grown up. For example, if it emerged that just six months before the birth of one of my interviewees, his mother's mother had died of a sudden heart attack, this would prompt me to wonder about the mother's psychological state, and whether she suffered from an acute bereavement reaction at the time of the interviewee's birth. Such circumstances could create an emotional distance between the young baby and his mother, a template that might then contribute to his ultimate sexual alienation from women during adult life.

I also used the middle hours of our conversation to take a full developmental history of the subject's own life, covering such areas as details of the birth and any birth complications, early breast-feeding or bottle-feeding, early toileting experiences, birth of siblings, early bereavements, discipline and punishment, physical maturation and developmental achievements, early schooling experiences, and so forth, leaving no stone unturned in my attempt to reconstruct as complete a picture of the interviewee's formative years as could be ascertained in the available time.

With three hours of interviewing already accomplished, we then began to examine the interviewee's sexual biography, exploring, for a further hour, a multitude of topics, ranging from the first kiss to the loss of virginity, the number of partners, thoughts about one's naked body, preferred positions, theories about sexual orientation, experience of fidelity and infidelity, and so forth. Few people would answer these questions in a restaurant, or over a cup of coffee in a friend's lounge. Psychotherapists, however, have developed the capacity, over decades of training and experience, to foster a trusting conversational intimacy, and I discovered, therefore, that after a full three hours of discussion, each interviewee responded to these many sexual questions with virtually complete freedom and lack of inhibition or restraint.

In the last hour, I finally broached the question of sexual fantasy. Generally, I began this section of the interview with a straightforward request: "I wonder whether you would now feel able to tell me about your favorite, most arousing sexual fantasy?" We discussed a host of topics, including the content of the fantasy, the frequency of the fantasy, subsidiary fantasies (such as one's "second favorite" fantasy), differences between masturbatory fantasies and fantasies during intercourse, and any shame or guilt about the fantasy. I also inquired whether any of the interview participants had either revealed this fantasy to another person or enacted the fantasy.

Extraordinarily, although the interviews lasted, on average, for five hours, virtually none of the participants excused themselves for a toilet break. I mention this small detail as an indication of how intense the interviews became and how deeply immersed each participant became in the discussion.

After the conclusion of the formal part of the interview, I administered a battery of psychological tests. These included some standard pencil-and-paper questionnaires, such as the Symptom Check List (90-Item Version), the Eysenck Personality Inventory, the Verbal Fluency Test, and the National Adult Reading Test. Additionally, I relied upon "projective" tests, more free-associative diagnostic tools that allow the interviewee to project his or her deepest fantasies onto a piece of paper (as in the famous Rorschach Inkblot Test). I used a simple drawing test, the Draw-a-Person Test, and a new variant, the Draw-a-Partner Test, encouraging subjects to use a pencil to draw pictures of both themselves and their partners. This copious additional data contributed to my greater understanding of the psychological world of each of the interviewees.

Then I conducted a debriefing, asking participants to reflect on the experience of being interviewed for such a long time. In this final section of the interview, I asked the interviewees how they felt about the time we had spent together, whether they regretted their participation, whether they had learned anything new about themselves, whether the interview had raised anything painful for them that they wished to discuss at greater length, and whether they thought that I might have managed the interview in a more sensitive way. Every single one of the interviewees found the experience worthwhile and edifying, and each stressed that he or she found it helpful to talk about sexual secrets, often for the very first time in their lives. Most left feeling great psychological relief and relaxation from having unburdened themselves to a sympathetic professional stranger whom they would never meet again.

As a final moment in the interview, I produced a "deconsent" form, also drafted by a lawyer, essentially a version of the consent form signed at the outset of the interview. Researchers must of course allow for the possibility that someone may consent to be interviewed at the outset of the project, and then change his or her mind later on. By offering both a consent form and a deconsent form, one affords the interviewee different opportunities to opt out of the project for whatever reason. In the British Sexual Fantasy Research Project, not one participant refused to provide informed consent, an indication that we had prepared the interviewees sufficiently for the experience and that they felt that we had treated them with interest, courtesy, and respect.

As each of the pilot interviewees departed, he or she received payment for the interview and for travel expenses, and I offered each person the opportunity to contact me in the future if something might have emerged from the interview that would require further discussion. In no case did I receive a follow-up telephone call or e-mail communication from any of the interviewees. I suspect that each regarded the interview as a discrete, self-contained experience that had served its purpose for both the researcher and the interviewee.

I shall discuss the principal findings of these interviews in the subsequent chapters, but needless to say, each interview produced an enormous amount of fascinating information that helped me to understand much more not only about the origins of sexual fantasies, but also about the role of sexual fantasies in our private lives and the role of sexual fantasies in our marriages or partnerships. It may also be worth mentioning at this point that none of the interviewees seemed to have any profound insight into the secret meaning or cause of his or her most private sexual fantasies. Whenever I asked anyone a question along the lines of, "Why do you suppose you become so aroused by the thought of sex with your sister-in-law, for instance, as opposed to sex with Kate Moss, for example?" I always received a blank reply. Virtually none of the participants had ever given much thought or reflection to the nature of his or her fantasy life, and most seemed quite baffled by the question. This piece of data alone made me realize that our sexual fantasies remain, by and large, an unprocessed, unsynthesized area of the mind, crying out for explanation.

Without doubt, the preliminary results of the ten pilot interviews proved sufficiently interesting to warrant the accumulation of larger-scale data. After all, the verbal confessions of a few volunteers could be regarded as "self-selected," and therefore potentially biased. To obtain data that truly reflect the population at large, a social-science researcher must study a substantial number of individuals randomly selected from different geographical regions of a country. If I had obtained information on ten people, and only ten, this data might prove very interesting, but it would not be very representative of British citizens at large. What if all ten interviewees just happened to be practicing sadomasochists, or born-again virgins, or what have you? It would be irresponsible, if not dangerous, to present conclusions based on such potentially unrepresentative data. Increasing the sample size dramatically, to obtain data on literally thousands of people, greatly reduces the likelihood of everyone having identical sexual biographies, until the chance of that becomes, in fact, infinitesimally small.

Utilizing the resources of the large team of research scientists, statisticians, and research assistants employed by YouGov, I could now access a unique panel of adult men and women of every age, religious persuasion, social class, occupational background, political ideology, and geographical region throughout Great Britain. The company's database of panel members has proved to be proportionally representative of the British population at large. In other words, let us say, for instance, that there might be 100,000 elderly female Labour Party supporters living in Scotland, 200,000 in the southeast, and 400,000 in the Midlands. In order for YouGov to represent this particular subsample with accuracy, staff researchers would recruit 1 such woman from Scotland, 2 from the southeast, and 4 from the Midlands to serve as long-term panel members. In other words, these seven women would join the YouGov panel, thus providing symbolic representation of approximately 700,000 elderly female Labour Party voters from those areas.

Not only does YouGov strive for proportional representation of geographic, ethnic, religious, sexual, and economic groups, but in constructing their panel, the YouGov staff also ensures that they will enlist panelists who represent the different newspaper readerships in the right percentages. Thus, in any YouGov survey, some 17 percent of the British respondents will be readers of the *Sun,* and some 3.5 percent will be readers of the *Guardian,* thus accurately reflecting national newspaper sales. In this respect, YouGov can speak with unusual accuracy about the tastes of the country, at the touch of a computer button.

Panel members receive small payments from YouGov for their time and trouble, ranging typically from fifty pence to one pound sterling per questionnaire, and they must each possess a computer, as YouGov polls men and women online. Thus, participation in a project is financially "incentivized," though to a very small degree. All of the information obtained from YouGov panel members is also coded anonymously so that none of the researchers posing the questions will ever be able to ascertain the name, address, telephone number, or e-mail address of any of the research participants. In this respect, YouGov conforms to the guidelines on confidentiality stipulated by the Market Research Society. YouGov has thus created a brilliant system whereby professional researchers and political parties alike can access the views of a random, representative sample of British subjects without violating the privacy of any of the adult men and women who participate.

Of course, it would be impossible to send a questionnaire to all 45 million or so adults in Great Britain. No computer would be able to process so much data in a meaningful way. Instead, YouGov ordinarily sends questionnaires to approximately 2,000 men and women from their database, and in most situations such a section of the panel will be considered scientifically representative.

After extensive discussions, I also undertook a pilot computer-administered survey of British sexual fantasies. Aided by a team of research colleagues, I devised a 52-item research questionnaire, which we sent to 3,617 British-based men and women from the YouGov panel, composed of 48 percent men and 52 percent women, reflecting the actual proportions in the British population—the very same sample of 3,617 Britons whom I had invited to participate in the face-to-face psychodiagnostic pilot interviews. This figure represents more than three times the number of respondents who would be approached in an ordinary national survey of this type. Approximately 40 percent of those polled responded to the questionnaire online within twenty-four hours, and the remaining 60 percent or so replied within seventy-two hours—quite standard response times for a research survey of this kind. YouGov's own in-house research has indicated very little difference in the data between those who reply quickly and those who respond a few days later.

In the questionnaire, we asked panelists to reply, in privacy, to a number of queries, ranging from the nature and frequency of their sexual fantasies to their background and childhood development, including a history of any child sexual abuse. As a psychotherapist, I particularly wanted to know whether a correlation could be established between early histories of abuse and later fantasies of abusing others or of being abused oneself. I already knew from the work of Nancy Friday and from research by a number of experimental psychologists that sexual fantasies of abuse—defined as harsh physical discipline or punishment, or as inappropriate sexual contact (either forced, unwanted contact between adults, or sexual contact with children)—would, sadly, be all too well represented within the general population.

The preliminary results of the pilot clinical interviews and the pilot computer survey of the British Sexual Fantasy Research Project helped me to appreciate a number of key findings:

- The vast majority of British adults *do* fantasize, indeed, quite frequently.
- Paradoxically, however, most adults never share their fantasies with anyone else, in part because of the great shame involved, as well as the great guilt, since most fantasies revolve around someone other than one's current long-term partner.
- Many fantasies contain strong imagery of sadism, masochism, and other forms of harm. If any of us could manage to put many of our more aggressive fantasies into practice, we would end up in prison.
- Contrary to expectations from the media, the film industry, and so on, a surprisingly small percentage of our fantasies concern so-called celebrities (entertainers, sports personalities, and politicians). Most of us fantasize about people whom we know, or, in many instances, about people whom we "create" in our minds, especially so that we may co-opt them to participate in our often subversive, sadistic, or masochistic internal dramas.
- In spite of the widespread fears of relating one's sexual fantasies to one's regular partner, in the preliminary survey a great many people expressed a keen interest in discussing their

sexual fantasies with a qualified mental health professional, thus suggesting a certain amount of curiosity, or perhaps concern, about the content of their sexual fantasies.

The preliminary questionnaire contained not only multiple-choice questions but also an open-text space in which participants could write out their most sexually arousing masturbatory or coital fantasy in as much detail as possible. Many of the responses to this open-text space appear in subsequent chapters of this book.

By now, I had accumulated not only data from my two decades of clinical psychotherapeutic experience, but also data from the ten preliminary psychodiagnostic research interviews and from the 3,617 computer surveys, complete with extensive information about the respondents' sexual histories and sexual fantasies. Although information on approximately 4,000 individuals (the combined total of the aforementioned data points) already constituted a very rich, robust, statistically significant body of evidence, I wanted to undertake even more extensive research.

I reasoned that, in order to make compelling statements about the nature of something so potentially ephemeral and intangible as a sexual fantasy, I would need to study the largest dataset that I could acquire. As a result of the pilot study data, I proposed to launch a full-scale national survey on the psychology of sexual fantasies, and with the aid of an advisory panel (consisting of a clinical psychologist, a marital psychotherapist, a child psychotherapist, a psychoanalyst, a team of adult psychotherapists, a statistician, a sexual health epidemiologist, and colleagues from related disciplines), I began to raise the necessary funds to undertake such a large piece of research work.

Throughout 2004, 2005, and 2006, I set about accumulating a much larger set of British adult sexual fantasies. With the further cooperation of YouGov, I sent a revised and expanded version of my 52-item computer-administered questionnaire about sexual behavior, sexual health, and sexual fantasy to 34,303 additional online panel members in November and December 2004, of whom 15,000 adults responded. Owing to the great length of the questionnaire, which required, on average, between thirty and sixty minutes of reading and responding time, not all of the 15,000 respondents completed the entire questionnaire, for whatever reason. But 13,553 of them did so in full, replying to every one of the fifty-two items on the questionnaire, thus providing me with an extraordinarily large amount of information.

This represents a 39.51 percent response rate (rounded to the nearest hundredth decimal place), which most researchers would regard as an impressive result for a research project of this nature. In view of both the sensitive nature of the questions and the sheer amount of time and thought required to answer this questionnaire, it would have been highly unlikely that all 34,303 online panelists would have responded, even with the token financial incentive, which on this occasion included the possibility of receiving a £50 prize through a draw. But we did collect partial data, especially full texts of fantasies, on 15,000, and complete data for each of the 52 questions from 13,553. YouGov assured me that this questionnaire could be described as both much longer and much more demanding than their average political poll, and yet we had a very robust and comparable response rate.

I supplemented the quantitative questionnaire results with a further set of 122 intensive, qualitative, face-to-face clinical psychodiagnostic interviews with British adults. This proved to be an extremely labor-intensive undertaking. I conducted the interviews principally during evenings and weekends, and, on several occasions, throughout extended sabbatical weeks and holiday periods. Participants were drawn from the larger YouGov panel. Each of these interviews lasted for approximately four to five hours, with most requiring five hours, exactly as in the pilot interview study. At the end of each interview, I administered the same battery of standard psychological research questionnaires and projective tests as before, also obtaining the necessary consent.

Additionally, I received a formal invitation from Channel Five Television, the British television broadcaster, to create a one-hour documentary about the psychology of sexual fantasies, commissioned by the head of science programming and by the same executive who had expressed interest in the project years earlier, who, by this point, had become the director of programs at Channel Five. This commission supplied some much-needed research funds; in addition, during the preparations for this program, which first appeared on British television in 2005, a team of specialist television researchers obtained personal testimony from other women and men who agreed to share their fantasies on camera, recruited through Web sites and personal contacts. Of course, I would regard these individuals, in particular, as highly self-selected, and although I did learn something from listening to their thoughts, the fantasies reported by these men and women do not figure at all in the data analysis. With the exception of two brief quotations, I have not drawn upon the experiences of these television recruits in the body of this book.

Finally, I established a Web site on which individuals from all around the world could record their sexual fantasies. This yielded some extremely interesting replies. I did not include the full text of the 52-item questionnaire on this Web site, as I suspected that few "surfers" would take the time to answer all of the questions. Instead, I encouraged those men and women (eighteen years of age and over) who found the Web site to provide "open text" responses of their fantasies, along with any information about their early childhood experiences that they might want to share. I have not included the information gleaned from the special sexual fantasy Web site postings in the final data analysis, in spite of the interest value.

To recap, then, I have now read firsthand testimony reports or listened to tape recordings of more than 18,000 British adult sexual fantasies. These data derive from the sources listed in Table 2.2. Please note that in scientific research, the capital letter "N" indicates the number of participants.

Combining the total number of masturbatory and coital fantasies that I have heard about in clinical assessment work and psychotherapeutic work over the past twenty years and more with the fantasies generated specifically for the British Sexual Fantasy Research Project, I have now studied more than 19,000 British sexual fantasies in total.

To ensure that the sample remains as representative as possible, I have drawn only from the results of the questionnaire sent to the members of the YouGov panel in conducting statistical analyses of the data. Any percentages or other statistical information contained in this book are based on the primary dataset from the 13,553 principal respondents. The lengthier vignettes and case histories derive principally from the confidential clinical psychodiagnostic interviews.

By early 2006, having accumulated this extremely large set of data, I began to embark upon the task of collecting data from outside of Great Britain. With the collaboration of YouGov, I launched a cross-national (Anglo-American) version of the Sexual Fantasy Research Project. I hope to gather comparative data from other parts of the world in years to come. In the meantime, we began by administering a revised version

---

TABLE 2.2

Sources of Data for the British Sexual Fantasy Research Project

1) Responses to the pilot computer survey of 2003 (N =3,167)

2) Responses to the principal computer survey of 2004 (N=15,000 partial responses, of which 13,553 individuals responded in full)

3) Data from the pilot clinical interviews (N=10)

4) Data from the principal clinical interviews (N=122)

5) Data from psychological testing of pilot clinical interviewees and principal clinical interviewees

6) Personal testimony from interviewees for the television documentary (used solely for background color and not as part of the formal data analysis)

7) Personal testimony from respondents to the specialist sexual fantasy research project Web site (used solely for background color and not as part of the formal data analysis)

8) Data from my public sector and private sector psychotherapeutic work with adults over two decades (used principally to inform my developing clinical and theoretical observations about the origins and function of sexual fantasy, but not recorded here in detail owing to the strictures of clinical confidentiality).

---

of the 52-item computer questionnaire to a group of American adults, males and females aged eighteen years and older, who represent every demographic group and every one of the fifty states. We surveyed 5,000 Americans and received completed replies from 3,433 of them. These respondents completed the survey about sexuality and sexual fantasies in exactly the same manner as their British counterparts had done two or three years earlier. Thus, combining the British data with the American data, I now possess a rich archive of full statistical data from a combined group of 20,153 British and American adults, as well as partial data and fantasies for several thousand more, totaling approximately

24,000 fantasies in all. Thus, the British Sexual Fantasy Research Project can claim to be highly statistically representative of the British population at large; combined with the American data from the international Sexual Fantasy Research Project, this dataset now represents, to the best of my knowledge, the largest survey ever published on the psychology of adult male and adult female sexual fantasies.

3

The Intra-Marital Affair: Staging Our Private Theater

My wife said her wildest sexual fantasy would be if I got my own apartment.

— Rodney Dangerfield

A Noah's Ark of Sexual Fantasies

Before we delve more deeply into the hidden psychology of our sexual fantasies—our secret psychological fingerprints of the mind—I would like to introduce you to the enormous breadth and variety of contemporary American and British sexual fantasies. The examples that follow are drawn principally from the computer-administered survey of the British Sexual Fantasy Research Project and the International Sexual Fantasy Research Project and from my direct, face-to-face, psychodiagnostic interviews with research volunteers. They are, for the most part, responses to the request to describe, in as much detail as possible, one's most sexually arousing fantasy. I have also included a very small number of additional fantasies obtained from the Web site that I established explicitly to elicit further fantasies. In every case, I have disguised the names of the fantasists, certainly those who participated in the psychodiagnostic interviews. As for the many men and women who shared their fantasies through the computer survey, I never knew their names in the first place.

AARON

Being stuck on a desert island with the blonde lady of my dreams.

STEPHANIE

I think of a man whom I know in real life. The two of us have a unique and electric sexual chemistry. So much so that strangers we see in public will ask how long we've been together and all that (even though he's not my boyfriend). I think of him teasing me with his lips—bringing them closer to mine and pulling away with the slightest brush of my lips. Constantly teasing. He brushes his lips all over my neck and down to my breasts and nipples all the while he's encircling me with his strong arms. His hands wander on my back smoothing out imaginary stresses. I feel him harden and he sighs while he strains against his pants and me. We're both rubbing against each other while our lips seek each other out. I wrap my legs around him and squeeze. He runs a finger down my back and squeezes my ass.

BEATRICE

Meeting a handsome rich stranger who then wines and dines me, a very romantic evening which ends with us making passionate love. I have multiple orgasms. Then, in this beautiful room, there appears a group of equally good-looking men. I first say, "I am not into group sex," but one holds my legs open, and another holds my arms, whilst a third licks and sucks at my breasts, then my clitoris, and thrusts his tongue repeatedly into my vagina until I am screaming for him to enter me. Then I enjoy a very energetic session with each one, repeating the holding down of me at first each time. (Writing this is turning me on.)

GARETH

Sex during a job interview with the interviewer.

DUNCAN

I meet a young White or Hispanic female. She has a pretty face, large natural breasts, long hair, plump, curvy buttocks, and big, smooth legs. She is just as much into me as I am into her. We wash each other's bodies, allowing our hands to roam freely over every part of each other. We step out of the shower and dry each other off with a thick towel. I give her a long, passionate kiss. Then I turn her around. She bends over, placing her hands on the commode or the sink for support. She allows me to slap her fat butt a few times. Then I commence to have anal sex with her. She becomes increasingly excited until she has a screaming orgasm. She squirts freely and shamelessly as she comes. Then I shoot a load of cum into her asshole. The End.

KAREN

Not willing to answer.

FREDDIE

I imagine an old-fashioned hunting party coming across a girl of about sixteen in the woods. After chatting to her and gaining her confidence, all but one of the men leaves her and he proceeds to kiss and caress her. After she becomes willing, he lays her along the length of a tree trunk. While he is kissing her, the others come back, and as she is so carried away she doesn't notice that she has each breast being fondled by different men, that her legs are being stroked by two more men, and that others are around watching. Gradually, her legs are pulled apart, and yet another man starts to lick her vagina. She, of course, becomes very aroused and starts thrashing around, at which point various objects are produced by the men. Starting with a banana, through to a cucumber and cudgel, eventually, the men start on her, both back and front, from the smallest penis to one belonging to an enormous fellow. She is turned over and generally used.

ISABELLE

I like fantasizing that I'm with the most gorgeous man who adores me and my body, and will do anything I ask. I'm not too kinky so it's not that exciting, but he will make love to me for hours and completely pay attention to my every need.

ORA

My partner asks if I can show his friend how to make a woman come by letting him watch me masturbate. I lay on the bed, naked, and start to rub myself. He brings in his friend. He watches me for a while and then starts doing oral sex on me while my partner watches. I end up having sex with the friend while my partner continues to watch.

HORTENSIA

Having sex in the shower with a complete stranger who I met that day.

UMBERTO

I am a 39-year-old Italian gentleman who loves the ladies (don't we all?). Although I would like to cheat on my wife, I am a good Catholic, and so, I never will. But I do fantasize about practically every woman that I meet. I can't actually walk down the street without eyeing up each and every single woman I see, wondering what her vagina looks like, what her arse and her breasts look like, etc. Sometimes I get so horny on the way into the office, walking down a busy street with lots of beautiful girls, I arrive with a big, stiff erection. So I go to the toilets and beat off before work, thinking about what I would do to some of the people I see in the streets. I am a real devotee of cunnilingus, and I would like to get some pretty blonde English girl and start sucking on her clitty, feeling the moist juices flowing out of her private place, and bring her to a fucking mind-fuck of an orgasm, right there on the street. My wife would divorce me if she knew how much I think about every other woman. Even older women arouse me. I know I could bring them much satisfaction.

EVERETT

I like to image that I am a doctor in charge of a prison-type hospital, and undress and examine the patients.

LEILA

Don't have any.

NANDO

In my fantasy I have mutual oral sex (69) with a much younger acquaintance of mine. Both of us have multiple orgasms and fall asleep exhausted in each other's arms.

MELCHIOR

Meeting Brad Pitt while exercising and he and I take a shower together and then go to a movie, followed by a really expensive dinner, and then checking into the Most Expensive Hotel in America and ordering room service for a week in which we watch porno and have sex several times each day. Also cuddling a lot and talking about what we could do and where we all could go and be together.

CATALINA

My girlfriend and I are having oral sex and one guy is watching us as he is masturbating but is not allowed to touch us, but he does cum all over my girlfriend.

PEDRO

I am a footman at Buckingham Palace, and one day, I am instructed to bring two young, pretty maids to the Throne Room, where Prince William and Prince Harry are waiting. The princes instruct me to bend the young ladies over the throne, and then lift up their short black skirts and pull down their frilly knickers so that their vaginas are showing from between their legs. I then have to unbutton the princes' trousers, and masturbate them both to erection, one in each hand. Prince William says, "Thank you Pedro, for your loyal service to the Crown." He and Harry then stick their throbbing penises into the vaginas of the serving girls, then they pull out and change places. I can see pussy juice on the princes' cocks. Soon, they cream off in the girls' cunts. The whole time I have been jerking off in the corner of the Throne Room, and my expensive livery gets covered with semen stains, much to the annoyance of the Lord Chamberlain and the Queen. The princes swear me to secrecy so I'm not allowed to tell their girlfriends.

QUENTIN

At my age, sexual thoughts don't occur.

ZEB

Satisfying a lesbian sexually.

RAMONA

In a vertical sun-bed with the fans blowing upwards.

XANTHE

This involves me as a doctor in a really sexy outfit. My partner is my patient strapped to the bed. I strip for him and make him watch since he can't touch me. I tease him with feathers and ribbons. I then mount him and have rough sex with him while he is tied up.

TYRONE

Having sex with the winners of a Miss Universe or Miss America pageant.

JEREMIAH

Bondage with my chosen other-sex partner leading to sex with that person.

VERA

My husband on an exercise bike. It was funny and we still laugh about it today.

WILSON

A threesome. I've never had this experience, but the idea has been very intriguing in the past. The fantasy usually involved a couple of my wife's friends along with my wife, when I was still married. The behaviors would be physical touching and alternating intercourse/oral sex (both giving and receiving). Nothing particularly clever in the fantasy, just the idea of being with two female partners. I never told her of this fantasy, nor did I ever act upon it (or even attempt to). Finally, neither this, nor any other sexual behavior was the cause of our divorce.

YOLANDA

My eyes meet with Antonio Banderas across a room and we are drawn to each other. As he reaches my side, his hand touches my arm and I feel like a bolt of energy has just shot up my arm. I'm at a loss for words, my heart is beating very fast, he cups my arm and leads me to an elevator and we get in. It goes up to his floor. We walk to his room. No words are exchanged at all. He opens the door and before it even closes we are all over each other. Panting, grasping, kissing. His lips are so hot, running all over my face and neck, and ears. He smells so wonderful. His hair feels so soft and sexy, his body so hard. We start ripping off each other's shirts, his hands grabbing and squeezing my breasts, his lips all over my chest. He pulls my bra down and starts sucking my hard nipples. I just feel like I'm going to faint, I'm so breathless. He really is working the breasts and nipples, nipping and tugging. I feel his hand slide down over my stomach, which is just quivering, and it slides down to my skirt, pulling the waistband open, and sliding his hands down to my panties. I'm running my hands all over his hard body. I can't believe how in shape he is, how hot to the touch he feels. I feel his fingers pull aside my panties and very softly I feel him running his finger around the outside of my lips. I know I'm very wet. He is talking the whole time to me, telling me how much he is going to fuck me, how hard it will hurt, how he is going to pound my pussy, that I'm going to be begging for more, how sexy he thinks I am. I almost come hearing the sound of his sexy voice. I hear myself start to plead with him to put his fingers inside me and he just gives a husky laugh, he rips off my panties and turns me around and bends me over and shoves me down on the bed and proceeds to tell me to get ready for his big dick, and the next thing I know, he is inside me, pounding away. It's unreal how far he seems to fill me up. He isn't a very gentle lover, but he has great thrusts in and out of my pussy. I feel like hot molten lava is just pouring out of me, my body tenses and I come. It's unlike any orgasm I've ever had. It seems to last forever, and when it's over I am so weak I can barely move. He then pulls out and picks up his clothes and dresses and walks out of the room, and doesn't say a word to me at all.

LYLE

Intercourse with a teenage girl.

KAT

Having a man masturbate in front of me or on me.

JOANNA

I am a 24-year-old woman, and my fantasy is about my younger brother, Wesley, who is 19, and very fit. I never used to pay him much attention, but in the last year, he really got tall (6 feet 1 inch), and he's started to get some hair around his nipples and in the center of his chest, and he's got some definition in his muscles, and now, all of a sudden, I am finding him very attractive. I know it's wrong, but there we have it. When I masturbate all by myself, I pretend that Wesley has come into my bedroom, drunk, with one or two of his hunky, randy teenage mates. The friends crowd around my bed, stroking their penises through their jeans, while Wesley straddles me. I pretend to be frightened, but secretly, I am loving every minute. Wesley tells me to be quiet, and that he will show me the proper way to enjoy a man's hard dick. He slowly unzips, pulls open the folds of his Levis, and I stare excitedly at his bulging crotch. He goads me into stroking his hard member through his boxers, and when I do, his snakehead pops out through the slit, already dripping with a bit of semen. Wesley's mates rip his shirt off, and then they take off their tops as well and they continue to pull on their penises and balls. Without any lubrication at all—not that I need any—Wesley plunges his fat cock into my quim, and after only two or three thrusts—because he is *so* turned on—he squirts a great big load of semen into my vagina, and I climax big-time. When Wesley has pulled out, he winks at his mates, and then one by one, they also mount me, squirting equally big loads deep inside me. I fall asleep very satisfied. I would just die if Wesley found out that I have these feelings, even though I'd secretly like him to know what his sister really thinks of him.

IGNACIO

Involves tying up my girlfriend between two trees in a public forest or park and performing oral, vaginal, and anal sex on her.

HERBERT

Gangbang with my wife as the center.

GLORIA

Just seeing my husband in his suit is enough to make me feel interested in him.

FERN

I am having sex with another woman, usually very feminine and of a smaller build. She is on top and I am wearing a strap-on penis.

EDOARDO

To be forcibly feminized into a chastised she-male, bound and kept as a sexual servant to my mistress, totally handing my life over to her.

DOUGIE

Attendance at a group sex session but not being allowed to join in, followed by selection of a pair of partners and having a personal session with them lasting all night. Engage in all forms of consensual sex in various positions.

CHAZ

I am a transvestite (trannie, if you like). One day, I go to a secluded park, all dressed up in a short skirt, bra and panties, and the whole gear, with wig and full makeup, looking better than most biological women. A husky, bear-like he-devil of a man sees me and approaches me, and before long we are snogging and running our hands all over one another's bodies. I get very turned on by this, and I get a big stonker, and before long, he looks at me and says, "Oh, my god, a chick with a dick!" I think this will turn him off and that he might hit me, but instead, he redoubles his efforts, and he sucks on my tongue ever more passionately, while he inserts his hands into my panties, and starts to fondle my hairy cock. Before long, another man— a total stranger to us both—arrives and he asks whether he can sit and watch us making out. We both nod affirmatively, and soon, this third man has got his cock out, and he is wanking for England! I am getting so turned on by all this masculine attention, and soon I become really, *really* hard, and think I will shoot my load. I am getting close, and then the third man leans over and tickles the underside of my nuts, and I spunk off all over both men.

BETTINA

With a famous rock star.

ALASTAIR

A student seduces a teacher.

ZANDRA

Lesbianism.

YOSEFF

Prefer not to disclose.

XENA

Being seduced by my doctor.

WILHELMINA

Most of my sexual fantasies are just from thoughts that pop into my head when I am feeling lonely mostly. Have the need to have someone close especially my husband who isn't always receptive. Fantasy is just about having a very sexual and loving relationship with another person, sometimes my husband, sometimes other men I know, and the person just makes you feel loved and wanted. Like I really matter. It is not only about the sex, but other feelings as well.

VICTOR

While watching a pornographic movie, I believe that it is my wife, myself, and another woman acting out what is on the screen.

ULRIKA

My current most sexually arousing fantasy is with a former art instructor whom I still have feelings for. It mainly involves kissing and embracing but also sex once in a while, and love always.

TARQUIN

Being tied up and told what to do. Anal sex, being spanked.

SPENCER

My wife and I have been married for seventeen years, and we are very happy most of the time. I love fucking her pussy as often as I can, but it always helps me if I let my mind wander. I find that this extra little bit of mind-play really helps to lubricate the situation. We have a young nanny, a Polish girl called Anna, who looks after our children. One day, I walked into the bathroom inadvertently, and caught sight of Anna, stark naked in the shower. Instead of blushing, she gave me a wicked come-hither look, and before long, one thing led to another, and soon, we were at it like rabbits, with me sucking on her clitoris, down on my knees in the bathroom, with my wife and children downstairs, within earshot. Within about five minutes, Anna started to come, and I had to place my hand over her mouth to stop her from shouting out too loudly. Nowadays, when I fuck my wife, my thoughts go to Anna, and her beautiful vagina, covered with a nice, trimmed thicket of pubic fur. I imagine sticking my tongue into her pussy, licking the clit and the labia, until she is soaking wet. I perform cunnilingus on her until my jaw fairly aches, but Anna loves every minute of it. Sometimes, I fantasize that I am sucking Anna off, and then, shock horror, my wife walks in and catches us. But instead of getting angry, she gets down on her knees, and she deep-throats my throbbing member, sucking me off in the best way possible, while I bring Anna off with my mouth. Spunk and cunt juice are flying everywhere, and we all collapse in a heap on the bathroom floor.

RICCARDO

Stockings and suspenders.

QUEENIE

Getting blindfolded by someone I love or admire, and being whisked away for a surprise romantic getaway in sunny climes. He takes the blindfold off to reveal a secluded white sandy beach in the heat of the day, champagne and strawberries on ice. The rest is inevitable.

PATRICIA

The thought of my partner being made to masturbate while watched by Margaret Thatcher and the Queen.

OSCAR

Vampire fantasy.

NANETTE

Watching partner have sex with a dominant person of same sex.

MIKHAIL

I would like to be tied up and then taken advantage of. I would like the man to be able to take full control, penetrative sex all night long with a lot of foreplay too.

Culled at random from my sample of approximately 20,000 contemporary, anonymous, American and British adult sexual fantasies, we have here a plethora of responses, a veritable Noah's Ark of private thoughts that will assist us as we begin our journey into the relatively uncharted terrain of the secret sexual mind. In this preliminary sampling of fifty-two fantasies, the whole panoply of American and British life parades before us: These fantasies range from youngsters such as nineteen-year-old Zeb, who yearns to have sex with a lesbian, to geriatrics such as the ninety-one-year-old Quentin, who claims that sexual thoughts no longer interest him. Nonagenarians may be pleased to learn that although Quentin may have abandoned his interest in sexuality, I have interviewed other people in their nineties who still maintain a full-blooded involvement in erotic thoughts and activities.

We have depictions of straight sex, such as Umberto, the "good Catholic" who loves every woman in the world, as well as gay sex, as illustrated by the forty-seven-year-old Fern, who wishes to engage in sexual activities with a woman who wears a strap-on penis. We have examples of tender sex, as illustrated by Isabelle, who enjoys "vanilla sex" with a gorgeous man, priding herself on being "not too kinky"; and then, by contrast, we have instances of rougher sex, such as the fantasy reported by Jeremiah, who has a huge penchant for bondage. Some of us prefer legal sex in our fantasies, such as Hortensia, who delights in a romp in the shower; whereas others become aroused at the thought of something illegal, such as Freddie, who entreats his male companions to rape a girl of "about sixteen."

Some of the fantasies concern our regular sexual partners, such as Wilhelmina's wish for more intimate contact with her husband, while others involve famous celebrities, epitomized here not only by Pedro's detailed account, in which he enlists the assistance of both Prince William and Prince Harry, but also by Yolanda's detailed description of her imaginary tryst with the actor Antonio Banderas. Still other fantasies revolve around ordinary, unknown individuals, often nameless and faceless, such as that of Duncan, for whom any White or Hispanic woman will produce arousal. Some fantasies contain no other people at all, such as the one reported by Ramona, who imagines herself on a vertical sun-bed, with fans blowing on her presumably naked or semi-naked body; and some even rely upon crowd scenes, such as the fantasy shared by Dougie, who expresses a penchant for group sex.

Karen has refused to answer the question, whereas Leila has claimed that she has no fantasies at all. One wonders what Karen's fantasies might be—perhaps they feel too spicy to articulate, or perhaps they may be very tame. In view of Karen's overly strict religious background, even a fantasy about simple kissing and cuddling would seem too dirty. And as for Leila, perhaps she really does have no fantasies at all, but then again, students of the human mind have known for thousands of years that our thoughts contain many layers, and that it might be possible to have a fantasy of which one has not *yet* become aware—an *unconscious* fantasy. Perhaps Leila's sexual fantasies remain temporarily submerged just below the threshold of consciousness, waiting to surface at any moment. In my research study, I interviewed quite a number of individuals who claimed to have had no sexual fantasies for many years, until some trigger experience (in some cases, even reading a book about sexual practices) facilitated the emergence of sexual fantasies into consciousness. I have also found that some people who report no fantasies at the outset of psychotherapy will do so after treatment has begun to unfold, once they feel certain that the psychotherapist will not be shocked, unlike their often puritanical parents.

As we read through the fantasies, we notice not only the wide range of content, revealing a breadth of secret sexual thoughts, but also an extraordinary diversity in terms of style. Some people have taken great pains to convey their sexual thoughts in exquisite detail, using unstintingly graphic language, as in the case of Spencer, the unfaithful husband who becomes obsessed with Anna's "beautiful vagina, covered with a nice, trimmed thicket of pubic fur." Oscar, by contrast, remains somewhat more guarded, revealing only that he becomes aroused by a "Vampire fantasy," leaving us to guess whether he actually dons the Bela Lugosi cloak and sucks the blood of long-necked virgins, or, rather, wishes for someone with sharpened incisors to sample *his* blood supply.

On the basis of these reports, it seems that some people want to be chained, penetrated, exposed, humiliated, hit, and seduced, such as Tarquin, who hopes to be spanked, tied, and anally penetrated. Ignacio, in similar vein, wishes to bind his girlfriend between two trees in a public location before penetrating each orifice. But others seem content with simple, romantic scenes. Gloria becomes easily satisfied, indicating that the mere sight of her husband in a suit will keep her smiling, while Riccardo can be pacified with just stockings and suspenders. Others make greater demands, such as Joanna, who, like a film director, stages a whole scene involving her younger brother, Wesley, and some of his drunken teenage friends. She needs to undress these lads in her imagination, so that they can eventually engage in full penetration, as part of a fantasy that includes an act of incestuous intercourse, per-petrated by her own brother.

One cannot help but wonder whether these fantasies might be the rantings of some sexually disturbed people, or, as I suspect, they repre-sent the broad diversity of fantasies enjoyed by ordinary citizens. We will, in fact, come to discover that even the most straightforward, "normal" people quite often have complicated fantasies, and that many of the ingredients of these fantasies will seem perplexing, and even contrary, perhaps, to the predictable logic of everyday life. For in-stance, why would Patricia become so aroused at the thought of her partner being forced to masturbate in front of Margaret Thatcher and Her Majesty the Queen? Many people would regard such a fantasy as "odd," to say the least. And why would a man wish to be feminized? And yet, Edoardo desperately yearns to be treated as a "she-male" and to become a sexual servant. The field of sexual fantasies raises many questions not only about what occurs in the minds of our friends, our neighbors, and our loved ones, but also about what actually constitutes a "normal" sexual fantasy.

Whatever the relative health or abnormality of one's fantasies, the vast majority of adults do seem to enjoy fantasies about someone or something *other* than their wives or husbands, girlfriends or boyfriends. In other words, most people will "cheat" while fantasizing, whether with a stranger in the park or with Margaret Thatcher and the Queen, thus engaging in what I have already identified as the intra-marital af-fair—a sort of extramarital affair that occurs within the relatively safe confines of one's mind. Most human beings have never shared the con-tent of their private intra-marital affairs with anyone, at least until now.

Many of us visit the cinema quite regularly, purchasing increasingly expensive tickets, buckets of buttered popcorn, and fizzy drinks; depend-ing upon our level of film-buffdom, we might treat ourselves and our families to a cinema outing once a month, or even once a week. But each of us enters another cinema much more frequently: the secret cinema of the mind. According to "Roy," one of the participants in my research project, when one fantasizes, "It's a little bit like shooting a movie in your head, and you're the director, you write the script, and you're the casting director, and you decide who gets to star in that little movie."

Roy could not be more correct. You will remember Jared, the young investment banker who would masturbate to pictures of Helga and

Ulla, his buxom German boxing buddies. Without doubt, one could argue that Jared engaged in moonlight employment as an honorary film director or theatrical stage director, carefully controlling the lighting and the sound, arranging the props and so forth, paying particular attention to the casting. He set the stage for his nightly masturbatory intra-marital affair with the same care that a good film director would employ when shooting a mainstream movie. However, unlike Federico Fellini or Steven Spielberg, who would no doubt hope that millions would ultimately attend their screenings, most of us would be utterly mortified if anyone else popped by for a viewing of the private theater of the mind. In this theater, admission is free, and we can, without censorship or restriction, openly acknowledge the contents of our more hidden thoughts and emotions.

Fleshing Out the Fantasy

On first reading, many people become either sexually aroused by the private fantasies of others or embarrassed by them. Some people will experience excitement, some revulsion, some shock and alarm, and some disinterest; still others will dismiss such fantasies as the product of disturbed minds. Our reactions will depend upon our level of maturity, our prior sexual history, and our general attitudes. But the more fully one becomes accustomed to the language of sexual fantasy and to the content of the fantasies, the more dispassionately one can analyze and evaluate their meaning. As you read the following fantasies, focus not only on the language and the content but also on the private emotional reactions that become stirred up inside of you, for this may provide a clue to the hidden meaning of the fantasy. For instance, if you feel horrified by every single fantasy contained in this book, it would not be unreasonable to assume that you might have grown up in a very restrictive household with parents who regarded play and the imagination as dangerous. If you find some of the fantasies arousing and only a few revolting, it may be that you have a more tolerant psychological character structure.

With reference to the fantasies that produce a reaction of disgust or horror, it would be far too facile to dismiss them as the rantings of a lunatic or sex maniac. Perhaps the person who penned the fantasy that causes you to experience revulsion may have unconsciously *wanted* other people to experience disgust, as a means of testing his or her lovability.

Perhaps that person wished to induce a sense of shock in someone else in order to repeat an earlier episode of having experienced shock himself or herself in relation to some childhood sexual scenario. We shall explore these dynamics in due course; in the meanwhile, try to monitor your own private repertoire of responses.

Let us begin to immerse ourselves more extensively in the database of material and allow the fantasies to speak for themselves. Here we have some more fantasies offered to the International Sexual Fantasy Research Project from our cross-sectional sample of ordinary adults:

RIDLEY

Playing golf with a woman for sex.

DUFFY

Sexual fantasizing is always a selfish act. Ejaculation rules my fantasizing. Any arousing image, usually from pornography, helps me ejaculate. I don't masturbate as much now because I have a partner. Fantasy has often changed. Currently I fantasize about a former roommate of my partner. It helps me ejaculate, which is more difficult now with onset of erectile dysfunction. Current partner jerks me off quite well; I reciprocate, giving her frequent orgasms. Dysfunction changed how I ejaculate, and penetration is no longer possible, but oral and manual contact still works. Erectile dysfunction makes imagining penetration of the roommate difficult because that is not real. During our usual sixty-nine oral and manual sex, I try to imagine butt-fucking her roommate, but I know that is no longer possible. Therefore this most powerful fantasy that I currently use is nonpornographic, being composed of only images of the other woman's face, memories of small talk we had in passing, and what I imagine to be signals of mutual attraction that passed between us when we were briefly alone one afternoon.

DYER

I undress a woman in white underwear, her panties soaked in vaginal juices. I smell her panties then slip my cock into her wet cunt. After plunging up and down I pull out and come in a spectacular splurge of semen over her breasts. I am still excited, and kiss her breasts, taking semen into my mouth, then kissing her on the mouth whereupon I come again inside her.

ANTONINA

I set up an ad on Craigslist saying I'm going to be in Louisville, Kentucky, for one night only. I tell my husband I'm going to visit my mother in southern Indiana and instead rent a hotel room at the Dixie Manor Motel (an adult hotel that has hot tubs and pipes porno into each room). I tell all the guys who are interested in the "rules" (not talking to me, no kissing on the mouth, no anal sex, must wear a condom), and set them up in groups of five or so at certain times . . . starting at 7:00 P.M. and ending whenever. At 7:00 I am naked in the bed in the hotel room, and wave after wave of groups of men show up. Some jerk off or have me jerk them off and leave. Others stay all night to watch. I have cocks all around me for hours, sucking and fucking.

REYNOLDS

Sex with two women. They use dildo and vibrator on each other. Taking pictures of full penetration of them and me and publishing them on a Web site.

HAILEY

Being serviced by two thin but big-breasted women.

BORIS

Watching two guys have full anal sex, with me masturbating.

JED

My wife is being fucked by several different anonymous masked or blurry faced men and women as I watch and masturbate. She looks at me longingly. The others may make her writhe with pleasure, but only I can bring her to the climax that she needs. She calls to me. She begs for more from me. I do not disappoint my lover. The others disappear from the fantasy, leaving us to our own peaceful intimate end.

CASSANDRA

Making love on a secluded beach or behind a waterfall.

MILLARD

Being tied up and submissive.

DAVIDA

My deceased husband having sex with a beautiful busty woman.

LYNDSAY

Giving a girl cunnilingus.

ELMER

Taking a woman in a corset FROM BEHIND!!!!!

DUCHESS

I fantasize about having an assertive partner (but no rough stuff) and having sex up against a wall or a staircase (inside a building or outside in the rain). If it's in the rain, I might wear a white T-shirt where you can see my nipples through it. Before there's actual penis/vagina penetration, I fantasize that I'm receiving oral sex while he fingers me and I picture all my juices dripping down his finger, then he sticks his tongue in me and has sex with me that way and he also licks around my anus. Sometimes I might fantasize that someone is watching us. When there's actual penetration, it's slow so I can feel him going deeper and deeper inside me. As we both get more and more excited, the pace quickens until we both climax.

FRANCO

Being groped, felt, touched, and stimulated by a large number of women. Hands and breasts are touching me all over, two women are stimulating my penis, one is masturbating me (with her hands) whilst the other is giving me oral sex. Another woman is sat above my face and I am giving her oral sex whilst she stimulates herself, and other women are stimulating her.

GARY

Shagging my secretary in the stationery cupboard.

HORACE

Being filmed, and then the filmer joins in.

ANIKA

I have met a really terrific guy online, who unfortunately lives 600 miles from me. Even though we both are married, we have spent many hours on the phone, as well as the computer. I have a fantasy about meeting him in a hotel, and having hot passionate sex for days, leaving all inhibitions at home. I fantasize about giving each other oral sex, him burying his tongue deep into my vagina while I feel his rock hard penis down my throat. Just as we are both ready to have an orgasm, he turns me over, and takes me from behind, with long hard strokes, until we both have an explosion of the most intense orgasm I have ever had. We both collapse and hold each other, kiss and taste the passion.

INGMAR

I would love to be with someone overweight but not super fat. She wears a lot of lipstick and kisses me all over and gets the lipstick all over. I then go down on her for hours. Maybe a friend shows up, maybe not. Then we have intercourse and I go down on her after that. This sort of happened a couple of times.

DWIGHT

Being dressed as a woman.

JUSTIN

Love a hairy chest, so often fantasize about getting naked with a handsome guy with a hairy chest and a big cock. We then passionately kiss and jerk each other off.

CY

Mutual masturbating.

KASPER

A friend's wife. I think she is the most beautiful woman there is. She has a body to match her beautiful face. Her personality is very stunning, caring, thoughtful, personally interested in me. I want to make mad passionate love with her.

MARGUERITA

That I am on an island stripped naked, blindfolded, and chained, and my partner has got me to no mercy.

BIRGITTA

Spontaneous sex in a public place with a stranger.

NORMA

Prefer not to answer.

DUTCH

We meet on a train. She shows off her shapely legs. We converse, flirt. She asks me to join her at her flat [apartment]. I forget my destination. Go back to her place and do it hard and dirty.

OLIVER

Don't have a specific fantasy.

ADDY

Being a queen and having to choose a partner, who, of course, is chosen by his stature and performance—each one has to have a different "speciality" as well as skin color, height. But all are very fit and gorgeous.

PETRINA

I fantasize about my deceased partner, that he is alive and we have wild passionate sex everywhere, hiding in department stores, on the boot of the car, just everywhere.

JEAN-BAPTISTE

I'm having sex with my girlfriend in an empty bar, and there's one girl watching us and she's feeling herself up. After a while my girlfriend goes over to the girl and they begin to finger each other.

QUINCY

Pornography.

JACINTA

Anything along the lines of *Basic Instinct*.

ROBERTA

My partner and I are on a secluded island. After a romantic picnic with wine, my partner begins to kiss my neck. Then he moves from my neck to my chest and begins kissing and sucking on my breasts while his hand moves down my thigh, then to my clitoris. His mouth moves down my body to the same area with his hands moving around to my backside. After a while he turns me over and then moves up my backside to penetrate my vagina with his penis. As things progress he gently spanks my behind while continuing to penetrate my vagina. Then he turns me around again and picks me up. I wrap my legs around his hips and he continues to penetrate me until we both orgasm. All the meanwhile we are kissing passionately all over each other's bodies.

SAMUEL

I don't think so!

CINNAMON

Doing it with another woman and having it rough and furious with a lot of oral, fingers, vibrators, strap-on action going on. Possibly having another woman helping out. Yum!

FLAVIA

When at work, the hunky lorry [truck] driver comes over to me, grabbing me by my tits and caressing them, slowly undoing my buttons on my shirt, and kissing me slowly whilst holding his penis against me, gradually working his hands down to my suspenders, and groping me, making me moan, then going on to his knees pulling my panties down and licking my pussy until I cum, and then he turns me round and then thrusts his penis into my now moist pussy.

TERRY

Being a woman's first partner.

URSULA

Swallow every drop of semen.

ELLIOTT

Having anal sex with at least two other men.

VERENA

My partner enjoying himself sexually in all sorts of ways.

SANCHO

I go to Las Vegas and hire an entire chorus line to spend a week with me. All of the showgirls are tall and beautiful and their job is to be nice to me all week—laugh at my jokes, tell me what a great guy I am, massage my neck, dance with me at nightclubs, etc.—and of course, have sex with me and with each other like crazed weasels in every possible position in the *Kama Sutra*.

WALLACE

Being seduced by an attractive woman in a loving and erotic way, perhaps in a shower at the gym.

GAIA

Something along the lines of the movie *The Story of O*.

REMINGTON

No thank you.

JAYSON

Mostly girls who are 17–19 years of age.

XENO

None.

LAZARUS

Role-playing with my partner as secretary.

HATTIE

Lying on the beach making love to my husband, wind blowing, sounds of the surf, nude.

YVONNE

Prefer to keep it to myself.

EBERHARDT

Remembering exotic and true sexual events from my past when younger.

ZARA

N/A.

LLEWELLYN

During a boring and stressful workday, I came to think about a female friend who I admire and couldn't get hold of. She has a great figure, nice boobs, and pretty face. It just came to me suddenly that I met her in her apartment after a dancing party. Both of us were sweating and she was shaking all over. I couldn't wait to rip her of all clothing, caressing her boobs, and gently rubbing her private area. She aroused me by moaning and I wasn't rushing to get into her, just playing with her body . . . she was more and more eager to have me into her body and finally, my dick slides into the warm and juicy heaven. Her vagina was tight and so warm that I have to control to prevent premature ejaculation. We change several positions, taking breaks to finally cum on her tits. It was such a great fantasy, though I will never get this woman.

I shall now provide some psychological observations of different fantasy constellations that have emerged in our selection thus far. In doing so, I hope to introduce readers to the ways in which a psychotherapist might begin to conceptualize the possible secret meanings of sexual fantasies—a style of thinking that will unfold throughout the remainder of this book.

On Touching One's Genitalia During Urination

Some of the respondents have refused to participate. Norma has preferred not to answer, and Samuel has chided us, "I don't think so!" Xeno has claimed to have no fantasies, whereas Yvonne does seem to fantasize, but has opted to keep her fantasies private. Zara has replied cryptically, "N/A"—Not Applicable. And Oliver, who does fantasize, has insisted that he has no special fantasy that really arouses him. So, in spite of the spate of more detailed, erotically charged fantasies, we still meet many people who struggle even to put their fantasies into words. In my research project, approximately 10 percent of American adults and 10 percent of British adults responded that they never fantasize. We cannot fully know what we might make of such data, especially when the rest of the adult population enjoys often very rich and compelling fantasies, many quite detailed in nature.

As I have already noted, I have met a good number of individuals over the years who, at the outset of their psychotherapeutic treatment, told me that they did not fantasize, but who, after years of therapy—having enjoyed the regular experience of talking about their intimate lives—gradually became more trusting and more comfortable. To my surprise, they did sheepishly begin to report that, yes . . . well . . . sometimes . . . when they had sex, or during masturbation, a fantasy would pop into their heads. Furthermore, when I conducted the five-hour-long clinical psychodiagnostic interviews with participants from the research project, I met a small number of individuals—all women, incidentally—who, at the outset of the intensive interview, insisted that they had never fantasized. But during our five hours together, these women eventually became more relaxed and began to disclose their fantasies.

So why did all the men in my interview study readily admit their fantasies, whereas some of the women would agonize before revealing theirs? Because I needed to understand all of the data in great depth myself, I did not enlist the services of any female colleagues to help me with the interviewing. It may be that some of the female research participants had concerns about confessing their fantasies to a male interviewer. For some women, it might feel rather too revealing to report sexual fantasies to a man; perhaps they would have found it easier to talk to another woman, rather in the same way that some women prefer to consult with a female gynecologist. But even though the presence of a male psychotherapist might have inhibited some of the female interviewees, this would hardly explain why the same thing happened in the computer-administered survey. Here, too, there were more women than men who claimed they did not fantasize. In that sample, all of the research participants answered questions in the privacy of their own homes or offices, with neither a male interviewer nor a female interviewer present.

On the basis of my clinical experience, I have come to suspect that men and women fantasize in equal measure, but that women experience much greater shame, even in the twenty-first century, about re-porting their private fantasies. Why should this be the case? Perhaps, once again, Sigmund Freud can come to our rescue. Back in 1925, Freud wrote a classic essay in which he suggested that our basic anatomical endowments serve as the foundation stones of our later sexual development. Whereas the male genitals can be readily seen, hanging and protruding between men's legs, the female genitals remain more hidden, more internal. Building upon Freud's observation, I have come to appreciate that these differences may have an influence on our readiness to talk about our sexual fantasies, most of which occur dur-ing masturbatory activity.

Over the years, I have also found myself wondering whether our dif-ferent patterns of urination—something that most of us do, by neces-sity, more frequently than masturbation—might have an impact on our willingness to fantasize and to share our fantasies. During most acts of urination, especially at a public urinal, men stand, touching their penises in order to control the stream of urine. Women, by contrast, generally micturate in a seated position, and in most instances have no reason to touch their genitals directly with their fingers when doing so. Quite apart from any masturbatory activity, or any soaping in the shower, most men reach maturity having the ordinary, normative expe-rience of touching their genitals several times a day, every day of the year, whereas women will not. It may well be that the greater visibility and availability of the male member allows men to enjoy a more perva-sive genital familiarity on a greater number of occasions, and this may contribute to a lessened degree of shame.

Of course, some men loathe their genitals—in particular, male trans-sexuals, who endeavor to have their penises removed by a surgeon. Many females, by contrast, derive great pleasure from the sight and the feel of the vagina, the clitoris, and the labia. One certainly cannot make any gross generalizations. But in thinking about the reluctance of Norma, Yvonne, and Zara to share their fantasies, I cannot help but wonder whether these women have come from sexually repressive homes, or whether they simply do not fantasize, or whether they do, in fact, fantasize but cannot bear to share these fantasies because of shame, possibly shame of a bodily nature.

And what of Samuel and Xeno? The former has told us quite simply, "I don't think so!" when asked about his fantasies, whereas the latter has insisted that he has none to share. Can we accuse Xeno of being a liar? Might Samuel be ashamed of his fantasies, and if so, what thoughts could possibly be housed in his mind that would cause him such internal mental anguish? Since I did not interview either of these men, we will never know. I have quoted them as evidence that both men and women struggle with their fantasies; indeed, representatives of both genders will, in some circumstances, refuse to share their fantasies, or state that they do not fantasize at all.

In the pre–World War II era, before Alfred Kinsey and his colleagues published *Sexual Behavior in the Human Male,* few people would have admitted that they practiced masturbation at all. The act itself filled most people at that time with shame and dread—shame for either not having a partner or for preferring self-pleasuring to intercourse with a partner, and dread at the thought of committing a sin or risking going blind, going mad, or developing hair on their palms. But in 1948, after Kinsey revealed that virtually every single human adult male indulged in masturbation, the taboo began to disappear. Today no one would be shocked to discover that one's partners, friends, neighbors, and family members engage in masturbatory activity. I suppose that a similar process of destigmatization began to occur in the wake of the publication of Nancy Friday's groundbreaking book *My Secret Garden* in 1973. In spite of Kinsey's and Friday's work, however, many people still suffer from shame about sexual fantasies. The fact that our minds have generated these sexual scenarios, large numbers of which do not concern our regular partners, still produces anxiety. In view of this fact, it should hardly astonish us that some people remain rather guarded or coy when asked to relate their most intimate sexual fantasies, even in the context of a completely confidential clinical research project in which we had guaranteed the participants absolute anonymity.

The Joy of Pain and Other Masochistic Postures

Clearly, Norma, Oliver, Samuel, Xeno, Yvonne, and Zara—the people who either refused to share their fantasies or stated that they have no fantasies—represent the minority. Most of my respondents offered their fantasies with little restriction or inhibition, some quite sketchily and others in much more detail. What else can we notice from some of the aforementioned fantasies? Some might be described as generous.

Verena, for example, has described her fantasy thus: "My partner enjoying himself sexually in all sorts of ways." Clearly, this woman relishes the idea of her partner receiving sexual pleasure. Does this indicate that Verena might be a sweetie, thoughtfully tending to the needs of her beloved, or might her fantasy be indicative of a more sexually *masochistic* position? In other words, might Verena be someone who holds herself in very low regard and does not believe herself to be entitled to sexual pleasure? She might be a woman who has sacrificed her own life and her own individuality for the sake of her male partner, putting him first in all matters, including in the bedroom. Once again, we do not know the full story, because I did not interview Verena directly. But on the basis of the many people whom I have interviewed or with whom I have worked in great depth, I realize that no sexual fantasy, however seemingly straightforward, can ever be taken simply at face value. When Verena informs us that she fantasizes about her "partner enjoying himself sexually in all sorts of ways," we must ask ourselves whether she really might be as selfless as she sounds, or whether she masochistically denies herself any pleasure. Perhaps she could be described as one of those proverbial "women-who-love-too-much." And perhaps, as a result of such sexual denial, she might also eventually come to hate the partner whose pleasure she places before her own. One can of course really go to town with all sorts of speculations about the hidden meaning of somebody else's sexual fantasy. And sometimes one will be quite wrong in these speculations. But as we study these fantasies in the thousands, we will develop a growing appreciation of some of the more hidden subtexts of a seemingly simple fantasy.

Verena's tendency to sideline herself in an arguably masochistic, self-dismissive manner might be quite covert to the untrained eye. In the case of fellow fantasist Marguerita, however, the masochism becomes much more apparent. Marguerita has admitted, "That I am on an island stripped naked, blindfolded, and chained, and my partner has got me to no mercy." Although this particular fantasy might produce sexual excitement in many female readers and in many male readers as well (allowing us to identify either with Marguerita or with her partner, or even with both characters), one wonders why Marguerita enjoys pretending to become helpless, naked, chained, blindfolded, and subject to the whims of her lover. Do we imagine Marguerita to be highly creative, liberal, and experimental, and hence unshackled by the strictures of normal bourgeois intercourse for procreative purposes? Or might there be other reasons for Marguerita's masochism?

Often, people who report masochistic fantasies, such as the experience of being tied up and used-and-abused by someone else, have endured early sexual experiences of a violent nature. By fantasizing about an abusive scenario in later life, they manage to *re-orchestrate* the earlier sexual scene, transforming it into something pleasurable. Psychotherapists and psychoanalysts refer to this phenomenon as the "eroticization of trauma." Once again, we do not know whether Marguerita experienced early sexual abuse herself—indeed, whether someone actually chained her up and treated her mercilessly—but this represents a serious possibility.

We know from my research project that many millions of people enjoy sexual fantasies of a masochistic nature; at a conservative estimate, roughly 30 percent of the adult population. It seems unlikely, however, that every sexual masochist experienced gross sexual abuse in early childhood. So how do we explain the extraordinary proliferation of sexually masochistic fantasies? Though such fantasies may result from early abuse, from my clinical experience I can also report that many people indulge in masochistic fantasies as a means of protecting themselves and their minds from an even more disturbing *sadistic* fantasy. Psychoanalysts have long known that when one works with a sexual masochist in psychotherapeutic treatment, an enormous amount of murderous rage will come spewing forth from the mouth of the patient in due course; in other words, beneath every masochist lurks an "unconscious sadist." Masochists work very hard to keep their more aggressive feelings in check by turning the anger *inward,* attacking themselves rather than their husbands or wives, boyfriends or girlfriends. It might be the case that if Marguerita had undergone psychotherapy, her analyst would have discovered a whole secret underbelly of bile and vitriol that she had never managed to express, and which she had transformed into a masochistic attack on herself rather than having to engage in a much more potentially destructive, sadistic attack on someone else.

One need not have experienced actual physical or sexual abuse in order to develop a masochistic fantasy. Many women and men have had depriving and depleted childhoods that have left them *feeling* abused or deserving of maltreatment, even though the actual maltreatment took more subtle forms. A masochistic fantasy could result from these sources as well.

Making Death Sexy

Two other fantasies in this chapter deserve particular comment, both concerning dead spouses. Davida has confessed that she fantasizes about "My deceased husband having sex with a beautiful busty woman"; similarly, Petrina has written, "I fantasize about my deceased partner, that he is alive and we have wild passionate sex everywhere, hiding in department stores, on the boot [trunk] of the car, just everywhere." One need not be a psychoanalytical psychotherapist to appreciate that both these fantasies offer confirmation of Sigmund Freud's original idea that the fantasy assists us in the fulfillment of a wish. Both Davida and Petrina have succeeded in using their minds to bring their dead husbands back to life. Davida's husband has returned from the grave in order to make love to a woman with large breasts, and Petrina's has become reincarnated but remains sexually faithful, if somewhat voracious. Many people would regard masturbation over the image of a dead spouse as far too painful, but for quite a number of individuals, this fantasy helps them to conquer the horrific finality of death, sometimes in a creative manner and sometimes in a less healthy manner. These individuals attack reality, quite understandably, by pretending that the spouse has not died.

Psychotherapists know from clinical experience and published case reports that many bereaved people experience auditory or visual hallucinations of brief duration in the immediate aftermath of the death of a loved one. An auditory hallucination may be defined as hearing a voice that no one else can hear, in this case the voice of one's deceased lover; in a visual hallucination, the bereaved individual actually sees something or someone that does not exist in shared reality, in this instance the ghost of the former partner. Many quite mentally healthy people in fact have such hallucinations in the wake of spousal or parental bereavement. Those who experience such hallucinations should therefore not worry, for it does not mean they have become certifiably insane. A grief-based hallucination serves as one of the many ways through which we manage the unbearable reality of the death of a much-missed partner. After the death of my own grandfather, my widowed grandmother—a very sane and healthy woman—told me that one day, shortly after his death, she saw my grandfather walking through the house. Obviously a hallucination, the image lasted for perhaps five seconds and then disappeared. Sometimes, when we cannot bear to let go, the psyche transforms the pain of our external reality. On this occasion, I believe my grandmother cleverly assisted herself in the necessary grieving process by invoking a visual image of my much-loved granddad.

Sexualizing these hallucinations also serves as a source of wish-fulfillment, and Davida and Petrina have done just that. These two clever, creative women have tried to reverse the reality of the death of their husbands by invoking them as living lovers. In most instances, such an eroticization of death serves a useful psychological function, helping us to bear the pain. Only when one cannot let go and move on will the sexual fantasy of a dead spouse become more pathological.

Years ago, at a psychiatric hospital, I treated a fifty-five-year-old woman who suffered from severe clinical depression. Both her parents had died thirty-odd years previously; but this lonely, bereaved woman could not separate from them, so much so that every night, at suppertime, she would lay three places at the supper table, one for herself and one each for her deceased mother and father. Simply unable to admit that her mother and father had died, she concocted a fantasy, albeit a nonsexual one, that supposed that neither had really passed away. Because she could not mourn the death of her mother and father—an essential part of healthy grieving—her clinical depression intensified, and for many years, until her psychotherapeutic treatment began, she suffered horrific psychological distress.

Let us now examine some more sexual fantasies, culled from the vast archive of both American and British sexual fantasies accumulated through my research project:

ZADIE

Being in a large Jacuzzi with my partner having wild sex, impossible with my disabilities, I'm afraid.

YUL

Sex with two women.

XENIAH

No fantasy, I am very happy with my husband, so no need.

WENDELL

At the age of eighty-five I do not get turned on. I am more inclined to laugh.

VICTORIA

Having my breasts sucked and having oral sex performed on me whilst doing the same for my partner.

URIAH

Sex with two women at the same time.

TESSIE

Being stripped by two or more other women and having one suck my nipples, and the other performs oral sex on me, then all three of us have sex together.

STRUAN

Being seduced by a lady and having her take me to bed, leading me by the penis.

RODELINDA

My next-door neighbor is a very handsome man, about thirty-five years old. I am fifty-two, but I look much younger. One day I am baking some cakes for my son's birthday party, and I find that I have run out of sugar. The party is due to start in an hour, and I ask my husband to dash to the shops to get some more. He is too grumpy and lazy, and he just sits in his chair, watching the football, and tells me to get it myself. I decide that I will go to see Theo, my neighbor. Maybe he will have some. I knock on his door, and I tell him my dilemma. He invites me into the kitchen while, in typical bloke-like fashion, he looks through his kitchen cupboards, unsure where he has put the sugar, since he never does any baking himself. As he strains to open the top cupboards, I can see the well-defined muscles in his arms and in his back. He looks just gorgeous, and I start to get a little bit excited. When he turns round, he can see that my nipples are a bit bigger than they should be. He notices, but he doesn't say anything to me. He just gives a bit of a half-smile. Theo tells me that he might have some sugar in a downstairs cupboard, in the cellar, and asks if I would mind accompanying him there. I follow him down the steps, and this gives me yet another opportunity to watch him from behind, examining his bum as it wiggles, and giving me another good look at his very fit torso. As we reach the bottom of the staircase, I decide to get bold, and I tell him that I hate my fat, lazy, sonofabitch husband, and that I need a real man to service me, to fuck me hard. Theo is a bit stunned by the boldness of my desire, but he is no fool, and even though I am almost twenty years older than he is, he knows a good offer when he sees one. Roughly, he slams me up against the wall in his basement, and immediately starts licking my prong-like titties, which have got even bigger in the last few minutes. This makes me so incredibly wet. He then unzips himself, and out flops the biggest dick I have ever seen in my life. It looks like something you would see on a horse—it's long, and firm, and thick, and covered in bushy hair. He roughly sticks his hand under my skirt, and rips the panties with one quick movement. He is so strong that he tears the fabric, and then, with my pussy exposed, he fingers me to check whether I am wet enough to fuck. He decides that I am, so he grips his big fuck-prod with two hands, and rudely shoves it up inside my cunt. I am screaming. It really hurts, but in a good way. All it takes is a few strokes in and out, and Theo deposits a great big load up my fanny. As he comes, he bites down on my earlobe, and this makes me come as well—one of my very best orgasms ever, leaving me wet and shivery. I thank him, and we arrange to repeat the adventure. I return home, and my sonofabitch husband hasn't even noticed that I'd stepped out.

QUINT

Being sexually exhibited by a "partner" to one or more other men, then having sex with one or more of them.

PENELOPE

Having sex with partner in a public place, e.g., a wardrobe in a department store! In a lift, or somewhere where we might be found at any moment.

OWEN

I imagine that I am a fourteen-year-old lad back at school—really I am twenty-nine. I had this very fit teacher, Mademoiselle McAllister, who taught us French. She wasn't especially pretty, but she had a great sexiness about her, and you could tell that she was always eyeing up the teen lads. In my fantasy, I imagine that I am walking home from school, and Mademoiselle McAllister drives by in her car, and says, "Owen, you look like you are carrying too many books—what a conscientious student you are. Would you like me to give you a lift home?" I gladly accept the offer, and think nothing more of it, until I notice that she is driving the wrong way, to her house, not to mine. "Come in for a drink before you start on your French verb conjugations," she says, and I follow her into the house. Mademoiselle McAllister tells me that she has been impressed by my progress in class, and that as a special treat, she will suck me off. I start to head for the door as I am a bit freaked out by all of this—I have not even kissed a girl my own age by this point, let alone the French teacher. But my knees give way, and she tackles me. I fall to the floor, and she starts pulling at my zip and at my belt, all at the same time. Soon, I am stripped bare from the waist down, and my fourteen-year-old prick, which has just started to get some pubic hair around it, starts to wave about. She gobbles my dick and she turns my winky into a huge member. I am worried that I am choking her, but she calls out to me in French, *"Ne t'inquiètes pas, mon petit"*—"Don't worry, my little one"—and I relax, as my cock fills her soft mouth. She starts to stroke my nuts, and then she goes down on them as well, what one of my mates calls "Gums on Plums." This makes me go wild. Then, she tongues around my ass crack, and that does it. I just come and come for what seems like five minutes. I fall asleep exhausted on the floor, and when I awake, she drives me home. My mum is worried that I'm so late coming back from school, but, cool as a cucumber, Mademoiselle McAllister just reassures my mum that she'd kept me behind for extra instruction. Too right!

NATALYA

Unexpected sex with a stranger, semi-rape fantasy, unwilling but seduced. Lots of oral sex, kissing, large cock, deep penetration.

MORGAN

Anal sex (me giving) with member of same sex (another male).

LUCIA

Seeing a person with a fat bottom.

KARL

Looking at the opposite sex and thinking what a good sex ride she would make.

JOSIE

Beautifully dressed man who resembles Elvis—being made love to gently but powerfully.

IGGY

Sex with an extramarital lover of many years.

HORST

The fantasy of having oral sex with the man that I truly love—not my partner.

GRETCHEN

Having sex with two or more women.

FELIX

Nylon, stockings, partially dressed women from the 1940s.

ELIZA

Almost always involves performing oral sex on some good-lookin' guy.

DELBERT

Having a teenage girl of around sixteen giving me oral sex, then have her beg me to give her sex for the first time.

CHARLENE

I'm alone with a woman. She has gorgeously round, pert breasts and long straight blonde hair. She is really pretty, sort of *Playboy* material. She's wearing just a thong and high heels. It's not a "love" kind of sex, it's an erotic kind of forbidden sex. She's doing everything to me and I in turn watch her strip and caress herself. Then one of her friends comes in—another long-haired blonde with pert breasts in just a thong and high heels. They start to fondle each other and lick each other—putting on a show for me. Then they rub me all over, playing with my breasts and pressing their bodies against me, over and over again, while one of them licks my clitoris faster and faster and faster until I come.

BEATE

Being surprised by someone who will not take "no" for an answer. Not rape, but insistent seduction, where he overcomes my protests and makes me want to submit. He would approach me from behind and slide his hands over my body, one on my breast, one on my genitals—firmly. He would kiss and nuzzle me along my shoulder and neck and push me carefully to the floor, where he would undress me and we would have sex.

ANDREW

Being on holiday and having sex with a complete stranger in the bushes.

Mental Infidelity

When considering this last cluster of fantasies, we can begin to see more clearly that many fantasies contain elements of wish-fulfillment. Zadie, for example, has imagined herself having wild sex in her Jacuzzi; but then, after indulging in this very pleasant thought, she laments that this would be impossible because of her "disabilities." Zadie has not specified the nature of her disabilities, but we might imagine that her body has become injured in some way, either through a congenital deformity, an age-acquired infirmity such as arthritis, or traumatic damage, such as paralysis or amputation. Whatever the reality of her bodily situation, Zadie has used her sexual fantasy to *reverse* the loss of her physical agility. By allowing herself to enjoy the thought of wild, passionate sex in the Jacuzzi, she frees herself, temporarily, from the limitations and encumbrances of having a real human body.

In similar vein, both Uriah and Yul permit themselves to enjoy the thought of not one woman, but two, a fantasy that Charlene, a woman, also shares. In real life, sex with multiple partners would be much more difficult to arrange. What if one partner becomes jealous of the other? Someone might have a sexually transmitted disease, or someone could become pregnant. In fantasy, however, one can indulge in sex with as many partners as possible without risking herpes, wounded emotions, or pregnancy. Such factors help to explain the potential appeal of *sexual fantasy* over *sexual reality*. The former may be safer and cheaper—one need never take one's fantasy out to dinner—whereas a real-life partner might come to expect all sorts of physical, emotional, and even financial caretaking.

Besides noticing how these fantasies fulfill many overt and covert wishes, one cannot help but notice how much sexual gratification the research subjects have derived from fantasies that involve physical contact with someone other than their regular partner. In other words, most people cheat in their fantasies. Of the previous twenty-six fantasies, culled randomly from my database, only four people—all women—specifically mentioned enjoying an erotic thought concerning their regular, long-term partner. Penelope admits that she fantasizes about sex with her partner in a public place; Victoria relishes the prospect of her partner sucking on her breasts; and Zadie, our disabled respondent, revels in the thought of sex with her partner in the Jacuzzi. Xeniah writes that she has no need for sexual fantasies, because her husband makes her very happy. Excepting these four and Wendell, the eighty-five-year-old man who claims to delight in laughter more than erotic excitation, all of the other randomly chosen fantasies in this section, twenty-one out of twenty-six, might best be described as transgressive forms of "mental infidelity"—cheating on one's partner *in one's imagination*.

Andrew yearns for sex with a stranger in the bushes, rather than on clean sheets with his wife of twenty years. Eliza does not particularly care whom she fellates, so long as he is a "good-lookin' guy." Horst tantalizingly notes that he wishes to have oral sex "with the man that I truly love," leading us to believe that this man must be his boyfriend, but then delivers the coup de grâce, clarifying that the one he truly loves is not his partner. Iggy craves sex with his "extramarital lover," while Josie hopes to find a man who resembles Elvis Presley. Natalya desires sex with a stranger, and twenty-nine-year-old Owen chooses to masturbate to the thought of Mademoiselle McAllister, the woman who taught him French at school fifteen years previously. Mental infidelity certainly ranks as one of the most prominent features in both the British Sexual Fantasy Research Project and the International Sexual Fantasy Research Project.

So why do we cheat on our partners when we fantasize? Why do so many of us think about our French teachers, or Elvis Presley, or anyone other than our wives and husbands, girlfriends and boyfriends, when we have intercourse (coital fantasy) or when we masturbate (masturbatory fantasy). In Chapter 6, I shall explore this material much more fully, but for the time being, let us speculate that our mental infidelities—fantasies of someone else—allow us to indulge in wish-fulfillment in the extreme. When we fantasize about sex with the French teacher, we can cheerfully put all thoughts about our spouses and domesticity aside. Many of the interviewees told me that they did not want to fantasize about the partner with whom they had had a row only hours before, the same partner who had spent all their money and had bored them with endless stories about their tedious work colleagues. According to "Declan," a thirty-eight-year-old truck driver who participated in my research project, "I love my wife, but she drives me fucking crazy. When we shag, her technique has really started to get on my tits. She always sucks my dick in the same way, and she's never been that good as a cocksucker. If I want to stay hard, I have to think about other people. Besides, I have to live with my wife all the time, and this gets boring. So when I have a wank, or when I shag my missus, I think of other women—gals that I have no connection to in the outside world, gals who I don't have to wine and dine, or listen to them bleeding bitchin' on about their sad, sorry little lives."

Riding Your Partner Like a Motorbike

Fantasies provide us with the opportunity not only to gratify our secret, forbidden wishes, but also to indulge in our wishes to *correct* reality. Remember Zadie, the disabled woman, who had become freed from her disability in her fantasy? Through fantasy, we can make "reality" as exciting as possible. Remember Josie? Why should she make love to her accountant husband when she could have fantasy sex with Elvis Presley? And what of Rodelinda, the fifty-two-year-old housewife, clearly unstimulated by her domesticity as she bakes a cake for her son's birthday party? She would much rather indulge a desire to fornicate with her thirty-five-year-old neighbor, Theo. Although I have changed Rodelinda's name, I do not know whether, in her original write-up of this fantasy, she elected to change the name of her neighbor. Could Theo be his real name? If not, one wonders why she chose that particular moniker, and whether she realizes that "Theo," in Greek, means "god" (as in "*theo*logy"). Why not make love to a god instead of the paunchy husband one sees all too frequently? Clearly, Freud made a very shrewd observation when he insisted upon the crucial role of wish-fulfillment in sexual fantasies.

But do fantasies satisfy only our more palatable desires for healthy sexual excitement and stimulation—a good old "sex session" from our favorite pop star or film star—or might they sometimes fulfill a more subversive function, gratifying some of our murkier desires? Psychotherapists and psychoanalysts have long appreciated that our behavior as human beings will be driven not only by the desire for satisfaction of our *erotic urges,* but also by the desire for satisfaction of our *aggressive urges.* Classical Freudian analysts have referred to this aspect of character as the "dual-instinct theory"—in other words, we become "turned on" by both sex *and* violence. And one need not search very far for confirmation of this notion. Indeed, even a brief perusal of any tabloid newspaper or Hollywood blockbuster will reveal our addiction to stories and scenes that combine the two. In fact, sex and violence often become intimately intertwined, and indeed confused, in the mind, so much so that overt references to violence become the mainstay of the sexual fantasies of many people. According to my survey results, literally millions of adult Britons and Americans seem to relish fantasies with violent content. I shall explore the details of this data in Chapter 13 on extreme sexual violence.

As troubling as this finding may seem, we simply cannot avoid the reality that for millions and millions of people, the idea of being harmed, or of causing harm to others, produces stirrings in the genital region. Although this book contains a welter of highly explicit and sometimes shocking material, I have had to curtail the number of violent fantasies as many may be too distressing to read. Some involved detailed scenes of Elizabethan-style torture, evisceration, and execution, which nevertheless ultimately resulted in orgasm for the authors of the fantasies.

Why do so many people find violent fantasies arousing? Apart from some clinical sadists and masochists who actively seek out physical pain in real life, the vast majority of psychic sadists and masochists would loathe actual pain but nevertheless become highly lubricated through their fantasies. Even relatively mild forms of this phenomenon may seem unpalatable to many people. Karl, for instance, enjoys looking at a woman and "thinking what a good sex ride she would make." Most women, I imagine, and many sensitive men, would find Karl's fantasy, particularly the language of his fantasy, very offensive. It seems to me that what he is saying is rather a different proposition from saying, "When I look at a woman, I become erect at the thought of what it might be like to have consensual sexual intercourse with her." His crude idea of treating her as a "good sex ride" pictures her rather like a motorbike. Does this mean that we might be clinically justified in diagnosing Karl as a cruel sadist who denigrates women and treats them as objects? Or might we conclude instead that Karl may simply be more honest than many about some of his most visceral desires? For all we know, Karl may be the ideal husband and family man, the sort who makes love to his wife in a tender and passionate manner after having put the kids to bed and done the washing-up. Does the choice of vocabulary in his sexual fantasy betray a wish for something less citizen-like? Compared to many of the more violent fantasies, some of which will be discussed later at great length, Karl's fantasy of a "good sex ride" seems somewhat tepid. Still, it contains a denigratory quality—thinking about taking a person with feelings and an identity and turning her into a "ride," rather like jumping into a bumper car at a fairground.

But men do not only perpetrate violent acts on others in their fantasy lives. They can also become the subjects or victims of violence that others perform on them. Consider the fantasy reported by straight man Struan, who wants to be seduced by a woman who leads him into the bedroom by his penis, or that of the gay man Quint, who wants to be exhibited naked in front of a group of other men, who then have sex with him. In reality, both of these sexual scenarios might be rather humiliating and even painful. Quint speaks of "being exhibited" as though he has become an object in a museum, not a full-bodied person in his own right—perhaps a gay male version of Karl's woman-as-good-sex-ride.

Of course, men do not have an exclusive copyright on violent fantasies. Many women also delight in thinking about violence. Many, in their fantasies, become the passive recipients of violent activities that become highly sexualized in the mind. Consider once again the housewife Rodelinda, who has abandoned her cake-baking in order to have illicit intercourse with her god-like next-door neighbor, Theo. According to Rodelinda, Theo "grips his big fuck-prod with two hands, and rudely shoves it up inside my cunt." In thinking about Rodelinda's fantasy, one wonders whether this might be described as a *sexual* fantasy, as a *violent* fantasy, or as something combining elements of both sexuality and aggression. Why does Rodelinda need not only the genital stimulation, but also the rude shoving of a "big fuck-prod," guided by two hands, in order to reach her orgasm? Natalya, another woman from the survey, craves "sex with a stranger," which she has described as a "semi-rape fantasy" in which she participates in an "unwilling" manner. Beate, even more extremely, yearns for a man who "will not take 'no' for an answer." She classifies this activity as "not rape, but insistent seduction, where he overcomes my protests and makes me want to submit." Many people would, perhaps, regard Beate's fantasy as a rape, in spite of her claims to the contrary. In any case, the element of violence becomes clear.

All of these excerpts show not only the ubiquitousness of sexual fantasies, with their pleasure and wish-fulfillment components, but also the more sinister side of fantasy life, namely the widespread occurrence of mental infidelity and the violence contained therein. Let us now examine some of the more specific fantasy constellations in even greater detail in an effort to understand some of the less readily articulated aspects of human sexual psychology.

PART TWO

A Cornucopia of Fantasies

Nine adulteries, 12 liaisons,
 64 fornications and something
 Approaching a rape
Rest nightly upon the soul
 of our delicate friend Florialis,
And yet the man is so quiet and
 reserved in demeanour
That he is held to be both
 bloodless and sexless.

Bastidides, on the contrary,
 who both talks and writes of
 Nothing but copulation,
Has become the father of twins,
But he accomplished this feat at some cost;
He had to be four times cuckold.
 —Ezra Pound, "The Temperaments," *Lustra*

4 Fantasy 101: Tales of Ordinary Explicitness

I'll let you be in my dreams
if I can be in yours.

— BOB DYLAN,
"TALKIN' WORLD WAR III BLUES"

Approximately 19 percent of the individuals surveyed as part of this study admitted that they find fantasies a great relief from the daily boredom of their lives and that the fantasies provide them with a private adventure. Similarly, some 21 percent of the respondents reported that they rely on sexual fantasies to lift their spirits. The largest percentage of respondents—at least 40 percent of males and females alike—confessed that they create sexual fantasies as a means of exploring different sexual thoughts and activities, many of which would not be easy to orchestrate in external reality.

Ordinary, straightforward fantasies about "vanilla sex" or "straight sex," without too many "extras," constitute a large proportion of sexual fantasy life. Approximately 58 percent of adult men and women have fantasized about their regular partners at some point. This constitutes a very large number; still, one wonders why the other 42 percent have not fantasized about their regular partners. Some might say they have no need to fantasize about their partners because they can make real love to them any time that they wish. Those who do fantasize about their partners may do so especially during periods of separation (an overnight business trip, for example); perhaps some conjure up sexual images of their partners performing illicit acts that could not or should not be practiced as part of their daily or nightly sexual repertoire. One of my research participants who often enjoyed vanilla sex with his wife would fantasize about sticking knives into various parts of her body, drawing blood, after mounting her. As we already know, we may find a huge disparity between the *ordinariness* of sexual behaviors and the *extraordinariness* of concurrent sexual fantasies.

I shall now share a large collection of unexpurgated sexual fantasies culled from both the British Sexual Fantasy Research Project and the International Sexual Fantasy Research Project. I have attempted to classify them into broad groupings, with each chapter in Part 2 covering a particular category. Some could be classified rather easily; for instance, a fantasy of sex with a pop star fits neatly into the chapter on sex with celebrities. However, other fantasies contain so much breadth and texture that they could have resided happily in several different chapters simultaneously. A fantasy about humiliating and raping a young family member, for example, could readily belong to the chapter on humiliation and shame, to the chapter on extreme sexual violence, to the one on pedophilia, or, indeed, to the one on incest. In such instances, I have endeavored to identify the primary source of excitation for the fantasist and to classify the fantasy accordingly.

The collection begins with fantasies that reveal sexual orientation. Although many people fantasize beyond their stated orientation, the bulk of British citizens fantasize *within* their stated sexual orientation. In other words, most practicing heterosexuals have heterosexually oriented fantasies, and most practicing homosexuals have homosexually oriented fantasies.

The database also contains many bisexual fantasies. A small percentage of individuals would define themselves as fully bisexual, enjoying male and female partners in equal amounts. For others, bisexuality might represent an occasional foray, either in external reality or in fantasy. People often assume that bisexual men and women must really be homosexual, but the fantasy data of the bisexual subgroup does not bear this out. Many bisexuals, in spite of their fondness for homosexuality, also derive great orgasmic pleasure from both heterosexual activity and heterosexual fantasy.

Here are some of the more "ordinary," but nevertheless explicit, fantasies conjured in the minds of ordinary Americans and Britons, providing evidence of our secret psychological cinemas.

Heterosexual Fantasies

CONNIE

My other half is a fire-fighter and that always gets me going.

NASH

I am a 42-year-old bloke, and I think of myself as pretty normal. When I beat off, I like to take my cock in hand, and I think of my girlfriend. We have been together for a good few years now, and believe it or not, the lady still floats my boat. If she is away on business which is often the case, I like to lie down on the bed, un-zip my trousers, pull down my pants, and start stroking Mr. Happy. I might use some baby oil and pretend that the lubrication is really her pussy juice. Then I will pump my dick up and down, and I'll just imagine that it's my girlfriend. I like to tickle my nuts when I have a fantasy like this, and I keep thinking that my hand and my girlfriend's hand are really one and the same. I don't like to wank off too fast. I try to make it last, and I always wait until the pre-cum starts gushing out of my piss-slit first. Because then the quality of the orgasm is usually always much better. I can't really see the point to a quick bashing of the bishop. That really doesn't do it for me. I have to make it a sensual experience. Sometimes I will dip my fingers into the pre-cum juices, and rub them over my tits, imagining that it is my lover's fingers doing the rubbing. I'll pull the foreskin back, and then roll it forward, just really getting into it. Then I like to fantasize that my gal and I have finally got down to some good, hard-core, solid fucking. I buck like a cow-boy—in and out, in and out—and I can feel the walls of her pussy contracting around my throbbing cock meat. Eventually, it all gets to be a wee bit too exciting, and I blow a load all over the sheets, pretending that the juice is squirting up her cunt hole. I then like to leave the cum all over my body, and just fall asleep that way, think-ing that when my gal returns from her business trip, we will proba-bly do this for hours. It will be even better in real life, of course, but the fantasy is still pretty fucking amazing.

ALONZO

Being in a wooded glen, beside a waterfall-fed brook. Partner and I get nude, enjoy the pleasure of sun and coolness on our skin, bathe, romance each other and eventually enjoy intercourse.

DAWSON

Log cabin in the middle of the winter with a warm fire, silk sheets, rose and jasmine petals everywhere in the cabin and on the bed. Candles everywhere. Hot, yet breezy environment. No touching of genitals for the first hour . . . just body touching and kissing for the first hour . . . then passionate and wild lovemaking in the end.

KATY

My fantasies usually take place in exotic places with my husband. Only the place tends to change as a backdrop.

SAUL

My partner and I win a contest, and are invited on an island resort, and in the middle of the afternoon she wants a little action, in bed of course, so I tell her that I'm going to take a shower first. While in the shower, she comes in, and then sex follows, in the most intimate ways I have never known was possible. And going back home, we went back totally refreshed and feel our sex life has been rejuvenated.

CLARK

Female asks Clark to take off clothing, Clark obliges, Female tells Clark to masturbate, Clark obliges, Clark lacks imagination, but Clark is happy.

RONALD

Love watching a woman deep-throat me until I reach orgasm and her swallowing.

ANTHONY

A horny lap dance from a girl with a shaved pussy. I had this once at a nightclub, and it made me incredibly hot, and I thought I was going to shoot a wad right then and there in my pants.

CORAL

Most of the arousal comes from the sensation of body heat and a sweet cologne smell. The kiss is fantastic and makes your legs weak. The strength of his arms holding you close to his hard chest and the feel of his arousal against your thigh. Then the feel of his penis penetrating makes me come which usually ends up being multiple times until it wakes me up feeling tingly all over. Actually it is better than actual sexual experiences.

GOLDIE

I'm a 29-year-old housewife and mother of two. Fortunately, my husband and I still have sex, in spite of kids waking us up every two minutes during the night for a drink of water or what have you. But when we do get private time, I still love sex with my gorgeous husband. When he goes away, I masturbate a lot, and I often masturbate about him. I imagine that we have sent the kids away for the weekend, and that we decide to have a dirty week-end at home together. After plying me with liqueurs, which I love, my husband decides to give me a massage with lots of creams and oils, and he gets my whole body warm and wet. He goes up and down my legs, kneading the muscles, like a professional masseur, and by the time his hand gets closer to my pussy, it is already very wet. He kisses me on the nipples while rubbing the back of his hand against my clit. I really get turned on when his wedding ring massages the clitoral hood, and this really sends me flying—something about the vibrations, and about the fact that the wedding ring means that he is married to me, well that really sends me sky-high. Before he's even got his penis out of his pants, I am cumming and cumming, like a porn star, really, because this beautiful man has got me so juiced up. Even though my pussy sometimes aches from all of the sensation, I know that he needs to get off, and I allow him to penetrate me for a deep vaginal fucking, the kind that he specializes in. Guess what? I have multiple orgasms.

HASKELL

I lie back on the bed completely naked, but without an erection. A lady dressed only in the sexiest lingerie ever climbs onto the bed, but does not undress or touch me yet with her hands. Slowly, she sits almost upon my face and she slips a hand into her panties and starts to masturbate herself and cums into her panties and just lowers herself enough to allow me to have the slightest taste of her juices with my tongue on her panties. She lowers herself further down my body and slowly gives me oral sex, flicking her tongue around my penis. She gives me slow lingering oral and then we continue to have slow passionate sex together.

LUKE

I was recently on a football coaches' course, and I would have liked one of the female coaches to come into the shower room and join me in the shower, and I end up performing anal sex with her.

CHARMAINE

My boyfriend and I are at Carowinds (an amusement park), and it is about closing time. And after we get off the last ride, I go to the bathroom, and when I come out, he starts kissing me and feeling me up. This progresses to him having me against the wall, and he pushes my shorts and panties aside and fucks me there.

GLORY

My ultimate sexual fantasy as well as that of most of my female friends from what we've talked about is simply having a loving, caring man who wants to take care of me and is cute, tall, and makes me laugh. We'd have fun together and he'd put me first in his life. We'd have sex during thunderstorms out in the woods or make out in the rain, or even do some wild stuff like sex in hotel pools where people could see us or on hotel balconies.

DESDEMONA

Having my partner make love to me, repeatedly bringing me to orgasm every time.

PRIYA

With my boyfriend, him undressing me whilst being quite forceful and dominant. Bending me over and taking me from behind really hard. Location depends—outdoors or indoors—it depends on my mood.

CONCHITA

Too private—but broadly speaking it is surrounded by mutual trust, consent, freedom, and love.

Homosexual Fantasies

NATHANIEL

Same-sex relations.

CORIN

Seeing my boyfriend taking off his shirt from behind still gets me instantly hard. I think about this all the time. He's so buff and I just get this terrific view of expanse of muscle, all defined and all mine!

GEORGIO

My boyfriend and I on a romantic weekend away. No one to disturb us at all, never leaving the hotel room for the whole time. Drinking nothing but champagne that is brought to our room and eating whatever we want—if anything. Being utterly pampered and able to do and have whatever we want but without having to get dressed or even lay eyes on anyone else.

CISSY

Being with another woman. Touching her and having her touch me. Feeling her suck on my breasts, and lick me in places that feel good.

GLYNNIS

She is wearing her red jacket which I love her in. She starts by undoing my top and taking off my bra, and then kneeling in front of me. She starts to tell me all the ways she loves me, and in between each way she licks at both of my breasts. She then lets me take off her top and her bra while we are kissing each other. Then it is my turn to lick and suck at her breasts which makes her so hot she starts to undress both herself and me. We then explore each other's bodies with both our hands and our tongues. As her room is small, there is only just enough room for us to lie down in front of her desk and we enjoy this as it makes it harder for us to move and all the while being as quiet as possible in case those in the other rooms hear us and come to see what is happening. After about an hour, we start to masturbate each other at the same time with our legs in between each other's. As we are both very aroused we manage to come very quickly—her first, and me not long after. We then lie next to each other, side by side, and talk. As she has another client I have to get up and go when the two hours of my appointment are over, but we make another date.

DALTON

I pretend that I am being fucked by Superman. He treats me just like Lois Lane, except in my version, Superman is a great big poof, but very masculine.

GISELLE

I'm a dyke, and I'm glad that I am. I would never want a penis inside my box, as it would hurt too much, and besides, I think they look disgusting. For me, it's a woman's body any time, especially a femmy, curvy lady with big boobs and a nice, tight, grippable bottom. I have a girlfriend of five years, and I often fantasize about her, but sometimes I will look at gorgeous straight women in the streets, or at restaurants, and wonder what it would be like if I suddenly got under the table, and shoved my head up under their skirts, and started sucking them out through their panties. I love the smell of a woman's vagina, all douched and perfumey, and I love, even more, sticking my tongue deep inside a woman's wet hole. I also have a big fantasy of seducing straight women, and letting them know what they've been missing all these years.

KRISTEN

Having sex with another woman/women. Having them taking the initiative, flirting with me and taking my clothes off, getting me to undress them and performing all sorts of sex acts with them.

SHELBY

Arriving unwittingly at a party for homosexuals. Having an innocent conversation with another man in a bedroom or chill-out room where there are other men who have been smooching and having foreplay. Suddenly, a group of men grab me and strip me.

I am struggling, but don't really want them to let go. Whilst they hold me, one of them performs oral sex on me and I enjoy it. They then tell me I have to return the favor—and eventually I enjoy it.

JON-ERIK

Being worshipped by a whole group of straight-acting (or straight!) guys. Sex worship defined as a group of them sucking me off at once, and the rest kissing me all over my body. All their attention would be on me.

BERNARDO

I just love wanking off over images of the guys that I saw at the gym earlier that day. I go to the gym a lot, maybe five or six times a week, and I really only go so that I can watch the other guys getting undressed in the changing rooms. I do a workout, but I could really do without it, if you know what I mean. I just like thinking about the perfectly chiseled torsos that I've seen in the lockers, and the cute bums and the dangly dicks. I especially like guys with circumcised cocks, and I imagine what it would be like to get down on my knees and maybe first masturbate them, then suck them, then bend over or offer my anus to them, and have them give me a really sturdy, fulfilling, satisfying fuck, filling my man-cunt with hot straight stud cream. I know I'm not the only one who has these thoughts, 'cause half of all gay pornography is about the locker room!

MALCOLM

I wanna be milked like a cow—maybe tied to a table while a guy grabs my udder and makes me squirt.

FLAME

Situation: A woman-only orgasm workshop in which we only wear sarongs, and during which, through massage and sexualized touch, we learn to recognize the erogenous zones of our own and other women's bodies. The environment is warm, comfortable with only cushions and carpets. Soft music, low lighting, and scented candles. The atmosphere is entirely warm and supportive.

RHIANNON

I really love it when my girlfriend just dives right into my vagina and licks everywhere. I used to be married to a man, and he was crap at doing cunnilingus. But my new lover (she's a woman, obviously) really knows what she is doing. She knows exactly where my G-spot is too, and she hits it dead center every single time, just like a champion darts thrower (excuse the phallic metaphor). She licks everywhere without any hesitation. She just goes for it. Guys keep making crude jokes about girls' pussies smelling like stale fish, but a woman's genital odor is beautiful, and guys who don't go down are missing something amazing.

MANNY

I meet a young good-looking guy, masculine appearing and well-muscled, short haircut, no kids, at least twenty years old, cocky. I challenge him. As described in the previous question, I fantasize about stripping down and wrestling. I always end up on top, and after holding him down for an extended length of time, I tie him up and force him to blow me, or I screw him. I tell him he has two choices, fight his way out of it or suck his way out of it. He does not want to blow me or be screwed so he fights, but I tighten up on the full nelson until he submits and lets me tie him up and do anything I want. Just writing this down is arousing.

Bisexual Fantasies

NIKOS

I want to have sex with a man and a woman at the same time. I like the combination of the man's manliness, hairy arms, chunky thighs, and the woman's femaleness, soft breasts, moist vagina, etc. I want to fuck a woman while a man is fucking me. That would make me feel very sexually satisfied, knowing that I hadn't missed out on anything.

WOLFGANG

I want to fuck my gorgeous, sexy, stunning wife in the cunt, while a handsome man, maybe somebody who looks a bit like

Robbie Williams or Jude Law, shoves his cock down my gob, and spunks off down my throat at the same time.

FANNY

I often fantasize about something that really happened. My ex-husband and I were in bed making love, when all of a sudden, my husband's ex-girlfriend, who was staying the night, climbed into our bed, unannounced and uninvited, but before long, we were all at it, and I had the best orgasm ever—my first "bi" experience, but certainly not my last.

ELAINE

In my fantasies, I alternate between guys and women, depending on my mood. If it's romance I'm after, then definitely cuddling and romantic dinners with a beautiful lady, but for sheer raunch and pussy-plunging, gotta be a bloke. Sorry, ladies.

JERMAINE

Three in a bed. A guy on my left side and a girl on my right side, each one caressing my tits and fondling my cock. We all have an orgy, with everybody penetrating everybody every which way. The girl puts a strap-on on her waist, and she fucks me and the other guy with a massive dildo. We all fall asleep in a great big pile.

CLEMENT

I am lying ill in a hospital bed, and then a male doctor and a female nurse come in to revive me. They pull back the sheets, exposing a big erection. The doctor tells the nurse to suck me to completion, while he then straddles my face and feeds me his cum. This makes my vital signs return to normal and the doctor—arrogant bastard—feels very pleased with his handiwork. They then move on to the chap in the next bed and give him some of the same medicine.

ADAM

I have this fantasy where my wife and I are in bed, and then a burglar breaks into the house. He holds me at gunpoint and then makes me strip, tying me naked to a chair. He then wanks himself and gets on top of my wife, and fucks her stupid while I get really hard. The sight of his cock plunging into her cunt makes me shoot a load every time.

KELSEY

A nineteen-year-old guy and his seventeen-year-old girlfriend. I give them a lift in my car as they are hitchhikers. I tell them that I will drive them 100 miles, as requested, but they must contribute to the petrol cost. They tell me that they have no money, that's why they are hitching in the first place. But they offer me sexual favors instead, which I gladly accept. So the nineteen-year-old guy sucks on my penis while his girlfriend sucks him off. The car is covered in cum stains by the time we are all finished blowing our loads.

The fantasies in this chapter serve as further testimony to the wide range of erotic life on both sides of the Atlantic Ocean, even though they represent the more tame and more ordinary ones in the survey. Of course, the bisexual fantasies, by virtue of the fact that most contain sexual acts with at least one male and one female simultaneously, may not seem tame at all. Many readers might regard anything involving more than two people as rather pornographic; but whether one wishes to categorize these fantasies as tame or spicy, they certainly pale in comparison with most of the myriad fantasies which now follow.

5   Group Formations: Threesomes, Foursomes, and Moresomes

I discovered my wife in bed with another man and I was crushed. So I said, "Get off me you two!"

—EMO PHILIPS

Please, Sir, I Want Some More

A surprisingly large number of adult men and women fantasize about sex with two or more people, anything ranging from an intimate threesome to a bacchanalian Roman-style orgy involving a cast of hundreds. Group sex and orgiastic sex may be a means of fulfilling deep erotic urges for maximum pleasure and erogenous stimulation, but these forms of fantasy might also serve as a means of defending oneself or protecting oneself from loneliness. Whatever the underlying psychological mechanisms, which will inevitably vary from individual to individual, the idea of threesomes, foursomes, and I what I have come to describe as "moresomes" certainly appeals to a great many adult men and women in contemporary America and Great Britain. The most popular forms of multipartner fantasies include:

- Sex with two or more men
- Sex with two or more women
- Sex with a man and a woman
- A threesome (genders unspecified)

- An orgy
- Watching a man and a woman having sex
- Watching two or more men having sex
- Watching two or more women having sex
- Being watched oneself during sex
- Being filmed during sex
- Being in a pornographic film

Sexual fantasies containing more than one other person serve a multiplicity of functions. On the surface, such fantasies allow for greater permutations of sexual activity ("one girl sucking my dick, another sitting on my face and another using a dildo on me," according to one of the male participants in the interview study). But psychotherapists and psychoanalysts have discovered that the wish to participate in a threesome may well have other unconscious purposes, which might include:

- An attempted repair of one's narcissistic injuries by possessing more than one lover simultaneously.
- A method for disguising deep-seated concerns about one's own genital or bodily inadequacy; thus, some men imagine that their female partner requires two penises in order to be satisfied, not just one.
- A flight from the deep intimacy required to sustain a one-to-one partnership.
- A means of exploring suppressed homosexual wishes in the heterosexual, and suppressed heterosexual wishes in the homosexual. For instance, a self-avowed heterosexual man may become aroused at the thought of having sex with his wife while another man also penetrates her. Even though the two men have no direct bodily contact with one another in this scenario, the heterosexual man derives secret excitation from the nearby presence of the other man.
- Perhaps most important, an opportunity to recreate the often pleasurable childhood experience of lying in a bed, snugly sandwiched between one's mother and father. Such early experiences not only provide the child with a sense of safety and comfort but also indulge the child's wish to separate the

parental-sexual couple, thus contributing to the little child's sense of omnipotence.

- Fantasies of groups can often be traced back to early childhood experiences of having had multiple caretakers during the first years of life. In my psychotherapeutic practice, I have found that many patients with promiscuous fantasies, or with fantasies of sex with large numbers of people, have had a great deal of inconsistent caretaking from a veritable committee of adults, rather than sustained caretaking from one or two principal caregivers.

- Voyeuristic fantasies stem, predominantly, from a heightened desire to peer through the keyhole of the parental bedroom, a phenomenon that Freud described as the "primal scene." Many small children cannot bear the experience of being excluded from the parental bedroom, and will therefore search for symbolic equivalents of reinserting themselves in the parents' bed by spying on the sexual activities of others. In this respect, all pornography contains elements of infantile voyeurism.

Herewith a sampling of fantasies involving group formations, which I have divided into two sections: first, fantasies of sex with more than one person simultaneously in which one participates actively; and second, fantasies of group sex, in which one watches as a voyeur.

Full-Frontal Participation
DORIAN

I fantasize of having a threesome in which my wife introduces another female into our sex life. In this fantasy my wife reveals she is bisexual and wants to have sex with the other female and me together. I fantasize that we all three engage in consensual sex, performing oral sex on each other, and I have vaginal and anal sex with both as they perform oral sex on each other.

CASEY

Well, I lived out most of my fantasies. But the hottest was being gang banged by a bunch of Latino and black guys. I was a willing participant.

FALLON

I'm nude, suspended comfortably over a banquet table of attractive people attracted to me. I'm dessert! I can swing myself before any of them so they can eat or lick or massage or anything else pleasurable. Whipped cream, cherries, dildos, and vibrators et al are all available to use on me.

BLAKE

Someone's penis in my anus and someone else sucking on my penis at the same time, and someone else sucking on my nipples while I jack off two of them.

EVADNE

My husband bringing two male friends home to share with me.

THORNTON

When I was in school, doing all the cheerleaders, have them all in a row and playing with each and fucking them for two minutes each, then going back and let each one play with the others while I take one on 'til she cums. There were five of them.

GROVER

Being fucked by ten young men with very large penises sequentially, and then having one or more of them put their hands/arms up my rectum until I climax.

ELROY

Probably having sex with my future wife and her three college roommates at the same time. It nearly happened once and I've fantasized about it ever since. The roommates bought me a pair of skimpy briefs as a Christmas gift. They all were persistently trying to get me to put them on and model them for them. I refused. Later that night, I came out of the shower with just a towel on and two of them, without the future wife around, tried their damnedest to pull the towel off. They didn't succeed. The fantasy begins with either or both of those episodes. Always with group sex between myself, the three roommates and the future wife. They all perform oral sex on me at the same time, leading to a mêlée of intercourse. Usually includes the future wife aiding the process throughout. One of those "if only" stories.

ZEBEDIAH

My most sexual fantasy is to be kidnapped and sexually assaulted by a beautiful black woman, an Asian woman, and a blonde woman. My fantasy starts off with them tying me down on a doctor's examining couch, then forcing me to excite their genital regions with my tongue till they orgasmed, then each of them taking it in turns to ride up and down on my penis till I came.

KRYSTAL

I have always wondered what it would be like to have two men work me over. I'd like to feel one licking and sucking on my pussy while I suck one of the cocks. I'd like both of them to play with my tits, licking and sucking on my nipples while they fingered my pussy. I think it would feel real good to have a cock going in my pussy and ass at the same time. I think if I ever had the opportunity to fuck two men at once, I'd go for it and enjoy every hour of it.

BREE

A gang-bang with sixteen army cadets, not really a rape though. Just cute guys queuing up to fuck me senseless.

HERMIONE

My fantasy involves myself, my boyfriend, and another girl. My boyfriend and I are in a red-light district in a hotel room above some seedy sex shops. We are having aggressive and passionate sex, when afterwards I hurriedly get dressed, run downstairs, and drag a prostitute from the street below, bring her into our room and have sex with her on the bed using fingers and toys, whilst he is sitting in the corner masturbating, watching the pair of us. As he is ready to climax I would walk over to him wearing nothing but a pair of black high heels, and I then have sex with him, with me being positioned on top whilst he continued to talk dirty to me, call me his dirty slut/bitch, until we both climaxed.

JENNIFER

My ultimate sex fantasy would involve me and my boyfriend and a large amount of other people, probably around thirty. We would be in a mansion (possibly Hugh Hefner's; in fact, it *would* be Hugh Hefner's). We are all gorgeous, including me—by that I mean we are all well groomed and clean and we have healthy attractive bodies (which myself and my boyfriend are/do in real life—this is not an imaginary, escapist sexual fantasy). My fantasy would begin late into the night. I am not interested in who we all are, how we got there or any of that shit. All I fantasize about is the fucking. Basically we are in very sumptuous surroundings and we are all gorgeous. Ideally there would be a huge en suite bathroom, also full of people fucking. I fantasize about different parts of that night. All of the different fucking. All of the different people I would fuck and how we would do it. I especially like to fantasize about this when I am with my boyfriend because his touching me—as well as my touching myself—makes it feel like there could be lots of us with some imagination. I don't find this fantasy hard to concentrate on either—it just pops into my head.

LAURIE

I teach an art class, mostly young women and young men. We often have life models, and these are sometimes so beautiful that they turn me on. I'd like to announce one night that the life model hasn't turned up, and that we all have to take turns stripping off and posing for the group; this way, I get to see the entire stunningly attractive class naked, especially the slim young men with long pricks and thick, heavy balls. I'd like to see them all getting hard-ons, and I make the class sketch their boners.

BONNY

Being in a car and having sex when a police car turns up and the policemen have sex with me as well.

HEATHER

I want my boss to come into the big open-plan office and tell us that today is "Sex Friday," and we all get to stop working early so that we can have sex with whoever we fancy. I really have the hots for two beautiful men who work at the adjoining desks— bringing new meaning to the term "hot desking." We instantly rip off each other's clothes, and before long the whole office is fucking, spunking, shooting female juice everywhere, and I am in seventh heaven with all these beautiful naked bodies. I can't wait to go to work next Friday.

DEBBIE-SUE

I am kidnapped by a man of a different race, and he takes me to his club house where all his friends are, both male and female. There is a bed in the corner and he takes me there. He assures me he won't hurt me, but he has never had sex with a white woman and he wants to. He makes me strip and stand there while he fondles me. He then has me lay on the bed and has two of his friends hold my legs wide open so he can have oral sex with me. Meanwhile, the friends then unzip their pants and encourage me to suck them off. As I start to climax, the first man then enters me with his large penis and he comes. After that, there are all kinds of positions including anal sex and having one of the females have oral sex with me, etc. It continues for several hours then he lets me go home as promised.

PAULO

I am hiking and come upon two men kissing. I hide in the bushes and watch as the two men start to undress each other. They begin to perform oral sex on each other, and I come out of the bushes. I tell them not to worry and I ask if I can watch. While I am watching, one of the men motions for me to come over and starts to perform oral sex on me.

ELDRIDGE

Having sex with multiple women who give blow jobs, jack me off, and want anal intercourse.

CURTIS

Having sex with my partner and her girlfriend at the same time. Often I have sex with my partner and then make her girlfriend eat her pussy while I screw her girlfriend. Sometimes the girls are on their side performing oral sex on each other while I come up from behind and screw one and then the other while they continue to have oral sex with each other.

GUDRUN

Having sex with more than one woman at a time.

Watching from the Sidelines

FORD

My most recurring fantasy is the one where my wife and I have been to a club. As the evening goes on she becomes more flirtatious and I begin to realize what is happening, and whilst I'm nervous, I continue to let her continue. She becomes obviously aroused on the dance floor and begins to attract attention to herself. We leave the club at the end of the evening with a mixed group and return to our house. There is more drink, and the atmosphere becomes more flirtatious. Some of the men begin to touch her and when she looks at me and I nod, she heads upstairs with them. I head up five minutes later to find them all naked. The men all have huge penises and I watch as my wife has sex with them all and writhes in ecstasy during the whole time.

DAVIS

Watching another man have sex with my woman partner.

ANNA

I am a young woman serving overseas and have been abducted and bound. I am forced to watch as a young Asian woman is initiated into anal sex and realize there is an anal plug in me. I start to squirm while bound and cannot help becoming aroused as the young woman is spanked and sodomized since I realize I am next. I usually climax soon after I visualize the man beginning to sodomize the woman.

DIRK

Watching my wife have sex with other men.

DAWN

I really get off on the idea of coming home from work, and finding my husband already in bed with my bestest girlfriend. They don't know that I've come home, and I sneak up and hide behind a large wardrobe where I can witness their sexual antics without being discovered. My girlfriend is pretty good-looking, and I know that my husband fancies the pants off her—who wouldn't—she's very striking. In the fantasy, he and she are already stark bollock naked and are clutching at each other's body parts like there's no tomorrow. He is pulling at her soft, firm round breasts, and she is tickling his pink nipples, getting them hard. I can see that he has a big erection, and that she has pussy juice moistening up her twat. Before long, he starts stroking the head of his cock against her labia. I know all about this since he does that with me in bed, and it just drives me wild with pleasure. Then she screams, "Big boy, shove it in, big boy, ride me, fuck me, fuck, AAAAAHHHHHH!" And then she climaxes. He needs a bit more pumping before he is ready to shoot, but shoot he does, and a whole wad of sticky semen spurts out of his penis, like a gushing geyser, into her waiting snatch. The whole scene makes me so horny, that I have been frigging myself from behind the wardrobe the whole time. I really lose the plot and masturbate to orgasm, suppressing my screams by biting down on my shoulder. Then I imagine that I have to go make dinner for the kids, and my husband comes down, pretending that nothing has happened.

FLEUR

Imagine my husband with his tart! I know they were into more kinky, instantaneous sex as they didn't have kids with them, and so could have sex during the day, every day. I imagine him being filthy, rough, and her not really enjoying it. I get my kicks from thinking he hasn't reduced me to that level!

MIGUEL

I have a really good pair of binoculars, and these allow me to look into the bedroom of the young couple who moved in next door. They leave their curtains open all the time, and at night, I use my binoculars to watch them making love. They are very free and uninhibited and they look like they're having a lot of fun. The man has a huge cock, and his wife just rides and rides him. They make a lot of noise, which I can hear from my house. This becomes the fuel for many of my fantasies, watching this couple.

DAVIDSON

I've just finished public school, and boy, did I get to see a lot of things there, especially other guys having sex. Unfortunately, being kind of ugly, I didn't get any, but I saw LOTS, especially pervy gay stuff, because that's what goes on in the English public schools, and anyone who says otherwise is lying. My fantasy is based on a real experience that actually happened when I was sixteen. I was lying in bed one morning—I shared a room with one other boy—and all of a sudden, this cute blondie boy who I've always fancied comes in and starts to sit on my suite-mate's bed. They think I'm sound asleep, and I don't disabuse them of this idea. Next thing I know, the blondie boy starts snogging the face off of my mate, and they're at it like rabbits. I pop a stiff woody in my pajamas immediately. I can hear that they're getting more vigorous in their petting, and soon, I hear clothes flying everywhere. I keep trying to sneak a peek but I'm scared they're gonna notice and then stop, so I keep my eyes tight, but I look every now and then for a few seconds of sheer heavenly delight. Before long, everyone has squirted spunk from the mutual masturbation and kissing, and I have shot my load too, without even touching my little snake. I just wished it was me getting the attention. Maybe at university.

LORENZO

I am a barrister. I get to meet a lot of very beautiful women in my line of work. As you would expect, my chambers charge very high fees, and sometimes the women clients start crying, explaining that they cannot meet the fees. I tell them that if they have sex with one another, and let me watch, I will waive their fees. I have assembled an entire anteroom full of obliging females, who strip off at my request, and lick each other's pussies, while I sit in a chair, with my hands in my trousers and pants, slowly jacking my penis to an erect state. I climax when the women do, and then go back to court to do a cross-examination, with spunk in my briefs.

GUY

When I was at school, the boys' and girls' changing rooms were right next to each other, and of course, boys being boys, someone had chiseled through one of the tiles in the wall so that the boys could see into the girls' changing room—fantastic! I remember one day, me and a couple of mates left a lesson early to catch the girls changing, and we looked through the secret tile, and we saw two gorgeous, gorgeous bust-heavy sixth form girls changing into their swimming cozzies. And then, just like if it was a porn flick, they started kissing each other and touching each other's breasts. They then just sort of giggled and not much happened after that, but I wonder what would've. I think me and the other lads all wanted to beat off right then and there, but of course we didn't, but in my fantasy, I imagine that the girls discover us peeping on them, and they come and teach us a lesson. They make us stick our heads under their skirts and eat them out—fishy smell, but very tasty—until they come on our faces, and they tell us to wank, but they won't let us come until they say so. Pretty kinky stuff, but a major wank fantasy of mine for years now.

6

Cheating: When the Intra-Marital Meets the Extramarital

A man has to do something to relieve the monogamy.

—Anonymous

Why on Earth Do We Cheat?

Why do so many of us cheat on our partners? And how to we define "cheating"? According to my research, approximately 55 percent of all adults have committed an act of *extramarital* infidelity at some point. But perhaps more shockingly, at least 90 percent of adults will engage in one or more *intra-marital* affairs at various points during the course of a marriage or permanent partnership.

Does it matter if we become intra-maritally unfaithful, masturbating to images of our next-door neighbors, our colleagues at work, strangers in the street, or celebrities on stage and screen? Clearly, some people do not mind in the least. "Missy," one of the interviewees in my study, told me, "I don't give a toss if my husband masturbates about other women. Why shouldn't he? I mean, I fantasize about other men, it's only natural. I mean you can't keep looking at the same body for thirty years without getting a bit bored. No, I don't have a problem with it. I mean, it's fine. I would get upset if I thought he was getting off on something dirty, you know, like teenage girls, or on really sleazy pornography. But if it's good clean lust about other women, and if he keeps himself to himself, then good luck to him."

Missy's chirpy, cheerful, tolerant attitude epitomizes that of many other Americans and Britons—but not everyone feels the same way. A substantial proportion of adults in both countries would find the idea of an intra-marital affair quite shocking and disturbing. Another female interviewee, a forty-year-old woman called "Alice," told me that she once arrived back home in the evening from a "girls' night out" with her friends only to find her husband, "Benny," sprawled out on the living-room sofa, snoring, with his hand inside his trousers and a pornographic magazine strewn on the floor nearby. Alice had never before suspected that Benny had ever availed himself of "girly" magazines, or indeed that he masturbated—he had always denied that he did—and catching her husband in this revealing posture caused her great distress. She explained, "I felt cheated and lied to, and that night, I told him he couldn't sleep with me in the bedroom. Yes, it does upset me, greatly, to know that he thinks about other women. I keep myself in good shape for him. I'd certainly never fantasize about other men, so why should he fantasize about other women? I think it's disgusting, and it has made me wonder how much I can trust him about other things."

Clearly, we have a wide range of reactions to the idea of the intra-marital affair. Some of us, like Missy, would tolerate mental infidelity and take it in stride, whereas others, such as Alice, would feel deeply aggrieved. Still others suffer from shame and guilt about such fantasies, regardless of whether their partners discover any tangible forensic evidence such as a pornographic magazine.

In 1948, Professor Alfred Kinsey and his coworkers estimated that approximately 50 percent of all married American men engaged in an extramarital act or affair at some point during their lives—a notably high percentage of the male population. Then, in 1953, they estimated that 26 percent of married American women did so as well. These were staggering figures, representing well over 100 million Americans in total during the immediate post–World War II era.

Subsequent studies using more refined methodology have confirmed the accuracy of Kinsey's original estimates: Roughly one-half of all married men, and about one-quarter of all married women, will have one or more extramarital affairs during their marriage. Subsequent researchers have categorized the extramarital affair, and one such team noted that affairs could be classified into one of three types:

1.   Primarily sexual affairs
2.   Primarily emotional affairs (not involving genital contact)
3.   Combined-type affairs (physical and emotional involvement)

Annette Lawson, a specialist researcher on the subject of adultery, has noted that extramarital affairs may be further subdivided into three other categories:

1.   "Traditional" affairs, in which the infidelity remains a conscious secret from the spouse
2.   "Parallel" affairs, in which the spouse tolerates or condones the affair, and may even be having a comparable extramarital affair himself or herself
3.   "Recreational" affairs, in which both spouses participate freely in an "open" marriage

Clearly, there seems to be no clear blueprint for modern marital life. One can remain completely faithful, be unfaithful occasionally, or be serially unfaithful, and so can one's partner, invoking either the wrath, toleration, or even encouragement of the spouse. In other words, no two couples will conduct their marital lives in quite the same way.

The American psychologist Dr. Don-David Lusterman has subclassified the different varieties of extramarital affairs in even greater detail, noting that an affair may be:

• Long-term, or short-term
• Secret, or not secret
• Purely sexual, or involving a discernible emotional attachment as well
• Heterosexual, or homosexual (in other words, having an affair with someone of the opposite sex, or with someone of the same sex)
• Involving physical contact, or with no physical contact
• Involving one other person, or many other persons

Based on his clinical researches with unfaithful individuals, Lusterman observed that normative life events may provide the immediate trigger for the affair. For instance, a midlife crisis, a parental bereavement, the "empty nest syndrome," or even unemployment may all serve as "risk factors" maximizing the possibility that one might engage in an extramarital affair. On the basis of my own experiences as a marital psychotherapist working with couples whose marriages have become threatened by the revelation of an extramarital affair, I would agree with Lusterman's observations.

Lusterman further theorized that whatever the trigger, extramarital affairs may serve a variety of functions. He observed that there are at least four different types of affairs:

1. The "exploratory affair," in which an individual tests out the strength of his or her marital relationship, as well as its desirability, by investigating whether he or she might find better sex, conversation, companionship—or indeed cooking—elsewhere
2. The "tripod affair," in which one's fears of psychological intimacy and of being enveloped by a potentially overwhelming partner become minimized through the act of infidelity
3. The "retaliatory affair," in which one seeks revenge on his or her partner in response to some perceived slight or injury
4. The "exit affair," in which the extramarital affair becomes the launching pad for extricating oneself from an increasingly disappointing marriage

From my own work as a psychoanalytical marital psychotherapist, I have learned that men and women may engage in extramarital, cheating behaviors for a large number of reasons. They include:

- A search for variety
- A creative search to fulfill unmet emotional or physical needs and wishes
- A need to affirm or reaffirm one's potency or desirability
- An attack on one's regular partner
- An attack on one's self, potentially sabotaging one's marriage and the stability of one's own family life
- A symptomatic cry for help, or a communication about distress in other areas of one's psychological functioning
- A reenactment of childhood trauma, especially a secret, unconscious identification with parents who may themselves have had one or more extramarital entanglements

- A protection against the fears of intimacy and merger with one's partner
- A safeguard against primitive anxieties of being engulfed by one's regular spouse or partner
- A manic defense against depressive anxieties

I Pledge to Thee My Troth

When I first laid eyes upon "Susannah," I thought she looked so prim and demure that she would not possibly be able to share her sexual fantasies with me. Indeed, she found it difficult to report her fantasy face to face and asked whether she could write it down. She spent a good thirty minutes composing her answer in a considered manner. Her fantasy, and those that follow, typify the widespread preoccupation with the extramarital affair and illustrate the great scope of infidelity, both external and internal, in adult life.

SUSANNAH

I am a 52-year-old housewife living in the countryside. I get pretty depressed much of the time, and my general practitioner put me on Prozac, but it doesn't really seem to be helping all that much. My husband is a wealthy businessman, but he is always away on travels and, as we never had any children, I spend a lot of the time on my own. Because money isn't a problem, we are able to keep the house in really good shape, and if I need some building or redecorating or whatever, then my husband is very generous with expenses, and I just call a workman. I get a secret sexual thrill from getting workmen in to do major construction or even odd jobs around the house. One day, I needed a new bathroom, and this young man, maybe twenty-eight or twenty-nine years old, called Omar, came to do the work. I greeted him at the door, and in he came, smelling a bit sweaty and reeking also of cigarettes. He wore ripped, paint-stained jeans and a smelly old cardigan, but he was good-looking, and he had about five days' worth of stubble on his face. I could see immediately that he had a ring on his third finger, which probably means that he isn't married, but rather just one of those trendy guys. I immediately started to get a bit short of breath, and I instantly had a fantasy that it would be great if he could screw me. I'm not that attractive, and none of the workmen who has ever come to the house has ever made a pass at me, but I hoped that in Omar's case it would be different. I set him up in the bathroom and offered him a cup of tea and some biscuits, but he refused. I felt upset as though he was already shutting me out. I kept knocking on the bathroom door every half hour or so to see if he needed anything—eventually I brought him some fruit juice and some muffins, and he seemed really pleased. I tried engaging him in conversation, but nothing—he just kept working conscientiously. My heart sank, because I have not had sex with my husband in about eight months, and I really hoped that something would happen with Omar. After about three or four hours, it seemed clear that he wouldn't be making any passes at me, and so I told him I was going to make a long phone call up in my bedroom, and that I would be back down to check on him in about an hour. I went up to my bedroom, locked the door, and proceeded to strip down to my slip and knickers. Then I went to the bedroom drawer and got out my vibrator, which I have been using more and more when my husband is away. I lay on the bed, shut my eyes tight and turned on the vibrator, bringing the tip to my left nipple and then my right nipple, through my slip. I imagined that Omar was here in the bedroom with me, had taken off his shirt revealing a gorgeous set of builder's pecs, and that he was the one using the vibrator on me. Once my nipples got really hard, I began to move the vibrator down to my knickers, placing the head of the vibrator against my growing clitoris and my moist labia, again, pretending that it was Omar who was gently prodding me with the vibrator. I imagined that I could smell his sweaty body and his cigarette smoke, and that as he massaged my genitals with the vibrator he would also be licking my nipples through the silky fabric. Gradually, I took off the slip and the knickers, and started to masturbate this time with my fingers, shoving a finger into my pussy, then two fingers and then finally three. As I withdrew my fingers, dripping with liquid, I rubbed the secretions over my nipples saying, "Yes, Omar, yes, let me take in your manly smell. Yes, Omar, yes, please fuck me now before my husband gets home." I pick up the vibrator again, and it slides easily into my passage. I have a strong visual image that the vibrator is Omar's stiff donkey-meat and that he slides it in, and then slides it out, thrusting with powerful biceps, fucking me like a train. All of this activity helps me to reach the most amazing of climaxes, and I come and come and come, better than any orgasm I've ever had with my husband, even though we've been married for twenty-four years. I get up, rinse off the tip of the vibrator and get dressed. I go back down to see Omar, who seems not even to have noticed that I was gone—it's clear that he could care less about me—and my depression returns. He does a wonderful job on my new bathroom, but at the end of the day, he leaves, and I never see him again. This makes me sad, sad, sad, and I have no one I can tell this to. I use this fantasy a lot on the rare occasions when I do make love to my husband.

PERCY

Watching two females have sex. Neither is my wife.

HESTER

Being in a hotel room with my ex-boyfriend, and while he is having sex with me, my current boyfriend rings me up on the phone, and whilst I'm talking to him on the phone, I'm trying not to scream out.

PHILIPPE

My ex-girlfriend invites me and my current girlfriend round for a dinner party. My ex says she wants to bury the hatchet and hopes that we can all be friends. I think this is a good idea and I say yes to the invitation. At the dinner party, we are all getting drunk and tucking into our pudding course. My ex goes into the kitchen to prepare some coffee. Unbeknownst to anyone but me, she crawls back into the dining room, goes under the table, and starts to rub my crotch through my jeans. I get really hard within seconds—she was always good at masturbating me. Then I feel the zip being undone, and within seconds, she's got my fat todger in her hand and then in her mouth, sucking me bigtime, while my current girlfriend sits at the table totally unaware of what is happening. I start to sweat with excitement. My new girlfriend asks what's wrong. "Nothing," I say, and I just continue to let my ex suck my willy. I spunk into her gob, and she takes the whole load. I can't believe that we have pulled this off, as it were.

LUCILLE

I have this fantasy of telling my boyfriend that I have been called to a really, really crucial, urgent work conference, and that I must leave the house one night at 7:30 P.M. In fact, I go to the lobby of a hotel in Central Manchester where I meet this incredibly stunning Italian man whom I bumped into at a drinks reception a few weeks previously. I've never done anything with him in real life, but in my fantasy we meet in the lobby, check into a room as "Mr. and Mrs. Smith," and then shag each other's brains out. The Italian guy is really well hung. He strips for me, slaps his dick across my face, comes all over my tits, and then, within seconds, he is hard again, and he fucks me, fucks me, fucks me. I go back to my boyfriend, who is asleep in front of the television, with some cans of beer by his feet. Uggghhh!

OTTOLINE

Having sex with my boyfriend while my ex-husband and his wife are close by.

MARCIA

Having sex with my ex-boyfriend while my current boyfriend is watching.

TAMMY

Being caught having sex in a hotel room and the maid joining in.

JEANETTA

Thinking about ex-boyfriend.

NIKLAS

To go to my friend's house, and he is in work. Then I talk to his sexy wife, and I teach her how to use the PC. I am touching her hand to guide her using the mouse. Then she kisses me and slides her hand up my shorts. Then she starts to open my shorts and give me oral. We end up having sex in the PC room as her husband rings to say he'll be home soon.

ELIAS

Cheating on my wife, and her finding the hotel receipts in my jacket pocket. I fuck her good and hard to shut her up.

FRANNIE

I am having an affair with a friend of my husband. He is repairing his car, lying on his back partly underneath it. I am wearing a skirt or dress, but no knickers. I approach him and bend to start unbuttoning his overalls. He knows it's me because he can see my ankles and feet. He asks what I'm doing and I tell him that I've come to give him a treat. He is already getting hard as I unzip his jeans under the overalls and he gets really hard as I squat over him and rub his penis against my labia. Then I squat lower to achieve penetration and move up and down until I have a vaginal orgasm, but he doesn't come. Then I let him get up and I lean against the car bonnet [hood]. He has his hands on the bonnet either side of me, and teases me with shallow penetration, and gives me a clitoral orgasm until I start to hold his hips and pull him into deep penetration, and we both climax together.

BREWSTER

Having a dinner party. I excuse myself to go to the toilet while my wife is serving the main course. A beautiful female dinner guest comes into the bathroom and starts to strip and snog me. We have mad passionate sex in the shower, and then we come back to the party, and no one realizes we've both been gone. My wife is still happily serving dinner, none the wiser.

EUGENE

I love my neighbor's cunt. I get really turned on licking her pussy while her husband and my wife are having drinks in their sitting room. I hope we get caught, then maybe we could all have a foursome.

7   I'm Ready for My Close-Up: Fantasies of Celebrities

You can't shame or humiliate modern
celebrities. What used to be called shame
and humiliation is now called publicity.
      —P. J. O'ROURKE, *The Enemies List*

In the 2003 pilot study of 3,617 British individuals, in the 2004 principal study of 13,553 British adult men and women, and in the 2006
study of 3,433 American adults, both male and female, I inquired
about the frequency of sexual fantasies involving celebrities. I did not
define "celebrity" in any special way; rather, I allowed respondents to
generate their own notion of what constitutes a celebrity. As one might
imagine, a tiny sliver of people chose politicians and classical musi-
cians, a larger proportion chose sporting figures, and the vast majority
defined celebrity as a star of cinema, television, or popular music.

A large number of respondents gave straightforward answers in
which they simply stated the name of some famous person. Some listed
more than one name, without elaborating further, and others went into
more detail, describing something about the fantasy in which the
celebrity appears. In the sample of responses that appears in this chapter, in the interest of saving space, I have included only some of the
more complex answers.

The celebrities named in the responses were primarily those of stars
who grace the covers of magazines and tabloid newspapers in America
and Great Britain, or in some cases, of those who came to fame in an

earlier generation. Clearly, in the private cinema of our minds, we often cast the same actors and actresses who appear in our favorite movies.

Roughly 25 percent of adults fantasize about celebrities, with men indulging in these imaginary encounters slightly more frequently than women. Interestingly, sexual fantasies about celebrities tend to predominate among the young; it seems quite clear that, as we age, our sexual interest in the current crop of celebrities diminishes. In view of the fact that the majority of film and pop stars tend to be youngsters themselves, this suggests that although an old man or an old woman may appreciate the attractiveness of a young singer or television host, the majority of people in their middle or late years still prefer age-appropriate partners.

When we do fantasize about celebrities, we engage in a variety of sexual activities in our minds, most popularly, conventional heterosexual intercourse, followed by oral sex or romantic scenes. Few respondents had fantasies of performing acts of extreme sexual violence upon celebrities, as the following sample reveals.

MORTIMER

Pamela Anderson in all types of ways.

ENRICO

Any sort of sexual contact with Scarlett Johansson would be ideal.

JANE

Andy Garcia, James Spader . . . just a regular fantasy about having sex with them.

ESTELLE

Antonio Banderas, Mel Gibson, an erotic body massage leading to rolling sex, then orgasming at the same time.

LAURETTE

Comedian/actor Hal Sparks. I fantasize about his character on *Queer as Folk* and being able to "turn" him straight.

SHANE

Christopher Reeve as Superman, in his Superman cozzie, before the accident, when he could give me a good fucking.

PACO

Great sex with so many celebrities including Sophia Loren, Kim Basinger, Lena Horne, Barbra Streisand, Condi Rice, etc., etc., etc.

PRISCILLA

Jude Law in the remake of *Alfie*. God, he shagged so many women in that film, and I want to be one of them. I have this re-current fantasy that I'm on the set of the film, and that Jude and I have to do a love scene over and over again. The director is not happy that we are just pretending to fuck, and he asks us "for the good of the film" and for "cinema verismo" if we can actu-ally have sexual intercourse without a condom. Jude instantly gets a stiffy and he rips my panties off. He dives into my snatch, licking and sucking for all he's worth, until his jaw hurts, and then, he plunges his hot piece of meat into my vagina, and he rides me like a dog in heat, spewing out a big stream of baby juice. I would love to have his child, as it would be beautiful I imagine.

JOAQUIN

Goodness, are you kidding? Modern celebrity is all about physi-cal attraction. I've fantasized about every hot actor, singer, sports player, or entertainment figure out there, and if I haven't I just don't know about 'em yet.

ERROL

Just straight sex with Heather Locklear, Barbara Eden, and some others I can't recall right now. Sorry, I guess I'm kind of boring as far as this goes.

STEFAN

Katharine Hepburn in *The Philadelphia Story* (time travel; guess who put the smile on her face at the swimming pool?).

GUSSIE

I've thought of having an orgy with the members of Duran Duran. I've also been "raped" by the guys in Cradle of Filth, Dimmu Bor-gir, and Type O Negative. I've fancied myself Elizabeth from *Pirates of the Caribbean* and had mad sex with Jack Sparrow (Johnny Depp) while Will (Orlando Bloom) was tied up watching us.

JOYCE

Sean Connery as James Bond (quite a few years ago), me as a Bond girl, a Pussy Galore figure, dominant with high-heeled boots, leather restraints, and whips.

SAMANTHA

Various movie/T.V. stars over the decades, e.g., Robert Wagner when he was in *It Takes a Thief;* George Clooney and Brad Pitt fight over me, and Pitt won; Don Johnson as Sonny in *Miami Vice* where I was a spy and we got together; Jon-Erik Hexum as a male prostitute in a house in Vienna that I owned and he taught me about doing it the correct way and then some; etc.

MARTA

I honestly have not ever done this. I cannot think of a celebrity I hold in that high a regard.

ISADORA

Gregory Peck. I guess this dates me. But I never saw such a handsome man in my entire life, well, with the possible exception of Robert Taylor and Clark Gable, two other old film stars of my youth. But Gregory is the mainstay of my fantasy. Yummy. I think he is dead now.

TILLY

Sex with David Cassidy when he was young, and also of fellating Prince William.

LARINDA

Jamie Foxx—I dreamt we were in a bathroom and I was getting dressed to go out and he kept talking to me seductively. We ended up kissing and I woke up before we did anything else.

DOBIE

Kim Novak when I was a teenager at sea in the Navy, having her to myself in my bunk when I came off watch.

ANTOINE

Just about any male star in which oral sex is performed. Many females in which oral sex and intercourse is performed.

ANDERS

Tom Selleck. I've always wanted to undress him and suck his dick and then tie him up and make him drink my piss. I want to torture his nuts (not too painfully), but to the point that he begs me to stop and is willing to do anything I want, if I will stop. I want to ride his dick until he comes multiple times inside me and then I want him to eat his cum out of my ass.

ANNE-MARIE

Gerard Butler, Ron Eldard, Ralph Fiennes, John Roberts (CNN news anchor). Basically, the fantasy is just meeting them at a party, or at a restaurant, or some shared hobby, hitting it off, and one laugh leads to another and we kiss passionately, go back to either one of our homes, kiss passionately, rip each other's clothes off and have sex. I fantasize of him kissing me on the neck which is very arousing, and I like to touch him all over (love the feel of skin) and run my hands through his hair. And more kissing. I prefer men with nice hair, so that's particularly fun to fantasize about. Pretty tame, huh?

HENRIETTA

When I was a little girl, about eight or so, I used to fantasize about George Hamilton. I saw him in a vampire movie then, can't remember the name, and I was in LOVE and couldn't stop masturbating at such an early age over him. Started when I was about eight or nine.

PALOMA

Doing doggie style with Jackie Chan.

PATRICK

I had a chance to go out with Marie Osmond and fantasized about having sex with her. Her flight was canceled and I never saw her. She was a friend of a friend.

LACEY

Jeanne Tripplehorn. I fantasize about the scene in *Basic Instinct* where she gets taken from behind.

LEE

Transsexual porn star Raquel. I want to French kiss her, suck her breasts, and penis, let her fuck my ass, and if I can get hard, fuck her ass.

EVAN

Jane Powell, a singer of many years ago. I used to dream about her being in bed with me.

GODFREY

I have masturbated to the thought of having sex with Freddie Mercury, as well as some gay male porn stars.

DERRY

Various tennis players (female), mainly spanking them.

MOLLY

Being spanked by Russell Crowe (if he looked like he did in *Gladiator*).

WESTON

Ann Miller while I was in college.

XAVIER

Every good-looking woman or girl I see on T.V. or the movies. Usually involves intercourse or oral sex.

HENDRIK

Pierce Brosnan, Hugh Jackman as a threesome.

URI

Sal Mineo, James Dean, Tab Hunter, having a friendship with them and sex too.

LELAND

Julia Roberts—being with her. Chris Evert—same as above. Other actresses and singers.

CICELY

Meg Ryan. Just sleeping with her.

SELMA

Mine is a rape fantasy involving Brad Pitt. I saw him in *Troy*, jumping around, showing off those tight buns and those chunky, muscled thighs. I just wanted to get right in the screen and hold him, and let him take me. I pretend that I am a prisoner from a slave galley in the ancient world, and Brad takes me along with several other maidens, all chained together, and he releases me, only to fuck my brains out and fill me with the hottest jizz ever. My job in the army camp is to be his little fuck-slut for all eternity, or at least until he gets tired of me and goes to fuck some other little bitch.

JOHANN

Sarah Michelle Gellar in a pirate costume.

LINDSAY

David Beckham. There was a show. Oral stuff happened.

PARMINDER

Yes. Drew Barrymore. Would like to do foreplay on her.

FAITH

I've had a sexual fantasy about an actor who was at one time on a crime show but I can't recall the name of the show or the actor. I was on the beach sunbathing nude and he came over to me and kissed me, and we proceeded to have sex.

COCO

Bruce Willis, started out with meeting him along the beach and ended up going to his house for a night of wild sex, and then afterward, it turned very gentle and tender. Parker Stevenson was another person in my waaaay younger years that I fantasized about, that was just pretty much straight sex with kissing, don't really remember too much else about that.

FABIENNE

Al Pacino . . . I prefer not to give details.

CECIL

Princess Di. Just a role model with perfect body, great smile, and loving every minute of it.

HUNTER

Britney Spears and other women I know as part of a game show where I meet like six or seven women. They are put behind a wall, nude, but I can only see them from the waist down, and I have to guess which body belongs to who and variations on that theme.

CHAVA

I would like to leave this blank. I have many male friends involved with the SAG (Screen Actors Guild) and AFTRA, and we are friends, very good friends, some I have known over thirteen years now.

ELIJAH

James Bond Girls.

JARVIS

Halle Berry. I would love to bathe her and wash her body with my tongue. Then bring her to the bedroom and lick her pussy from behind including her anus, then she sucks my penis until I ejaculate and I ejaculate all over her body including her hair and breasts. Then Jennifer Lopez comes in and I bathe both of them at the same time, licking and sucking every inch of their bodies, and do it all over and over again.

RAYMOND

At my age it's all wishful thinking. It used to be Ava Gardner and Rita Hayworth for a torrid affair.

HOWARD

Jessica Lange in her role as King Kong's lover whilst Kong gently examined her breasts and I beheld her beautiful legs.

BERGER

Seth Green, Topher Grace. That would be one hot man-on-man-on-man action.

DELILAH

Elvis—just romantic kissing and hugging.

KERMIT

Have fantasized on most male film stars, also Madonna.

CYRIL

Halle Berry. Me as James Bond.

DARIA

Nobody who would be thought of as a celebrity in the popular sense. Not having a T.V. helps a lot in being immune to their charms.

LICIA

The *Desperate Housewives* gardener.

DAPHNE

Matt Damon. We would meet and really get to know each other, become friends, and then he'd sneak me into his hotel room. . . .

LAWRENCE

Kate Hudson. Kate and I slip into a room with no windows and a lock on the door. We quickly undress each other and she becomes aggressive. We have sweaty, powerful sex in many positions until we both come together.

RAMONE

Yes. Too numerous to make explanation practical.

RAFI

Diane Lane, about her movie *Unfaithful*.

NOEL

Angelina Jolie. After she has multiple orgasms from various means, I lay her on her back and lay her arms to her sides. I take her arms and hold them, but my arms are coming from just under her legs (not holding them up, per se, just slightly). I then pull her to me, using her own body against her to give a feeling of being dominated without all the bondage and such—works great for the wife.

HEIDI

I go on holiday and meet Arnold Schwarzenegger. He takes me to his five-star hotel, he begins to undress me, sucking and biting my breasts. He tears off my clothes and begins to lick me all over. He puts me on the bed. I feel his arms around me, then he takes me roughly. I have orgasm after orgasm as he fucks me again and again, but he does not cum. I so want him to cum. When I ask him why, he says he wants to be dominated. I bind and gag him on the bed. I suck his cock hard and ride him but he does not cum. I take his gag off and ask him why he still hasn't cum. He asks me to humiliate him. I stand up and just let my bladder go, my piss washes all over him, and his cock pumps semen everywhere. He looks longingly at me and sighs, "Thank you, will you do this to me again?"

SANBORN

Having someone famous begging me.

SHERILYN

Several pop stars especially when growing up such as David Cassidy, and then it was just plain straightforward sex.

AVA

Bob Marley. I feel his body underneath me, his tool working on me. I grab his long sexy dreadlocks, pull him up towards me. He knows how to rock the rhythm. All the time he's biting my shoulders and neck, talking sweet nothings in my ear in that Jamaican accent, he's pulling me closer and I'm pressing further down. . . . Until the climax . . . but it doesn't stop there.

KENDALL

Pamela Anderson—on a leash.

APRIL

Orlando Bloom and myself having wild sex during a thunderstorm on top of a castle involving many sexual positions.

STAVROS

Marilyn Monroe and Kylie Minogue. Being lured into their bedroom for a night of sheer passion.

CHRISTOPHER

A lot of female celebrities, too many to list, mostly just straight sex except with Madonna, that is more B.D.S.M.

CONSTANCE

Various racing drivers.

FARRAH

Britney Spears—lesbian sex.

GEORGIA

Dennis Quaid, being in his arms kissing and making love.

RANDOLPH

I remember watching Princess Anne's wedding on telly years ago when I was a young teenager and had just started masturbating. I thought she was the most beautiful woman I had ever seen. I used to jerk off thinking about taking her in her wedding dress, ripping it off, sucking on her nipples, and then diving my dick into her vagina and thrusting until she and I both came together. It's now more than thirty years on, and I still return to that fantasy more times than my wife will ever know. It's something about those early wanks that were so amazing—especially when you had to do it under the duvet at boarding school so that the other boys and Matron (!) wouldn't find out about it.

DELLA

In the past, John Cleese, Michael Palin, Rowan Atkinson, any tall, thin, dark-haired/dark-eyed comedian. Sex is funny and I used to want to experience it with someone who is really funny themselves.

WILBUR

Goldie Hawn. Licking ice cream off her body, all over.

BRIDGET

Robert De Niro. We meet on a cruise liner, have casual sex, but gradually fall in love. I don't think I'd really like him if I actually met him, though.

DARCY

Margaret Thatcher. I was the office boy, and she gave me a blowjob in Number 10.

HELMUT

Angelina Jolie as Tomb Raider, dressed in leather. She ties me up and rapes me, again and again.

MARTINA

Viggo Mortensen from *The Lord of the Rings*—use your imagination you dirty people!

NOELLE

Denzel Washington in the back of a limo with the roof open and then standing up having it from behind while driving down Times Square . . . yipeeeeeeeeeeee.

WILFRED

Kylie Minogue, after studying her wax model in Madame Tussaud's, but in reality I know it will never happen.

TUCKER

The American actress-singer Cher (that shows my age!). Her costume was often brief and very sexy in the videos promoting her songs. She presents as being proud of her looks. Fantasy: consensual B.D.S.M. (Bondage—Domination—Sado-Masochism). Cher as a willing slave dressed in a very skimpy fishnet outfit.

NABIL

Elle Macpherson forcing me to make love to her.

WINSTON

Ben Affleck. My friends know this and refer to him as my boyfriend. General gay stuff.

MARIN

Hugh Grant and Tony Blair and Cherie Blair. For some reason I am invited to 10 Downing Street. I am dressed very smartly. There is a party going on and there are many famous people there. Cherie asks me if I would like a tour of No. 10. We go upstairs, and the minute we enter the bedroom, she forces me onto the bed. Her tongue goes down my throat and her hand goes straight up my skirt. I am in awe of her and I just relax and our tongues meet. I open my legs and my skirt rides up, and her fingers enter me. I am wet to her fingers and have no knickers on. She says nothing but rips open my blouse, kissing and biting my breasts hard, dominating me, kissing down to my waist. She spreads my legs further apart and she tongues my hot wet cunt. I am hers and will do anything for her. I begin to cum, and I buck hard against her tongue. I scream as I cum harder than I ever have before. I black out. As I come round Cherie has pulled a very long dildo from a cabinet drawer. She is laying next to me, feeding this long dildo into herself. "Welcome back," she says. "Do you want me to fuck you with this, you slut?" I murmur weakly, "Yes, please." She stands over me with a wicked smile, the dildo buried in her own wetness, and she slowly pushes the long pink dildo into my wet hole. "I am going to fuck your cunt so hard," she says, as she begins to rock forward into me, the dildo sliding in and out of our hot cunts. She swears at me, all the time telling me how she is going to cum, and how hot her cunt is. I have never heard such coarse language before and it turns me on. I hear voices in the corridor but Cherie does not seem to care. Tony and Hugh Grant walk into the room like a pair of Cheshire cats, their smiles set in place. Next thing I know, Hugh is putting his hard cock in my mouth. I suck greedily as Cherie continues to fuck me, swearing sexually all the time. She changes position and is more on top of me. Then as I am sucking the sweet cock of Hugh's, Tony begins fucking my arse which is wet from my and Cherie's juices. I try to scream but gag on the cock in my mouth. Cherie is screaming and calling me her whore, her slut, as she cums again and again. Then I feel Tony jerk inside. My arse is filled with hot, sticky cum, and Hugh shoots his load into my mouth. I gag and swallow the cum. All the time I am cumming and cumming. I feel hot and exhausted. Tony and Hugh both start getting dressed and Cherie sags on top of me, exhausted. As Hugh and Tony leave, Tony says, "Thanks, you little slut, not a word to the press, and we can do this again sometime." Cherie hasn't finished. As she pulls the wet dildo from herself, it is still in me. She begins to suck her juices from it, slowly sliding her mouth up and down its length. She begins to lick her husband's cum from my arse and fuck me gently with the dildo. I begin to cum again as she sucks greedily her husband's cum from my arse. I cum and fall into a sleep.

TISH

A man who was a mixture of The Rock and Vin Diesel. This nonexistent man and I engaged in kissing and sexual intercourse.

EMILIO

Kylie, Madonna. Madonna sitting on my face whilst I perform oral sex on her and Kylie riding my cock and masturbating herself, then they swap positions and Madonna rides my cock and lets me take her up the ass.

DAISY

Robbie Williams—the ultimate bad boy! Turning the table on his dominant character! Using toys and restraints. . . .

JEROME

When I grab my dick, I like to think of Britney Spears in her schoolgirl uniform with bunches. I'm not a pedophile, and I know she's over eighteen, but I really like the uniform thing, and she fills it better than anyone I have ever seen. I like to imagine I'm her headmaster, and I call her in for a punishment and discipline session after school, since I know she's been naughty. I pull her to me, and she starts to struggle, but eventually I find her little love button and start to rub her clitoris up and down and soon she is grinding into my fingers with the same rhythmic motions that she uses in her video. She tells me to put my finger into her cunt, and it is already very juicy and wet, and I sprout a huge woody. I push her down on her knees, and in really rude language, I say, "Britney, suck me off, you cunt. Suck it, you bitch." She does what I tell her, and my rod really fills up her mouth. I bang into her face, into her jaw, really fucking her mouth hard, and she's gagging. Then I pull out and squirt my load all over her uniform. I wish I could do this for real. My pants are full as I am typing this, so I'm gonna have to go and wank off now. Thanks for that you guys.

EILEEN

Joaquin Phoenix dressed as a priest. Johnny Depp dressed as a gypsy.

MARILYN

Depends what you call a celebrity in relation to oneself. I happen to know a few celebrities. Was even married to a sort of celebrity. But I think you mean with people one does not know, an image. So, probably, no. As a teenager, perhaps, but those fantasies did not include "sex" as you define it, and they were all people famous in the horseracing world. I admired the world (still do, although I don't have fantasies about people in it these days), so perhaps that is what is important. My sexual fantasies about being cuddled amongst the straw were my attempt to become closer to that world, to be enfolded in it. Oh, I think I did have one or two fantasies about Bruce Springsteen at one time, but I can't remember what they were.

CHRISTINE

Prince Charles (when younger). I was in a cottage and it was heavily snowing outside. His car breaks down and my cottage is the only house for miles. He is freezing cold and wet so his clothes come off and I offer to give him body warmth in bed. . . .

JETHRO

Liz Hurley, Kate Winslet and Daniel Craig. Fucking the women; fucking the man.

GAYNOR

ROCK STARS WILD SEX.

KARINA

More like multiple male stars going through my mind during sex.

PIERRE

Having sex with local T.V. news presenter on her desk whilst live on T.V.

MIKE

Tying up the Queen and Margaret Thatcher together with rope, then fucking them, one after the other.

CAROL

Tom Cruise, Robert Redford. Just that they actually want ME, very romantic, lots of cuddles and kissing, passion and desire.

ILANA

Mario Lanza—being sung to and loved by him.

FERGUS

Sex with Raquel Welch in the movie with the roller derby, on the rink while skating.

KIRBY

Paris Hilton. Having a tit wank.

PHILIP

Yes, pretty much any female pro tennis player.

DARIUS

Nicole Kidman. She is perfection.

PETRA

Serena Williams. I just want to be squeezed between her thighs.

GABRIELLE

Nick Nolte, who has aged with me throughout the years!

FREDERICA

Being cuddled by Bill Clinton.

LEON

Living with Marilyn Monroe, having her urinate on me while sitting on my lap in the toilet and having anal sex with her. Masturbating between her breasts, watching her masturbate as I come on her face, have her give me oral. To have oral and anal sex with Catherine Deneuve.

STEVIE

Keanu Reeves, licking me all over, then making wild passionate love.

CILLA

Harrison Ford in his Indiana Jones roles, after being saved from extreme danger.

FERDINAND

Prince William. I was in a parking lot, and he called me over to his car and wanted me to give him a blow job. I, of course, complied.

SEAMUS

I couldn't care less about celebrities.

RANDY

Having sex with Hillary Clinton in the White House. She would be wearing black garter belt and black bra.

FABIO

George Michael, having him re-enact the infamous toilet scene, but me being the cop!

CATHLEEN

Errol Flynn, Rhett Butler in *Gone with the Wind,* George Peppard, Steve McQueen, King Charles II (!). Generally very "girly" romantic fantasies!

NICOLE

Kevin Costner, tying him up and seducing him and teasing him till he can't take it any more, then having wild sex.

CORT

Ashley Judd. Regular sex, I think she is beautiful and sexy.

DALE

Fucking Lady Helen Windsor.

BERTIN

Isabelle Adjani in *La Reine Margot.* Womanhood doesn't get much better than that. The sex scenes are so erotic.

NINA

Dustin Hoffman. I was his Mrs. Robinson in the film *The Graduate.* Mel Gibson, passionate rough lovemaking with him in his role in *Braveheart.*

ANN

Being spotted in a crowd by Sean Connery and whisked away for sex.

CASIMIR

Just fantasized about having oral sex with Teri Hatcher. Eating her out and letting her suck me off.

EDMOND

Madonna and her husband at the same time, being fucked by him whilst going down on her.

COURTNEY

I am me and consider myself a celebrity, so no need.

MARCY

I have imagined that I have re-enacted the scene from *Cocktail* with Tom Cruise where they make love under a waterfall, after stripping off underwater in front of each other.

TODD

Jennifer Aniston. We were simply happily married and having normal sex.

DUSTY

Gregory Peck—years ago! Very romantic and normal.

CARLA

Barry Manilow—anytime and anywhere!

KLAY

Bo Derek. As a teen, *10* made quite an impression!

MILES

Movie starlets.

CYNTHIA

Kevin Sorbo—imagining having normal (penis in vagina) sex with him in a tender and loving way.

DURHAM

Doris Day, just ordinary sex.

CLORINDA

Oliver Reed and Tom Jones taking me to bed and having their way with me.

ANALEESE

Yes, and it's none of your business.

FINN

I have had fantasies about porn stars. Just fantasizing that I was taking the role of the male star having sex with the female. I guess that's because they get to do things which my wife wouldn't want to.

AVIVA

Colin Firth. Who hasn't?

JANIS

Barry Gibb. Saw him in a white suit looking very sexy.

MARY-CATHERINE

Jude Law, Dustin Hoffman, George Clooney, George Michael, Freddie Mercury, John Lennon—mainly center on a global theme: being taken by surprise—rough sex.

ROMY

I do not believe in the existence of "celebrities."

CARLOTTA

Burt Lancaster. Dreamed I was having sex with him. Was so sorry I woke up.

DEE

Hiring Richard Gere as the *American Gigolo,* and having the night of my life—all for me!

JESSIE-MAE

None—I prefer real people.

PAMELA

Josh Hartnett on a boat.

TAD

Not applicable. You lot are really sad. I can't believe you ever were capable of thinking of this crap. I only entered this survey to show you that there are real people in the world who are normal and I thought I'd take you for the money. Sad.

8　　Is Your Wife a Lesbian?
Is Your Husband Homosexual?
Is Your Gay Lover
Really Straight?

*Vita hominum altos recessus magnasque
latebras habet.
[A man's life contains hidden depths and
large secret areas.]*

—PLINY THE YOUNGER

The Case of the Strap-On Dildo

Data on sexual orientation reveal that most Americans and Britons exist somewhere on a continuum ranging from extreme heterosexuality to extreme homosexuality. Many straight people would be deeply angered if anyone dared to question their heterosexuality, just as many gay people might be highly insulted if anyone impugned their sexual orientation credentials.

Consider this fantasy, provided by "Ulrich," a fifty-two-year-old participant in the Sexual Fantasy Research Project. Ulrich told me that he had never entertained a homosexual thought in his life. Of course, Ulrich will happily give his male friends a great, big strapping bear hug in a bar, but any other expression of intimacy with another man, either physical or emotional, would be anathema. Consider Ulrich's favorite sexual fantasy, which revolves entirely around the female genitalia:

I love CUNT!!! That is the only thing that I fantasize about—cunt, cunt, cunt and nothing but cunt. It seems pretty normal to me. What guy doesn't? I masturbate myself to an orgasm at least five or six times a day, and when I jerk my cock, I like to talk dirty to myself. I will say things like: "I'm masturbating my penis, pounding my pud, beating my meat, and wanking my fat todger." Then I'll say: "I'm gonna slam my stick into a nice hairy gash, into a juicy drippy wet twat, and I'm gonna make the bitch scream. I love staring at a hairy cunt, and I'm gonna ram my rod into her gaping hole, and fill her up with cream." I don't know why but I get really turned on when I talk dirty to myself. I use a lot of porn—magazines and the net—and I love to look at pictures of women getting fucked by big cocksticks, with hairy dongers shoving in and out of their gashes, with guys slamming their hairy nuts against the hairy pubes of their holes, filling them with dick, with spunk. I love cunt! Give me more.

When I first read, and then reread, Ulrich's proto-heterosexual fantasy, I did find myself wondering why he took the trouble to provide such a vivid description of women "getting fucked by big cocksticks, with hairy dongers shoving in and out of their gashes, with guys slamming their hairy nuts against the hairy pubes of their holes, filling them with dick, with spunk." Some psychological commentators might jump to the conclusion that Ulrich becomes excited, at least in part, by the thought of the male member. Having talked to Ulrich directly, however, I developed the strong impression that he would be tempted to punch anyone who made such a suggestion to his face, or even behind his back.

I have included Ulrich's fantasy in order to broach the subject of *complexity* within sexual orientation. On the basis of the questionnaire results and my clinical interviewing, I can confirm that, although the vast proportion of Americans and Britons do profess to have a reasonably clearly defined sexual orientation (e.g., heterosexual, homosexual, or bisexual), many people have the capacity to maneuver, either to a large extent or to a more limited extent, along the sexual orientation continuum. Some do so only occasionally, as in the case of "Romney," a highly experienced heterosexual who has bedded many women during his thirty-three years, but who arrived at a psychotherapy session in a state of panic because, over the weekend, he had had a nocturnal emission in his sleep while dreaming about an old male friend from boarding school. Once, and only once, at the age of twelve years, he and this friend had engaged in mutual masturbation. Romney knew that such an ejaculatory experience did not negate his highly satisfying relationships with women, or indicate, necessarily, that he might be a "closet homosexual." After exploring the meaning of his dream, he became calmer. He arrived at the conclusion that a part of him craved affection and recognition from men in his life, especially from his somewhat distant father, whom he could never please. After discussing his homosexually tinged dream, Romney managed to realize that "maybe we all have a bit of a queer side to us, and if we do, well then, so what?" He responded to the unexpected eruption of homosexual thoughts with relative equanimity.

Many other fundamentally heterosexual men and women, however, become more disturbed than Romney did when gay and lesbian thoughts begin to cross their psychological threshold. I have met gay and lesbian patients who become equally troubled when they find themselves unexpectedly aroused by a member of the opposite sex.

Sexual orientation seems a straightforward matter for some people, especially for those who live at the extremes of the orientation continuum; but for a great number of adults there may be small or large areas of gray, which can produce a mixture of excitation and confusion. Our brains work with such lightning speed that within the first two or three seconds of meeting another person, most of us have the capacity to determine whether a particular individual may be male or female, old or young, kindly or cruel, vivacious or depressed, rich or poor, stylish or slobbish. Utilizing not only our visual apparatus but also our unconscious intuition, we can absorb an enormous amount of data that provide us with telling clues about someone's personality. Such clues will also help us to make our own private diagnosis of someone else's sexual orientation and sexual life.

In our increasingly sexually liberated culture, many of us enjoy being able to obtain the full measure of someone else, and we often make extremely rapid and supremely confident judgments about others on the basis of superficial characteristics. How many people still adhere to the stereotype that all lesbians wear their hair in a short crop, or that all gay men have pierced ears or limp wrists?

Over the years, I have met quite a number of lesbians and gay men who *do* conform to these physical stereotypes, but I have also encountered many who do not. Furthermore, I have interviewed women with extremely short, spiky hair who turn out to be married with four children, and men with effeminate features who prove to be compulsive womanizers. Additionally, I have met lesbians who would make Claudia Schiffer seem masculine, and gay men who could drive a steel-plated tank through a desert storm. Although we often enjoy our rapid, amateur diagnoses of the sexual lives of other people, we may frequently be quite wrong, because one cannot tell simply by looking. Sometimes we can guess whether someone may be gay or straight with unerring accuracy. But at other times, even experienced psychological professionals will be caught out.

It can be difficult enough to ascertain someone else's sexual orientation just by looking, but imagine how much more difficult it can be to determine someone else's sexual behaviors, let alone his or her sexual fantasies. Many years ago, I saw a middle-aged man in consultation whom I shall call "Mr. Erlenmeyer." Referred by his family physician, Mr. Erlenmeyer presented as rather effeminate. His head drooped to the left in a jejune manner, and he wore a chunky silver ring on the middle finger of his left hand; he had a long mane of peroxide-streaked hair, and a tattoo on his right forearm. On the basis of these physical characteristics, I assumed he must be homosexual. This gentleman then surprised me when he began to speak about his wife and his two daughters. The consultation proceeded in an ordinary manner as he talked about his depression, his work inhibitions, his various psychosomatic symptoms such as migraines and stomachaches; and then, after approximately forty minutes, he told me that he really had come about a sexual difficulty. "Aha," I smugly thought to myself, "this man will now confess his secret homosexual liaisons." But Mr. Erlenmeyer surprised me further, revealing that he had a mistress called "Gwendolyn" whom he beat with a riding crop. He had begun to feel guilty about cheating on his wife, who had sensed that he might be having an affair.

How might we define Mr. Erlenmeyer's sexuality? Would we understand him as a heterosexual man? Would we suspect that because of his effeminacy he must really be homosexual, but does not know it—evidence of what psychoanalysts have often called "latent homosexuality"? Mr. Erlenmeyer identified himself as straight, never once offering any indication of sexual interest in other men.

Another patient, whom I shall call "Mr. Frankenberg," arrived at my office complaining that he had lost all sexual interest in his wife.

He had a pierced ear and a small mustache, and once again I entertained the possibility that he must really be a gay man. Mr. Frankenberg then revealed that his sexual interest in "Mrs. Frankenberg" had begun to dissipate after he had commenced an extramarital liaison with "Drake," a young man who worked in his office. "Aha," I thought, once again, "the pierced ear and the mustache really are dead giveaways." Three weeks later, Mr. Frankenberg arrived for his session and informed me that he had something rather unexpected to tell me. "More revelations of covert homosexual sex?" I wondered in silence. In fact, Mr. Frankenberg admitted shamefacedly that he had just met a beautiful woman whom he adored more than his wife and more than Drake, and that he wanted to discuss the advisability of leaving both of them for this new lady.

How would we describe Mr. Frankenberg? Would we regard him as an essentially heterosexual man who happened to stray from time to time? Would we conceptualize him as bisexual, able to enjoy physical relations with members of either gender? Would we classify him as homosexual, sleeping with women as a defense against his ostensibly true homosexual nature? And does it really matter? No doubt a panel of mental health professionals, sexologists, and members of the general public would all have their different views about Mr. Frankenberg. He, however, refused to define himself, informing me one day that although he may be confused, he would not live his life in "tiny boxes."

These two brief vignettes provide a glimpse into the potential complexities of erotic life. Over the past two decades, I have encountered a multitude of patients whose sexual lives challenge every one of the ordinary, workaday assumptions we cherish about the nature of human sexuality. I can recall a number of similarly telling cases:

- A twenty-nine-year-old male patient called "Zachary," married to a beautiful wife with whom he enjoyed a great sex life, told me that at the age of ten, he had masturbated with another boy at boarding school. To this day, no amount of satisfying marital sex could ever equal the thrill of his prepubescent masturbation.
- A thirty-nine-year-old gentleman called "Yoram," also married to a beautiful woman, used to sneak out of the marital home at night to have sex with male prostitutes, but only if these men would don a pair of panties and a bra that Yoram had borrowed from his wife's wardrobe.

- Perhaps more unexpectedly, a sixty-two-year-old woman called "Elsa," a life-long lesbian, arrived at my office in great distress because she had recently found herself quite attracted to an elderly gentleman who reminded her of her late father. Elsa had never slept with a man before and had begun to worry that her life would be incomplete if she did not attempt penetrative intercourse with a penis before dying.

These sorts of cases certainly challenge our notion of sexuality as a monolithic creation. My colleagues and I have encountered gay men who find themselves becoming erect in the presence of women, straight women who lust after homosexual men, lesbians who fantasize about heterosexual men, and straight men who, during a drunken escapade, have experimented with another man. Does anybody have a clearly consolidated sexual identity, or has everyone become confused? Perhaps psychotherapists meet only those people who do struggle with sexual confusion.

The most challenging case that I ever encountered, from a classification point of view, involved a male-female couple called "Pablo" and "Leonore," both aged forty-two. After years of vigorous lovemaking, Leonore purchased a strap-on dildo shaped like a penis. Pablo would insist that Leonore wear the strap-on dildo around her waist, and he would urge her to penetrate him anally with the dildo. So, here we have a situation in which a seemingly heterosexual married couple perform intercourse, reversing the traditional positions of "penetrator" and "penetratee," with Leonore actually pretending to have a penis, which she would insert into her husband's rectum. Would we understand this as a colorful sex encounter between two married straight people, or do we regard the sexual activities of Pablo and Leonore as an indication of great mental turmoil resulting from the fact that Leonore does not know whether she has a penis or a vagina? Or perhaps the fact that Pablo craves anal penetration by a strap-on penis might indicate a primary homosexual preference? In truth, this couple presents so many challenges to orthodox theories of sexuality that I hardly know where to begin in my attempts to theorize.

If sexual behaviors can confuse us and force us to question our notions of classification, then just imagine how complex the situation becomes when we take sexual fantasies into account. If we become foxed when we try to guess whether someone sleeps with women or with men, the guessing game becomes infinitely more problematic when we try to predict what someone else will be fantasizing about during intercourse or masturbation. If we experience difficulties predicting sexual behaviors, we must lay down our arms in defeat at the prospect of anticipating what someone else's masturbatory fantasies might be. One cannot tell just by looking; indeed, one could not tell what someone else fantasized about even if one had access to a diary detailing his or her full sexual history. My research reveals that some people who have never had a homoerotic experience in their lives fantasize extensively about homosexual encounters, and that people who have never had a heterosexual experience in their lives will nonetheless fantasize copiously about the opposite sex. In the world of sexual fantasy, all the rules and conventions become challenged. The examples that follow fall into three basic categories:

1. Brief, general fantasies about unexpected forms of sexual orientation.
2. More detailed fantasies about complicated expressions of erotic orientation.
3. Fantasies written by heterosexual males who enjoy the thought of lesbianism, from which they become excluded—a situation that many experts regard as a compelling psychological puzzle. After all, if a heterosexual male enjoys intimate contact with women, why should he remain a voyeur rather than a participant?

The Panoply of Erotica:
Creative Fantasist or Just Confused?

RUSSELL

Being tied to a chair and made to watch another man make love to my wife.

SANDY

Being with a young guy, age eighteen, and taking each other's clothes off, and sucking on each other's cocks. Slow French-kissing together. I am not gay but have erotic thoughts about this. Then watching two sexy women I know who are lesbians, seeing them make love to each other.

TAYLOR

Usually a threesome with two men, two women, or one of each. Lesbian fantasies also.

AMBROSE

Me and other straight guys on a weekend away where we get drunk/carried away, start messing around, stripping, etc.; usually leads to massage and then group masturbation and giving each other a hand.

UNDINE

Being with another woman and having her be submissive while I pretend to be a man and take her from behind doggy style.

SALVADOR

A woman is being fucked vaginally by a number of men, and each one comes inside her. When it is my turn, I fuck her with another guy (i.e., double entry), knowing the other guys' come is helping us to get into her vagina. The thought of having my dick rubbing up against another guy's dick, with all that come, and that we can come together inside her too, is what really does it. Sometimes I will add to the fantasy by licking the woman's clit and the other guy's dick and balls as he rides her, savoring the come that is oozing out of her from all the other guys before us, before I enter her as well. I am actually gay, but I have often fantasized about having sex with a woman, but with other guys involved. Of all the fantasies that really "rock my boat," this is the one.

ELEANOR

As a lesbian, strange though it may sound, I fantasize most often about straight sex with a random stranger with whom I could have one day/night of easy, fast, abandoned sex. In reality, this would probably not be very pleasant, but I miss something about straight sex . . . the physical obviousness of it perhaps.

CAMPBELL

Standing naked behind another guy with my erection in between his legs wanking him off over a lady on her back frigging herself off in front of us. Once she is covered in spunk, I get to lick it off and fuck her up her ass doggy-style.

VERONIQUE

Watching a man and woman having sex, and me masturbating at the side. As a lesbian that's a bizarre turn-on.

SANTIAGO

Going to a club, getting hold of a mega-busty woman, taking her home, and then finding out she is a transsexual.

WANDA

I imagine that I am a young girl, say about eighteen years old. I venture into the sand dunes behind a gay nudist beach (naked of course) and either I am accosted by, or I accost, two gay studs who proceed to have the most outrageous gay sex in front of me.

COLLIER

My (current) favorite sexual fantasy involves swinging and seeing my (female) partner have sex with another man while I have sex with his (female) partner. My partner wants to see another man give me oral sex during this scenario also and when I am feeling really horny, I do think about this sometimes. During this fantasy I want to see my partner have lesbian sex with the other woman, including oral, digital masturbation, dildo/vibrator action, and double-ended dildo as well. I also think about spit-roasting my partner. We often talk about this type of scenario during sex and both get aroused by the thought of it.

SIDNEY

Watching my wife being subjected to sex by a number of male strangers with penises in vagina, rectum, and mouth. Four men playing with her breasts (one squeezing and kneading a breast and another playing with the nipple), whilst she masturbates the other men (one with each hand).

RENATO

I want to have sex with the man next door. I have a fantasy that when our wives go out, we go to each other's gardens, strip off and do it doggy-style on the grass, shooting cum everywhere, especially in our anuses and on our backs.

RHONDA

In my fantasy I have a penis but I'm still a woman. I have sex with a woman, who admits it's the best ever.

LIAM

Meeting a group of ladies in a smart hotel. The ladies are dressed in business suits or cocktail dresses. They flirt with me and I get a little tipsy. They take me off to the ladies' toilet where they slowly reveal their stocking-clad legs and pretty lingerie. With me naked and kissing and licking any flesh I can, things start to get heated. It is at this point that I try to give oral sex to one lady, and to my horror I discover a large, very erect cock in her panties, which is swiftly pushed down my throat. I am held down and soon have my ass and face fucked by this horny group of transsexuals. When they have finished with me they take turns to piss in my ass and shit in my mouth just to make sure that I am fully humiliated.

KENDRA

My most sexually arousing fantasy is having sex with a dominant female who is also a hermaphrodite.

MARTHA

Kissing a woman's breasts as a man takes me from behind.

NICOLETTE

Having sex with two men and a woman at the same time, she kissing my breast, a man kissing my vagina and exploring my vagina with his fingers, and me giving a blow job to the other man.

PANDORA

My biggest fantasy would be just me and another woman but she would arouse me more than any man ever has or would again.

NEHEMIAH

Sex with a transsexual. Having them bent over forward and entering them from behind.

RUFUS

Sex with my male mate and best female friend (not my girlfriend) at the same time, stripping down to underwear and spending the night all locked up together in a room, with a big double bed, giving and receiving sexual pleasure.

JENNA

I'm tied to a bed by two women. They tear my clothes off, then undress each other. Then my husband walks in. They tie him to a chair, and make him watch as the women begin to kiss my breasts, lick my nipples and gently bite them, then one of the girls starts kissing down my belly till she gets to my vagina which she gently teases by kissing and licking, and then the other girl goes over to my husband who has an erection, and starts to give him oral sex. This goes on for about an hour, then we all get on the bed, and have the best sex ever.

STACEY

As a transgendered person, my chief sexual fantasy is of having sex with a person I love in the gender role that I would prefer.

Let us now examine a number of more detailed fantasies involving some sort of mixture of heterosexuality and homosexuality in both male and female adults. As you read through these fantasies, consider whether these individuals might be secretly gay, secretly straight, confused, or legitimately bisexual. Perhaps we have to admit that we simply do not know.

DONNIE

I just joined the army a few years ago. It's pretty exciting, the basic training, but I haven't seen any fighting yet. The best part so far is the friendship with the other lads who are great—all really fit boys, and some are cute and hunky—phwoarrh! Basically, I like screwing chicks, but these lads in my troop are so hot that I like seeing their cocks in the showers, and in the army there's plenty of opportunity for group nudity and getting your cocks out, so I don't complain one little bit. My best mate is called Luther. He's twenty-one just like me, and from the North, also just like me. He has the most beautiful body—smooth, lean, tall, fit and well muscly from all the training. He also has an incredibly fit girlfriend, Merry, who I never met, but he talks about her so often that I feel I know her. Luther keeps a piccie of her in his locker and underneath his pillow on the bed, which he shows me from time to time. She is beautiful—long silky blonde hair, and nice firm, bouncy boobs. I can't see her nipples from the photographs, but I imagine what they look like. I love to masturbate, but I don't get to do it that often, 'cause there's always the other lads around, and although you would think we all spend our time wanking off together, that doesn't happen as much as the general public would like to think. But I do sometimes get a private moment or two in the bog to shoot my load, which I need to do. If I have more than five minutes by myself, you know, enough time to really enjoy myself, then I think about having a threesome with Luther and Merry. In my fantasy, I am in the barracks, just looking after my kit, or some shit like that, and Luther and Merry come back from the pub, very drunk and messing around with each other. Next thing I know, Merry is flat on her back on the bed, and Luther is lifting up her skirt, and tugging down on her panties, so that I soon see her nice trimmed bush, and her cunt hole. He tugs on his belt, loosens his fatigues, and out pops Mr. Big, that's my special name for Luther's throbbing piece of donkey-meat, 'cause he has a big one. I'm not very good at measuring, but it must be eight or nine inches of prime man-length, and it looks so tasty. All of this stripping and exposing gets me very hard, and I watch as Luther rubs the head of his prick against Merry's clit and cunt lips. This makes the head of his cock very wet and very shiny. Eventually he shoves his pole into her pussy, all the way up to the hilt, up to his pubes, which he trims—I caught him in the showers once doing that, and I knew then and there that he was a dirty old stomper. He slams his meat in and out, in and out, and before you know, Bob's your uncle, and he is letting a big load of dick juice into her cunt, and she's gagging for it, screaming her tits off. This gets me so hot that I look at Luther, and Luther looks at me as if to say, "Go for it, matie, boy," and I do. I get my cock out, and it's not as big as Luther's but still pretty massive, and I take his place, launching my torpedo into her warm wet place. The best part is that I can feel Luther's spunk inside her cunt. I've been inside enough cunts to know the difference, and it is definitely his spunk, and that makes me shoot a big bucket of cum cream into her twat. Luther doesn't know that I feel this way about him, and I wish he did 'cause it would be excellent if we could do this in real life, and not just in my fantasy, wanking in the bog, with all the other lads having a piss nearby.

ANSON

I have a very horny one, and it goes like this. I'm eighteen, and pretty good-looking, at least my girlfriend thinks so. When I beat off, I like to think about going to visit my dad's younger brother, my Uncle Hal, who is about thirty, and he's good-looking too. I don't think he's gay, but he's not married, and my mum has certainly wondered about him. In the fantasy, my parents have gone away on a long trip, and they want to make sure that I get three meals a day and that I'm looked after, so I move in with Uncle Hal in his flat. On the first night there, I go to bed, but I'm having trouble sleeping. Uncle Hal comes in and asks me if he can get me anything. I tell him I'm all right, and he says it's really lovely having such a nice, presentable nephew staying with him. He sits on the edge of the bed, and asks if that's OK, and I tell him, "Yeah, sure." We chat for a little while, and he starts asking me about my girlfriend, and he wants to know all the details— what's she like, what does she look like, etc. Half an hour goes by, and I'm still wide awake, and Uncle Hal tells me that he will give me a back rub, as this will really help me to untense and fall asleep. I turn over on my front, and I start to feel real good as Uncle Hal pushes his strong fingers into my neck and shoulder muscles, and I can feel all the tension disappearing. Uncle Hal tells me I have nice broad shoulders, not bad for an eighteen-year-old, and he wants to know if the rest of my body is as well developed. For some reason this question gets me extremely horny and I start to get a bit of an erection. When he asks me if I've gone through the change yet and whether I have hair on my dick, I get hard, and I pop a big fat cock. I think Uncle Hal knows, because he can tell that I'm shifting my position and starting to grind my pelvis into the mattress. Before I can say anything else, my uncle has reached under my waist, and he's grabbed my dong and gives it a good grope. He then gets very dirty, and says, "Is this what you use to fuck your girlfriend?" I nod that it is. He then says that he wants to make sure that I'm giving it to her good and proper, and he asks me to describe how I fuck my girlfriend in full detail, not leaving anything out. I start to explain, but he says, "No, no, you'd better show me. Take your clothes off, and pretend to fuck her, like she's here on the bed." I do as I'm told, and soon I'm totally 100 percent naked, and I enjoy the feel of Uncle Hal checking out my tits, my cock, my waist, my legs, etc. I get on the bed and pretend I'm lying on top of my girlfriend, and I start to hump the mattress, stabbing my dick into the sheets. All this friction makes it even harder, and I'm getting pretty close to coming. I notice that Uncle Hal has been playing with himself the whole time that I've been fucking the mattress, and as he starts to moan, I get really hot, and before you know it, I blast my seed all over Uncle Hal's sheets. This makes him go all hair-trigger, and he wanks himself off shooting his cum all over the bedroom.

LETITIA

My husband is a very good lover, and we have been happily married for over thirty years, but he will never perform cunnilingus on me. I have tried many times to get him to go down on me, but he says that he can't bear the taste. This makes me feel sad and dirty, and I wish there was something that I could do about this. I keep myself clean, and I always shower very extensively before sex, but still he won't lick me out. Sometimes when he is nibbling around my inner thighs—that's as close as he'll get with his tongue to my vagina—I like to imagine a beautiful woman, maybe twenty-five years old, in between my legs. She has no problem with mouth-action, being a woman herself. I like to fantasize that she runs her smooth tongue over the labia, up and down, and then moves on to the clitoris, just gently flicking her tongue over the hood. This is such a delicious sensation, that when my fantasy combines with the actual sensation of my husband working on my legs, I feel that I am ready to orgasm. But the twenty-five-year-old goes further, and she really buries her tongue deep inside the vagina, and starts to stimulate the internal vaginal wall. Apart from my husband's penis and my own fingers, oh, yeah, and the gynecologist's fingers and speculum, nothing has ever gone into my pussy area in this deep way, and I am floating in the air. I really love the thought of cunnilingus, and although I wouldn't know where to get any (as I am not computer-literate, and we live in a small town), I wish I could get my hands on some lesbian videos, so that I could watch other women being tongued in this way. Oh, I'm glad you asked for full accounts of our sexual fantasies, because if there are any men reading this, for god's sake, be a man and lick out your wife. It won't kill you, and she'll be grateful forever.

WLADISLAW

I am a married guy, and my wife and I have been married for fourteen years. We have two great kids, and we also have good sex. I love the feel of my penis in her vagina, and I love the warmth and closeness of her vagina muscles pumping the sperm out of my penis as well. It makes me feel very manly and very satisfied. I do have a sexual secret, which is that whenever I fuck my wife, I always think about men. Apart from a bit of mutual wanking with a neighbor when I was thirteen, I have never done anything with guys, nor do I intend to, but when I wank, it is men that I find attractive. But I would really never want to sleep with one. It sounds odd, I know, but I find the male face really attractive, ditto the male body. But for pure physical sensation, it is a woman with whom I want to go to bed, specifically my wife. Does this mean I'm bisexual or does this mean I'm gay and don't really know it? Who knows? Maybe I'm hetero but just like the look of guys. After all, I'm a guy and I love my penis and my masculine body, so why shouldn't I like other men's fit bodies? When I have sex with my wife, I do like to fantasize about men, and I have one or two fantasies that really get me turned on. There is one in particular, and it's about watching guys pissing. I think it's a real turn-on to see a nice big man with hairy arms and hairy wrists pulling his pisser out of his pants at a public urinal and then having a nice powerful splash up against the porcelain of the urinal. This makes me really hard. In my fantasy, I am standing next to another guy who is taking a piss, and I reach over and grab onto his dick and hold it for him while he pisses. Sometimes I imagine that the guy is a famous guy, especially young pop singers, like Robbie Williams and Will Young. Sometimes I'll even imagine that Robbie is taking a slash and that Will Young is pissing next to him and gradually, they grab each other's dicks and hold them for each other while pissing. This gets me so aroused that all I have to do is think about this, and I'm stiff, and whatever my wife is doing, I go up to her and rub my dick against her bum signaling "time to go to bed." I gave her the shagging of her life.

VENETIA

I love to fantasize about lesbian sex. I'm a forty-two-year-old woman, married, mother of a beautiful little boy, and generally happy in my life. My husband is not the best lover in the world, but he is tender, attentive, never hurts me (unlike an earlier boyfriend who used to sodomize me in the bottom). But all in all, I prefer to think about women when I am in an aroused state. I really go for the typical traditional glamour girls, women like Elizabeth Hurley and Nicole Kidman. I look at pictures of them, and I just can't believe how stunning they are. I would like to look like these women, and get the admiration of men (and women) from all around the world. In my fantasies, I dream that Nicole Kidman, Elizabeth Hurley, and I are all actresses starring in the same film, and we get picked up from our hotel together in a big stretch-limo, and then have to go to makeup together at six in the morning before being brought to the set. We have a really kinky costume designer who insists on dressing us personally, and of course we have to wear such tight dresses that there is no room for undergarments. The costume designer gets to us after we have finished in makeup. He says, "Ladies, now I would like you to take off all of your clothes, every single stitch, so that I can sew you up into your costumes." We all do as we are told, and I am standing there, watching Liz Hurley and Nicole K. stripping, removing their jeans, their blouses, and their bras and panties, revealing the most gorgeous bodies. Nicole has red pubic hair, and Liz has dark hair but very closely trimmed. The girls look at my genitals too. We are all a bit embarrassed about having to get naked before getting into our dresses, especially with the costumier there, but we are all professionals so we just get on with it. But as time goes on we are all starting to get hotter and hotter from looking at our gorgeous bodies (I have one too). The costumier says he has to leave us for a bit to get some safety pins, and there we three are in the room, totally naked. Nicole cracks a joke and says it's really bizarre to be standing there naked, and Liz and I just giggle. Nicole decides that it would really help us in our love scenes with our male leads (Brad Pitt, Tom Cruise, and George Clooney, respectively) if we could practice our kissing. Liz and I both think this is a great idea. Nicole crosses over to Liz and grabs her head tenderly, stroking her long back hair. I am running with vaginal secretions at the sight of Liz and Nicole tonguing each other. Nicole then comes over to me and repeats the process, sticking a delicate tongue into my warm, waiting mouth. Liz surprises me by coming over and stroking her hands up and down my flanks, paying particular attention to my rounded bum cheeks. Nicole's hands also start to stray and gently move down to my nipples. She continues kissing me while she tweaks my breasts and my tits. I decide to be really daring, and without any preparation or prompting, I move my hand to Nicole's vagina, and I put my finger on her clitoral button with unerring precision, eliciting a giant moan of pleasure from Nicole's beautiful lips. Before long, we are all massaging each other's clitorises (clitores?). Before the costumier comes back, we are all climaxing again and again. Now where can I get an Actor's Equity card?

SUGAR

I know that it's pretty normal for women to have lesbian fantasies, but I have them all the time, even when I'm being penetrated by Lars, my partner of seventeen years. I have lots of different lesbian fantasies, and although I do like penises, I much prefer breasts and vaginas, they're just so much more soft and sensual and well, beautiful, like a painting. I prefer really girlie women, very feminine ones with soft creamy white skin, pink nipples, and a nicely trimmed thatch over their clitoris and vagina. I work in a gynecologist's surgery as a receptionist, and so I spend the whole day watching a long queue of young women going in and out of the consulting rooms. Most of them are very young, very sexually active. Sometimes, even though I'm not supposed to, I will read their files. I do have access to them. If there is a particularly attractive young lady I'll get very curious and imagine what kind of sex life she has and what kind of sexual problem she has, and if she is very, very beautiful, I will often go straight home and masturbate about her and wonder what her vagina looks like, and what her breasts look like. I get very jealous of the doctors in the practice (it's a group practice) because they get to see vaginas all day every day, and I wish that I had done medical training because then I too would get exclusive access to naked female bodies. There is one incredibly beautiful redheaded woman who is twenty-two; I know from the notes that that is her age. She has unbelievably good skin, really lustrous complexion, and I love it when she comes in for an annual check-up, not least because she is so friendly to me as well (not in a sexual way, just kindly). In my favorite fantasy, I tell her that the doctor is being delayed, but if she wants to follow me, I will show her into the consulting room. I tell her to get her skirt and her undies off, not in a creepy way mind you, just in a nice way, and she does. So I get a good look at her vagina—the hair around it is golden. I have her put her legs in stirrups, and I take a really good look. I would like to go down on her and lick that beautiful part of her anatomy, but professionalism (and fear of discovery) prevents me from doing so. I just frig myself like mad when I leave the room, wishing that I had such a beautiful vagina.

Men Who Love Lesbians

For many, the male penchant for lesbian fantasies and lesbian pornography remains the gold-standard test of heterosexuality. Why confine oneself to only one woman when one can enjoy two or more women making love to one another? On the surface, the male heterosexual consumption of lesbian iconography seems quite straightforward: Straight men enjoy the sight of naked women.

But as feminist writers have noted repeatedly, although on the surface a male fantasy of lesbians appears to indicate a love of women, such fantasies in fact express hostility toward women because they serve as a pornographic objectification of females in a male theater. Psychoanalytical research indicates that there may be another component of the male love of lesbianism. The noted New York–based psychoanalyst Ethel Spector Person has wondered why these men become so aroused at the thought of two women making love to one another, instead of becoming more aroused at the prospect of making love to the women themselves. Person has suggested that such men might harbor secret fears about their own potency and their own capacity to satisfy women. Most men have concerns at least at some point during their lives about the size or the erectile abilities of their own penis; therefore, the lesbian fantasy not only gratifies the pleasure in observing the naked female body, but also relieves the man of the burden of having to satisfy the women himself. Professor Person has also noted that many of the men who enjoy lesbian themes may themselves *identify unconsciously* with women and with women's bodies. Rather than enjoying watching a man and woman making love—that is, having a fantasy in which the man can imagine himself in the position of the other man—the men who prefer to watch two women imagine themselves in the position of one or both women. The lesbian fantasy, devoid of any male figure, also eliminates any masculine competition; in other words, the male fantasist will have no other masculine rival, no father figure, no brother figure, no boss who could possibly threaten his sense of potency.

In discussing the excitation of lesbian fantasies with men undergoing psychotherapy and with men who participated in my interview study, I have discovered that many of them experienced a marked episode or episodes of maternal deprivation, often of a gross nature, during the first five years of childhood. Such an experience, I believe, can stimulate a craving for extra-*maternal supplies,* and the fantasy of more than one woman engaging in sexual activity gratifies this wish.

The heterosexual male preoccupation with lesbianism serves as an illustration of the multilayered complexities of erotic orientation and desire, as the following set of fantasies will show. Do these reports reveal evidence of passion for women, or, rather, hostility, or some combination thereof?

ALEJANDRO

Watching and joining in with two gorgeous women would be my ideal fantasy.

SPALDING

Having sex with a neighbor when yet another neighbor (also female) stops by the house and we ask her to join us. I enjoy each of the women and enjoy watching the two women give each other orgasms.

MONTY

My main and repeated fantasy is about having sex with women, not one woman in particular, but just the idea of lesbian sex. Usually they are giving me oral pleasure, or we are kissing.

DAKIN

Lesbianism of any form.

FRANCESCO

My wife having an orgasm with another woman.

KIP

My favorite sexual fantasy is about my wife. She's a hot-looking thirty-six-year-old, but most men say she still looks in her twenties, with big, bouncy tits to prove it. I am so proud of her that she keeps herself looking so good. In my best wank fantasy, I imagine that I come home early from work one day, and to my surprise, I find my wife with her tongue down the throat of the eighteen-year-old daughter of our next door neighbor. I'm not a child molester or anything like that, but I would bang this girl at the drop of a hat, she's so hot, and I'm always undressing her with my eyes, wondering what her cunt and pussy lips must look like when she's naked. Anyway, in my fantasy, my wife gets there first. These two are tonguing each other's mouths, and the temperature is getting hot. I hide behind a cupboard, but already this girl-girl action is making my rod get a bit bigger by the second. Next thing I know, my wife starts to tweak the young girl's tits (let's call her Anita). She's tweaking Anita's tits, and before long, both bras are off, and they start rubbing their nipples together. Oh boy, my dick is straining so much that I have to undo my trousers and my belt, and I just start rubbing my dick through my pants. My wife then starts to suck on Anita's tits. I guess they must have seen me or heard me, because at this point, my wife yells out, "Hey, Kip, come on in and join me and Anita—if you're man enough." I rush in, cock first, and I shove my boner down Anita's throat. She's never had cock down there before, but with my wife stroking her fanny, she starts to get into it. Before too long, buttons are flying all over the place, and eventually we're naked. But as I fuck Anita, and as my wife sucks my balls, I think how hot this is, and I wish this could really happen. But unfortunately, my wife is pretty conservative, and if I made any moves on Anita, her dad would probably rip my head off. I have a younger daughter myself, so I know how protective fathers can be. But as a wank fantasy, this one is great.

HANS

Watching two girls kissing, having oral sex and masturbating each other.

ELLIS

I just love the thought of wanking over two ladies eating out each other's pussies. A beautiful blondie girl eating out snatch is my favorite turn-on. I really need the girls in my imagination to get into it in a big way—you know, not just porn-style licking—but really chowing down, like they were having their last meal. I'd love to see them pinch each other's nipples while 69-ing, and then letting all the pussy juice drip down their thighs. I masturbate really hard, chafing the skin, when I think about this. Sometimes my dick gets red raw, and I break the skin, but the thought of these carpet munchers really gets me blowing a big wad of cum all over my belly. I wish these lesbians were there to lick it off my stomach, and also off the wall of my bedroom, 'cause when I shoot, the cum flies over my shoulder. I suppose I'd be a good porn star one day. One day, maybe, who knows?

9   On Genital Exhibitionism

Kleiner Mann hat auch sein Stolz.
[The little man also has his pride.]
— GERMAN PROVERB

Mini-Exhibitions

Exhibitionism forms a normal part of healthy human development. It would be a matter for concern if the teenage boy did not, at some point, show off his biceps, developed from many workouts at the gym, or if the teenage girl did not, at some point, flaunt her growing breasts by wearing a tight shirt or sweater. To refrain from appropriate displays of body parts might indicate a deep sense of shame about one's body, which might be indicative of depression or other psychological difficulties.

However, what happens when men and women display their genitalia in public as well? Most mental health professionals would regard genital exhibitionism, otherwise known as "flashing," as a worrying symptom. Even the seemingly simple act of a man in a raincoat flashing his penis to an unsuspecting female bystander can provoke years of traumatization in the victim. And though most flashers do not engage in physical contact with their victims, a substantial proportion, approximately one-third, will proceed from flashing to more serious acts of interpersonal violence. In fact, long before he became a multiple murderer, the infamous Jeffrey Dahmer exposed himself at the Wisconsin State Fair, an early warning sign of the devastating sexual behavior that would follow.

Although exhibitionism can be a clinical-forensic reality, most Americans and Britons manage to confine their exhibitionistic strivings to the realms of fantasy or to other more sublimated forms of display (e.g., holding court at a dinner party, chairing the village fair, starring in the school play). My research has revealed, interestingly, that younger members of the population seem to enjoy exhibitionistic fantasies more than their elders—perhaps, in part, because these twentysomethings and thirtysomethings have not yet established themselves in the world and still have a deep-seated need to be seen in all ways, even bodily.

As I explained in my study on *Exhibitionism,* published in 2001 and based in part on my clinical psychotherapeutic work with flashers, the roots of exhibitionism stem from deep anxieties about bodily adequacy. In that short book I adumbrated a number of reasons why some men, in particular—the primary perpetrators of flashing—commit acts of genital exhibitionism. These include:

- A defense against castration anxiety, using the exhibitionist act as a means of enforcing masculine potency
- An expression of sadism toward women, especially hatred toward the mother
- A means of narcissistic display in an otherwise "unseen" person
- A protection against intercourse with women, who may be construed as dangerous or castrating
- An expression of a masochistic impulse to be caught, imprisoned, and punished
- A vehicle for transforming aggressive desires into sexual desires, thereby rendering them more ego-syntonic to the patient himself.

The vast majority of those who fantasize about exhibitionism will never commit an arrestable sexual offense. One wonders, however, to what extent the dynamics of clinical genital exhibitionism apply as well to those for whom exhibitionism has become a primary source of masturbatory or coital fantasy stimulation.

JIM

Having sex with my partner outdoors and perhaps a few people watching, but I don't know that they are.

CARTER

Being caught masturbating by a stranger.

VICENTE

I live on the fifth floor of my building. I like sticking my penis out of the window and wanking, hoping that someone will see me. I never let the cum fall on the ground, but I would like to. I just worry that it would hit someone.

LUCYANN

Sitting on the balcony of my flat [apartment], with my legs wide open, masturbating in front of the hot teenagers (seventeen, eighteen, nineteen) who live next to me. They see my vulva, and they get their dicks out and masturbate along with me. They squirt their cum onto me, even though they are many feet away.

MELVIN

Getting my dong out, and wanking in front of a group of young girls, aged 18–20, and getting them all heated up. I flash my dick at the cutest of the girls, and tell her, "Suck it, baby, suck it." She gets down on her knees, and eats my schlong up, and I spunk down her gullet. Then her friends queue up for a heavy helping of Melvin cream.

CHANA

Being forced to an orgasm whilst in a crowded train. I am not allowed to draw attention to myself and have to reach an orgasm just as the train pulls into a station, where there are people waiting to get on the train. The man bringing me to the orgasm is always behind me and I never see his face.

BOSWELL

Whipping out Mr. Floppy, and letting everyone take a good, close look.

GERMAINE

Being a stripper.

BREANN

Various sex in public places, but out of sight: changing rooms, trains, cars, beach, park, office, etc. And spectacular scenic spots:

Eiffel Tower, Grand Canyon, outer space, etc., places that are man-made or natural wonders that excite the senses. The risk of being caught is a big turn-on. With a partner or fantasy-figure, rather than a stranger.

ARDEN

Being a rock chick, and having to strip off in front of a heaving, sweating audience of guys and ladies, all admiring my body, and screaming for me to perform my hits. This really gets me going. I guess I like the unadulterated admiring from so many strangers who are all fantasizing about me. I like the idea of hot teen guys wanking over my posters on their bedroom walls, just like I used to do with David Essex and David Cassidy.

GLENDA

Being romanced and seduced by a stranger, then making love to them in a place where someone else could find us.

WEBSTER

Having to strip off in front of a group of seventeen-year-old girls who look at my penis and laugh at it as it bobs up and down in a state of semi-erection.

GUILLERMO

I'm gagging to have sex outdoors with everybody looking at me humping my missus. The crowds cheer as I thrust my cock in and out of her dripping twat, and I squirt lots of spunk into her, making her moan. The guys all want to take their turns, and I tell them they can have sloppy seconds.

KATARINA

Being filmed masturbating.

DILLON

Spontaneous sex in a public place with a stranger.

BOBBI-JO

Slowly stripping someone, then slowly stripping myself in front of them, turning them on, but they are not allowed to touch me.

MINA

Having sex knowing you are being watched through a two-way mirror.

HUD

The guys on the rugby team hide my clothes as a practical joke, and they make me go out of the changing room fully naked into a whole throng of female fans. They wolf-whistle when they see what I have hangin' between my big fat thighs, and that night, I pull.

ETHAN

Catching my partner unaware and having sex from behind while in a public place.

FIDEL

I love to be out in the open. Sex in fields or on the beach, or any-where with the threat of being caught.

LACHLAN

Having sex with my wife, out in the open, with strangers of both sexes watching.

GARTH

Sunbathing nude in the sand dunes and being watched and filmed in revealing poses.

HENRICUS

The thought of being watched while I am having sex.

DIANE

I saw Kathleen Turner in *The Graduate* in the West End, totally starkers as Mrs. Robinson. This got me so horny, not 'cause I fancy women, but because it would excite me to be naked, and make some young teenage boy's cock leap into action when he saw my pussy and breasts.

LAVINIA

I want to be totally naked in front of my husband's friends, and let them parade me about and examine me. Then, when they have taken me in with their eyes, I want to be fucked good and hard by each and every one of them.

LURISSA

About being in a porn film and being watched whilst I am made to perform sexual acts.

WYATT

Having sex in front of a large audience.

LEONARDO

Having sex outdoors and the thrill of being caught.

BONITA

Another woman or man joining my husband and I. Anal and vaginal intercourse with both men at once.

EVELYN

Sex in a pool.

MALA

Having sex with another female while two men watch, then the men join in.

Maxi-Exhibition

DIMITRI

I am at a party in some swanky house in Mayfair. Everyone is dressed in fancy clothes. The ladies wear gloves and ball gowns, and the men are all in penguin suits. I am looking particularly handsome tonight, and I am in a horny mood having just taken some cocaine before arriving at the party. We all sit down at a very long dining table. There must be twenty-five or thirty guests seated, all getting stinkered on fine champagne. There is also a whole fleet of servants in liveried uniforms waiting to serve us. I am seated in the middle of the table, with two beautiful, big-titted blonde Sloane Rangers on either side of me. Somehow the conversations turns to sex, and one of the S. R.'s just asks me point-blank how big my dick is. Suddenly, the whole table is hushed with silence, and people just cannot believe the outrageousness of this question, especially in a Mayfair house. I am unfazed, and I tell her I'm packing twelve-and-a-half inches. Her jaw drops in disbelief. In real life I have nine-and-a half—pretty big by anyone's reckoning—but hey, this is my fantasy, so I add another three inches. "It's true," I say, and the Sloaney bitch challenges my honesty. Suddenly all the other ladies and men at the table start to get in on the act. The hostess says, "I know, we'll all play a game. Why don't all the women unzip the trousers of the men seated next to them? That's it, just get their dicks out, get them hard, and then we'll have the butler go round and measure. The winner will get to show off his cock in the middle of the table and fuck whichever lady he wishes." Everyone starts to get very nervous, especially all the stuffy aristo blokes with the diddly dicks. I say that I'm man enough to take on this challenge, and I shame all the other men into playing. This said, the game begins, and I get the two Sloane bimbos unzipping my fly and yanking out my schlong that's over a foot long, with change. The other women are unzipping their men, and everyone else apart from me has turned scarlet red with embarrassment. Everyone looks in my direction, and their eyes just pop out of their head. The women all want to suck me, and the men look like they want to cut my dong off with their butter knives. All the ladies have got their men's dicks out of their penguin pants, but mine is so big that it takes two of them to yank it out, and it's still coming, because there's so much of it. Finally, fed up, the hostess yells at me, "Come on already, Dimitri. Get your cock out." Soon, it is all out on display, a great big hosepipe, the sort you might see on a fire engine. It hangs down to my knees. The hostess then tells all the men to stand on their chairs, with their trousers and boxers down at out ankles. I'm the first up, because I have pride. The other limp-dick fairies get up slowly, afraid to show off their teeny tiny pricks. The hostess then sends the butler round with a ruler, and he starts to read off the measurements: "Lord Windsor, five inches, Lord Cavendish, six inches, Lord Shithead, four inches, etc., etc." He then gets to me, and my dick is longer than the ruler, "Crown Prince Dimitri, twelve inches and change, milady." Everyone starts to applaud, and all the ladies are salivating because they want to suck me off. The hostess has me stand in the middle of the table, and she tells me I can take any of the ladies, and roger them senseless in front of the whole dinner party. I choose a rich bitch with huge knockers and big nipples. I rip her dress off, throw some dishes to the ground, and then lay the bitch down on the table. She whispers, "Please don't split me open." I start to tease the head of my cock against her clit. My cock is so big that I can only get my hands around the tip. I ask two of three of the other guys to help me guide it into the girl's honey pot. I pound my prick into her twat, nearly splitting her open. All the other guests are getting really excited seeing me move my meat that they all start to jerk off and frig themselves. Some of the ladies grab candles from the candelabra and start to fuck themselves, while the blokes are grabbing for the pats of butter, lubricating their dicks while they wank. I love being on display. I fuck the bitch until she passes out, and I deposit a whole ocean of cream into her little quim. I really am a member of the aristocracy—a minor member—but that's the only "member" about me that is minor!

10   The Erotic Smorgasbord: Fetishism, Transvestism, Homeovestism, and Other Forms of Object-Love

Some minds speak about things, and some minds speak the things themselves.
—Friedrich von Schelling, quoted by Ralph Waldo Emerson, *Journal*

It may be a surprise to discover that a proportion of the population derives its primary erotic thrills not from a *person* but, rather, from an *object*, whether that be an item of clothing, a particular piece of fabric or some other texture, a slice of rubber, leather, a kitchen utensil, or a fresh vegetable. Although many people might well enjoy the sight of a sexual partner dressed in a basque or a skimpy thong as an occasional treat, most do not, as a rule, require these items of clothing in order to become excited; for the fetishist, the transvestite, or the homeovestite, these objects become *de rigueur,* and large numbers of these individuals will find arousal difficult without the requisite costume or prop. For these men and women, the costume becomes a ritualistic part of love-making, whether masturbatorily or with another person. In this respect, the use of the costume or the prop underscores the potential theatricality of the sexual life.

Although fetishism, transvestism, and homeovestism represent three different sets of desires and form part of different erotic subcultures, I have chosen to group them together as each concerns sexual arousal contingent upon the presence of an external, physical object. Briefly, "fetishism" might be defined as the erotic thrill provided by the presence of any physical item imbued with arousing qualities; most popularly, fetishists will become excited by such items as rubber, leather, boots, sneakers, high heels, ribbons, fur, and other items too numerous to mention. Generally, each fetishist will be aroused by one very particular fabric or texture. "Transvestism," by contrast, might best be defined as the strong desire to dress in clothing generally worn by the opposite sex (especially men in dresses). Some people will become aroused by dressing-up in transvestic fashion, whereas others will be excited at the prospect of making love to a transvestite. Lastly, "homeovestism," a little-known variant of transvestism, may be defined as the penchant for wearing items of clothing belonging to another member of one's own gender (for instance, a man who enjoys dressing in the clothes of another man). This will often involve men with homosexual inclinations stealing or borrowing the clothing of another man, and then masturbating.

It would not be helpful to attempt a potted explanation of such complex psychological constellations here; suffice it to say that most of the psychoanalytical theories of transvestism and homeovestism indicate that the practitioner or fantasist struggles with an anxiety about core gender identity. Herewith, we have a small selection of fantasies involving clothing and other physical objects of arousal.

TALBOT

You wanted to know what my most arousing fantasy is; well I'll tell you. It's leather. Don't ask me why, but ever since I was a little boy, I found leather really stimulating, and now that I'm a grown-up, I can't get enough of it. I grew up on a country estate, and we had lots of horses in the stables, so maybe it's something to do with all the saddles and all the other leather equipment (boots, crops, etc.)—who knows? Anyway, I am 100 percent heterosexual, and I love fucking women—every chance I get—but the whole experience becomes much more sexy when the woman is wearing leather garments, or if I am wearing leather garments, or both. I just love the smell and the feel and the texture—it's weird, but if I see a woman in leather, especially boots or hats, or even carrying a handbag, I just get hard. My key fantasy involves

Diana Rigg in *The Avengers*. She was the wet-dream of my boy-hood years (what boy my age didn't wank off to Diana?). I even had a magazine with her in it, and I would ejaculate onto her face in the magazine. I did this so many times that eventually I couldn't open up the pages. In my fantasy, Diana comes into my bedroom, dressed as Mrs. Peel, wearing just a long pair of black leather boots. She announces herself as Mrs. Peel, and I tell her, "Peel back my foreskin, Mrs. Peel," thinking she will find this witty. Without hesitation, she comes up to the bed, and reaches into my jockey shorts, and takes out my todger, and then, as in-structed, she peels back the skin, and takes my cock-head in her mouth. I can smell the leather of her black thigh-length boots, and I can see her fingering her pussy as she sucks my dick. Diana, the leather, and the blow job all combine into one great big head-rush, better than any drugs that I took in the 70s, and I just lose it. I blow my wad into her hot, warm, wet mouth, and my spooge just drizzles down her cheeks and onto her tits, and one or two drops of my baby-juice even get onto her boots. Fantastic! Thanks, Miss Rigg!

GRIFFIN

I like to dress up in my flatmate's underwear. He's good-looking and a stud. He has no idea how much I fancy him. I will some-times take his undies out of the laundry basket, have a good sniff, and then wear them to work. I have a hard-on all fucking day long, and then when I come home at night, I have a fantastic wank in his pants. Then I put them back in the laundry basket and pretend that he knows.

LUIGI

You may think I'm a bit of a perv, but I love to take a scrubbing brush and massage my cock head with it, then my pubes, then my arsehole. The brush kind of hurts, but I get the most massive stiffy. I can't masturbate anymore without Mr. Brush.

CASTOR

Watching pretty women or girls who wear stockings and sus-penders, etc., stripping.

VERN

I love ribbons. I wrap them around my cock until they threaten to cut off the blood supply. Then I slather baby oil over my erect cock and jerk myself off. The ejaculation is fantastic, and I fall asleep with my cock covered in spunky ribbons.

MARLO

My partner dressed in uniform—it would really turn me on.

ATHENA

I start making love to a beautiful woman, only to find out that it's really a beautiful man done up as a lady. It's a transvestite! This fantasy really arouses me, but I wouldn't want to do it in real life. But in fantasy, I kind of get the best of both worlds.

FINTON

I get really turned on by women's panties. I love to nick some panties, and rub them all over my tits and my cock. Then I shoot into them, and let the semen dry. Sometimes I will wear the panties, if I can get my cock stuffed into them that is.

JAMES

All my fantasies start with footwear. I'll see a woman out wearing high heels or knee boots and that will start me off. I fantasize about being dominant at first, leading things on, but once it gets to the bedroom, the woman takes complete control, making me her sex toy, licking her heels, then her pussy, but she's never satisfied, so she takes a belt to my behind and I have to lick her all over again. Sex is then at her pace. She uses her mouth and breasts to stimulate me, keeping me on the edge, putting the pointed toe of her boot in my mouth while fellating me to stop me making any noise. We finally have penetrative sex, and after coming, she lets the cum dribble out of her, down her legs, and I have to lick her boots clean.

DANI

That my partner works as a security guard and asks me to steal some underwear. He then takes me to a private office to strip-search me and when he finds the underwear, spans me as a punishment.

SHAW

Rubber, rubbing against rubber, and wanking off in the process.

HEINZ

Feet and socks, especially if they are smelly and stinky. I've been a foot fetishist for about twenty years.

ROLANDA

My partner wearing latex.

HELOISE

I'm having sex with three women and one man. The girls are in fetish rubber and one is licking me out, the other is dangling her tits in my face, and I am sucking them (she has a rubber head mask on and only her face is visible). The last girl has her pussy hanging over my face and I intermittently lick her and then play with the other girl. The girl that is licking me out is interrupted by a guy ramming me with his huge penis and she licks his firm stem before he forces his way in. Once he has, she reverts her tongue's attention back to my clit while holding my hips in place for his hard shafting.

GRANIA

Licking the feet of a very sexy young man.

EPHRAIM

Woman with shoulder-length hair (any color) dressed in white underwear and wearing stockings and high heels.

CALEB

Being tied up and forced to worship another man's shoes/ trainers/feet. The other guy's wearing sports kit.

BROGAN

Lately, I find that the best way to get off is to take a hairbrush— usually I take my girlfriend's, and when she goes out, I will rub the hard bristle against the tip of my dick, and also against my testicles, rubbing the brush back and forth. It hurts a little bit, but it gives me a great sensation, and I shoot all over the place. Later that night, for instance, when my gal and I have sex, I think about someone taking the hairbrush to the underside of my big fat balls, and just stroking the bristles against my hairy sac. I also sometimes imagine someone sticking the end of the brush up my arse, and this makes my nuts get even tighter, hugging the base of my penis. I spunk masses just doing this and thinking all about this. Amazing!

FELICIA

Being forced to have sex by a group of women whilst dressed in their clothes.

DAYTON

I really get off on other guys' pants. Whenever I go to the gym, I like to hang about in the changing room when all the other guys have gone into the shower or the sauna. I keep close watch on all the pants. Some guys lock theirs away in a locker, but others, the more rugged ones, just leave them on the benches or on hooks. If I think it's safe, I like to sniff a couple of them, especially the crotch. If there's a pubic hair or two in it, it's a bonus. If there was this epidemic of stolen pants from the gym, I'd be in trouble, but once every two or three months, I nick a pair, and then I take them home, and sniff them, and then put them on, and I jerk off like crazy, thinking about the guy who wore them. I think of these stolen pants as trophies, and I call them "spunk rags." I never wash them. At the moment, I have about eight, and it's my collector's collection. I just wish I had the guys who went with them, but whenever I put on a pair of these spunky pants, I get instantly hard and have to pull myself off.

HUGH

Satin shorts. That's what I fantasize about. It has to be satin; otherwise, it's no good. I go to this shop in Soho which sells them, and they all know me there. I love to go in and try on all the different types in the changing room. One of the really embarrassing things is that the pants are so tight, and when I try them on, I get so aroused and my penis gets so big that it's hard to stuff the thing into the pouch. I buy them, go home and masturbate. I don't think about anyone in particular, just the shorts. I'm married, by the way, with four kids, and I have a great sex life with my wife. She doesn't know about the shorts, but I have bought her a lot of satin over the years, and it definitely helps our sex life.

DRUSILLA

I don't just fantasize, I do it. It's dildos, strap-ons, vibrators, and even toothbrushes, also carrots and bananas—cucumbers are usually too thick. Anything that I can stick up my pussy, I do. Toothbrushes are great, 'cause you can really let rip with the bristles on your clit, and that makes me lose it right then and there.

BOBBI

I have a secret: I wear men's clothes. I like to get as butch as I can, and go out and seduce women or gay men. They actually think I'm a man. I frig myself off just thinking about some of my many conquests over the years. I'm really looking forward to reading your report on sex fantasies, because I think this is a very important subject which most people get very hot under the collar about and don't understand how important fantasies are, especially in this climate of sexually transmitted diseases.

11   Humiliation and the Infliction of Shame

Quant à vous, le nouveau, vous me
copierez vingt fois le verbe ridiculus sum.
[As for you, the new boy, you will write out
for me twenty times the verb ridiculus sum.]*

—SCHOOLTEACHER TO CHARLES BOVARY,
IN GUSTAVE FLAUBERT, *Madame Bovary:*
Moeurs de province

A Host of Humiliation Fantasies

Throughout the course of interviewing, I talked to many men and women who told me they fantasized about being humiliated or about humiliating others. Some would enjoy alternating from one of these positions to the other. In clinical practice, the humiliation fantasy ranks as one of the most popular subtypes of sexual fantasy. Humiliation fantasies generally involve some sort of bodily degradation, either the enforced exposure of one's own body or of someone else's. Common humiliation themes might include:

- Forcing another person to strip
- Being forcibly stripped
- Forcing another person to masturbate
- Being forced to masturbate
- Forcing another person to perform sex acts
- Being forced into performing sex acts

- Urinating, defecating, or spitting on another person
- Being urinated, defecated, or spat upon
- Shaving the body or body parts of another person
- Having one's body or body parts shaved
- Inspecting the body or bodily orifices of another person
- Having one's body or bodily orifices closely inspected

Humiliation fantasies stem from a great many different biographical sources and serve different psychological functions. The dynamics of humiliation will be explored more fully in due course.

Some research participants shared their fantasies in a calm and proud manner, while others did so reluctantly, full of deep shame and embarrassment. Here I offer first some brief fantasies from the large computer-administered survey, and then some much more detailed fantasies involving humiliation drawn from both the computer survey and the psychodiagnostic interviews. As you read through this assortment, bear two key questions in mind:

1. What sort of childhood events might have contributed to the development of these sexual fantasies?
2. How and why do these fantasies produce orgastic *pleasure*?

WILLIAM

Turning up to an address, where I am grabbed from behind. I am placed into a blindfold and then moved into a room. I am then handcuffed and restrained before someone else comes in and strips me off. He proceeds to lick my genitals and then takes me to the edge of ejaculation, before stopping. Then he starts to have sex with me, penetrating me, and then stopping. It carries on like this before someone else starts to urinate across my body. As that is done, the first person starts to perform oral sex on me, taking me to ejaculation. I am then released and moved out from the address, not having seen anyone.

VLADIMIR

Forcing a young woman to strip.

CARINA

Being drugged so I don't know what's going on, and then being brought to orgasm, then penetrated by two men.

UPTON

Being abused and dominated by a team of sixteen-year-old football players, after their game, sweaty and muddy and in kit, being humiliated and made to do stuff for them.

KARLEEN

Being kidnapped by a terrorist gang, and stripped, and having my bodily cavities investigated. Then fucked and fucked by one guy after another. It's so bad, and yet so good.

MARITZA

I am in a room with women and men. They are not people I know in real life, but in the fantasy they are known to me. I am tied by wrists and ankles between two pillars, by chains and leather strapping. I am wearing stockings and shoes. The chains can be used to make me stand or sit, controlling how I am positioned. A mixture of men and women, all dressed in a mixture of leather and rubber, take turns in controlling me. I am whipped, paddled, verbally abused, have nipple clamps added and pulled, eaten out by both men and women. No more than two at a time but the others watch. Sex is both anal and vaginal. The women use dildos and strap-ons.

LILA

Being forced to masturbate in front of the nuns at my school when I was a girl. In my fantasy, I am a grown-up, and yet the nuns still make me feel very small. They were real sadists, but this fantasy arouses me for some peculiar reason.

SKIP

Being medically examined by a lady doctor wearing suede and leather clothing. The procedures involve an enema, internal rectal examination, testicle manipulation, and catheterization. Finally the administration of anesthetic gas by mask until consciousness is lost. Upon coming round being masturbated to ejaculation.

GIOVANNI

Walking into a room with two beautiful women who don't notice I'm there, watch them play with each other, then one notices me and beckons me over. They both begin to play with me. As I become more aroused, one of them lies me down and ties my hands, so I'm powerless. They then take it in turns to use me without letting me ejaculate for a long time, and eventually getting me to ejaculate on them.

DUNSTAN

From being at school, being taken to the bushes by sixth formers and forced to strip naked in front of them, then perform acts on them like sucking them or rimming them and having sticks and their cocks up my ass.

MYLOS

Being dominated by a mistress, preferably my wife.

JOCK

Having anal sex (fucking) with a man aged 16–21 whilst he is tied up, and spanking/whipping the same man.

ENID

I'm working in a men's prison in the office, when the inmates take over the prison. They force the governor to perform oral sex on some of the inmates and bugger him and generally abuse him. They also turn their attention on me, forcing me on my back on the desk. The men rip at my clothes enough to reveal my breasts and crotch. To start with, the ringleader makes derogatory remarks about me as he sucks my breasts and slips a finger into me. All the other men are watching and touching themselves as they are getting more and more turned on. Other men restrain me so that the ringleader can do what he wants. He forces his cock into my mouth and makes me suck him off. All the time I am getting more and more wet. His excitement grows and he walks round to the other side of the desk. He plunges his cock deep into my pussy and starts to pound away, groaning as he does. The governor is forced to watch. When he's shot his load into me, they make the governor suck out all the cum. Then the next inmate gets to take his turn. . . . That's usually enough to do the trick.

CHEYENNE

Wetting myself and then being humiliated for it by being made to wear and use nappies, plastic pants, and being dressed as a very young (18-month to 2-year-old) girl.

MORRIS

A hot footballer, taking a dump on my chest, rubbing it in, and then making me suck his fingers clean.

MONIQUE

Being caught breaking the law and given the choice of appearing in court or being spanked or caned by an authority figure.

DASHIA

Arriving at a man's house, being forced to strip down to my underwear, having a collar put round my neck, and led into another room, giving the guy a blow job, being handcuffed, then spanked either by hand or with a cane, made to stand in the corner of the room until I wet myself, having the wet underwear stuffed into my mouth, blindfolded and tied up and placed in a cage or cupboard for a few hours, urinated on, taken out of the cage, and used for rough oral and anal sex, then allowed to wank off in front of the man, then tied up and returned to the cage.

FELICITY

Tying up another person and humiliating them naked.

CHLOE

I like being urinated upon and urinating on my partner if allowed. Masturbation is also a useful diversion.

CHANDRA

There is a plane crash in the desert. I am thrown from the plane unconscious. I wake up in a luxurious room in a desert palace. I am told I am being cared for but I am actually being held as a sexual prisoner by the Prince.

TORI

Being caught out with no underwear on, or having to work somewhere with no underwear on, with people getting glimpses.

SPIRO

Being dressed as a girl and being spanked and used by a group of people.

ANN-ELIZABETH

Lying on a bed dressed all in red when a man walks in with a sailor outfit on, telling me that I am a naughty, dirty girl, and that I need to be punished.

REGINA

Dominant sex, almost being a slave to a much older and unattractive man. This would involve him letting his friends use me as well. Filming me, humiliating me. Not physically, but verbally abusing me at times.

Maxi-Humiliations

Most of the fantasists who replied to the survey provided me with rather concise, telegraphic descriptions of their humiliation-oriented intra-marital affairs, but others took the trouble to respond at much greater length. The fantasies that follow reveal a great deal about the hidden contours of the mind of the humiliated or humiliating person and about the attendant rage that invariably follows an episode of humiliation. The vast majority of the respondents reporting humiliation fantasies enjoy the thought of humiliating others or vacillate between thoughts of being humiliated themselves and perpetrating humiliation upon someone else. Strikingly, quite a sizable proportion of these detailed humiliation fantasies involve interactions among homosexual men. It would be worth wondering at this juncture why themes of humiliation feature so prominently among the subgroup of gay male respondents, but not among lesbians. No doubt, many homosexual men will have internalized a great deal of homophobia during their lives,

thus contributing to the wish to eroticize their shame, rather than suc-
cumb to it more completely, and this may serve as a partial explanation
of the profusion of extended homosexual humiliation fantasies.

HOWELL

I like to pretend that I'm a customs officer at Heathrow, and that
my job is to make sure that no illegal immigrants enter the country, especially in view of the terrorist activity of late. One day, a
whole group of Hispanics come off a flight, and they have rather
dodgy documents, so one of my men calls me over to check out
these six young Latin-looking guys to see what the story is. I tell
these men to follow me and my colleague into a small interviewing room. They look frightened but they have to do as they are
told because they have no choice. With a fierce look in my eye,
letting them know I mean business, I make them strip. The men
look shocked, and one of them says, "This is England, you can't
make us strip." I say, "Wanna bet, you greasy Spic?" and I punch
him in the stomach. My mate and I start to kick him about, and
then I shout to the others, "Strip. Now." Naturally everyone
obeys, and before long, we are standing in front of a group of
young Spanish guys, all pretty rugged and handsome, and all totally naked, at my mercy. I start to get a whopper of a boner in
my trousers. I go up to each guy in turn, and I start inspecting his
body, my eyes penetrating him like lasers, and you can see the
men sweating, because this is really uncomfortable, and that excites me even more. I call them filthy pigs, and tell them that they
are bringing filth into the country, and that they have to be disinfected. I start with one man, and we make him bend over so that
his hairy arse is on display. My junior colleagues put a special
clamp device on his Spanish man's arse which holds the cheeks
open, and then I spray some disinfectant into his cunt-hole. He
screams from the stinging, but it is good for him. I then repeat
this process, cleaning out the bums of all the other five men.
Then I make them peel back their skins to check for dirt on their
cocks, and I make them pair off, and lick each other's cocks
clean. They find this disgusting, as they are clearly all heterosexual, but they must do as they are told, or else they know they'll
get a good hiding. As an extra, added punishment, I have them
sit on buckets, and take a crap in the buckets, one after the other

so that everyone can see them taking a shit. I then force them to piss while crouching over the shit-filled bucket, but I have one condition: they must not aim their penis into the bucket. They have to let their dick hang loose, and if it happens to fall over the edge of the bucket, then too bad, they will have to piss on the floor. When this happens, I then make them lick up the urine. Some of the Spics start to retch, but I show no mercy. Finally, as part of the disinfection process, I hand them all razors and shaving foam, and I tell them that, one by one, they have to stand in the center of the room and shave their pubic hair off, making themselves really smooth. This really does it for me and my mate, and we both cream off in our pants watching this happen. I really wish that some hunky customs officer would stop me next time I go through Heathrow—I would love to be strip-searched, with someone invading each body cavity.

IMMANUEL

I run a really large company, and I'm worth a fair bit of money. My employees find me a bit intimidating, and I like exploiting that image, because I know it makes them work harder for me. I have a couple of young ladies who work for me as temps, secretaries, personal assistants, that sort of thing, and most of them are pretty good-looking. One, in particular, Cherisse, has a great set of boobs and a nice-looking face. She is also pretty flirty. In my horniest sexual fantasy, I imagine that one day I call her into the office, and I tell her that I am going to fire her for no reason at all. She looks shocked and begins to sob: "No, you can't do this to me. My boyfriend is on disability, and we have a young son, and I'm the sole bread-winner, yadda yadda yadda yadda." I tell her I don't give a fuck, but if she does me a special favor, I may be inclined to change my mind. "What do I have to do?" she asks, with tears streaming down her face. I say that it would help if she could start by taking off her skirt, and her stockings, and her shoes. She looks shocked and humiliated, but she obeys because she knows she needs the job. Wow, there she is in a tight top with only her panties on. I walk around her again and again, patting her bum cheeks through the silk panties, and I am really enjoying the touch of her soft creamy skin. "I'm just gonna pull your pants down, and if you try to move, you're fired," I say. She keeps crying, but she stands there, motionless, and down come the panties, revealing a nice trimmed bush, and lovely pink pussy lips. I gently run my index finger over her clitoris and labia, and within a few seconds, her whole cunt starts to get a little wet, and pretty soon, the bitch is dripping wet. I stick my finger in firmly, and start to move it around, getting her all squishy. She has trouble standing up straight because the fingering of her genitals has made the bitch start to squirm. I like this very much, and I start to pinch her tits through her top, but then I tell her firmly, "Get naked, now, or suffer the consequences." Soon, she is bare, completely bare, the way I like it, while I am fully clothed. I start to suck on her nips, and I tell her to finger herself. She won't do it, but I shout at her, and soon she does as she is told. "You're a good little secretary, Cherisse, and if you make yourself come while I'm sucking on your nips, then maybe . . . just maybe . . . I won't fire you." Cherisse obeys, and her breathing intensifies as first she shoves one, then two fingers into her pussy area. Before you know it, Bob's your uncle, and the bitch is writhing and moaning, and then shooting her lady juice onto her finger while I suck at the breasts. I'd love to do this to some of my workers, but some jerkoff has now made this kind of thing illegal.

MURDO

I'm a 46-year-old welder from Aberdeen, and I work for a big construction company with lots of other guys from the building trade—welders, carpenters, electricians, and so on. We recently took on a new apprentice welder called Scott—sixteen years old— who is under my supervision. What a hot-looking lad he is— blond hair which flops down over his forehead, long eyelashes and a girlie face with soft skin, just barely enough stubble to be shaving maybe every other day. He has a great bod, with a broad chest and wide shoulders that taper into a great tight waist and good strong chunky hips and thighs and nice solid legs. I nearly cream myself whenever I look at him. None of the other men knows that I am a raging woofter so I have to keep my lust for Scott to myself. Scott himself is definitely not gay—pity, cause he'd make a great homosexual, but he's not, so that's that. He doesn't have a girlfriend, but he talks about girls as if he means it. Still, I can dream, and when I go home at night, I wank off to Scott several times. In my fantasies, I imagine that I call him into my office and tell him that as part of his initiation as a welder, he has to let me inspect his body and for this he will need to get totally naked. Scott looks a bit surprised, but like most confident straight kids his age he thinks, "Well, what the hell, if that's what I've got to do, then let's get on with it." He immediately wastes no time and strips off his T-shirt in one swift motion, exposing that amazing chest with tufts of wavy, sweaty blond hair under his arms that get me instantly aroused. Then he shucks off his jeans, and stands in front of me in just his white linen boxers. I think I can see an erection straining in the boxers, and I tell him, "Whip 'em off, sonny boy." He winks at me, knowing that I'm enjoying humiliating him like this, and he slowly pulls the boxers down to the middle of his thighs, letting me have a really good look at his uncut cock, which must be seven or seven and a half inches long (I pride myself on being able to tell the size of a man's dick just by looking). I tell him that as part of his becoming a professional welder, he has to show me just how well he handles his blow-torch, and I tell him to pump his cock up and down a few times, and then to slap it against his belly. This he does with gay abandon, and then I can't restrain myself any longer, and I leap upon him, and toss him off, catching his geyser of cum in my throat. I tell him to suck on my dick, and he hesitates, but I pull his head into my stiffening crotch and I rape Scott's throat. Oh if only Scott knew what he was missing, I could show him so much pleasure. It hurts so bad that this fantasy will never, never come true. But still, it's a great fantasy, and I live in hope. Wanking over the straight lads is so much more exciting because the anticipation is always highly exciting. If a gay boy offered himself to me it would feel too easy, too much of a throwaway. So bring on Scott and all of his straight mates for some good sucking, wanking, and maybe even a fuck session or two.

BARNABY

I am a retired copper. I worked for many years for the police, out in the Midlands. When I was in my twenties, I had a pretty good body, and a lot of the guys that I had to arrest for one thing or another would offer me sexual favors if I let them go. Of course, I never did, 'cause that would be unprofessional, but the temptation was huge. But once, I did have to arrest this 21-year-old bloke—a really cocky lad with a cheeky grin. I thought he was very attractive. My colleague and I locked him up in a holding cell, and then my colleague went off duty. This kid was a real troublemaker, and he kept shouting at the top of his lungs, threatening to kill himself. I went into the cell and told him that he would have to give me all of his clothes, except for his pants. He refused, and I said that it was for his own safety, in case he tried to hang himself with his belt or shoelaces, or even the legs of his jeans. He eventually obeyed orders and handed over all his clothes, and he stood there, almost naked, except for a skimpy pair of boxers. He had a completely smooth body except for little patches of dark hair under his arms, which really turned me on, I confess. In my fantasy, I return to his cell some twenty minutes later, and I tell him that we are worried that he will strangle himself with his underwear, so he'd better hand over his boxers. He refuses to comply with my orders, so I start shouting at him to obey. He looks scared, poor lad, but he does as he is told, and he yanks the boxers off, revealing the most gorgeous-looking cock you've ever seen—thick and veiny, with lots of curls. I tell him to bend over and touch his toes, and if he doesn't, he won't get out of this cell alive. By now my penis is really big and I unzip myself, and shove my meat up his unlubricated arse. He screams for mercy, but as he is a criminal, I fuck him savagely. Eventually I release a flood of jism up his back passage—it's a great feeling to spunk inside this lad. And as I am squirting a load, I'm also using my fist to wank him off, and we both spunk together. It's reasons like this that I loved being a copper.

ORVILLE

When I was in my twenties, I was in the armed forces—I'd better not say which branch—but I was. I'm now sixty-eight. Me and my mates used to have a little game which we would play to welcome the new recruits. I think about this a lot, especially when I masturbate, and sometimes I like to re-enact it with my partner (male—also in his sixties). Whenever a new lad would join the forces, me and these two mates, let's call them Rog and Dennis, we would take the lad out and get him to have a few pints, be all matey with him, you know, make him think that we were going to look after him, take him under wing, that sort of thing. After a few beers, we'd go back to our cabin (we were often out in the field when we did this) and then we'd pounce on him when he would least expect it, push him down on the ground, and then pin his arms and legs—usually by one of us sitting on his chest, which winded him, and then one of us on the arms and one on the legs. In this helpless, passive position, we'd unbuckle his belt, and then shuck his combats down to his ankles. By this point, the new recruit would be screaming his head off, but we'd tell him to shut the fuck up and this would be his test of manhood. We'd take turns then, Rog, Dennis, and me, rubbing his penis through his shorts until he got hard. We told him that if he got hard, this would prove he was a fag and he'd get kicked out of the forces (remember this was forty years ago and you would get discharged). The lad would wrestle and wrestle and say that he was no fag, but we kept rubbing his dick, insulting him, calling him names, really making him squirm. We'd then strip off his shorts, and cover his balls in boot black, which is bloody murder to get off one's ball sack afterwards. All the other men would then see him the next day in the showers and would know that he'd been "done." We'd then grip his dick and do what we call "forced-wanking," jerking his penis up and down, running our hands over his foreskin. We told him that if he shot his load, this would prove he was a fag. The poor kid would squirm and squirm, and try not to get hard, but who wouldn't in this kind of situation? After he shot, usually over the hands of whoever had the job of doing the final wank, the person doing the wanking would then rub the cream all over the lad's face. We'd then leave him there, covered in cock juice and often crying his eyes out. We'd then take him out for another beer and tell the kid he was a real man and well done to him for making it through and that he'd do very well in the forces. Of course he'd get teased the next morning in the showers, but in a good sort of way. Rog, Dennis, and I did this with about twenty lads in all over the years. We never met one who didn't get a stiffy and shoot his wad. This only proves what I have always suspected, that all men have gay tendencies.

EDGAR

I'm a prisoner in a really rough prison institution, and I'm straight. My long-suffering girlfriend comes for a visit, and we chat through the Perspex partition, and we have a tearful good-bye. It will be four weeks before she can come and see me again. As soon as she goes, the chief warden assembles all of the other prisoners and the screws in the main hall, and he says, "Edgar, we have reason to believe that your girlfriend gave you some drugs on your recent conjugal visit, and we will have to search you. The screws have already turned your cell upside down, but they've not found anything yet, so prepare yourself for a full body cavity search." I get really scared about this, and I say, "Does it have to be here in the main hall, with all the other lads watching? I'd be too embarrassed." The warden replies, "Definitely. Here in the hall, with everyone watching. I will not have any secrets in my prison. All right, get your shirt off." Embarrassed and blushing, I remove my T-shirt, revealing my hairy, chiseled chest. "Right, Edgar," cries the warden, "lift your arms above your head, and show us your armpits—sometimes guys like to hide drugs in their hairy armpits." I do as I am told, but I feel totally and utterly humiliated, and all the other screws are watching me, along with all my cellmates and the other lads on my wing of the prison, about thirty guys in all. Two of the hunkier screws start to walk around me, examining under my arms. The warden tells them to pull on the hairs under my armpits, and to run their fingers through it, checking for drugs. They find nothing, but all of this close body contact, combined with the fact that I just saw my girlfriend, has made my dick get a bit stiff. The warden then tells me to take off my shoes and socks, which I do, and I hand them to the screws. They check inside the socks and the shoes, removing the heels, and even sniffing the insides, like sniffer-dogs, checking for drugs. Again they find nothing. The warden is convinced that I must be hiding drugs somewhere, so he forces his screws to continue with the strip-search. "Trousers off, now, you fucking piece of prison shit," he barks, and I slowly and blushingly unzip my trousers, and shuck them down to the floor, and step out of them, so that I am left in just my briefs. The screws examine the trousers, and they run their hands up and down my hairy legs, just to make sure. I know what's coming next, and then the warden walks up to my face, "All right, punk boy, get 'em down. Now!" I have no option but to remove my briefs, even though all the other lads are smirking and laughing, and I am turning pink. I don't want them to see my cock, but it seems I've no choice so I do as I'm told, and down come the briefs, exposing my cock, my thick, tangly bush, and my hairy low-hangers. The warden calls for surgical gloves. He is going to continue the rest of the strip-search himself. As he snaps the gloves on his hands, my dick gets a bit stiffer. He comes over to me, and grips my cock in his plastic-covered hand, and gives it a good tug. He then inspects my pubes. "There's too much bush there for me to get a good look, so we'll have to shave this prisoner." Before I have time to react, two of the screws pin me down, and the warden winks at two of the hunkier lads who share a cell with me. One of them squirts Gillette shaving foam on my bush, and holds my cock up, while the other one takes a disposable razor, and removes my glory. I want the floor to open up and swallow me, I am so humiliated, but my dick doesn't care. It's as hard as ever, and I'm starting to leak a bit of cum-juice from the tip of my uncircumcised meat. They stand me up again, and parade me in front of the other guys. The warden shouts at them that anyone caught smuggling drugs, or even suspected of smuggling drugs, will be subjected to the same punishment: a cock shave. The warden then says, "Well, now that his cock is cleaner, I can see that there were no drugs hidden in his hairy bush, but what about under his foreskin?" He shouts at me to pull my foreskin back, but I refuse. He then slaps me in the face, and once again, two of the screws pull my hands behind my back, restraining me, while the warden, still wearing the plastic surgical gloves, pulls my foreskin back, revealing a nice, juicy, purple cockhead. The whole place goes into an uproar with all the guys hooting and hollering, and calling out, "Faggot, fairy, pussy!" The warden then slips behind me, and with no warning, sticks two fingers up my bum hole and jiggles them around, checking for drugs in my arse. He finds nothing of course, but the feeling of being finger-fucked in this way makes my dick go even harder. They force my mouth open to make sure I have no drugs in my cheeks, and then the warden even sticks a finger up each of my nostrils, looking for drugs. I want to die by this point. I say, "You've invaded every hole in my body, but you haven't found anything, so please let me go." The warden gives me an evil grin, "Sorry, man, not until you've jerked off for us. We can't have you go around the prison dripping your precum onto the floor, can we now?" I scream a defiant "no," but it is useless. The warden has all of the thirty prisoners queue up, and he tells each man to grip my dick and give it five tugs. One by one, each of my fellow inmates wanks me up and down five times. All in all, I receive 150 tugs on my todger. When they have finished, I am so close to coming that I am seeing stars. The warden comes up one more time, and he yanks my dick so tightly that I just explode, all over his surgical glove. It's the best cum session I ever had in my life.

PRAKASH

My fantasy involves dressing up. I have a really stunning, sexy girlfriend, and she gets off on watching me strip out of my man's clothes and getting dressed up in hers. When we have sex, she lies on the sofa, a bit like a queen in a Persian court, barking out instructions, while I, her humble servant, must do everything that she says. First she has me remove my shirt, and when I have done this she makes comments about my manly chest. Then I have to take off my shoes and socks, and then my trousers. I stand before her in just my Calvins, and I start to get erect. She tells me that I do not have permission to be hard in her presence, and that I must stand there until the erection goes down because she "has plans for me later on." She leaves the room, and I wait there, semi-nude, feeling just plain stupid, trying to think about anything that will make my dick go soft so that I can obey my mistress's command. When she returns half an hour later, my dick is limp, but the very sight of her, now dressed in something diaphanous, makes my cock stiffen again, and she gets angry, so we repeat the process. When she returns a second time, my dick is still stiff. "Oh for fuck's sake, would you just relieve yourself already so that your cock will go soft, otherwise it'll never fit into my skimpy little panties," she hollers. She calls her girlfriends in to watch, and they all sit on the sofa as I am forced to lower my underpants, revealing a big, thick, brown, bushy penis with a long foreskin. "Now," she commands, and I take my penis in hand and start rubbing my fingers over the foreskin, pulling it back. I feel completely humiliated, especially once the other girls start to giggle, pointing at me masturbating in their presence. Eventually, I get into the whole thing, and my cock is bursting to the point of explosion, and before I know it, I shoot a great big geyser of sperm onto the floor. "Down on your knees, slave, and lick it up," shouts my mistress. This time I am really humiliated, but I obey, and though I have never had semen in my mouth before, I do as I am told, and lick up the messy puddle of spunk that has come out of my long, brown penis. Then my girl-friend/mistress tells me, "Now that we have de-spunked you, your penis is shriveled, so now, you can get into my used panties." She hands me a pair of tiny, frilly, purple silky knickers, and I get dressed in them. I feel completely ridiculous because my physique is not built for these tiny panties, but I put them on with all her girlfriends staring and laughing, and my cock—now soft—gets covered by the sexy material of the panties. I have so much pubic hair, since I do not trim like women do, that it juts out from the sides of the panties and from the waistband. I just look stupid. But we continue, and then the other women help me to wear first a bra, then a black silk blouse, then tights, and fi-nally a really tight pencil-skirt. They give me heels, a blonde wig, and then apply some makeup as well, turning me into a some-what believable girl. I feel feminized, embarrassed, but my cock is becoming stiffer and stiffer. "A chick with a dick," they all shout, and I cream in my girlfriend's tight little panties.

TOMASSO

Whenever I jerk off (which is two or three times a day, 365 days a year) I have the same fantasy, but it's a good one, and it always does the trick, leading me to a powerful, powerful high-octane climax. This is what I wank about: I'm a 22-year-old university student (male), and me and my mates are known on the campus as party boys; in other words, we like a good time and we go out drinking whenever we can. Often we don't get back from the pub till really late, and sometimes we will buy beers and go cruising along the motorway. We are often not back in halls of residence until 3:00 A.M. or 4:00 A.M. This happens certainly every Friday and Saturday night, but increasingly during the week as well. My mates Billy and Jake are swell guys—all straight—and we would do anything for each other. We are like brothers. Well, here is the fantasy in more detail. You see, one night, the boys and I go out drinking, and we're not back until 5:00 A.M., and although in reality there really is no one to tell us off, in my fantasy there is a halls monitor, who is a beautiful blonde woman with lovely, pert breasts. Her job is to wait in the entrance hall of the dorms, and to note the names of any university students who come back after midnight. When Billy, Jake, and I walk in—all drunk—at five in the morning, this blonde, whom I call Phyllis, gives us a stern look, and she tells us that we will be punished, and that owing to the lateness of the hour, our punishment will be severe, in front of the entire school. We are all so drunk, we don't take Phyllis seriously; instead, we just laugh it off, and crash out in our respective dormitory rooms, and awaken with throbbing hangovers. Suddenly, there is a knock at my door, and a similar knock at Jake's and Billy's doors, which I can hear as their rooms are just a wee way down the corridor. I scream out, "Get the fuck away, I'm sleeping," but to no avail; and suddenly the door to my room opens, and in walks Phyllis in a very tight-fitting sweater with three very large, very muscular guys whom she tells me are the campus police. Before I know what is happening, the guys bundle me up in my blanket and carry me out of the dorm, just like a sack of potatoes, into a waiting vehicle, where I am joined by Billy and Jake. I am just in my boxers, and so is Billy, but Jake is starkers as he sleeps in the nude, and the cruel campus police took no mercy on him, not even letting him put on a pair of pants. Something tells us that the punishment is going to be more cruel than we had thought. We are driven to a holding cell, somewhere to the north of campus, and pushed out of the van and into the cell, which is bare, with just a big bucket, and chains on the walls. The guards chain us to the walls—we try to resist, but we are all hung over, and besides, we are much smaller guys than these campus police guards—so it is really useless to try to fight. After we are kept waiting, and waiting, for a couple of hours, Phyllis comes in, in her tight sweater, accompanied by three more college girls, none of whom we have seen before. We are dying of thirst by this time, still hung over, and I ask for water. "Why of course," says Phyllis, and she gets a big liter bottle of mineral water, and holds it up to my lips. Remember, my hands are tied with the chains so I can't even lift the plastic bottle. I only want a few sips, but Phyllis holds my head by the hair, and she forces me to drink the entire liter bottle in one big gulp. I nearly choke in the process but I do it. Two of the other girls are performing this same force-feeding of mineral water on my mates. The girls then produce more bottles of water, and even though we think our drinking ordeal is over, they force us to down another liter, and soon our bladders are swelling and our stomachs have got real bloated. Then the guards arrive with some stools, for Phyllis and the girls, and they just sit there, facing us, looking smug, staring at us without saying anything. Billy and Jake and I are confused: why are they here, what are they doing? What's gonna happen to us? Thirty minutes goes by and no one says a word, then forty-five minutes, and finally sixty minutes. Me and the lads are starting to squirm, because we not only feel like shit from all the booze of the night before, but we are all getting desperate for a slash. Finally, Billy breaks the ice, and says he has to use the toilet. The girls remain silent. Billy starts to beg, but all to no avail. Clearly, this is the punishment, these girls are just going to watch us piss ourselves. There is a bucket, but it's too far away, and the girls are certainly not going to bring it to us. I am starting to feel real pain—nothing worse than needing a wee and not being able to. I feel most sorry for Jake, who is totally nude, whereas at least Billy and I are wearing shorts. The girls just stare, and their silence is starting to freak us out. Eventually, Jake breaks down—he can't hold his piss in any longer—and he starts to leak. After a few drops of piss fall to the floor from his dangling dick, he says, "Oh, fuck it," and out it comes, and he pisses all over his legs, his feet, and of course the floor. With that as our signal, both Billy and I can hold it in no longer, and we release our bladders too, absolutely soaking our underwear in hot streams of piss, so much so that you can clearly see the outlines of our dicks through the wet pants. We are all feeling humiliated, and we think this will be the end of our punishment, but no such luck. The girls then talk for the first time in hours, and Phyllis, the ringleader, tells us that because we have been naughty and have stayed out past our curfew, our punishment will become more severe by the day. Tomorrow, she tells us, we will all have our arseholes shaved; the next day, we will be forced to masturbate to orgasm in front of all the other female students at the university; and then on the final day, we will have metal probes inserted into our urethras (our piss slits) with all of the faculty watching. We break down in tears at the thought of these disgustingly humiliating punishments, but there's nothing we can do. In my mind, I go through each of these painful rituals—the arsehole shaving, the public masturbation, and the probing of the piss slit, which is excruciatingly painful—but it is really good to have Jake and Billy sharing the pain with me—at least this way we can support each other. This fantasy gets me so horny, and because the story is so long and so detailed, I can always find a point at which I spunk all over the room. I usually don't make it to the piss-slit torture. It's often just enough to wet myself and have my arse shaved that brings me to a whopping great knuckle-sandwich of a wank.

MARIANGELA

I am a 24-year-old woman living in the north of England. Sadly I have had lots of medical procedures over the years because of an early spinal injury that has colored my life in many ways. Over the years I've had lots of surgery and lots of medical examinations—some very sensitive, but often very insensitively done, of the "get-your-kit-off" variety. My favorite fantasy during masturbation (I don't have sex with men) concerns a medical examination by a surgeon. I go into his office, and he has a whole group of young male assistants there. In his gruff manner, he introduces me to Dr. A., Dr. B., Dr. C., Dr. D., and Dr. E., his junior colleagues and assistants, who will be helping him with the examination. The surgeon tells me that because of the nature of my medical condition, he will need to do a full body examination, and that I must be totally naked so that my clothes will not interfere with his access. The examination begins, and as I am nervous and fumbling with the buttons on my blouse, the surgeon shouts out, "Oh for god's sake, I haven't got all day, will one of you just get this lady's shirt and bra off already." Dr. B., a young, hunky twenty-something doctor, obliges and he roughly undoes the buttons, almost ripping them in the process. But he does the job, and he gets my skirt and blouse off. Next I start to get off my shoes and stockings, but again, I am taking too long, and the surgeon signals to Dr. C. to rip these off quickly. It feels like a forced stripping. And before long, I am made totally naked, with the young doctors holding my clothing. I am acutely ashamed of my naked body with six men staring at me, but in spite of trying to cover my nakedness with my hands—one across my breasts and the other across my genitals—the surgeon pushes these out of the way and puts his cold stethoscope on my chest. The junior doctors crowd around, seeming to take an interest in the surgeon's examination, but actually I can see that they are staring at my vagina and my nipples, and one of them, Dr. C., begins to get a hard-on which I can see through his trousers. I tell the surgeon that I am feeling extremely humiliated being so naked in front of the doctors. With a knowing leer on his face, he surprises me and asks, "Would it help if you weren't the only naked one here?" "Yes," I say, "that would help me a lot." "All right," says the surgeon, "choose one of my colleagues here, and tell him to strip." I choose Dr. E., who has the nicest body and the cutest face, and I nod in his direction silently. Dr. E. looks completely baffled by this request, but the surgeon—his boss—tells him to stop being such a "pussy" and to get undressed so that the patient will feel more at ease with being naked. The other young doctors start smirking as Dr. E. removes his tie and starts unbuttoning his shirt. The surgeon shouts, "So you gentlemen think this is funny? Well you can all strip off as well." Before I know it, the surgeon has made all five doctors take off all of their clothing. The doctors strip to their briefs and boxers, but the surgeon stares them down until they are completely bare, as am I, and I can see their dangly cocks. I am now feeling so much more relaxed because I am not the only naked one. The surgeon tells the naked doctors that it would help to relax me if I had an orgasm as that would put my mangled body in a less tense condition, so one by one, the naked docs walk up to me, stand between my open legs and finger my clitoris. They queue up, rubbing their cocks against each other's bums, and then they start on me, with their dicks standing up to attention. It is all getting very steamy here. Then the surgeon tells the lads to fuck me individually, and they go at it, in alphabetical order, with Dr. A. slamming his cock up my fanny, thrusting in and out until he squirts. Then Dr. B. goes at me, and then the rest until I have love juice from five doctor dicks dribbling down my thighs and onto the floor. Then, just when I think there is no more sex to be had, the five naked doctors lift the surgeon up, and carry him—torpedo style—shoving his face in my twat, and he starts to lick up all the cream. I explode with a huge multiple orgasm that goes on for what seems like hours and hours—very satisfied with my medical care.

12   Incest: Do We Really Fancy Our Family?

Naturam expellas furca, tamen usque recurret.
[Even though you drive out nature with a pitchfork, yet she will always return.]
— HORACE, *Epistles*

The Devastations of Incest and Other Forms of Sexual Abuse

As a psychotherapist, I spend much of my professional life dealing with the psychological consequences of early childhood sexual abuse. Fortunately, the vast majority of men and women in America and Great Britain today have had the protection of growing up in households where their caretakers have treated their bodies with concern and respect. Sadly, however, many youngsters, including infants as well as toddlers and other small children, have suffered varying forms of early sexual abuse at the hands of mothers, fathers, grandparents, aunts or uncles, siblings, housekeepers, au pairs, family friends, and neighbors, as well as total strangers.

Though exact figures remain unclear, carefully conducted research studies have suggested that at least one-third of all American and British children will have endured inappropriate sexual treatment at the hands of an older person by the time they reach adulthood. Lloyd deMause, director of the Institute for Psychohistory in New York City and a preeminent authority on the subject of domestic abuse, has studied the incidence and prevalence of child sexual abuse for over forty years. In his many publications, most notably in his books *The History of Childhood* and *The Emotional Life of Nations* and in the pages of the *Journal of Psychohistory,* he has documented systematically that throughout the centuries young people have suffered from sexual abuse during infancy and childhood to a much greater degree than we would ever imagine. In his landmark essay "The Universality of Incest," which appeared in the *Journal of Psychohistory* in 1991, deMause presented compelling evidence that the true incidence of child sexual abuse may be much higher, suggesting that at least 60 percent of girls and 45 percent of boys in America experience some form of sexual abuse.

What exactly constitutes child sexual abuse? As one might imagine, abusiveness exists along a spectrum, encompassing everything from an adult groping a child's genitals, buttocks, or nipples, to the insertion of objects (whether a penis, a finger, or a nonbody part) into any of the child's bodily orifices (whether mouth, vagina, or anus). The abuse may be perpetrated by a single person, or in extreme cases may be enacted by a group of people, as in a pedophile ring involved in the production of child pornography.

In view of our increased knowledge about the *extreme* forms of child sexual abuse such as pedophilia, child pornography, and multi-perpetrator cult abuse, some people often overlook the impact of the ostensibly more "mild" forms of abuse. But in my experience, any inappropriate behavior, whether a sexual act, a sexual glance, or even a sexual innuendo, can potentially threaten the child's sense of bodily safety. For example, I vividly recall the case of a twenty-eight-year-old woman who once, at the age of five years, had stumbled into her father's bedroom and caught him with his penis exposed, masturbating to explicit pornography on a videocassette. Although her parents had always treated her body with all due respect, and though she was a physically fit and attractive person, this young lady has, to date, never had a boyfriend or a sexual relationship of any kind, and she remained very frightened by the sight of the adult male penis. One need not be penetrated or even physically touched in order to feel sexually abused.

Psychological and psychiatric researchers have devoted a vast amount of study to the nature of child sexual abuse, and particularly to its consequences. We now know that child sexual abuse (whether "mild" or grotesque) will have adverse consequences for one's general well-being; furthermore, the earlier and more extreme that abuse, the greater the damage will be. As a result of the investigations of the many clinical and empirical researchers in this field, we know that survivors of childhood sexual abuse will be:

- More likely to suffer from anxiety
- More likely to suffer from eating disorders (e.g., anorexia nervosa, bulimia nervosa, bulimarexia)
- More likely to engage in forms of self-harm (e.g., cutting oneself with a razor blade, burning oneself with a cigarette)
- More likely to become sexually promiscuous
- More likely to have fragmented attachment relationships
- More likely to suffer from major psychiatric illness (e.g., clinical depression, borderline personality disorder)
- More likely to fail in education due to lack of concentration
- More likely to suffer from spurious physical pains and other psychosomatic ailments
- More likely to experiment with prostitution, or to become a full-fledged prostitute
- More likely to abuse drugs and other substances
- More likely to abuse alcohol
- More likely to suffer from deep anger and aggression
- More likely to engage in criminality
- More likely to have a sleep disorder
- More likely to abuse one's own children or the children of others

These symptoms represent only a small fraction of the devastating consequences of early childhood sexual abuse.

In our zeal to rout out the child pornographers and other practitioners of pedophilic perversions, we often forget that the vast majority of child sexual abuse takes place within the child's home, and that, indeed, roughly one-third of all sexual offenses against children will be perpetrated by other young people, often older brothers and sisters. Therefore, although we need to continue to devote our energies to the eradication of *extrafamilial* abuse (i.e., sexual abuse occurring outside the family), our greatest danger remains *intrafamilial* abuse (i.e., incest occurring inside the family).

Before we attempt a more thorough understanding of the incest fantasy, let us immerse ourselves in some representative ones. Some of the fantasies reprinted below involve children, but others do not. The common denominator is that they feature family members, whether children or adults. For more on sexual fantasies involving children and teenagers, see Chapter 14.

NORMAN

Undressing slowly, and making love to my sister-in-law.

TADEUSZ

I go to see the mother of my daughter-in-law. I knock at the door, and she opens it. I ask her to turn round, she does, and I put my hands on her breasts. She unbuttons her blouse and I take her bra off and fondle her breasts. She pulls me into the bedroom (it's a single-story house), and then unzips my trousers, pulls them down, and my pants, puts my penis in her mouth, then we proceed to the bed and have intercourse. Just after that, her daughter comes in and says she wants to be shagged, so I strip her off and proceed to the bed and have intercourse with her, then the mum again, and so on. Another is where I see our next-door neighbor bending over in the garden tending her plants. I go down, lift her skirt over her head, pull her pants down and enter.

JADA

I fantasize about my boyfriend having sex with his younger sister (who is three years younger and who is very attractive), and they are afraid of being caught, but very turned on, and they know that they are doing something wrong but they are really enjoying it. I will either see it from my boyfriend's view, or his sister's view, or both, whatever I feel like. It usually starts that they are playing around in the bathroom, and he touches her by mistake on her breasts (she only wears knickers, or a towel), and they joke about it, but continue to touch each other, and it leads to him giving her oral sex and then full intercourse. All the time they have to be very quiet as the rest of the family is downstairs and they might get caught.

REMI

Anal sex with my brother, and maybe one or two of his hot friends.

NESTOR

Sex with my partner and one of her sisters (she has two).

QUINN

Sex with mother-in-law and wife.

ROBBIE

Oral sex with my sister-in-law, i.e., I lick her clitoris and labia while finger-fucking her, and she sucks my penis.

NICK

Fucking my cousin who is a babe. I've always fancied her, and in my wank fantasy, I do. It's great. Thanks for that.

GUIDO

I have the most gorgeous stepsister who has great tits. I've never done anything with her, but I'd like to nail her. She doesn't know how I feel about her, but I toss off a lot just thinking about her nipples, her breasts, her curves, and everything else about her. I'd also like to come on her face. I also have a fantasy of getting caught red-handed, in the act, maybe by her father.

WAYNE

My girlfriend is really turned on by her uncle. He's hankered after her, and she's turned on by this. She stands in the kitchen listening to him closing the door on the last of the guests. Hears the click of the door shutting and the sound of her uncle, a big unattractive fat guy, pausing, turning and coming down the corridor towards the kitchen. She sleeps in the kitchen, her bed is in the corner. He comes in and says, "Well." Smiles at her. All that follows is completely soundless, he never speaks except to wonder at himself, and she acquiesces silently, in delightful submission. He kneels in front of her, undoes her buttons, she's pounding with excitement, he suckles her little breasts and shuffles her across the floor backwards towards the bed, eventually getting up and walking her towards it. She puts up minor resistance, and him pushing her on turns them both on further. He pushes her head down to suck his dick and then with a groan he lets her fall backwards on the bed. Kneeling before her he opens her legs and inserts himself inside her, and she's dripping wet but awfully tight, so he has to ease in very carefully so as not to hurt her too much. But the fact is that he does hurt her a little.

HOPE

My boyfriend and his brother. We talk about lots of things and I end up kissing the brother. My partner sees us but doesn't mind, and the two of them undress me and remove everything below their waists. They both use their hands to stimulate me before they take me, one up the rear, one up the front, and the one be-hind is touching my breasts. After they finish they swap places, stimulating me some more and saying, "I'm f****** gorgeous," while I massage their willies, until they're ready to take me again. After they've finished this time, each one takes turns in going down on me and kissing my body until the pair are turned on again, when one takes me from behind while I go down on the other. They swap places again after they've finished, so they can both experience the sensations. After the fourth time is over we are all exhausted and talk quietly amongst ourselves while I lie there wrapped up between the two of them and we all sleep like that, then we wake up and they are both turned on and want to take me like the first two times again.

BUCKY

Having sex with my daughter.

FREYA

My boyfriend has a twin brother who sneaks into bed with me. I know it's not really my boyfriend but I pretend that I think it is.

CROSBY

I am laid under the sink unit repairing a leak and my sister-in-law unzips me and performs oral sex on me.

YVONN

Group sex involving mother and son.

NORTON

Watching my mother as a younger woman having sex with several older men. In a gang bang.

ZEKE

Having consensual and loving sex with a mother and her young daughter together.

LUPE

I'm really ashamed of my fantasy, because it involves my teenage son Jorge, who is seventeen years old. Jorge is very much the man of the house because I divorced his father when Jorge was a little boy. In the last year, he has really shot up, and he has turned into a beautiful young man—beautiful on both the inside and the outside. He looks just like his dad—tall, lean, dark, and brooding—and though his father was a shit, a real bastard, he was the man who made me come more than any other. He gave me the best sex I ever had. When I am alone at night in my bed, which is every night by the way, I have this really erotic fantasy about Jorge. I imagine that I hear him cry out from his bedroom, which is just next door to mine. Being a good Latina mama, I rush into his room to find Jorge masturbating his penis, pulling on the foreskin and rolling around in the bed with pornography magazines in bed with him. I walk into his room, and he just gives me a filthy look as if to say, "Why don't you join me, Mama?" I tell him he is a wicked boy, and he will be punished for his sinfulness (we are a very religious, Catholic, old-fashioned family). But Jorge tells me that he knows I have been single for too many decades, and that if I don't have sex with him tonight, I will turn into one of those elderly widows with dry vaginas! I am amazed by how frank and how dirty Jorge is being, and this gets my vagina very wet. All the time he continues to pull on his penis, up and down, up and down, and he is dripping lots of juice from his cockhead. He shocks me and says, "Mamasita, if you love your little Jorge, you will suck me off." I tell him he will go to Hell, but he pulls me forward, towards his penis, and he pries my jaw open, and tells me to suck. Before I know what is happening, I am deep-throating my own son, and it tastes delicious. I tug on his furry nuts, and he reaches over and pinches my titties through my nightgown. I keep sucking until he blows his wad down my throat. I want to spit it out, but he tells me that a good mother must swallow. I do as I am told. Meanwhile, my fingers are rubbing my labia like a goat in heat, and soon I have the wettest orgasm. If Jorge knew he would be horrified, but I find his body very sexy, and I have this fantasy about him at least once a day, sometimes twice.

KYRA

My masturbation fantasy is based on real experiences that I have had for the last couple of years. I am now nineteen, but when I was fourteen, my Uncle Hutch who lived not far from my parents used to invite me round for visits. My parents loved Uncle Hutch and still do, so there was nothing to suspect—they just thought he was being friendly—which he was in his way, I suppose. Uncle Hutch used to give me sherry when I went to his house, which I thought was totally fantastic as my parents would never let us touch a drop of alcohol. I guess the buzz from the sherry and being alone with my uncle got me a little bit horny, so although I was a bit freaked out the first time it happened, I eventually got quite used to the idea of unzipping Hutch's fly and, at his request, yanking on his enormous cock. He used to spurt his cum in my face, and then he started to put his hand under my blouse and into my knickers. I had never even had a real boyfriend at that time, so this was technically my first experience of sex, and even though I know it was wrong, it did excite me and made me quite wet. I had my first orgasm ever when Uncle Hutch put his hand into my pussy and started to finger my clitoris and vagina, and I came loads. This all continued in secrecy for some time—several years in fact. One day, when I was about seventeen, I came out of Uncle Hutch's house at about five o'clock in the afternoon, and as I started to turn the corner, I bumped into my cousin Ben, who is the same age as me, clearly headed in the direction of our uncle's house. I asked him what he was doing, and he looked embarrassed, and said he could ask me the very same question. Eventually, after some probing, it all came out that we were both going to Hutch's on a regular basis for these special niece and nephew meetings. Ben and I got to talking, and we confessed that we found the whole thing very erotic in a naughty way, and that neither of our parents knew what the hell was going on. One day, I was due to see Uncle Hutch, and Ben and I decided to surprise him by showing up at the same time. Hutch answered the front door, and he looked a bit shocked to see his niece and his nephew at the same time, but he is a canny guy, and he immediately took in the situation and invited us both in, giving us beers and sherry, as always. Hutch didn't waste much time to tell Ben that it would be really exciting if Ben started to kiss me, which he did, and then Hutch had Ben fondle my tits through my shirt. Eventually, all three of us started stripping, and Hutch encouraged Ben to start rubbing his nineteen-year-old penis up and down the length of my clitoris, which was very wet now. Ben's dick looked like a diving board at a swimming pool, sticking out at a full ninety-degree angle from his thicket of light brown pubic hair. Uncle dared me to suck it, and it didn't take long before Ben squirted a big puddle of semen in my throat. I swallowed it, and then Uncle Hutch stuck his tongue down my throat and scooped it out. This got him so hot that he told us both to bend over the couch, and then one after another, he fucked us both in turn, Ben up the arse, and me in the vagina, but from behind. I always masturbate about this, and I can get off within literally minutes.

SELENA

My father is on the living-room floor with my mum's clothes on—stockings, suspenders, dress—and he is being fucked by two men, spit-roasted on our living-room floor. I can't believe what I am seeing, my father is helpless and is being fucked hard at both ends. I sit on the sofa and pull up my skirt and finger myself while I watch my father being roasted. The men do not look at me, they just pump my dad. First, one cums in his mouth, the other cums in his arse, and I cum on the sofa. The guys say, "Thanks, same time next week," and leave the room. My dad looks at me and says, "Don't tell your mum but I love cock." I say, "I won't but you will have to fuck me." He looks at his little princess and starts to take Mum's clothes off. I say, "No—in Mum's clothes." He smiles weakly and I tell him to lie down. I sit on his hard cock facing away from him. I ride his hard cock as I cum. I shit myself all over his stomach; as I do this he empties his cum into me. He is totally degraded, and I get up and look at him smiling on the carpet. I stand up, walking round to his face, standing over him. I tell him to open his mouth. I piss on him.

LENI

I spend a lot of time thinking about pretty much all the members of my family, certainly my two older brothers, certainly my father, and also my mum from time to time. In my fantasies, I imagine lots of group scenes where the whole family goes at it at the same time. In my favorite fantasy, my two brothers come into my bedroom late at night, both dressed in their pants (they are in their twenties now, and in my fantasies they are in their late teens). They jump into bed with me, one brother on either side, and they cuddle up to me, both rubbing their cocks on my body, up and down, up and down. I pretend to be asleep, but actually I am wide awake, and I am getting really turned on—it's terrifically arousing. My parents hear all the rubbing and the grunting of my brothers from their nearby bedroom, and they come in, shining a torch on the bed, shocked to find the three of us going at it. My mother pretends to be shocked, but my father is already popping an erection, and he climbs on top, rubbing at my breasts. My father goads my brothers to start to get more adventurous with me: "Go on," he says. "Get her knickers down and start to play with her clit." My older brothers do exactly what Dad says, and I get really moist, especially when Claude, my oldest brother, sticks his forefinger into my vagina. My brothers are doing a good job, rubbing, fingering and all of that, but Dad gets impatient, and he pushes my brothers out of the way and says that he will give a demonstration of how to have intercourse properly, so he gets on top of me, and he sticks his penis inside me while the brothers masturbate each other. Even Mum starts to finger herself through her nightgown while Dad starts penetrating me. His sweat is dripping onto my face, and I don't mind at all because it feels fantastic to be filled by his giant cock. Dad thrusts in and out over and over again, and I am amazed at how long he can sustain his erection, much longer than the brothers, much longer than any boyfriend I have ever had. He just keeps going, and I feel like he is riding me like a bull. I have a great orgasm when I come, and so does the rest of the family, including Mum. My dad shoots inside of me, and my brothers squirt over each other, and all over Mum.

LEO

No—but it involves my mother-in-law!

GUSTAVO

I was fucked by my father when I was sixteen. I often wank off just thinking about that.

LAVERNE

We are already in bed, my boyfriend having his hands tied to the bedposts and blindfolded. I am fucking him, hard and deep, when I become aware that we are not alone. His son (twenty-five years old) has called around to the house, and he has heard us upstairs and comes to see what the noise is. He is standing just inside the door, all in black: boots, jeans, tight T-shirt, and his ankle-length black leather coat. As I catch his eye, he smiles at me, and pulling out his dick and starting to stroke his hard-on, gestures to me to continue with his dad. I beckon him closer to us, and start to fuck my boyfriend again. His son is wanking to the side of us, and then, as I carry on with his ass, the son leans forward to start to fuck his dad's mouth. He then climbs up onto the bed, one knee either side of my boyfriend's head, leans forward, and we start to deep kiss, while we each carry on screwing Dad. Then, his second son (ten years old) comes in, smiles, strips, and joining in, starts to wank his dad and play with himself. I usually come at this point.

CONSTANZA

My sister's husband. He's very well hung, and sister isn't good enough for him. Well I think so.

RENEE

It's shameful, but I do get off on the thought of being in bed with my dad. This never happened in real life though, just in case you're wondering.

ROLAND

Is it sick to fancy your mother? Well I do. I mean, she is pretty hot at thirty-seven. I am seventeen, and so that means she had me when she was twenty. Anyway, she's still pretty fit, with nice titties and a good wiggly bum. And what's more, there's something a bit dirty about her. Ever since my dad left when I was five, she's told me again and again that I'm the man of the house, and that she relies on me to protect her. She's had a lot of boyfriends—all of them are idiots—and since Chris, there hasn't really been anyone serious, which allows me to fantasize all the more. I know that my mum masturbates 'cause I've found a few soft porn mags under her mattress. Sometimes when I come back home from clubbing with my mates, I'll get into bed, strip off totally starkers, and then rub some baby oil onto my willy, getting it real good and hard. I just keep rubbing and rubbing trying not to shoot my wad, which is difficult since I am always on a hair-trigger, but if I feel myself getting hard, then I'll slow down, squeeze the head of my cock and wait a little bit before starting up again. Sometimes I will wank like this for hours. Whenever I have this kind of slow wank, I will fantasize about my mother calling me into her bedroom and luring me over to her bed. She purrs, "Roland, you're the man of the house, so show me how the man of the house treats the lady of the house. Mount my cunt, son." Her crude language really shocks me but arouses me all at the same time, and I start tenting in my shorts. I climb on top of Mum, and I rub my dick up and down her fanny, mixing my pre-cum juices with her cunt juices until we are both dripping wet. She moans, "Get it in me, get it in me now, son." Every time she calls me "son" this makes me go even harder, and I stuff my prick-stick into her cunt. It's a bit looser than my girlfriend's twat—well, it would be, after all Mum has had four children—but that gives me room to stick two fingers in alongside my fat cock, and Mum starts going crazy because my dick is stimulating the deep inside walls of her vag, while my fingers are stroking her clit. She rubs her hands on my peter, and then she runs her red fingernails up and down my back, almost drawing blood, as she pulls me deeper and deeper into her vag. I pump her like I am riding a bucking bronco, and she keeps calling out, "That's my man of the house. You're the man of the house." Mum reaches down and sticks a finger into my arse-crack, and then tickles the under-side of my ball sac, and boy, that really does it, and off I go, fill-ing her pussy with lots of white glue. I make a mess of her insides, and then, when I go limp, I fall off her pussy and watch my spunk slip out of her. She pulls me close, sticks a tongue down my gullet and kisses me hard and deep. She stares me in the face and whispers, "You're a good little man. You're the man of the house."

STANLEY

For me, it's got to be my brother's wife. My brother—two years older—is a bit of a wolf when it comes to the ladies. He's always brought home some real stunners, but last year he started bang-ing Nancy, or as my sister and I call her "Nancy of the Knock-ers," because of her two humongous tats. Nancy is totally devoted to Frank, my brother, and I doubt that she would ever cheat on him, but in my fantasy, the whole family goes away for the weekend to celebrate my mum's eightieth birthday, and we are all sharing a big cabin with lots of bedrooms. Frank gets completely hammered at the party, and he falls asleep, as do the other family members. Nancy is up in bed, reading, with Frank next to her snoring really loudly. I see the light on under her bed-room door, and I gently walk into the room and quickly assess the situation, so I ask Nancy if she'd like to join me in the bar for a nightcap. She is excited, as boring Frank is snoring, so she throws on a robe over her see-through nightie, and puts on some sexy slippers with furry trim and high heels, and joins me in the bar area of the cabin. We are sipping some vodka martinis and getting pretty sloshed ourselves, and then bang, all of a sudden Nancy tells me that Frank has not been a very devoted husband. Turns out he's been having an affair with some slag in his office, and he and Nancy haven't done the business in several months. She tells me that she's so sexually frustrated that she's thinking of taking a lover. I see this as my cue—my invitation—and I lean over and start to stroke her curly, wavy hair, and then insert my long tongue into her mouth and start kissing her, almost sucking off her mouth. The passion gets more and more intense, and I get really turned on, as does Nancy. Suddenly, even though we're in the bar, a communal area, buttons start popping and clothes start flying, and soon I'm naked, and climbing all over Nancy and those gorgeous watermelon breasts which Frank has left completely unattended. I know it's kinda kinky for a brother to fuck his own brother's wife, but what the fuck, it's a fantasy, and I'm gonna pop my wad. So I lay Nancy down on the floor, give her cunt a good tongue cleaning, and that gets her good and ready to receive my cock in her mouth. I fuck her face, and then, just as I am about to come, I slam my meat into her cunt and in only three thrusts of my hips, I deposit a big tablespoon of jizz into her fanny and she squeals like a pig. It's the best orgasm I've had in ages, and I collapse on top of her completely satisfied. The vodka martinis and the excellent sex means that we are both completely spent, and I fall asleep on top of Nancy, with my limp dick still inside her vagina. In the morning, the rest of the family creep out of their bedrooms, and they discover me and Nancy of the Knockers asleep, and with our naked bodies intertwined. I have quite a job trying to talk my way out of this one.

RUBY

Definitely my dad. He raped me when I was ten, and when I was eleven, he brought one of his disgusting pervy mates round and they raped me together. In my fantasies, I imagine that I am seeking revenge. I get him all aroused by doing a little dance for him wearing only my bra and panties. When I see him getting hard, I unzip his trousers and pull his thing out. He tells me to suck his cock just like I used to do when I was a little girl. I put his disgusting prick in my mouth, but instead of giving him the blow job of his life, I bite down really hard, drawing blood, and I just keep biting as hard as I can. The bleeding won't stop, and soon the fucker hemorrhages to death. This fantasy gets me really hot.

Displaced Incest: Masturbating about Teachers, Bosses, Nurses, Doctors, and Other Older People

I wish to conclude this chapter with a further selection of fantasies that I call "displaced incest" fantasies. I suspect that many people become aroused by teachers, doctors, bosses, and other authority figures in part because they function *in loco parentis*—in the place of parents—by looking after us, often tending to our bodily needs and physical safety, as good parents would have done. Therefore, I do not regard an adult crush on a teacher as a neutral sexual choice, on the whole, but rather as a vestige of some sublimated incestuous feelings that one may have experienced in relation to early parental caretakers. A representative sample of displaced incest fantasies follows.

BRANDY

My boss, in the bath, getting very soapy with me, washing me, and drying me and then having a fuck.

ANTONIA

Being a maid in a big house and the master of the house comes home and finds me masturbating. So he takes me in his study and makes me drop my knickers. He starts to spank me on the bottom and then he finds out how wet I am and calls me a dirty slut and makes me suck his cock and lick his balls. Then he fucks me hard.

BRUCE

Being involved with a teacher while still at school, going back to when I was a schoolchild.

ROSABELLA

My boss. He tells me that I can get a promotion if I let him pee on me.

NINTOCHKA

I get really turned on by this man in my office who I'll call Julian. He's a barrister, and I work as a personal assistant to one of his colleagues. We have barely anything to do with each other because I don't work for him, and I rarely see him as he is out at court, but when I do see him, I get incredibly randy and want to have sex with him. He is happily married with kids by all accounts and he does not ever seem to notice me. I often dream about him, usually first thing in the morning when I am having my bath. I imagine that I am working late one night in the office, and my boss has gone home. Julian is also working late, and his P.A. has had to go home early to look after her aging mother, and Julian desperately needs some preparation done on a brief which has to be completed at once. He tells me that he knows it is not part of my job description to work on his stuff but he would be ever so grateful if I could help out. I am secretly thrilled but try not to show it, and I tell him it would be a pleasure to be of service, so I grab my pen and pad and I go into his office. The case concerns adultery and it's all about this man screwing another woman, and so Julian has to go into all the saucy details of what the man did. As he proceeds I am trying to take dictation but the account of the sex between Julian's client and the other woman gets me so hot that I drop my pen on the floor. Julian rushes to pick it up—it's fallen between my legs— and he looks up at me, handing me the pen. Before I can say thank you, Julian has grabbed me by the shoulders, and he starts snogging me like no one has ever snogged me—firm, masculine, passionate, and sensual. I can feel his stubble on my cheek, and his tongue pressing between my lips. His tongue starts to dart round inside my mouth and I am getting wetter and wetter. With animal passion, Julian pushes all the papers off of his big secretary-desk and he pulls me on top of him. I run my fingers through his salt-and-pepper hair and I hoist up my skirt to straddle him. I cannot really believe that this is happening but it is and I am in heaven. Julian starts to shove his hand up the skirt and he begins to massage my muff through my panties and my tights. I can feel his wedding band rubbing against my clitoris and this gives a beautiful sensation. Also, the presence of his wedding ring reminds me that we are doing something really dirty and that also becomes a wonderful turn-on. Suddenly the gentlemanly barrister becomes more like a caveman, and his Etonian manner gets cast aside as he starts ripping at my fishnets and pulling on my panties. Eventually, he gets me nude from the waist down and pulls me onto my back with my legs in the air, and he buries his face into my muff, sucking and licking, and generally performing cunnilingus on me better than anybody has ever done. Some of my boyfriends have gone down on me over the years but I have always felt that it has been a great effort for them, but with Julian it feels right, it feels natural, and he does it so well. I can feel his beard stubble against my swelling pink clit, and that makes me go to heaven with what feels like a five-minute orgasm. I nearly pass out from fainting, but Julian won't let me go to sleep. He just keeps licking my pussy until I have to push him away because I just can't bear the pleasurable sensations any longer—it almost hurts from the multiple orgasm—so I grab Julian by his shoulders and push him back up to my mouth. We kiss some more and then I start to work on him, unbuttoning his black tailored trousers, and releasing the most beautiful, clean, long and thin penis I have ever seen. It's a very elegant-looking cock, exactly what you'd expect from a man in his position, and it begins to swell in my hands. I take his dick into my mouth and he whispers, "Oh yeah, suck my rod, suck my rod." It feels great in my mouth—so clean, so tasty, and I just can't get enough. I'm slurping on it, and he is massaging my scalp at the same time. Eventually, after applying lots of rhythmic pressure, Julian announces, "I'm gonna blow, I'm gonna blow—please . . . swallow . . . my . . . come." He shoots a whole spoonful of spunk into my mouth, and of course I swallow every little drop. We both collapse on the desk and wake up next morning, still in each other's arms, ready to begin the next day at work with none of our colleagues being any the wiser.

TINO

A nurse. Definitely a nurse. I'm her patient in a hospital, and she has to give me a sponge bath. When she gets to my cock and balls, I get nervous, but she tells me, "Relax." So I do and she starts washing. It doesn't take long before I've unleashed a big bucketful of cum on her hands. I ask her to lick it off. She does lick it off, then kisses me, passing my jizz back and forth between our mouths. Cool!

NEELY

I am undergoing an intimate medical examination in front of a woman doctor and a group of female medical students. The doctor shows the students how to masturbate me to orgasm, explaining what she is doing all the time. All through this, the lower half of my body is exposed.

JULIO

Role-playing teacher/student, or doctor/patient.

COSETTE

Best fantasy was one I had about a teacher when I was at school. He was a physics teacher. I always fantasized about us having sex in his classroom, me in school uniform.

DOV

A bossy woman like a schoolteacher telling me to strip, and obeying her every order.

DONATELLA

Details vary, but a general theme of mine is submission, always with someone I know. For a while now I generally have fantasized about my boyfriend's dad's friend. He is forty and I am twenty, although it's not his age which turns me on, it's him. We are never alone together and have no real reason to ever be. I fantasize about some random event that gets us alone under plausible circumstances, but he forces me to have sex, not rape as such, but just ignoring my half-hearted protestation. It would be fairly rough and aggressive sex. I also fantasize about sex with my boyfriend where it's more submissive but in a planned way, such as being tied up and blindfolded, with mild violence such as scratching, slapping, and biting.

DOMENICO

Having sex with a schoolmistress.

ALGERNON

Humiliation and sex with elderly granny type—oral, vaginal, and anal—and fisting.

LAURENT

Having sex with nurses while in hospital and letting them masturbate me.

MARY-MARGARET

Domination by a beautiful woman or women. In the picture they are authority figures like a teacher or boss at work. Sometimes I am made to kneel beneath their desk between their legs, and pleasure them. Sometimes they tease me without relief, then make me serve them. Sometimes it is the other way round, and I am in control.

JOHNSON

When I lost my virginity to an older woman, and smelled the WONDERS of a lady's GARDEN for the first time.

FLETCHER

An older lady taking me in and having me make love while she wears a girdle.

SAFFRON

Being fingered by my gynecologist and also his nurse.

DEAN

Girls in uniform, nurses, policewomen, etc.

ISEULT

Sex with a doctor.

JOSEPH

When I go to the doctor's, and the doctor is female, and she has to give me a full medical. As the medical progresses she becomes aroused as I'm on the couch. I then start to feel up her legs and take off her white coat to find her to be naked underneath, and she gives me a blow job and then joins me on the couch for full sex. Then afterwards she gets dressed and fills in the paperwork, and I leave as if nothing out of the ordinary has happened.

13

Can I Be Arrested
for My Fantasies?
Extreme Sexual Violence

Quelques crimes toujours précèdent les
grands crimes.
[Some crimes always precede great crimes.]
— JEAN RACINE, *Phèdre*

As we have already observed in the previous chapters, a great many sexual fantasies contain violent ingredients, whether physical violence toward oneself or another, or psychological violence toward oneself or another. In fact, some distinguished investigators, such as the psychoanalyst Robert Stoller, have speculated that aggression may well be the very fuel of sexual fantasy, the key to arousal. Most forensic mental health practitioners, those who have worked with dangerous men and women in high-security institutions, would agree that patients who perpetrate sexual violence have often experienced gross abuse (whether sexual, physical, psychological, or any combination thereof) during early childhood; and these experiences provide the template for the eroticization of cruelty in later life. Here we have a small selection of fantasies involving sexual violence toward other adults.

DANNY

It is about arousing other people, against their better judgment, to an almost unbearable degree.

FRANCINE

Being held against my will, normally by a group of people who have the "right" to (e.g., travelling in a third-world country and being stopped by the police, taken to a "prison"), and tied up in some way with my clothing ripped, and people looking at me as a sexual object, and then a man raping me (except I enjoy it).

ALBERT

Being abused physically and verbally by a dominant woman, preferably known to me (friend or colleague).

BENITO

Tying my girlfriend up with silken cords, blindfolding her and forcing her to submit to my tongue as I caress her intimately.

DELIA

Being a sex slave in a high-class brothel-type establishment. Lots of sexual torture.

MILTON

You'll think it's sick, but sometimes when I wank, I think about my girlfriend's head being cut off by an executioner. It's then put between my legs, and I jerk off onto her head.

RICHARD

Being tied/strung up and forced to watch as partner is fucked . . . then being forced to clean semen from partner's body.

PALMER

My Mistress has dressed me as a whore, in a micro-miniskirt, white fishnet stockings, large breasts glued on with a satin blouse over the top. Heavy makeup. I am placed over a chair or a horse, my feet adorned with ten-inch ballet heels and my ankles spread as far as a spreader-bar will go. My Mistress proceeds to pull up my skirt and start beating me with her hand before moving to a tawse. Once she is satisfied that I have cried for long enough, she roughly impales me with her strap-on and uses me roughly. At one point, she cries out and someone new enters the room, a naked man who Mistress directs to use my mouth. Mistress, the man, and myself all orgasm at the same time.

AGNES

I'm a governess in, I think, a Victorian household. The wife is an invalid and the husband's very sexy in a quiet sort of way. He likes the way I look after their children, and that I'm strict, but never cruel. He comes to me one evening and says that he has a problem. His wife is too ill to have sex with him and he has been with a prostitute and feels that he needs to be punished. He asks me to punish him by caning him. I comply, going into the role of schoolmistress chastising a naughty schoolboy. He enjoys it so much that he is very hard when I've finished. He thanks me for it but I tell him that I haven't finished yet and take him in my mouth and suck him off.

IVANNA

Being tied up in a prison camp and having guards rape me to get out information.

FLO

I'm a colored slave girl and I'm lined up with other slaves, and rich plantation owners come along and poke and prod me, and feel my breasts, and put their hands up my skirt to feel my pussy. I get picked, and am taken to the plantation on the back of an open wagon where I'm taken to a cabin and prepared for the "massa" by two big black women who try and warn me about what he's going to do to me (presumably it happened to them). I'm all washed and ready, not knowing exactly what's going to happen, and I hear his footsteps on the wooden porch outside. I'm shaking with fear . . . but also anticipation. I know the rest of the women are in the next cabin and know that I'm about to go through. . . .

ANGELIQUE

Being gang-raped by a gang of handsome builders who take it in turns to fuck me.

CASSIUS

Fantasies about the corporal punishment of late-teenage school-girls, particularly caning schoolgirls in uniform!

OSMOND

Shoving my hard throbber into a slut's cunt and squirting juice into her pussy, against her will.

GWYNETH

Having sex with a fat middle-aged man, who I am not attracted to . . . but he finds me very attractive. I'm doing it because I have to, because I could get in serious trouble if I don't.

NOAH

Cock and ball torture. I like having my nipples pierced while a dominatrix is tugging on my testicles and tackle.

BILLIE-JO

Being gang-banged by a group of black men and feeling completely powerless. Scenery varies, but essentially I am always being used and never in control of the situation.

LENNY

Being used and abused by a dominant active lad. Someone who knows what they want! Being tied up and blindfolded, having sex outdoors in pubs and clubs, etc.

CLARA

I want nipple clamps on my tits. A man puts them there, and then leaves them for about four hours. Then he buggers off. By the time he comes back, my tits are aching to be sucked and my pussy is dripping wet. The man tugs roughly on the nipple clamps, and I have the most juicy orgasm of my life.

SAL

Gang-rape at the gay sauna where I command a group of guys to fuck an extremely beautiful guy and come all over him.

TULSA

My sexual fantasy comes in several parts. In the first, I am naked, except for a dog collar, in a cage, and at the mercy of a sophisticated, latex-bound dominatrix who is verbally abusing me and prodding me with a riding crop through the bars. Then she drags me out and makes me crawl at her feet. She then restrains me on a cross and whips me across the buttocks and genitals until I beg for mercy. Then she takes me from the cross and fucks me in the mouth with a strap-on dildo before penetrating me. As a treat for being a good slave, then she lets me suckle her nipples. I am then dressed as a French maid including the frilly or lacy underwear, and makeup, and have to serve at a dinner party where I am sexually abused by her female guests and also made to suck one of the male guests while being penetrated by a dildo and whipped by my mistress.

GUNILLA

I am submissive by nature and tend to have similar storylines, whereby I am made to become a slave, to be impregnated, to be stripped of everything except for a collar that I must earn to please my master. The whole thing involves becoming an object, not a person, and involves training such as being forced to wear internal devices permanently, having to beg to have them out to use a toilet, all at my master's discretion. I also have many facets in it where I am publicly whipped or flogged with onlookers whilst I am shaved (head) and made to thank my master for teaching me a lesson.

ULF

Being raped by a group of women—held down and used by them, aroused to orgasm.

PASCAL

My girlfriend dressed as a nurse, tying me up and dominating me.

HUGO

Taking a female spy into a cell, securing her to the bars, stripping her, using various instruments of pain on her to obtain confession, and then raping her every orifice before casting her over to the troops to have their way with her.

IGOR

Kidnapping a teenager, then phoning her mother, telling her that I have her daughter. Take the mother to the place where her daughter is and can see us. Making the mother have sex and perform sexual acts under threat that if not she will never see her daughter again. Then put the mother in a room and get the daughter in and do to her what her mother and I did, with mother watching from the other room.

ESSIE

Getting fucked good and hard and rough by my husband. In real life he's pretty gentle, but S and M scenes really turn me on, and I masturbate with a vibrator thinking about what it would be like if he could actually bring himself to tug tightly on my titties or shove the vibrator roughly inside my cunt. I have asked him to be rougher, but he says he loves me too much to hurt me in this way. I really want rougher, more vigorous sex, and I want it now.

MAUREEN

I fantasize of having sex with men and women, and I like to touch and grab my nipples when arousing myself. And the harder and rougher I get, the better it is.

NEDDA

Being taken from behind roughly and having my hair pulled at the same time.

PRUDENCE

A toned-down version of *The Story of O.*

EVA

I am lying on a bed and I am being raped by a stranger, usually a repairman, gas man, etc. He is being very rough and thrusting a huge penis into me, and I am trying really hard not to like it but my body is becoming more and more aroused and he is saying things like, "What will you tell the police? That you were raped but you had an orgasm?" And he sneers and laughs at me as I start to come.

ROWENA

Being gang-raped.

VANYA

Having sex with someone I know who is in their early twenties and then taking their mother by force at the same time.

YANNIS

Taking all my enemies, anyone who's ever been cruel to me, and fucking them until they bleed to death.

BIANCA

Being seduced by a terrorist and sodomized, raped, and impregnated by him and then sold on to another such person. Not as myself but as the persona I assume in my fantasies.

GERTRUDE

Gang-raped.

CRAIG

Being whipped and urinated upon.

ELENI

I imagine that I'm in a situation where I'm alternating between dominating and being dominated. I put myself into the head of one, then the other person, within the scene. It's a fairly aggressive fantasy—there's spanking or caning where it hurts the recipient, but both people know it's actually a turn-on for her and me. There's usually an element of being "forced" to do things, being under someone else's power—and that's often a woman, although the sex is mainly hetero. I'll imagine having nipple clamps put on, being spanked, being forced to give head to someone, or sometimes having someone go down on me while they're being spanked.

FINCH

I'm not going into detail. Involves bondage, forced exhibitionism, voyeurism, multiple men, non-consent.

GERALDO

Tom Cruise and Penelope Cruz, tied up.

BRUNO

My fantasy is pretty full-on, in-yer-face, but you did ask for my most "sexually arousing" fantasy, so here goes. I'm a very kind man, would never hurt a fly in my life, never have, but my sexual fantasies are always pretty rough, involving fucking women really hard and just basically treating them like pieces of meat. When I meet a new woman at work or in a bar or wherever, I instantly imagine what her tits look like under her top and then I work down to her pussy and bum, gradually undressing her with my eyes. I've slept with a fair few women over the last thirty years, so I can tell pretty much what a woman's body parts will look like. After I've done this, I imagine what it would be like to fuck her, since, in my mind, she's already fully nude. The women in my fantasies are always strangers—sort of composite figures—and usually have blonde hair, you know, like an old film star, maybe Lana Turner or someone like that. The hairstyle is really important, because I like short, wavy, bouncy hair. Someone like Cher with long stringy hair just leaves me limp. Once I have undressed the woman, I like to slam her body up against a piece of furniture, usually a bar or a table, a bit like that scene in the Lana Turner film *The Postman Always Rings Twice,* and also the remake with Jessica Lange. I push the woman onto the table, and I call her "bitch" and I tell her that I'm gonna fuck the living daylights out of her until she won't be able to stand up any more. I get my dick out and show it to her. My dick is pretty big, about nine inches long, and it's quite fat too, and the bitch gets very scared. I can see fear in her eyes. I move up to her face, and start to pistol-whip her on the cheeks of her face with my cock, and this makes me start to drip pre-cum onto her lips. I tell her to lick the pre-cum and to make it look like she's really enjoying it. The bitch obeys my orders and then, just to show her I mean business, I then slap her with my fists and she screams, getting me hard and harder. I then position the bitch so that the top half of her body drops off the table with her blonde hair and head hanging over the side, but her bum and legs are still on the table. Her stomach muscles aren't strong enough to pull herself up so she just dangles like a marionette. I tell her that if she locks her legs around my waist that way she won't fall off. The bitch does as I tell her. Then, now that we are in position, I shove my dong into her pussy, slamming really hard. My cock really stretches her cunt, and she is screaming. I cream off in her pussy, and I always get her pregnant. Sometimes I pretend that I have venereal disease or something like that and then I tell her that I've just passed it on to her and she starts screaming and crying. I cum buckets.

DERMOT

It's a pretty sick one, but I'm sure you've had worse. I'm in the R.A.F. (Royal Air Force), and my plane is shot down somewhere in the Middle East, and I'm captured by a group of terrorists who lock me up in a cell. They tell me that unless I give them all the R.A.F. secrets—information about planes and flight paths— they will kill me. But first, they torture me in all kinds of really cruel ways. First, they tie me to a rack, and beat my bare feet with a bamboo rod and then with a metal rod. I'm told from my buddies in the R.A.F. that this kind of torture can kill a man right off because apparently you can get a brain hemorrhage. I scream, and I bite my lip until I draw blood, but I survive the torture. But they decide to turn up the temperature since they see that I can obviously take it. They offer me the chance to free myself by giving them military secrets, but there is no way that I would betray my country. Next they pull out my eyelashes one by one, and then when I still won't talk, they get a man they call "The Dentist" who is clearly anything but. But he does have a huge pair of pliers, and he prizes open my mouth, and yanks out some of my molars without anesthetic. I can't help screaming, but still I won't talk. The torture goes on and on for weeks, but still I don't fold. Finally, the chief of the terrorists tells me that in spite of all their efforts to get military secrets, they have failed, and therefore, they have no option but to behead me with a ceremonial sword. As they tie my hands and hold my head by the hair, about to be killed, I ask for a final request. I tell them that I want to have one last wank. They don't know the English word "wank," so I start to rub my dick and show them. They take mercy on me, and allow me one last wank telling me that when I ejaculate that is when the sword will take off my head. I start wanking for England, literally, and as my balls tighten the executioner prepares his sword. I shout out that I'm coming, and as I do, they execute me in one swift motion. Sick, but horny.

LORELLE

Saddam Hussein. That's my fantasy. Everybody thinks he's ugly and evil and disgusting. I know he's a brutal dictator and a tyrant, and all of the world hates him, but I think it would be really great to get fucked by him, really really hard and just treated like a piece of meat. Sometimes when I'm alone in the house, I close the curtains in the bedroom and lie on the bed dressed in only my bra and pants, and I close my eyes really tight and start fingering myself down below, and then I like to pretend that Saddam has broken into my house and he holds me hostage. The United Nations is out hunting for him, and when they find him, he tells them that unless they leave him alone, I will be killed. He yanks me out of bed and holds a knife to me at the window so that all the patrol cars outside can see that he is armed, dangerous, and means business. There is a standoff as the authorities decide on the best course of action, so Hussein and I have lots of time to spend together. He tells me that to pass the time he will treat me like the dog that I am. He makes me cover my face, and then he tears my undergarments off of me, and turns me onto my stomach, pulling my buttocks up into the air like an animal. He then pulls out his dick, only five inches in length, but quite fat and quite rank in smell, and he starts to jerk himself to an erection. I guess he is going to penetrate me from behind, but instead, he surprises me, and he sticks his dick into my bottom, anally raping me and leaving a big deposit of cum up my ass. This hurts like hell and I start to bleed from the ass, but I'm also really horned up by the whole process, and my vagina is tingling with pleasure. I ask him to please fuck me up the twat but he refuses. He says he has already given me his precious seed. I beg for more cock from the great dictator, but he won't perform any more. He drags me back to the window, naked, with blood trickling down my thighs, and he holds the knife to me once more so that all the military personnel outside can see. Suddenly, there is a shattering of glass, and someone has thrown nerve gas into the window, and both Saddam Hussein and I are knocked out. When I awaken, I am naked, in an army hospital, with a couple of armed soldiers surrounding me. They ask me how I am, and I tell them I still need a fucking, and that although Saddam raped my ass, he did not finish me off. The Western soldiers take pity on me, and one by one, they ram their hard cocks up inside me, and this makes me go ballistic, and I come and come and come and come, thinking that it is Saddam Hussein's five-incher inside of me the whole while.

14   Teenagers and Children

God guard me from those thoughts men think
In the mind alone.

> —WILLIAM BUTLER YEATS,
> "A PRAYER FOR OLD AGE,"
> *Parnell's Funeral and Other Poems*

Flirting with the Underaged

Although most American and British adults seem to prefer other adults as sexual partners, a substantial number of individuals have indulged in fantasies about young people. Approximately one-third of the male population has had one or more sexual fantasies about a teenager aged sixteen years or older, while nearly 10 percent of men have had a sexual fantasy about a teenager or a child aged fifteen years or *younger*—a fantasy which, if enacted, would constitute a gross criminal offense. Women seem to fantasize less frequently about teenagers aged sixteen years or older, and very rarely indeed about teens and children aged fifteen years and younger.

The attraction to those aged fifteen years or younger stems from a multitude of sources, ranging from a sadistic desire to harm a person to a more infantile wish, on the part of the adult, to recapture some of his or her youthfulness through an identification with the body of the teenager. Let us examine what various American and British adults have written about their sexual fantasy interest in teenagers, both over and under the age of consent. In this section, I have included fantasies that refer directly to a sexual interest in teenagers as well as some incorporating a symbolic sexual interest—for example, those featuring adult partners dressed as schoolgirls or schoolboys. In some cases, the fantasists have not indicated the age of the young person in question, and I have therefore given fantasists the benefit of the doubt and classified the lust-objects as older teenagers, although without more detailed information, one cannot be absolutely certain as to the most correct classification.

RYAN

I like to role play with my girlfriend. One of our favorites is schoolteacher, me, and student, her. She will dress up in a school dress uniform, short pleated dress, loose puffy shirt, and matching vest. I am giving her instructions, and for every wrong answer or childish attitude we become more intimate, until finally we have sex.

FRIEDRICH

Girls from ten to fourteen.

RYAN

Girlfriend dressing up as a schoolgirl with pigtails.

ERNIE

Friend of my daughter's comes to my bed during the night and I wake up to find her straddling me.

NELSON

Group sex with my wife, two daughters, Gillian Anderson and Julianne Moore, and four other men. With all and every combination we can devise.

ED

Generic schoolgirl fantasy, faceless teen of indeterminate age (but probably under age), lifting her skirt and masturbating for me, before allowing me to take her virginity roughly.

BURTON

Providing instruction to a young teenage girl in how to please a man with vaginal, manual, oral, and anal sex, with the assistance of her mother and/or sister.

CHANDLER

Deflowering an innocent-looking young girl with small breasts outdoors.

AUDREY

Gang-bang orgy involving me and a dozen or so violent, black teenagers.

HORTON

Have a Japanese schoolgirl start feeling me up on a crowded train, then getting off the train and having full sex somewhere.

NICHOLAS

I'd like to be a teacher to a group of lads just shy of their six-teenth birthdays. I'd make them run around outside, get all sweaty, and then personally escort them into the showers. You can guess the rest.

CORINNE

Introducing shy and nervous teenage boys (and there are some) to lovemaking and intercourse.

PANCHO

My daughter's female friends, aged sixteen, come to the house, and believing me to be asleep, start to play with my penis. I "wake up" when I have an erection, and show them how to mas-turbate me. After I have come, I show them how to masturbate each other, using fingers and tongues. I join in, and as each of them comes, my real climax shudders through me.

ANDI

Having another woman treat me as her baby, examining genitals and telling me to be a good girl while she looks at and strokes my clitoris.

EBENEZER

I get off on the thought of being dressed as a baby, in nappies, and jerked off. I did this once with my girlfriend, and it was incredible.

The Mind of the Child Molester

Nothing could be more devastating to a child than to suffer sexual abuse at the hands of an older person, whether a fully grown adult or indeed a teenager. Psychotherapists regularly devote years and years to helping survivors of early childhood sexual abuse to recover from the myriad emotional ravages that result from such experiences, which often blight every aspect of a survivor's life. I remember working with one patient who had been abused by both her father and brother before the age of ten. I first assessed this woman on a bright, breezy summer day, the sort of day most people enjoy. As the woman entered my office, she exclaimed, "I hate warm days like this, because you can see people with shorts, and short-sleeved shirts, and lots of exposed flesh. Most people love that, but I can't walk down the street without all this flesh reminding me of my sexual abuse."

A small percentage of adult men and women rely regularly upon sexual fantasies of young children, and in some cases, even of infants. Fortunately, very few act out these fantasies in reality. Mental health professionals and law-enforcement agencies do struggle, nevertheless, to know which fantasists—if they could even be identified—would be most at risk of committing such devastating violent sexual crimes on infants and children.

Adults who fantasize about children tend to exhibit greater degrees of psychological disturbance than those who direct their fantasy lives to older teenagers. Therefore, it would be fallacious to compare a man who has lustful thoughts about his neighbor's fifteen-and-a-half-year-old daughter to one who fantasizes about a child under the age of five, even though both scenarios would be illegal, if acted out in reality. Most individuals with pedophilic character structures have suffered devastating abuses in their own childhoods, and they often unconsciously inflict abuses on other young people that are similar to the ones they themselves suffered, in a desperate attempt to expunge some of the painful memories haunting their mind. Here we now have a sample of some of the potentially pedophilic fantasies.

TANDY

Tickling my daughter's vulva. She's eight. I would never do it though.

MONROE

Most of my fantasies are based around stories I have read, mostly involving effeminate, sexually willing young boys (1–15) forcibly cross-dressed, becoming the passive (oral and anal) victim of the sexual attentions of slightly older girls and boys.

ZACHARIAS

A boy, about fourteen, and his girlfriend, twelve, visit me and ask me to teach them about having sex. Reluctantly I agree, and take them to a bedroom. I get them to undress each other, then to get on the bed. I then instruct them in the various sexual organs, using crude rather than medical terminology. I then show them how to perform oral sex on each other whilst I watch. I then show them how to have sexual intercourse, which they do. Whilst watching them I undress and start to masturbate. They ask me to join them on the bed, which I do. We continue touching each other's bodies. I then have anal sex with both before the girl performs oral sex on me until I climax in her mouth.

EAMON

Sex with a beautiful young teenager or pre-teen whose parents are my captives after their defeat in battle.

CORBY

I am a young boy delivering newspapers. As I am passing a home, I hear a female saying, "Get your trousers off." (This bit actually happened.) I stop to listen and the female pops her head out of the window, sees me and asks if I want to join in. I say "yes" and she comes downstairs to get me. She strips me as soon as I get in the door and leads me upstairs by holding my penis. When upstairs we perform all sorts of sexual acts while the male watches and, sometimes, joins in.

DANA

Observing (peeping) at children exploring and enjoying each other's pleasure. The learning curve. Something that evaded me as a child. Also, another is to hold captive a female I hate and her family, and force them to commit sexual acts on each other. I would then exact my revenge on the person that had caused this situation and "bonk" her in front of her family, hoping she would show her pleasure to those at large.

JUANITA

Initiating a young boy into the joys of sex.

LOGAN

I am staying in a hotel. There's a knock at the door and an attractive dark lady asks me to help her with her zipper. I say, "Up or down?" and she meets me in a kiss, saying, "Whatever." I peel her out of her tight satin dress, and she swallows my cock with glee, saying, "I want it! Shoot on my tits!" I spray her and there's another knock at the door. I ask who it is, and it's her husband. She lets him in and berates him for his small cock, saying it's his fault she has to go door to door to find satisfaction. I interrupt saying they can discuss that on their own time. My cock is hard and I am not finished. I tell the husband to take a seat and watch his wife get sodomized properly. Maybe he will learn something. "Better yet, get on your knees and get her backside ready for use." He licks her hiney, but before he's done, I make him put me in her. I ride her hard, slapping her ass and pinching her nipples. She cries tears but bucks like a bronco. He says, "Be careful, don't hurt my wife." I slap him hard in the face and shove my cock in his mouth. I whisper angrily, "Don't you ever tell me anything about how to fuck your bitch, bitch." I lay back on the bed and she licks my ass while he drains my cock yet again. She orders a pizza to my specifications from room service and makes me a drink, and he lights my cigarette. I watch TV and smoke while each services one of my hairy nuts. The pizza arrives, he pays, they thank me, and leave. I am working on my second slice when there's another knock on the door. A hot little early teen is standing there in the hall wearing P.J.s, with feet! She says, "Mom told me there was a guy over here with a big . . . pizza, and I just love . . . pizza. Can I come in?" I say, "Sure, but if you want pizza, you gotta let me see those little titties." She pulls off her top and steps inside. I admire her buds and say, "Look, I am going to break a lot of laws with you tonight, but for now let's eat pizza and watch *Lost*." She says, "That's my favorite show too." So we have a nice evening of pizza and TV. At 11:00 P.M., when the news comes on, I duct tape her to the countertop and with a vibrator and my tongue, change her views forever about how many orgasms are acceptable in an evening's encounter.

15   Sugar and Spice and Everything Nice

Marriage is popular because it combines the maximum of temptation with the maximum of opportunity.

— GEORGE BERNARD SHAW, "MAXIMS FOR REVOLUTIONISTS," IN *Man and Superman*

After reading through the texts of the fantasies presented in previous chapters, one would be well justified to think that not a single American or Briton loves his or her spouse. In many cases, this would be quite true. As a marital psychotherapist, I can attest that many people do indeed wish their spouses dead. But if you are among those who still prize matrimony, take comfort, for you are not alone. In fact, in spite of the soaring divorce rates and the ubiquity of infidelity and sexually transmitted diseases, marriage remains our preferred state of habitation. In our fantasy lives, we do think about our sisters-in-law, our teachers, our neighbors, Bill Clinton and Tony Blair, Britney Spears and George Clooney, satin underwear, carrots and cucumbers, and a host of other people and objects too numerous to mention; but, we also fantasize about our regular, long-term partners, although not nearly as frequently as our partners might wish.

One must, in the first instance, make an important distinction between the frequency with which adult men and women fantasize about their partners during solo masturbation and the frequency with which they fantasize about their partners during sex *with* them. When people have sex with their spouses or their "significant others," roughly two-thirds of them do think about their partners with noted frequency, whereas roughly one-third will think about their partners very infrequently or not at all. Interestingly, we find almost no difference between males and females, so in the case of the very large percentage of adults in heterosexual relationships, women seem not to be more intra-maritally loyal than men, and vice versa. One must not forget, of course, that although many adults think about their husbands and wives, boyfriends and girlfriends with great regularity during sex, they also fantasize about much more besides. Perhaps unsurprisingly, as the typical adult ages, and as his or her relationship with a key lover develops over the years, fantasies about the partner appear less and less frequently. In fact, the research data from the International Sexual Fantasy Research Project on both sides of the Atlantic revealed that roughly 90 percent of all adults will be thinking about someone else, other than a spouse, during sex with their partners for a substantial amount of lovemaking time.

When adult Americans and Britons masturbate by themselves, with no wife or husband cuddling next to them in the bed, the mind becomes even more fertile, and the rate of intra-marital fidelity plummets. In fact, during masturbation, only one-third of adults, on average, will concoct a sexual fantasy about their partners on a regular basis. Nonetheless, many people still cherish sexual excitement from their long-term marital partners, as the following fantasies testify.

AMY

Husband masturbating.

MARY-LOU

Taking a nice hot bath with my man, and then screwing after. We screw through the night, pause for breakfast, and then we do it again. Beautiful!!!!

BOB

Being woken up for sex with my wife, watching her strip and making me have oral sex with her.

BRITTA

Being alone without the children.

DONNA

Having sex with my partner.

ELVIRA

Being romanced and kissed all over by my partner.

FRANCESCA

Being alone with candles and a real fire, with my husband.

MARNIE

I want my boyfriend to fuck me stupid. I love the feel of his thick dong going in and out of my pussy lips. I cum like there's no tomorrow. I wish I could do this with him all day. It's such a drag that tomorrow's Monday.

GONERIL

Being woken from my sleep by my partner for sex at any time, night or day. It has to be in a bed, in a very romantic and caring way.

AURELIA

Gentle sex with an understanding man.

HELEN

My boyfriend waking me up as he comes inside me.

ISIDOR

Orgasm at same time as partner.

JOAN

Sex with my husband in a field during a thunderstorm, not wildly exciting, sorry!

OTTO

Seeing my wife naked.

MARVIN

With my wife of forty-five years.

PEGGY

Log fire, wine, my husband, loads of time, just us.

NIGEL

Normal sex with my wife.

KESHONDRA

No fantasy as such, just some days I just think it would be nice to have sex with my husband that evening.

QUANESHA

Having my husband make love to me in unfamiliar surroundings, and on the spur of the moment.

LOUELLA

I like to be kissed all over my body and be aroused by it, and do the same back to my partner. I do not know what else there is in having sex.

BENJAMIN

At the moment it is that my lover who died last May comes back to me one night and we have one last time together making love.

REGAN

Lots of kissing and cuddling with my partner ending up with long slow sex.

ARVID

Having sex with my partner in the open in various situations, e.g., under a waterfall, in long wet grass, in a summer meadow on a hot day, swimming nude together, and making love in the water.

ZENOBIA

Making love with my partner in long grass in a field or meadow, totally naked, running or being chased through the grass, skinny-dipping in a river.

WARREN

Being with my wife.

UMA

Having my back massaged and leading into sex with my partner.

TANIKA

Being made pregnant again by my partner.

VIRGINIA

Nothing as a fantasy—it is the actual which turns me on—my partner's look, behavior, smell.

MACK

Having sex with my wife for hours. Oral sex, anal penetration of my wife, and sex in various positions.

YASMINA

Just being treated nicely and affectionately by my partner in nice surroundings with low lights, romantic music. Taking each other's clothes off and making love on the floor.

RUDOLPH

The love of my wife.

CAROLA

In a log cabin on a snowy day in front of the fire in candlelight with my partner.

DURSLEY

Memory of my late partner.

HYDE

Just me and my wife kissing passionately and making love for most of the night.

ELSPETH

Remembering the past—my husband is now impotent.

FENELLA

Just having my husband alive again to make love to me.

KILLIAN

Sex with my partner.

BERTHA

Being sung to or played to on an electric guitar, sexy music or song, e.g., salsa style.

STERLING

Having sex with my wife with a lot of oil.

ARCHIE

Being with my wife.

CRESSIDA

Making love with my man, my gorgeous man.

TASHA

Very romantic with my boyfriend saying very loving things to me.

DINA

In the bath with bubbles and John.

PART THREE

The Origins of Sexual Fantasy

Love looks not with the eyes, but with the mind.
And therefore is winged Cupid painted blind.

—WILLIAM SHAKESPEARE,
A Midsummer Night's Dream

16　The Underbelly of the Normal Fantasy: Erotic Freedom or Sublimated Sadism?

Quite apart from the way passion
dominates and fetters a person, he is also
tied up in many necessary relationships.

—JOHANN WOLFGANG VON GOETHE,
Kunst und Altertum am Rhein und Main

The Ultimate Strip Poker Game

In Part One, I reported that virtually every sexually mature adult generates sexual fantasies. Often highly pleasurable, often destructive and troubling—sometimes a mixture of the two—sexual fantasies can be accessed through the clinical interviewing process and through psychotherapeutic work as well as through the ordinary confessions of ordinary members of the public. In Part Two, I provided a large selection of representative fantasies, sketching the widespread erotic preferences of British and American women and men.

In Parts Three and Four, I shall attempt to provide some understanding of *why* we fantasize and to suggest some of the hidden, unconscious functions that fantasies may serve in our lives. I shall also broach the exceedingly complicated question of the relative "health" or "illness" of a particular fantasy. If someone has a sadomasochistic fantasy of being beaten by a partner, for example, what might this indicate? Does it mean that:

  A.   This person must be "disturbed," "perverse," "twisted," or what have you, in desperate need of help?
  B.   This person might actually be quite clever, allowing for the expression of destructive impulses in the relatively harmless arena of fantasy?
  C.   This individual might be more sexually liberated and creative than the average Joe or Jane?
  D.   This individual struggles with aggression, and that such a struggle may be manifest not only in the overtly sexual part of his or her life, but also in the nonsexual parts as well?

In other words, can we dismiss our fantasies as just harmless private entertainment—assuming that a bit of kink never hurt anyone—or do our fantasies actually govern our lives in other respects?

I propose to begin my psychological analysis through a description of the case of "Callum," one of the adult volunteers whom I interviewed for the research project. This gentleman had developed the most unusual and colorful of poker games in his mind.

When I first met Callum, I thought to myself, "What a traditionally masculine chap." A strapping, six-foot-tall man with a muscular, barrel-shaped chest, Callum squeezed my hand with bone-crushing intensity. He lumbered into the room, sprawling on the sofa as though he owned it, legs spread wide in a cocky, confident manner, and he bellowed, "So, what's this interview about?" A forty-two-year-old building contractor with a gravelly *basso profundo* voice, Callum had volunteered to participate in the research study, eager to earn some extra cash.

I explained the purpose of the interview, which Callum did in fact already know, as he had talked to my research assistant at great length on the telephone beforehand. "Sexual fantasies?" he queried. "I've got lots of those. Which one should we start with?" Comporting himself with all the delicacy of a bull in a *corrida*, Callum created the impression that nothing fazed him at all and that he maintained total control over every aspect of his life.

I provided Callum with further information about the research project, and I explained that it would be helpful to know about his sexual fantasy (or fantasies), but that first, I wanted to learn more about him as a person—how he spent his time, what sort of family he had come from, and so forth. Only then would we discuss his sexual biography and his sexual fantasies. Callum launched into the interview with great verve, and he talked virtually nonstop for four hours, answering every one of my questions in quite illuminating detail.

In spite of Callum's evident helpfulness, I soon observed that his mood seemed never to alter. He used the same super-confident tone of voice to describe every single feature of his life. Then he told me that he had recently earned a lot of money as a building contractor. I could well understand his sense of pride and accomplishment—hence the qualities of authority and certainty in his speaking voice. Likewise, when Callum told me that, as a child, he had excelled in football at school, I could also readily appreciate his surety. But when he told me that his "mam" had died shortly before his eighth birthday, he did so with all the detached calm and clinical coolness of a seasoned wartime correspondent, as if reporting: *"Government officials from the White House have just confirmed that Callum's mother has indeed died, leaving her son in the care of his disinterested father."*

I became quite concerned when I heard that Callum had lost his mother at such a young age, and I must have naturally contorted my facial muscles, as psychotherapists often do, imagining how he might have struggled with grief. Callum no doubt saw the change in my expression, and he immediately reassured me, "Don't worry, it's fine. She's at peace, and we all had to move on." Although I said nothing at the time, I sensed that his external confidence might well have masked an internal state of fragility, one which might feel too painful to experience, and therefore must be defended against with this tough-lad character armoring.

I do not doubt that many people can and do survive all sorts of bereavements, impingements, and abuses with considerable resilience, and that we do not all crumble into a heap in the wake of a sad life event. Some of us can even survive truly awful experiences and still manage to function. I must confess, however, that in my work as a psychotherapist, I have never seen a young child survive the death of a parent without paying some sort of emotional price. In most cases, the child will become either quite fragile and delicate, prone to any number of character disorders or other more severe forms of mental illness, or, by contrast, grow up to become a tough nut, generally lacking in sympathy, despising dependency and vulnerability in anyone else, sometimes becoming thuggish and even entering into a life of crime. I had begun to suspect that Callum's leg-splaying, macho posturing and his rugged braggadocio as a muscled laborer might have functioned as a protective suit of clothes, designed to cover up the more tender, hurt, bereaved boy.

We persevered with the interview. After discussing the death of his mother in a matter-of-fact manner, Callum explained that his father remarried approximately six months after her death, and that, apparently to everyone's great pleasure, he had chosen for his new wife "a real hottie with big bazongas." I blinked with a certain amount of surprise and incredulity when I heard Callum describe his new stepmother in such a highly sexualized fashion. Would an eight-year-old boy whose own mother had only recently died really be in a fit state of mind to appreciate the breasts of his new stepmother? And even if this proved to be the case, would he really refer to his stepmother's bosoms as "bazongas"? I instantly wondered whether any inappropriate sexual activity might have taken place between Callum and his new "stepmam."

I asked Callum to describe how his relationship with his father's new wife unfolded, and whether the constant presence of the new woman in the house made him pine for his own mother even more acutely. "Naw," said Callum, "it all worked out just fine." He then paused for the first time in the course of our interview, became a bit sheepish, and revealed, "She did catch me once jerking off in the toilet when I was about thirteen." Callum certainly is not the only person whose fumbling adolescent attempt at masturbation has been interrupted by an untimely parental intrusion, but I did wonder out loud how and why his stepmother happened to enter the bathroom at that time. To my surprise, Callum informed me that she did not exactly "enter" the bathroom, because in his family *everyone* walked around naked and no one paid much attention to closing doors; so, technically, his stepmother did not intrude upon Callum in mid-masturbation: "She was just walking by down the corridor."

Callum anticipated my next question, and he revealed that he did not mind his attractive stepmother catching him with his trousers down; in fact, it had rather excited him. He had just begun to develop postpubescent genitalia, and he explained that he rather enjoyed exhibiting himself in this way.

As our conversation continued, I asked Callum to describe his sexual and marital history. I imagined that he might be married and might have fathered a few children, but, in fact, Callum blushed when he told me that he had never had a relationship with a woman that had lasted for more than four months. In spite of his well-developed physique, his burly features, and his success as a building contractor, Callum had never managed to keep a girlfriend. Once again, he knew that I would be curious to hear his explanation as to why he found a long-term relationship so challenging. "Well," he professed, "I just like to park my engine, drop my bombs, and then disappear." Callum giggled to himself, and he shared his private mirth with me, "It's like my mate Harry always says, about me and women . . . I just fuck 'em and move on."

I found myself very preoccupied with Callum's vocabulary. I have certainly talked to many men who regard women as essentially sexual objects whom they "fuck" and from whom they then "move on," but Callum had used a much more idiosyncratic description, analogizing himself, and in particular his genitals, to a World War II fighter pilot, parking his "engine" and releasing his "bombs." I wondered what his girlfriends would think if they could hear him speaking in such an unarguably denigratory manner? Can it be a surprise, therefore, that his relationships lasted for such a comparatively short period of time?

After discussing his sexual history, revealing that he must have bedded more than 100 women over the past twenty-five years, Callum proceeded to share with me his most arousing masturbatory fantasy. I shall now present the fantasy in Callum's own words:

> It's all based on poker. You see, I'm a very keen poker player, and I play a game every week with my mates, Harry and Charlie, who work with me, and four or five others. We all enjoy the game a lot, and I'm one of the better players, and I've won a considerable little pot over the years. But you see, although these guys are my mates, they're not much to look at. [*Laughter from Callum.*] I'd never want to play poker with ladies in real life because I don't think they'd be good card players, you know, not competitive and all that. But when I jerk myself off, I like to pretend that instead of guys in the game, it's just me and a whole bunch of ladies—maybe five or six of them, and just me, the only guy. Because there are no other guys about, I suggest we play strip poker, and the girls are really up for this. Anyway, we're playing hands, and each time someone loses a hand, off come some clothes. Eventually, we're all stark naked, and I'm sitting

there with all these naked ladies, and I've got a big stiffy on, and I need to do something about it. So I suggest we make the game a bit more interesting: Since there's no more clothes to lose, what about playing "dares"? You see, I've devised this system. Each of the cards has a special sex act attached to it, and each of the colors, red or black, means that either *you* have to do something to one of the girls; or *they* have to do something to you. You see, black means the guy does something to the girls, and red means they do it to you. And the numbers go like this: If you draw a 2 from the deck, that means nipple play. If you pick a 3, that means vagina, 4 means prick, 5 means ass, 6 means sucking, 7 means jerking off, and so on, you see. Picture cards are all wild, and you can do whatever the hell you like. Oh yeah, and the ace means you have to stick a finger up the ass, either the girl does it to you, or you do it to the girl. So to give you an example, if I draw the 6 of clubs, that means I have to perform cunnilingus on one of the girls, because 6 means sucking, and a black 6 means I have to do it to her. If I picked the 6 of hearts instead, it would mean that I could choose whichever girl to give me a full blow job. After we finish playing, I line up all six girls, on their backs, in a row, like a can of sardines, and I fuck them each in turn, like a conveyor belt, one after the other until they're so exhausted that they just fall asleep, fully satisfied. I must have about ten or fifteen orgasms in the fantasy, and when it ends, I shoot a lot of semen. That's the fantasy. Unlike some guys, who like a quick jerk-off, and then zip up, I like to take my time, and this one does take time, but it's worth it. [*Laughter from Callum.*] I bet you haven't heard that one before. If only I could find a way to market this poker game, I bet there'd be lots of guys who'd want to play, and lots of girls also.

Callum had guessed correctly that I had not encountered such a strip poker fantasy before, and I certainly marveled at the detail of his masturbatory entertainment. He presented quite a contrast to the elderly gentleman I had interviewed earlier that very morning who claimed to have only one simple, straightforward sexual fantasy: "I fuck my wife." When I asked for elaboration, the interviewee replied, "I told you, I fuck my wife. No frills, just straight fucking. That's it." I found myself wondering why some people seem to have rather sparse fantasies, and others, such as Callum, have invented long and intricate tales of sexual experimentation.

I asked Callum whether he had any sense of *why* this particular fantasy appealed to him so much, and whether he had any idea at all how and when it had first developed. Helpfully, Callum provided a crucial piece of biography: "I've been jerking off to this one ever since I can remember. I think it got started when I heard that my dad and my mam used to have a poker game, before my mam passed on. I don't think it was strip poker, in fact it *wouldn't've* been strip poker, but one of the boys at school told me about strip poker when I was ten or eleven, and I remember thinking, that sounds pretty hot."

Evidently, the image of the poker game had fascinated Callum from an early, impressionable age. But why did the poker game become such a primary focus of eroticization in his mind? After all, many boys and girls grow up in households in which one or both parents play poker or some other card game, but I would guess that rarely, if ever, would the poker game become such a salient, defining feature in the postpubescent central masturbatory fantasy. It seems likely that Callum had used the setting of the poker game as a vehicle through which other wishes could be expressed.

On the surface, Callum's fantasy, albeit rich in its description, seems to fit perfectly with his "normal guy" persona. What card-carrying, self-confident, red-blooded heterosexual male would not enjoy the fantasy of being the only man in the room, enveloped by his own harem of women, with all the participants stripped naked, waiting to perform sexual acts upon one another? The fantasy contains no elements of gross perversion; in other words, it harbors no pedophilic component, no wish to inflict bodily pain upon the other participants, and so forth. So does the fantasy really require any commentary? One could argue that this fantasy fully establishes Callum's credentials as a gold-standard heterosexual man.

On rereading Callum's fantasy, I do, however, wonder whether it might be as straightforward as it first appears. Naturally, I remember that this man has bedded approximately 100 women in the past twenty-five years of his life, and has not managed to maintain a relationship for longer than four months with any of them. Could it be that Callum has simply had a run of "bad luck," or might his sexual biography indicate a real deficit in his ability to forge an intimate, committed attachment relationship? And might this vulnerability manifest itself in the masturbatory fantasy as well? Perhaps the masturbatory fantasy even enforces the wish to have superficial sexual contact with lots of women, rather than with one permanent partner.

Although I met Callum on only one occasion, I have met other Callums in the course of my psychotherapeutic career, men who bed large numbers of women in a promiscuous Don Juan fashion. These men evoke a lot of jealousy in more traditional, single-partnered men, often eliciting such comments from their mates as: "You lucky bastard, I wish I could sleep with as many women as you do." But in fact, when Don Juan arrives at the psychotherapist's office, he will invariably come to complain that although he has engaged in sexual activity with a seemingly endless stream of women, he *also* suffers from depression and from a lingering sense of emptiness, lamenting that all of this erotic activity lacks any meaning or deep satisfaction.

The ancient Roman littérateur Juvenal, author of the famous *Satires,* opined famously, *"voluptates commendat rarior usus,"* which translates colloquially as "All pleasure's no pleasure." In this vein, consider the famous filmic example of *Alfie.* Although the main character, brilliantly portrayed by Michael Caine, and more recently, in the remake, by Jude Law, leads a seemingly enviable life, owing to his spectacular talent at bedding any woman within his radar, most viewers will ultimately become enveloped in a sense of despair, owing to the lack of any sustained intimacy in the protagonist's life.

I recalled Callum's description of intercourse with a woman. He had characterized his sexual activity thus: "I just like to park my engine, drop my bombs, and then disappear." On the one hand, this sort of comment seems prototypically macho, indicative of a swaggering man who enjoys good, solid sex with a woman. But on the other hand, Callum's description also reveals a great deal of hatred and hostility toward women; in spite of his professed "love" of women, he has chosen to describe the sexual act as a military expedition in which his penis becomes a fighter plane with an "engine," and his sperm become "bombs" waiting to be dropped, after which he will disappear. Callum's language would probably horrify a great many women, and no doubt many men as well.

In my interview with Callum, I gently inquired whether he thought his fantasy contained any elements of hostility to women, but in his brash manner, he simply refused to countenance this idea and brushed me aside, claiming, "It's just a normal fantasy, with lots of babes. I *love* women." No doubt Callum does love women; but speaking psychotherapeutically, I suspect that he also harbors long-standing and deep-seated resentments toward them which manifest themselves not only in his aggressive, militaristic language but also in the fact that he cannot tolerate being with any one woman for more than four months. When he masturbates, the women become interchangeable objects, without names or personalities, who have one function and one function alone, to be lined up like a can of sardines and penetrated.

In view of Callum's history, both his denigration of women and the particular contents of his favorite masturbatory fantasy begin to make sense. Although we do not know much about the quality of the interactions between Callum and his biological mother, particularly in light of the fact that he claims to remember very little about her, I suspect that her death had a strong impact. As I have already indicated, it would be rare indeed for a bereaved child of eight to remain unaffected, if not traumatized, by such a profound loss. When a small child loses a parent, most will manage to cope with the bereavement *if* the surviving parent or caretaker allows the child multiple opportunities to mourn the death by attending the funeral, by reminiscing about the deceased, by telling stories, by enjoying photographs and home movies, and so forth. This constant engagement with the dead parent will allow the child to "let go," while still clinging to an internal image of the parent. When the surviving parent tries to "move on" quickly, to forget about the partner who has just died, any number of symptoms will develop in the offspring, including depression and often one or more varieties of psychosomatic illness. No doubt Callum's father did the best that he could in such troubled circumstances, but it seems evident that the father had found the loss of his wife too painful, and so he replaced her immediately with the "hottie" with the big "bazongas."

One might argue that a working father needed a new wife at the earliest opportunity to help him with child care, and that, by remarrying so quickly, he should be applauded for having speedily arranged a replacement mother figure for his young son. But I propose that by remarrying at the first available opportunity, Callum's father transmitted to his son a notion that one woman can be readily substituted for any other—just like the women in Callum's bed, and like the women in the poker game, where it becomes immaterial which woman draws the 3 of diamonds, as long as someone performs a sexual act on Callum or he performs one on one of the nameless, faceless girls.

In my clinical practice, I have worked with a number of men over the years who have lost their birth mothers before the age of five, due to illness in most circumstances. In virtually every case, the men became sexually promiscuous in later life, having internalized multiple models of female caretaking from the biological mother, the stepmother, the nanny, and so forth. Of course, many promiscuous people have a living mother, so it would be too crude to explain all adult rapacity as an attempt to deal with actual bereavement, but I will endorse the view that early maternal bereavement becomes a reasonable risk factor for the development of later promiscuity, either in reality or in fantasy.

So, because of the way in which the family handled the bereavement, Callum began to treat women as disposable. He also harbored a deep fear that if he became close to any woman for more than a short time, she too might die, just like his mother. By killing them off at the four-month mark (or sooner), Callum managed to protect himself from the prospect of another woman dying on him.

His denigration of women became more pronounced when his father married the seemingly erotic stepmother, who later caught Callum masturbating in the bathroom. This no doubt excited him, and like any childhood or adolescent sexual experience, it left a profound imprint on his subsequent adult sexuality. An episode such as this one might have given Callum the message that any woman might be his for the asking, or for the taking. In his memory, the hot young stepmother did not blanch when she saw his penis. She did not run away in horror. But nor did she close the door, encouraging him to keep his sexual behaviors private.

By setting his fantasy in a poker game, Callum has succeeded in bringing back to life something that his biological mother had enjoyed, namely, the very poker games that she had played with his father. Although he claims not to remember much about his mother, and that he does not miss her, I suspect that this boast of self-sufficiency may be a highly developed defense against the fact that he misses her deeply. By invoking the poker game, both in real life with his friends and in his masturbatory fantasy, Callum succeeds in recreating an aspect of his dead mother's world, thus revivifying her in a symbolic manner.

But in the fantasy, Callum does not masturbate to an image of his mother and father playing ordinary poker; instead, he imagines a group of strangers playing *strip* poker. Many people imagine themselves being stripped in their fantasies, but in Callum's case, having come from a home in which people did not close the door to the bathroom, anyone could see his genitals at any time, as happened with his stepmother; thus, nudity featured prominently in his late childhood and early adolescence. I wonder whether Callum experienced not only excitement, but also some shame, at having his stepmother observe his teenage masturbation ritual.

In his fantasy, by contrast, no one walks in on Callum masturbating in the bathroom; instead, he becomes the *master* of the stripping—he casts the game, and he takes off his own clothes, under fully controlled circumstances. Through the poker fantasy, Callum succeeds in transforming the trauma of bereavement and genital exposure into the triumph of control. He has no dead women in his fantasy. His masturbatory thoughts contain only healthy, living women, a perfect antidote to the real-life experience of his mother dying; and if, for some reason, one of the fantasy women should die, then he has a whole set of spares with which to replace her. In fact, he estimated all of the women in his fantasy to be roughly twenty or twenty-five years of age, the very age of his own mother at the time of her death.

The poker game fantasy permits Callum to satisfy all sorts of interrelated psychological needs and desires, but above all, the fantasy allows him to express his aggression toward women. Although he thinks of himself as a man who loves women, in reality he finds them frightening and often becomes quite hateful toward them. I wish to propose that he still hates his mother for dying, and that he also hates his stepmother for being a sexually arousing and intruding figure rather than a maternal one, because an eight-year-old boy whose mother has just died needs to have a nurturant stepmother, not a "hot" one.

The psychoanalytical interpretation of one's own sexual fantasies, or of the sexual fantasies of another person, should never be undertaken as a cavalier party game. Even well-trained mental health professionals must proceed with caution when unraveling the patient's unconscious narrative. We know that the hidden meanings of a patient's sexual fantasy may be as complex, multidetermined, and convoluted as a seemingly bizarre dream. My colleagues and I would, I trust, never rush to claim that we *know* what someone else's fantasy or dream might mean. Instead, we prefer to offer informed speculations, based upon what we have come to learn about the patient in question and what we have already discovered in our work with other patients who present in similar ways. We cannot ever attain absolute certainty in our psychological detective work; instead, we present hypotheses to our patients, using these observations as a starting point for a psychotherapeutic conversation.

If Callum had come to see me as a long term psychotherapy client, instead of as a participant in a research project, I would have begun a very slow, methodical, and gentle exploration with him about the possible meaning or meanings of his masturbatory fantasy. At the end of this process, I might have remarked: "I wonder whether your preference for treating women as sardines in a can, as objects upon whom you drop 'bombs,' gives us a better sense of some of your more complicated feelings toward women, particularly women who may have let you down?" A defensive patient such as Callum might engage with these ideas, or more likely, might tell me to jump into a lake. Sometimes a patient will not be ready to work on a particularly frightening idea at an early stage in treatment, and the psychotherapist has the latitude, indeed the obligation, to return to these moments of vulnerability at a later point, when the patient feels stronger and therefore better equipped to confront his or her difficulties.

Had Callum entered psychotherapy, I suspect that during the early months of treatment he would have continued to act on his erotic impulses, bedding scores of young women, but would then start arriving at his sessions telling me about the frequent disappointments, fights, and break-ups, and about how he had begun to find masturbation so much more satisfying than intercourse. If, at that point, he could be brave enough to reveal his secret masturbatory fantasy about the poker game, we would have much more data to work with concerning his objectification of women and his hostility toward them, and yet, also, his wish to find a way to be with them. One must not forget that even though Callum abuses his poker ladies, he also deeply craves female companionship and female caretaking. Callum's strip-poker fantasy contains a hopeful element as well—that somehow he will find a way to interact pleasurably with women.

After a time, if Callum could develop the capacity to remain in psychotherapy—and not discard his therapist as he does his women—we would then work together to develop a role model of psychological intimacy and longevity of relatedness, a template that could be used in his erotic life with women. My colleagues and I have all worked with men similar to Callum, and sometimes, after years of painstaking work, we watch them become transformed from Casanova-style "love rats" into more solid, reliable lovers with one partner. Critics often accuse psychoanalysts and psychotherapists of having become the handmaidens of bourgeois morality, turning sexually polygamous, liberated partygoers into conventional, monogamous, suburban householders. When treating promiscuous patients—promiscuous either in fantasy or in reality—we must, of course, avoid the crude temptation of becoming Dr. Frankensteins of the mind, reshaping these patients in our own sexual image. But as we allow our patients the opportunity to express hostility toward early caretakers, we find that they will naturally abandon their proto-promiscuity and begin to yearn for more sustained intimacy, in part because they no longer find one-on-one relationships quite so deadly or threatening. Above all, we strive not to impose a sexual lifestyle upon our patients, but rather to explore the arenas of woundedness in their biographies that prevent or inhibit them from experiencing the potential joys of interpersonal contact.

Hidden Hostilities in the Masturbatory Arena

Callum's fantasy of the strip-poker game reminds me of many of the other fantasies contained in my research project, seemingly "normal" fantasies about sexual interactions that do not contain extreme violence such as rape or murder, but that nevertheless involve aggressive features. The fantasist in question will usually deny that the masturbatory story contains anything untoward. But I wonder. Let us study the following fantasies from ordinary American and British men and women, all of whom live *outside* the prison system, men and women who, for the most part, cherish fairly traditional sexual relationships.

NEAL

Spanking and having sex with a secretary dressing in blouse, skirt, and high heels or boots.

OREN

Dressing my partner in kinky underwear and tying her to the bed.

PARTHENOPE

Being used as a sex slave by a master or mistress to service friends.

QUISHA

My fave fantasy is kind of like a rape scene, but with no violence. I'm tied up, blindfolded and forced to have sex and perform all duties. I'm very frightened, but very turned on. I am completely dominated. There may be one or more people involved, or perhaps a whole gang of really horny, sexy young men. All very fit with no beer bellies. The Brad Pitt type of man. Mmmmmmmm. I DO NOT WANT TO BE RAPED IN REAL LIFE THOUGH— IT'S A FANTASY.

AVERIL

Pinning the man down and covering his eyes so he can't see his hands, and I do what I like to his body.

CORDELIA

I sometimes imagine a group of men masturbating over me while I lie on the floor. They would cum all over me.

PERCIVAL

I like to dominate a straight man and fuck him till he comes.

The influential Hungarian-born, British-based psychoanalyst Dr. Michael Balint, a leading figure in the mental health profession during the 1950s and 1960s, argued that in a sensitive sexual relationship, neither partner should ever bite the other. I do not suppose that Balint had Hannibal Lecter–style biting in mind, but, rather, the more frequent form of nibbling in which lovers will often engage during sex. Balint regarded sexual biting as an expression of infantile, regressed behavior, an expression of primitive sadism, and thus cause for concern when it became a feature of lovemaking. Although I do not myself have a fixed viewpoint about biting or not biting, nibbling or not nibbling, during lovemaking, I suspect that Balint's condemnation stemmed from his recognition that biting can contain elements of deep cruelty. Certainly, if a stranger suddenly pounced upon you and bit your hand, you would want to call the police immediately, and most people in that situation would do the same; private views of biting during sexual intercourse, however, may vary. But Balint, like Freud before him, not only appreciated that lovemaking contains hostile elements, but also understood that, in many instances, the arousal required for lovemaking can actually depend upon the very presence of such hostile elements.

In examining the previous set of fantasies, we can come to appreciate the role of hostility contained in them. None of these fantasists reported a sexual fantasy involving soft breezes, Caribbean beaches, and piña coladas. On the contrary, these fantasies, though not extreme by comparison to others that we have already encountered, particularly in Chapter 11 on humiliation and in Chapter 13 on sexual violence, do contain, nonetheless, aggressive or secretly sadistic ingredients. This particular cluster of fantasies boasts spanking, sexual slavery, rape, enforced cunnilingus, degradation, and forceful sex.

Neal, for example, yearns to spank his secretary, whom he wishes to have attired in blouse, skirt, and high heels or boots. To the average reader, Neal's fantasy might evoke a number of reactions: some may find it arousing or wish to try it themselves, some may admire Neal's so-called erotic freedom, some may regard it as denigratory to women, and some may diagnose Neal as a perverse, sadomasochistic fetishist. Should we regard Neal as a decent chap who just happens to crave a bit of role-play from time to time, or do we conceive of him as a disturbed person of the type we wish to protect our wives and daughters from, and certainly our secretaries? In the consulting room, I have met many Neals over the years who enjoy erotic coital or masturbatory fantasies based on spanking. I would estimate that 90—if not 95—percent of these men had never, to the best of my knowledge, laid a hand on a woman in an unpleasant manner. Most of them treated women with respect and dignity.

Other men, however, do sometimes turn their fantasies into reality. I remember one patient in particular, with whom I worked many years ago, who engaged in frequent spanking behavior, which he regarded as "no big deal." I had become aware of the way in which his preference for spanking emerged after his wife had become sexually anesthetic and would no longer perform fellatio upon him. This sexual "upset" served as the immediate trigger to the development of the spanking fantasy and the spanking behavior. But upon further examination, I learned that, as a little boy, this patient had received frequent spankings from his mother; therefore, when he became angry at his wife, he not only would discharge rage toward her for withholding fellatio, but would also, symbolically, manage to attack the abusive mother of his childhood at the same time.

On the surface, Neal's brief fantasy, sixteen words in length—
"Spanking and having sex with a secretary dressing in blouse, skirt,
and high heels or boots"—may hardly shock an enlightened, contemporary audience. Indeed, compared to the case, reported to me by one
of my colleagues, of a sex offender who used to roam through crowded
streets stabbing random, anonymous women in the buttocks with
sharpened scissors, Neal's fantasy seems positively tame. Nevertheless,
Neal's fantasy reveals traces of what I refer to as "the ordinary sadism
of everyday life." Remember, we have no evidence that Neal would
ever smack his secretary, even if she appeared to consent. He has reported a sexual *fantasy*, not necessarily a sexual *behavior*, but even so,
it contains a potentially aggressive ingredient. He has created a special
scene, with a special costume, in which a punishment, however mild,
might be administered.

This particular fantasy of spanking one's secretary naturally reminded me of the film entitled, quite simply, *Secretary*, in which the actor James Spader portrays a lawyer who hires a young woman, played
by the actress Maggie Gyllenhaal, in a secretarial capacity. The secretary soon discovers that her duties include being spanked on the bottom while wearing a short skirt and heels, as well as submitting to a
variety of sexual acts. Although she seems to agree to her boss's requests for spanking and other forms of comparatively mild sadomasochism, one wonders about her capacity to provide informed
consent, as earlier in the film we learn that she has a history of psychiatric disturbance and that she engages in quite marked self-destructive
acts of cutting herself with sharpened implements. On the surface,
James Spader's smacking might seem just a bit of kinky office fun, but
as one explores the psychology of the situation more deeply, one discovers that what at first appears as consensual adult role-play may, in
fact, be the reproduction of an earlier set of traumatic situations for
both parties. Eventually, the so-called mild sadomasochism develops
into full-blown humiliation as well as other forms of physical and psychological cruelty.

It would be easy to become po-faced, like the psychoanalyst Balint,
and dictate that in healthy sexual interactions one should never bite,
and further, one should never smack or spank; and yet, in my psychotherapeutic work with couples, I have met many men and women
who enjoy performing *Secretary*-style scenarios in their erotic life,
claiming that it spices up their romance. And many of these people,

though issue-laden, have never suffered from gross sexual traumas or engaged in other forms of self-destruction such as anorexia or cutting. According to my research, millions of Americans and Britons have had spanking fantasies. Although it is impossible to say whether those who fantasize about spanking and those who fantasize about being spanked constitute two completely separate groups—one could, after all, enjoy both positions—we can reasonably conclude that approximately 7 percent of the population has derived sexual pleasure from fantasies of spanking in one form or another. To make matters more complex, many had parents who spanked them in early childhood, but others did not.

Here we reach a point of complexity and heated debate, both in clinical psychotherapeutic circles and in general public discourse. If two parties consent to a spanking scene, should we call the cops, call the shrinks, or just leave well enough alone? And if the spanking remains confined to the world of private masturbatory *fantasy,* what then? Should we telephone the thought police, in case a man or woman fantasizing about spanking should then move from thinking about it to a full-fledged enactment? And even if the psychological spanker never lays a hand on another person, will he or she be pregnable, nonetheless, to being *spanked down* in some symbolic form, such as in the boardroom, perhaps?

In clear-cut cases of actual sexual perversion, such as pedophilia, rape, intrafamilial child sexual abuse—in other words, any attempt to derive orgastic satisfaction through harm of another person, either physically or psychologically, often both—I would not hesitate to alert whatever combination of psychotherapists, psychiatrists, social workers, probation officers, lawyers, police, and cognate professionals one needed in order to arrange for both the victim and the perpetrator to become physically safe and receive appropriate psychological treatment. But as mental health professionals, and as members of the public, we all encounter cases that may not be so clear cut, such as the enactments in *Secretary,* or the fantasists reported in this chapter. Quisha, for instance, has stressed very clearly that, although she enjoys the fantasy of being tied up, blindfolded, dominated, and raped by one or more flat-stomached men, preferably Brad Pitt, she would never wish to experience such an event in real life. And in typing her fantasy for me on the computer, Quisha chose to use all capital letters, noting "I DO NOT WANT TO BE RAPED IN REAL LIFE THOUGH—IT'S A FANTASY," thus underscoring that incalculably important difference.

Most of us would regard blindfolding, domination, and rape as forms of violence; and if Quisha's "fave" fantasy ever turned into reality, then there really would be tremendous cause for concern. But as Quisha keeps her thoughts of rape confined to fantasy—a fantasy shared by millions of women and men—should we send all of these people to psychotherapists, allow them to continue with their fantasizing, or simply sit on the sidelines lamenting and worrying about the state of a mind that would enjoy a fantasized experience of rape? I regard myself as neither qualified nor inclined to pass judgment on such a complicated and contentious matter. Having thought about the relative health or illness implied by sexual fantasies for many years, having talked to thousands of men and women about their sexual fantasies, and having read transcripts of literally tens of thousands of sexual fantasies, I have come to realize that it would be easier to adopt a quick, entrenched position on these matters than to think them through adequately. Indeed, I have been struck by how rapidly my colleagues fall into one of six categories:

1.   Those who regard Neal-like and Quisha-like fantasies as the products of deeply disturbed minds and traumatized childhoods.
2.   Those who regard such fantasies as "small potatoes" compared to those of the real-life rapists, pedophiles, and murderers with whom they have worked.
3.   Those who conceptualize such fantasies as symptoms of unresolved aggressive conflicts that will interfere with the fantasist's daily functioning.
4.   Those who believe that such fantasies may be symptoms of unresolved aggressive conflicts, which may remain safely encapsulated in a secluded part of the mind, thereby not interfering with other areas of functioning.
5.   Those who regard such fantasies as a potentially creative means of dealing with aggressivity.
6.   Those who throw up their hands in abject frustration, caught between their psychoanalytical instincts to rout out pathology and their sexually liberated wish to be compassionate, tolerant, and open-minded.

Over the course of my career, I have at various points adopted each of these six postures, and so I must now acknowledge the sheer difficulty of making pronouncements about the private sexual fantasies of others. I suppose that I have now arrived at an amalgamated clinical viewpoint, recognizing that, to the best of my knowledge, no one has ever entered treatment solely to discuss a sexual fantasy. Clients come to see me and my colleagues for all sorts of reasons: depression, anxiety, marital strife, addictions, job loss, bereavement, ennui, creative blocks, and thousands of other reasons besides. Our task remains not that of the judge who passes sentence on the sexual fantasies which may emerge, but rather as someone capable of providing an opportunity for an intelligent conversation, to inquire whether a fantasy might be related to other areas of trouble. If I discovered, for example, that Quisha found herself getting "fucked," "fucked up," or "fucked over," not only in fantasy, but in her job, her marriage, her relationships with girlfriends, and her encounters with siblings and parents, then, and only then, would I become more inclined to regard her sexual fantasy as a pathological manifestation that might benefit from treatment, rather than simply as an expression of an erotic preference shared by millions of others.

Returning to Callum, let us revisit his fantasy of playing cards with a group of women, in orgiastic fashion, in which he and the women remain on erotic tenterhooks, uncertain which card will be drawn next, unclear as to whether, upon drawing the next 3 or the next Jack, they will be fellated, penetrated, or licked, or will do this to someone else. Should we classify Callum as a secret sadist? Or does his fantasy express an erotic freedom that the more sexually repressed among us desperately crave or punitively condemn—sometimes both?

Callum certainly had become mildly depressed from his many disastrous attempted relationships with women, experiences that had caused him considerable despair, so much so that I actually referred him to a psychotherapist colleague for treatment. Nevertheless, in spite of his psychological difficulties, through the course of our interview he struck me as a loyal friend, a witty conversationalist, an engaged citizen who undertook charity work, an accomplished member of his chosen profession, and a man with many earnest and engaging qualities. I could not dismiss him or diagnose him readily as a deviant, a pervert, a satyr, or anything else sexually untoward. Instead, I would regard him, like most people, as a "mixed picture," beset with injuries and vulnerabilities, and yet boasting talents and abilities as well.

I do believe that if Callum's mother had not died at such a young age, or if his father had managed to facilitate a more mature mourning process, Callum might have had a different type of sexual fantasy. I would also argue that if he had not suffered great loss from the death of his mother and inappropriate erotic stimulation from his step-mother, his sexual fantasy might have involved fewer women. So, one could establish a psychologically compelling case that Callum's sexual fantasies stem directly from his biography. And yet, I know that many men (and perhaps many women) would become sexually aroused by Callum's fantasy, or might enlist this fantasy as a masturbatory aid or as a means of spicing up their own sexual lives; and most of these people will not have lost a mother at a tender age, or have masturbated in front of their stepmother with the bathroom door ajar. Thus, trauma and history seem to pervade our fantasy lives, but trauma and history cannot explain the fullness of our erotic complexities.

17   "They've Scraped Out My Soul": Struggling with Shame and Humiliation

Strange fits of passion have I known:
And I will dare to tell,
But in the Lover's ear alone,
What once to me befell.

—WILLIAM WORDSWORTH,
"STRANGE FITS OF PASSION HAVE I KNOWN"

Deborah's Menstruation: Do I Have Cancer of the Cervix?

Of the many fantasies reported in the earlier chapters of this book, scenarios of humiliation and shame certainly occupy a huge role. Indeed, I received so many fantasies about being humiliated, and the converse, about humiliating others, that these could have constituted, quite readily, a separate volume. In both the 2003 pilot study and the 2004 British principal study, and in the 2006 American principal study, humiliation and shame featured in quite a seminal way, and thus these fantasies deserve particular explanation, not least because of the important light that they can shed on understanding other types of fantasy constellations.

As children, many, if not all, of us will have experienced shame—that aching, agonizing emotional pain that results from some sort of humiliation. According to the pioneering psychoanalyst Erik Erikson, one of Freud's most acute disciples, deep-rooted shame invariably involves exposure of the body in some way. We tend not to experience shame unless someone has made fun of, or criticized, our body, or a body part, or some bodily function. Whether being forced to wear a dunce cap in the schoolroom, a pernicious pseudo-pedagogical practice still utilized in some cultures, or being called names such as "fatso," "four-eyes," "greaseball," or whatever, the impact of early shaming can be devastating. Even as adults in the workplace, we tend to internalize episodes of office tardiness, sloppiness, or negligence as reflections of our very physicality.

Over the years, during the course of consultation work, I have heard thousands of stories of shame. Let me offer some illustrative examples from the biographies of women and men who have endured a lifetime of shame, resulting from a series of dreadful pre-adolescent experiences of feeling bodily exposed. I shall begin this exploration of the psychological meaning of sexual fantasies involving shame and humiliation by describing the dream of a reasonably healthy and well-adapted middle-aged woman. This study will provide the groundwork for our subsequent thinking about the widespread nature of humiliation and shame in the many different aspects of our lives.

"Deborah," a forty-six-year-old teacher, first entered psychotherapy because of debilitating feelings of self-loathing. She hated her body, her face, and her voice; she told me that she believed she sounded like a man, although I thought she had a rather pleasant, traditionally female timbre to her speaking voice. Although not classically svelte, Deborah had a perfectly well-proportioned body, and many men and women would certainly have called her attractive.

Deborah reminded me once again that each of us possesses two distinct bodies: the *external body* that others see, and the *internal body* that we carry around inside our head. The latter might be described as a mental, visual representation of our body often tainted with residues of childhood trauma. A huge disparity may exist between the external body and one's own private conception of one's body. My colleague Professor Susie Orbach, a London-based psychoanalyst, has referred to this phenomenon as the "false body," wherein our archaic experiences and internal perceptions color and distort our capacity to inhabit or enjoy our bodies. Deborah had a fine external body, but a deeply damaged internal one.

She came from a very poor, working-class family, and, tragically, her mother had died shortly after Deborah's eleventh birthday, leaving her with a bereaved, depressed father and two younger brothers. Because her father worked in a factory twelve hours a day, Deborah had to take responsibility for the care of her younger brothers, Henry and Lon. Some months after Deborah's mother passed away from cancer of the cervix, Deborah became fully pubertal and began to menstruate. With no mother at hand to instruct her about the menarche, she experienced great shock at her first period, and she remembered very clearly how she could find nothing other than a white towel in the bathroom to stick between her legs in makeshift fashion. According to Deborah, "The fact that the towel was white made it even more horrific for me as a little girl, because the white of the towel really showed up all the blood. I thought I was hemorrhaging, and I thought that I, too, would die, just like my mother."

Deborah felt too ashamed, embarrassed, and afraid to reveal what had happened to either of her brothers or to her father. Unable to talk about her experience with a trusted adult woman or a friend, as most emotionally nurtured young girls would have done, Deborah kept her bodily changes completely secret. In the course of psychotherapy, Deborah revealed that she had become absorbed in ruminations about her body, and we discussed the possibility that although these thoughts had plagued her, they had also allowed her to cleverly protect her mind from even more distressing thoughts about her mother's death.

Since she had no one with whom she could discuss feminine hygiene and puberty, and because her school had provided only the most rudimentary instruction in anatomy, biology, and sexual health, Deborah became very much adrift in the sea of bodily changes. As an eleven-year-old, she also became one of the first girls in school to menstruate and to acquire secondary sexual characteristics (body hair, breasts, and so forth). Far too busy at home caring for her siblings as well as for her father, Deborah did not ordinarily begin her homework until nine o'clock in the evening, by which time she had become too tired to concentrate properly. When she did skim through her reading for class, she would often fall asleep over her books, and she had neither the energy nor the inclination to have a bath or even a shower before bedtime. In the morning, she awoke to an early alarm, fixed breakfast for the boys, and walked them to school, as their father would already have left for the factory. Thus, for long stretches, Deborah did not have time to wash herself properly, and she often went to school with stringy, greasy hair.

One day, during lunch in the school cafeteria, Deborah sat down at a table across from two boys and began to eat her lunch. As soon as she had tucked into her spaghetti Bolognese, the two boys looked at each other, lifted their trays, and moved to another table. Dumbfounded, Deborah continued with her lunch, but from across the cafeteria, she could see the boys laughing at her, pointing at her, and then clutching their noses. Eventually, six or seven boys began to chant, "Deborah smells, Deborah smells," all pinching their nostrils as a means of communicating that she emitted a horrid odor. As the weeks went by, Deborah acquired the cruel nickname "Stinky Debs," and some of the boys would write this with marker pen on her locker. No matter how many times Deborah rubbed off the offending words, someone would repeat the insult, and the name stuck. She had become the whipping girl for the entire class. As Deborah explained to me in a psychotherapy session years later, "You know they say 'Sticks and stones may break my bones, but names will never hurt me'?" I nodded affirmatively. She then stared at me, and murmured, "It's just not true."

Deborah's depression became more acute, and eventually the head teacher referred her to an educational psychologist, who helped her to deal with a new symptom that had developed: a total inability to concentrate on her lessons. Sadly, her mind had become so absorbed with the accusations of being smelly that she could no longer attend to her academic studies. Deborah did use her sessions with the educational psychologist—a man—to talk about her difficulties at home and the death of her mother, but she simply could not muster the courage to tell him about the insult "Stinky Debs" and the horrid chanting. It all felt far too painful. Besides, she did not know whether the smell emanated from sweat under her arms or from the menstruation.

In my experience, these sorts of childhood humiliations exert a traumatic influence on the development of the personality. Episodes of bodily shame become deep scars that do not heal easily. I have seen young children whose parents have slapped them, kicked them, and punched them, calling them "stupid," "fuckwit," and many other names besides; and although these verbal assaults and cruel calumnies do hurt, none of them leaves the child with the searing predominant sense that his or her *body* might be disgusting. But Deborah felt that she had a disgusting body, and no amount of showering or sanitary towels could erase the shame of that humiliation in the lunchroom.

When I met Deborah, she told me that at the time she had thought that she, like her mother, must have cancer of the cervix. Why else would she be bleeding from between her legs, and why would her blood be emitting such a fetid odor? Heartbreakingly, even though she had received support from an educational psychologist, she had felt she could not trust him enough to verbalize the full extent of her shameful feelings. In desperation, she carried these taunts and accusations of bodily shame and humiliation in her mind for more than thirty years, during which time she never had a boyfriend, and never had sex, always thinking herself too dirty and disgusting, imagining that if she dared to flirt with a man, he would undoubtedly rebuff her for being bloody or smelly.

In our therapy sessions, Deborah worked very hard to confront some of the terrible memories of childhood, and she began to make great progress. After three years of once-weekly meetings, she started to develop a much more enhanced sense of self-esteem. As a result of our work, and as a result of her bravery in sticking with the often difficult psychotherapeutic process, she bounded into my consulting room one day announcing that she had met a young man at work whom she fancied. She spent the entire fifty-minute session talking animatedly about "Asher," describing his many positive features in great detail. I felt rather like a proud parent at this point, secretly hoping that something creative and joyful might develop between Deborah and Asher.

After a stream of increasingly successful dinner dates and visits to the cinema, Deborah told me that Asher had actually invited her away for the weekend. At this point, the couple had done nothing but kiss, so the idea of spending a weekend away and sharing a hotel room would inevitably force the question of sex. The virginal Deborah wondered what penetration would be like—indeed, what a penis would be like, as she had never seen the genitals of an adult male up close. Excitedly, she purchased some new clothes for the occasion, and she told me all about the perfumes and scented bath lotions that she had stockpiled, consciously wishing to introduce some "erotic smells" into the picture. Unconsciously, she hoped to cover up the aroma of sweat and menstrual blood that still lingered in her mind from her painful eleventh year.

I very much hoped that her first experience of adult sexuality might be a success. Unfortunately, after her weekend away, Deborah sat down in my consulting room and burst into tears as she started to provide an account of what she tellingly described as her "*dirty* weekend" with Asher. On Friday evening, the couple had enjoyed a lovely meal and had drunk much wine; afterward, in their suite, Asher began to caress Deborah. All went according to plan until the moment when Asher delicately removed her underwear and started to perform cunnilingus. At this point, Deborah became completely hysterical and started to shout and scream. Asher tried to calm her, explaining that he really liked to "eat out" a woman's vagina, and thought that she would be pleased since many men dislike this particular act. But he could not possibly know that his very visceral use of language—"eat out"—caused Deborah to become even more distraught, and she grabbed her underwear and retreated into the bathroom. This outburst spoiled the entire weekend, and Asher, naturally, experienced a great rejection as well. The weekend terminated on a very sour note. By the time Sunday afternoon had come round, Asher had stopped speaking to Deborah, and they drove back to London in stultifying silence.

This poignant, heartfelt vignette illustrates the enormously lasting power of early bodily taunts and insults. Such bodily humiliations not only sting at the moment of injury, but continue to suppurate throughout the adult life cycle, often denting or even damaging potentially pleasurable areas of our lives, such as the arena of consensual adult sexuality. Many women would have relished a tender lover such as Asher; but for Deborah, the exposure of her genitalia, and the fear that she would somehow contaminate Asher with her eleven-year-old's odor, proved too overwhelming. As a result of these mental gymnastics, she developed a transient hysterical neurosis, and in doing so, spoiled the weekend, secondarily protecting herself from the possibility that her genitalia might still smell. Naturally, we had to devote many months of psychotherapeutic sessions to the task of unraveling Deborah's psychological turmoil.

Shortly after the calamitous weekend with Asher, however, Deborah became extremely angry toward him during one of her psychotherapeutic sessions. She muttered, "He's a sex maniac. He tricked me into thinking that we would have a romantic weekend, but all he wanted was sex. And he's filthy, trying to lick my vagina, when he barely even knew me." Of course, I allowed Deborah to rant and vent her feelings of anger, however justified or unjustified these might seem to an external observer. Personally, I felt great compassion for Asher, who sounded like a kindly man, consciously unaware of the complex character that he had taken on board when he began to date Deborah.

At her next session, Deborah explained rather sheepishly that she'd had a "horrible, horrible" dream that had caused her to awaken in a sweat. She had dreamed that Asher had come to her house and had tried to break into her bedroom to rape her. Deborah endeavored to escape from Asher's evil clutches and had raced into the bathroom, just as she had done in reality on the "dirty weekend" in the country. In the dream, however, Asher broke down the bathroom door and started to wrestle Deborah to the floor. In desperation, hoping to avoid rape, Deborah had taken the metal brush from beside the toilet, which she had described as "more like a poker for the fireplace," and hit Asher on the head, causing him to drop to his knees. Taking advantage of his now supine position, Deborah had shoved his head into the toilet and then proceeded to flush it so that dirty toilet water kept washing over his head. As the dream continued, Deborah flushed again and again until the pipes started to backfire and copious amounts of urine and feces emerged in the bowl, covering Asher in excrement.

In true Freudian style, we spent a good deal of time trying to analyze the unconscious meaning of Deborah's dream. In November 1899, Freud published his magnum opus, *The Interpretation of Dreams,* a work of such landmark importance that his publishers decided to print the year 1900 on the title page so that his volume would be associated with the turn of the new century. In *The Interpretation of Dreams,* Freud posited that every dream contains a secret wish, and that the clinician must assist the patient in uncovering the hidden wish that seeks fulfillment in a dream—a wish that may be so taboo that it cannot easily be ratified or even acknowledged in waking life. Although subsequent generations of psychoanalysts and other mental health professionals have questioned the validity of Freud's hypothesis, I have always found his insistence on the dream as the expression of an unconscious wish to be a very useful starting point in the complicated and challenging art of dream interpretation.

Reduced to its simplest elements, Deborah's dream draws heavily upon some of the actual imagery of her thwarted weekend with Asher. The couple begin to have sex, Deborah revolts, and she runs into the bathroom. But at this point, the dream veers in a different direction.

Instead of weeping, as she did in real life, Deborah fights back, and instead of sulking, Asher breaks down the bathroom door to gain access to Deborah. As the dream becomes fiery and violent, it seems like a none too thinly veiled disguise for Deborah's secret wish to be penetrated; but then, instead of consummating the relationship, she arms herself with an extremely potent phallic rod (the metal toilet brush), and instead of being the passive woman about to be penetrated, she becomes a more active, almost caricaturedly masculine basher, hitting Asher over the head. She thus becomes the perpetrator, not the victim. Then, she immerses his head in toilet water and flushes until the pipes burst, and eventually Asher becomes covered in urine and feces, and therefore, no doubt, quite foul-smelling—completely shamed and humiliated.

Ingeniously, Deborah's unconscious mind had taken a recent real-life adult situation and turned it on its head. In other words, in the hotel room, she suffered from a deep bodily anxiety that she might be emitting an awful odor and that therefore Asher could not possibly perform cunnilingus on her; but in the dream, Asher becomes the one who smells, and far more dramatically than Deborah ever would have done.

In her dream Deborah has not only succeeded in transforming a recent painful adult experience into one where she feels herself to be the victor, but also managed to incorporate early traumatic childhood ingredients into her internal theatrical drama. By attacking Asher in her dream, she has also generated a successful symbolic attack on the two boys from the school lunchroom and all the other young lads who humiliated her for being smelly. Deborah in this scenario remains clean, untarnished by menstrual blood or foul smells; and Asher, the young man, a symbol for all taunting lads, contains all of the messiness and dirtiness. After all, he planned the "dirty" weekend. Thus, one can proffer the hypothesis that Deborah's dream serves as a brilliant example of Freudian wish-fulfillment wherein Deborah becomes transmogrified into the non-smelly, active perpetrator of violence; Asher, by contrast, becomes the repository of everything rancid and foul. From a wish-fulfillment perspective, Deborah has cunningly managed to become active and clean instead of passive and dirty (as she would have felt herself to be in childhood); additionally, she has succeeded in discharging her hatred and aggression toward boys and men, identifying with the aggressors of her childhood, and thereby giving them a taste of their own medicine.

Though the dream provides some crude fulfillment of a childhood wish and of an interrelated adult wish, it also waves a red flag—a potential danger signal, if you will—for both patient and psychotherapist, warning that some psychological conflict remains as yet unresolved. According to modern psychoanalytical clinicians, the dream becomes the arena in which unresolved psychological difficulties can be fruitfully explored. At this point in her life, Deborah had still not buried the specter of her childhood humiliation or of the shame and feelings of aggression that had followed suit; therefore, the dream became a vehicle through which she could temporarily transform the trauma of her childhood into something that her mind could more successfully manage.

So how does Deborah's dream relate to our more primary interest in sexual fantasy? It demonstrates that by utilizing the mechanisms of dream analysis, we can extrapolate some working principles for understanding the nature of sexual fantasy. After all, sexual fantasies might be described as reverie-like *dreams* that take place while one remains *awake*. Many people masturbate in darkened rooms, often a bedroom, with their eyes closed, in a reclining position; therefore, the physical similarities between one's body during nighttime dreaming and during sexual fantasizing cannot be ignored.

Unfortunately, Deborah never felt sufficiently comfortable to relate her masturbatory fantasies to me during the course of treatment. Sometimes I ask patients directly about their sexual fantasies, but at other times I proceed more diplomatically, waiting until the patient brings such material directly to me. In Deborah's case, I do not know what stimulated her masturbatory routine. Perhaps nowadays, having studied the subject in greater depth, I might have felt more inclined to inquire in a direct manner; but at the time, I did not do so. I strongly suspect, however, that there may be a marked similarity between the content of Deborah's nighttime dreaming life and her waking masturbatory fantasy life. I have come to believe that just as dreams can often help us understand masturbatory and coital sexual fantasies, the analysis of sexual fantasies may be able to assist us in the art of interpreting dreams.

Working psychoanalytically with Deborah taught me very powerfully about the ways in which early experiences can sear themselves into the cortex of the brain and about how the mind must find a creative solution to help alleviate the painful memory of an early humiliation. One of the defense mechanisms that we use—first identified by

Anna Freud—namely, "identification with the aggressor," becomes a clever means of turning our pain into something more pleasurable. By becoming aggressive and sticking Asher's head in the toilet bowl, Deborah used her dream life to make Asher into the smelly one. The early insults and taunts for having dirty hair and unwashed genitalia mortified Deborah, so much so that in one of our sessions of working together, she screamed, "Those boys at school . . . they hurt me so much, *it's like they've scraped out my soul!*"

On Being a Faggot: The Story of Milo

Unlike Deborah, a psychotherapy patient with whom I worked for many years, "Milo" volunteered to talk to me as part of the Sexual Fantasy Research Project. A twenty-nine-year-old gay man from a tiny village, Milo instantly told me that he found his sexual fantasies "quite troubling." Like a great many of the men and women who participated in my clinical research interviews, Milo had two sexual fantasies that brought him continued orgastic release.

Markedly feminine in his manner, Milo looked more like a woman than a man, with long, seemingly tinted eyelashes, pencil-thin eyebrows, which looked impossibly well sculpted, three or four gold rings on his fingers, and a long, silken shirt that trailed down below his knees, reminiscent of the young Boy George. The son of a domineering mother and an absent father, Milo conformed to every stereotype of homosexuality that appeared in mid-twentieth-century clinical psychoanalytical textbooks.

Milo spoke with tremendous frankness and with remarkable composure and fluency; I had the sense that he had narrated his fantasies before, and he had absolutely no trouble at all revealing his favorite sexual fantasies in close detail. He boasted with pride: "There's two, one in which I am active, and in the other, I'm passive." I will now relate Milo's two favorite masturbatory fantasies in his own words:

Both fantasies involve me and a straight boy—any straight boy—and when I say "boy," of course I mean over the age of eighteen. But he's probably not much older. In my "active" fantasy, I'm in a club—a straight club—and I see this cute, cute guy on the other side of the room. I go over to him and buy him a drink. He looks at me pathetically, and knows I'm "bent" as hell, and he pushes

me away. But I'm not gonna be undone by him, so I slip a drug
into his beer which he's drinking from the bottle, and he begins
to get a bit woozy. In this condition, he accepts my invitation to
go back to my place for more beer and to watch straight porn. I
get him back home, and I have him sit on the sofa, and then I
pretend to get us some beers, but instead I come back with duct
tape and rope, and when the boy's not looking, I creep up behind
him, and tie him up real quick-like, and stick a nice piece of tape
across his mouth. Even though he's much bigger than me, he suc-
cumbs, and I have him where I want him. Then I take out a
pocket-knife, and I start to cut off his clothes—I take off his
shoes and socks first, then I rip his jeans, his shirt and finally his
undies. He's completely naked, and he has fear in his eyes, but
I'm laughing. By now the drug has worn off, and he's wide
awake, and he knows exactly what's happening, and that he's
been tricked. I then turn really nasty, and I start slapping him in
the face, and I take a riding crop and start bashing his nipples,
and his penis, and also his balls. He starts crying because he has
no idea how he got into this dreadful situation. But he can't
scream with the tape over his mouth. He tries to get up, but I
smack him on the face real hard, leaving a red mark. Then I get a
video camera, and my computer, and I tell him that I'm about to
humiliate him, and broadcast the whole fucking scene on the Internet, and that I've stolen his address book with all the e-mail
addresses of his friends and family, and that I'm going to send
them to the web-address of this little scene, so that they can all
see that he's not a straight boy after all, he's really a fucking
poof, and he likes being fucked up the arse by a pretty boy. I aim
the camera so that it focuses on his torso, but I am out of shot,
except for my hands and fingers. First I turn on the camera, then
I tweak his tits, and get them really hard so that they're standing
up like sausages. Then I run my finger down his treasure trail
into his pubic region, and then I tug on his dick and I start making disparaging comments about his dick, and say it's pretty pathetic for a straight boy and that there's no way it could ever get
hard enough to fuck a girl. I start to masturbate his penis, and you
can see that he's sweating, turning red, and dripping with sweat
which is falling from his forehead. He's getting pretty close to coming, and I tell him that he can avoid the indignity of spurting off in

front of friends and family. He looks at me pleadingly as if to say, "What do I have to do?" I tell him that I won't toss him off completely if he says a mantra. He looks at me with raised eyebrows. I tell him that the mantra is . . . [Here Milo paused for about fifteen seconds for dramatic effect] . . . the mantra is, "I'm a fucking faggot, and I like cock in my throat and cock in my arse. I'm a fucking faggot, that's what I am." The straight boy nods that he understands what he has to do to avoid getting his spunk all over the camera lens, and so I rip the tape off his mouth real hard, removing some of his stubble in the process. "Say it," I tell him, and so he does, but with a real quiver in his voice: "I'm a fucking faggot, and I like cock in my throat and up my arse." I say, "What are you?" And he says, "I'm a fucking faggot." I tell him he's a good boy, and then, even though he's crying from all the shame, I still tug on his dick until he spurts, and then I wet myself laughing at his pathetic state, tied, covered in spunk, and humiliated in front of all his friends and family on the Internet.

Do you want to know the other fantasy? It's the same as the first, except in the other one, the passive version, it's me who's kidnapped, and spunked off by a straight boy, and he calls me the queer faggot, and all my friends and family see it.

After reciting these two fantasies, both variants of the same theme, Milo paused for breath. I found myself somewhat shocked, not so much by the content of Milo's fantasies, but by his seeming facility at relating these fantasies to a total stranger—and a mental health professional at that—with such straightforwardness, as though I had asked him to name his favorite color or his favorite breakfast cereal.

I asked Milo whether he could reflect on these two fantasies and tell me what he thought about their power over his mind. At this point, the otherwise intelligent, well-educated young man became silent and pensive. He retreated from raconteur mode and suddenly seemed quite bemused. He shrugged his shoulders, announcing, "I don't know . . . I don't know why they're such a powerful turn-on, but it works for me every time. I sometimes get men that I pick up to act this out with me. One guy was pretty rough—a genuine straight boy—who really enjoyed making me squirm." When I pressed him for further understanding, Milo simply shrugged once more, thereby illustrating one of the key principles about sexual fantasy: For something to arouse and excite us in such a potent way, *its origins must be unconscious, and most probably rooted in early traumatic experience.*

I did not have to search far to gain a better understanding of Milo's sexual fantasies. When we came to explore his childhood, he told me in no uncertain terms that his mother had undoubtedly wanted a daughter, not a son, and that she used to let him play with her clothes, or dressed him up in her 1970s miniskirts and 1960s Twiggy-style boots. He became known as a "pretty boy," and all the girls used to love putting makeup on him. In the school plays he would invariably be cast in female roles, garnering local acclaim as a very credible Cleopatra. A prototypical "sissy boy," Milo became living proof of the research of the American-born psychiatrist Richard Green (now working in Great Britain), a specialist in sexual orientation and gender nonconformity research, who has found that the vast majority of boys who later become homosexual men could be characterized as having suffered from the so-called "sissy boy syndrome" in childhood, preferring to play with dolls instead of trains, and so forth.

Although Milo's mother tolerated and encouraged her son's effeminacy, Milo's father became outraged and tried to send him to a psychiatrist. When Milo refused to go, his mother supported her son. The father would tease Milo and speak of him as "my other daughter" (Milo has an older sister). Milo claimed that the family used to find him amusing, but when he related this information to me, I thought I could detect a trace of split-off sadness and disappointment on Milo's face and in his tone of voice.

Milo experienced a real sense of confusion at home, not knowing whether to think of himself as a boy or as a girl. The confusion became intensified at school, when he would spend all of his afternoons playing "house" with the girls instead of running around the playing fields with the other lads. The real torment for Milo occurred, however, on the athletic field. He developed a clinical phobia of balls—quite literally. If he saw a football, or a soccer ball, or even a tennis ball, he would flinch and start to sweat. He told me that he had "disgraced" himself as an athlete and that all the other boys used to shout at him quite regularly, calling him a "faggot" or "fairy," but mostly "faggot." Can it be any wonder, then, that years later, when Milo learned how to masturbate, he would incorporate the malicious, soul-scraping comments (to borrow Deborah's metaphor) into his repertoire of self-stimulation?

In Deborah's dream of sticking Asher's head into the toilet, she managed to make somebody else into the smelly, fecal person. In Milo's sexual fantasy, his mind permitted him to turn an anonymous "straight boy" into the victim. But because the mind keeps very accurate records of our life histories, Milo could not quite manage to forget that before he became the perpetrator, he had spent a good deal of his childhood being tormented himself by the prototypically masculine, heterosexual, gender-confirming boys. And though it seems clear that in Milo's first fantasy he manages to derive orgastic pleasure from treating the "straight boy" like a "faggot," he also has the reverse fantasy, which serves as a more literal reenactment of the actual experiences of heterosexual boys cruelly teasing him in childhood.

How can we understand Milo's sexual fantasy of humiliating another man? Should we characterize it as a sick, bizarre, cruel perversion, laced with sadism and masochism? Or do we approach his movie of the mind in a more compassionate manner, regarding it as an understandable means of trying to master a trauma from many years previously, a trauma that had caused him to question his sense of maleness and his very sense of self, and that had resulted in stinging, scarring shame? Different mental health professionals would adopt different stances on this matter. Frankly, I would position myself somewhere in the middle of these two viewpoints. Although I understand Milo's need to turn somebody else into a "faggot," thus relieving himself of the awful memory of being so insulted, he has, in the process of "faggotizing" someone else, engaged in an act of the type that Anna Freud referred to as identification with the aggressor. She regarded this as one of the classic defense mechanisms of the unconscious mind whereby we avoid psychological pain and a sense of victimization by becoming as cruel as the people who had harmed us originally. In this way, we pass on the abuse to someone else. Now, in real life, Milo treats heterosexual men with kindness and respect; only in his *fantasies* does he torture them. Since he practices cruelty only in his fantasy life, in a sense Milo has become a kinder citizen than the boys who insulted and humiliated him at school. But one wonders, does this sadomasochistic humiliation fantasy have a cost for Milo?

Whatever the potential advantages or disadvantages of Milo's fantasy life, he has certainly managed to take a soul-destroying experience and turn it into a source of sexual pleasure. In doing so, Milo has engaged in a mental strategy that psychotherapists and psychoanalysts would regard as quite normal in people who have endured physical, sexual, or emotional abuse. In our growing body of experience, we find that those who suffer early humiliations will either reenact them by passing the abuse on to somebody else (identification with the aggressor) or reenact the abuse privately, inside their heads, in the form of a sexual fantasy. Although the fantasy can be experienced as both sexually arousing and sexually soothing, it also, on many occasions, can be psychologically disquieting.

I recently read a case history about a male patient undergoing psychotherapy who reported a very similar masturbatory fantasy to Milo's. In 2002, Eric Sherman, a psychoanalyst in New York, published an account of a homosexual man called "Kevin" who would masturbate to a fantasy of tying up a heterosexual male, then calling the man a "faggot," just as Milo had done. As a boy, Kevin suffered similar verbal jeering to that inflicted upon Milo. As Sherman has written in the American clinical journal *Psychoanalytic Dialogues*: "Kevin began dreaming up fantasies of getting even by beating up his tormentors and humiliating them by calling them the same names they called him. In his fantasies, he felt strong, masculine and in control. The weak and feeble boy in the gym was now dissociated and identified as the other—the tied-up adult, the raped child, the helpless one who felt the pain." Over the course of treatment, Sherman also discovered that as a young boy Kevin had suffered sexual abuse at the hands of his stepfather, "Fred," who would force Kevin to perform fellatio. Afterward, Fred would instruct Kevin, "Wash your hands when you get in, so your mother won't smell anything."

Milo and Kevin have much in common. Both men have utilized humiliation fantasies as a mainstay in their masturbatory repertoire as a means of dealing with early slanders and verbal attacks. In Kevin's case, the desire to seek revenge had become compounded by the fact that his stepfather had raped him orally; therefore, the wish to retaliate became quite pronounced in Kevin's personality structure. But we regard such highly aggressive wishes as unacceptable in our culture; to soften them, therefore, we sexualize them—we eroticize them—turning something awful into something pleasurable, something which had once occurred in reality into something safely confined in the prison-house of the mind.

As with most of the fantasists reported in this study, Milo's fantasies function in a double-edged way. He lessened the blows of early shame and humiliation by inflicting the experience on others; though soft-spoken in his day-to-day life—more civilized than the bullies who verbally assaulted him—in his masturbatory routine he becomes as aggressive as the original perpetrators. Like most of us who fantasize, Milo's sexual fantasies bring him bodily pleasure, resolve a psychological conflict, and serve simultaneously as a painful reminder of an early wound.

The Abu Ghraib Syndrome

During the summer of 2004, a series of shocking photographs appeared on the front pages of many of the world's newspapers. They depicted a group of American soldiers, led by the now infamous Lynndie England, humiliating a group of Iraqi prisoners captured during the recent war against the regime of Saddam Hussein. According to press reports, the American soldiers forced the Iraqis to strip naked, to display their bodies, to pose in all sorts of humiliating sexual positions, and to endure other indignities, such as being forced to contravene their Muslim dietary codes. The pictures proved so graphic that many people wondered at the time whether someone had "doctored" them, shocked that the American soldiers appeared to be enjoying such perverse forms of torture. Indeed, one could not escape the sexual element, as millions of people found themselves staring at the photographs of the nude Iraqi men while Lynndie England and her fellow soldiers stood by with contemptuous, triumphant grins on their faces.

At the time, journalists in many countries kept asking in dumbfounded tones: How could such disgusting behavior have occurred? How could well-trained soldiers force other soldiers to remove all their clothing and assume humiliating sexual postures, including feigned anal intercourse and group orgiastic sex? The reporters kept insisting that such behavior could only be described as *unthinkable,* a truly bizarre aberration of conduct that must be immediately investigated and punished.

I must confess that the actions of the American military personnel—though certainly reprehensible—did not surprise me. First of all, innumerable historical precedents of captors treating their prisoners with abominable cruelty litter the pages of our history books. One need only examine the protocol of the Nazis during World War II to remember that when Jewish people and members of other oppressed minority groups first arrived at the concentration camps in Germany, Poland,

Russia, and other parts of Eastern Europe, those not immediately executed would be forced to strip naked, and many would be subjected to invasive and humiliating medical examinations.

Second, I had already studied the transcripts of more than 3,000 British sexual fantasies by the summer of 2004, as part of my pilot computer survey, and the reports from Abu Ghraib did not strike me as that unusual. In fact, I wondered why we had not seen *more* instances of enforced stripping and sexual humiliation in our history books and newspapers, because the events at Abu Ghraib corresponded all too closely with a great many of the sexual fantasies which form a part of this study. Remember, Deborah had dreamed of shoving her boyfriend's head into a toilet overflowing with feces, and Milo had fantasized about forcing a "straight boy" to ejaculate before a video camera connected to the World Wide Web. In Chapter 11, on shame and humiliation—replete with some of the most graphic fantasies contained in this book—many of the respondents reported fantasies of humiliating their imaginary "captives" by stripping them, shaving them, ejaculating on them, and performing other acts of nonconsensual sexual cruelty. The crimes of Lynndie England and her military colleagues may be regarded as a concretization—an *explicitization*—of the very same acts that one can find as a mainstay of ordinary American and British sexual fantasy life. After all, there may not be much difference in terms of content between the behavior of the American soldiers at Abu Ghraib and the fantasy of "Howell," the participant in my research project who imagined himself to be a customs official at Heathrow Airport, just outside of London, degrading illegal Hispanic immigrants trying to enter Great Britain. Of course, Howell's desires seem confined to fantasy, whereas, to the best of our knowledge, Lynndie England and her companions acted out their tendencies. Though there is an enormous difference between fantasy and action, I propose that the roots of sexual acting-out stem first and foremost from previously existing conscious and unconscious fantasy constellations, in other words, scenarios already formed in the mind as a result of early aversive and often traumatic experiences.

Most of the fantasists quoted in Chapter 11 provided anonymous written accounts of their fantasies. I never met Howell, or Immanuel, or Barnaby, and therefore I can only guess at what sorts of childhood experiences they must have endured. On the basis of having encountered similar people in my consulting room over the years, however, I can speculate that they must have suffered shameful experiences them-selves; like Deborah and Milo, they likely had experiences as children that prompted them in adult life to enjoy inflicting humiliation upon someone else or to relive the experience of being humiliated. Fantasiz-ing softens the blow by combining the experience with an orgasm, al-most as a "treat."

When one has suffered from trauma (whether physical, sexual, or psychological), one cannot escape it; tragically, it seems to be one of the great truisms of human psychology that if one has been traumatized, the original trauma will keep seeking expression. A more emotionally robust or resilient person with a greater security of attachment during infancy will, in most cases, be better equipped to deal with a subse-quent trauma than someone with broken attachments, but every sur-vivor of a trauma will feel the impact to a certain extent. Fantasy becomes one of the many arenas in which our traumas keep reappear-ing, reminding us again and again of their devastating impact, often outside of conscious awareness.

When a young person such as Milo suffers sexual taunts and humili-ations, it becomes difficult to repress them entirely; the sexual fantasy provides an outlet in which the individual can attempt to manage the trauma by making the experience more pleasurable. As one of my pa-tients once said to me: "Brett, I live in a mental prison, but while I'm in it, at least I can make sure it's well decorated."

In reading the full-length fantasies on shame and humiliation re-ported in Chapter 11—a small selection of many comparable fantasies in the large data set—one will be immediately struck by the number of homosexual men represented there: Howell, Murdo, Barnaby, Orville, and Tomasso—as well as one self-identified heterosexual man, Edgar, who enjoys the thought of being humiliated homosexually in a prison setting. One wonders whether these gay men had endured humiliating experiences during their earliest developmental years; after all, most of them would have reached sexual maturity at a time before homosexu-ality had become more socially acceptable, long before the introduc-tion of civil partnerships, which became ratified in Great Britain, for example, only in 2005. Sixty-eight-year-old Orville—the former En-glish armed forces conscript who, with his mates "Rog" and "Dennis," would assault and humiliate the new recruits, covering their scrotums with boot black—would have become sexually active long before 1967, the year in which homosexual relations between consenting adult males became legalized in Great Britain. Therefore, many of these men would perhaps have endured similar taunts and calumnies to those Milo had experienced, and possibly worse, being called "fairies," "pansies," "poofs," and a host of other deeply insulting epithets.

As my patient Deborah knew only too well, and as a century of clinical experience has confirmed, the age-old adage about "sticks and stones" may well be untrue. I can think of dozens of patients who have arrived at my consulting room in floods of tears because someone or other had hurled a nasty insult in their direction. These insults damage the burgeoning sense of self, and if one becomes the subject of an insult at a very early, impressionable age, the impact can be very destructive, causing not only deep shame, but, as we have seen in some of the more extended humiliation fantasies, also the desire to retaliate.

According to my research, literally millions of people in the United States of America and Great Britain enjoy masturbating to stories of shame and humiliation. In real life, we would be devastated if someone humiliated us in a public forum, so why should scenes of humiliation arouse us in our private fantasies? Why do we not simply dream about nice, sweet, simple sexual scenarios of making love to our regular partners? And whence do these fantasies of bodily exposure and bodily humiliation originate? Surely not everyone with a humiliation fantasy has endured vicious name-calling in childhood or adolescence?

In reading and rereading these fantasies of humiliation, I became struck by two particular observations:

1. A large number of the fantasies involve body parts being forcibly displayed.
2. A large number of the fantasies depict the body as dirty or smelly in some way.

Let us examine each of these features in turn.

In Howell's fantasy of embarrassing the illegal Hispanic immigrants, he forced them to "Strip. Now." Further, he inspected their bodies with eyes that penetrated "like lasers." Immanuel, the chief executive of a large corporation, threatened his unwitting female employee and forced her to remove her clothing in order to keep her job. He saved the last item of clothing, her panties, for himself, and eventually she stood in front of him "completely bare, the way I like it," while he remained fully clothed. Murdo, the middle-aged welder, performed a similar routine on his sixteen-year-old apprentice, Scott; while Barnaby, the retired policeman, theoretically hoping to prevent a young twenty-one-year-old criminal from strangling himself with his underwear, insisted that this young man surrender his boxers. Orville, the army officer, stripped his vulnerable new recruit; Mariangela, the young woman confined to a wheelchair, fantasized about her many physicians undressing themselves so that she would not be the only naked person in the room. By contrast, the three remaining fantasists in this collection, Edgar, Prakash, and Tomasso, did not strip anyone else; instead, they became aroused when others required them to strip or to be stripped. Edgar, a self-proclaimed heterosexual man, received a thorough examination from the prison guard, ostensibly searching him for drugs, while Prakash and Tomasso endured stripping punishments at the hands of young women, Prakash having to undress and masturbate in front of a group of women, and Tomasso—along with his friends Billy and Jake—being chained to the wall of a prison, urinating upon themselves, and having metal rods inserted into their urethras, their clothes being removed in the process.

The fantasy of being stripped and having one's body examined serves several interrelated psychological functions. By masturbating to thoughts of being stripped and examined, the eight men and one woman in this cohort engage in an act of exhibitionism. Most normal boys enjoy running around naked at some point during their early development (at ages two, three, or four), displaying their genitals. At this age, the so-called "pre-oedipal" period of psychosexual development, little boys become enamored of the penis, of its impressive ability to discharge urine, and of its difference from the genitals of little girls. Child mental health professionals might even express concern should the boy refrain from such activities, as this might indicate a great sense of shame about the body and about masculinity. But if boys grow older, past puberty, and *continue* to flash their genitals in public, this could be classified as an act of male genital exhibitionism, the most commonly diagnosed and perpetrated of sexual offenses. In my clinical experience, genital exhibitionists suffer from a deep sense of castration anxiety (a fear of losing their penises) and from a sense of feeling unimportant in the world (as though no one has noticed them or taken them seriously). By exhibiting their genitals, these men often attempt to induce unsuspecting bystanders to stop and stare and then to expostulate: "Goodness what a large penis you have! What a big, tough, phallic man you are."

Of course, girls also enjoy running around naked during early childhood. But according to classical Freudian psychologists, this exhibitionistic behavior becomes increasingly less prominent as the years unfold. Interestingly, very few women engage in acts of public genital exhibitionism—virtually all those arrested for the offense are males.

By exposing the genitals exhibitionistically, whether in fact or in fantasy, these men, in particular, manage to convey, both to themselves and to others, that not only do they have a penis, as opposed to a vagina—in other words, they really are boys, not girls, as they often fear, especially if taunted about their masculinity in early childhood—but also that the penis has survived any threats or attacks. Thus, these fantasies assist them in feeling potent, either because they succeed in taking charge of another man's genitals or because they are able to demonstrate that they have very visible penises themselves which others might enjoy examining in detail.

Additionally, exhibitionistic fantasies containing elements of humiliation serve as a secret, unconscious means of reversing what I suspect might well be a series of early episodes of bodily humiliation of some kind. By revisiting an infantile or childhood experience of humiliation, and by attaching a masturbatory or coital orgasm to the experience, the fantasists in question render something once painful into something now pleasurable. Thus, pain becomes pleasure, and the threat of castration becomes the thrill of exhibition.

But these fantasies also serve another purpose. As I indicated earlier, many of them involve dirtiness and bodily odors. For instance, in Howell's fantasy, he has insisted that the illegal Hispanics remove their clothing, only to discover that they are "greasy" and sweating like "filthy pigs," and therefore he decides they must have their buttocks spread open and disinfected and their penises cleansed of any smegma. But curiously, once he has had the Hispanic men disinfected, Howell forces them to urinate, to defecate into a "shit-filled bucket," and then to remove their pubic hair so that they will more closely resemble prepubescent children.

I suspect that, without knowing it, Howell has found himself trying to come to terms with early experiences of toilet training, of childhood soiling or incontinence, and of being proclaimed dirty or smelly by his mother or some other caretaker. The average human infant will soil at least six nappies per day, so we often forget that as infants all of us spent a great deal of time being stripped of our diapers, and having our buttocks and genital regions inspected and then washed, only to soil ourselves again after another feed. This constant cycle of having a grown-up remove our clothing, without our permission, to check our bodies for urine and feces, examine our diapers, and then clean our intimate bodily cavities may produce a combination of pleasure and a sense of invasion for the human infant—pleasure because of the joy of being cleaned and tended, but invasion if the mother, father, or caretaker engages in the diaper-changing ritual with resentment, disgust, or gruff gestures that might cause the infant discomfort.

When Howell arranged for the Hispanics in his fantasy to be stripped and disinfected, only to become soiled once again, he had unwittingly restaged the ordinary toilet-training battleground of every baby. And when Howell concluded his fantasy, confessing, "I would love to be strip-searched, with someone invading each body cavity," he managed to give away the·game, secretly admitting that although he had enjoyed performing this stripping ritual on someone else, he remembered both the joy and the potential humiliation of the time when his mother or father would have done this to him. Perhaps Howell's mother washed his penis or his rectum overzealously during toilet training, and perhaps these sorts of experiences contributed to his eroticization of the bathing, disinfecting, and soiling processes which then became such a mainstay of his fantasies.

As with all the fantasies contained within this study, it would be foolish to suggest that one *single* early childhood experience would cause us to have a particular fantasy in later life; however, I do wish to propose that early infantile and childhood ingredients serve as necessary *preconditions* for the establishment of later fantasy patterns. With reference to the specific fantasies concerning humiliation and shame, I would argue that they assist us with the *mastery* of early experiences of shame, whether due to invasive toileting or to insults and assaults on our sense of bodily cleanliness, integrity, or potency. A small child whose mother cleans his anus in a rough manner, and who, later on, becomes the subject of jeers and taunts at school, may become vulnerable to the eventual development of fantasies of either being humiliated in adult life or causing someone else to be humiliated. Often, the fantasist will *alternate* between a fantasy of being humiliated and causing humiliation, struggling mightily with the feelings of aggression that always ensue when one has become the victim of bodily shaming and other forms of early traumatization.

Although we like to imagine ourselves as the architects of our own fate, choosing our own life paths and our own erotic preferences, my research has led me to the conclusion that large numbers of people do not command their own sexual minds. Rather, sexual preferences and sexual fantasies become forged by early impressions, often as a result of shame, of humiliation, and, as we shall now discover, of sexual trauma.

18   Case History: Paris and the Ginger Pubic Hair

Each had his past shut in him like the leaves of a book known to him by heart; and his friends could only read the title.
— VIRGINIA WOOLF, *Jacob's Room*

The Man with the Razor Blade and the Shaving Cream

"Paris," a forty-nine-year-old male nurse, boarded a train to London in order to participate in the International Sexual Fantasy Research Project. A slender man with a shock of white, wavy hair, Paris bounced into the interview room and wasted little time in telling me his favorite sexual fantasy. In fact, before he had even settled down on the sofa, he stressed, "I really have only *one* favorite sexual fantasy, and I have it every time I do the business, you know, every time I jerk off. Do you want to hear it?"

As I have already noted, in the course of my clinical interviews I would invariably spend the first four hours talking about the interviewee's current life, infancy, and childhood, and additionally, I would take a full family history. Afterward, I would ask for details of sexual behaviors. Then, and only then, would I tentatively raise the more private, more delicate subject of sexual fantasy, asking softly whether the person seated opposite would feel comfortable describing a preferred sexual fantasy used either during masturbation or during intercourse with a partner. But Paris subverted my usual interviewing process. In fact, he could hardly wait to share his fantasy with me. I nodded my assent that he would be more than welcome to describe his favorite fantasy. He began:

Well, it's pretty easy to describe. It's the same one I've been having ever since I began wanking off, which must have been when I was about fourteen, fifteen, something like that. Here goes: I'm gay, you see, so it's a gay fantasy. I'm tied to a bed, it's an ordinary bed, in a darkened room, I don't know where, and somebody has cuffed my hands over my head, and tied me to the bedposts, spread-eagled like, you know? Anyway, there I am, tied to the posts of this bed in this dark room, and for some curious reason, I'm wearing a T-shirt which is quite sweaty, but I have nothing on the lower part of my body, no trousers, no pants, nothing. So I'm feeling pretty vulnerable, pretty exposed, but also pretty excited, 'cause my penis is on display. Suddenly, this man comes in, he's a big man, but I don't know who it is because it's dark and I can't see his face. This strange man comes up to the side of the bed, and he's carrying a razor blade and some shaving foam. He surprises me 'cause he squirts the shaving foam all around my pubes—my pubic hair—and then he rubs it in, and I am getting turned on from all this. He puts even more shaving foam on my bush, and then he takes the razor, and with, you know, up-and-down strokes, he removes all my pubic hair, every last wiry whisker, until I am shaved clean down below. Then, the man puts the foam and the razor down, and he starts tugging on his own dick, which is pretty massive, and he starts wanking while hovering over me, and I am still chained up to the bed— just my hands are chained, by the way, my feet are kept free for some reason. Anyway, he keeps wanking, and wanking, and I can see his dick getting more and more stiff, and then presto, he shoots a big wad of cum all over my chest—a big puddle of cum, and then he just turns around and disappears. This gets me so horny, that as I'm wanking, this is the moment when I go over the edge, and I squirt my own load, and I shoot buckets of cum on my chest. It's really arousing, and it does it for me every time. Well, that's the fantasy. Is that the sort of thing you wanted?

Paris surprised me with his exceptional frankness. Most of the people that I interviewed, both before and since, needed at least four hours of preparatory conversation before they felt sufficiently comfortable to talk to me about their private sexual fantasies, but Paris launched in with no restraint. In fact, I had the impression that he could not wait to tell me the fantasy, possibly out of nervousness, possibly out of a wish to shock, possibly as a result of his deep comfort with the fantasy, or even as a result of his deep *discomfort* with the fantasy. I could not be certain. In any case, at this point in the interview I became increasingly intrigued by Paris's fantasy, wondering why—out of all the possible erotic scenarios that one could sculpt in one's mind—Paris chose to masturbate to this particular internal movie of being chained to the bed, shaved, and masturbated upon by a strange man.

I explained to Paris that I very much appreciated his candor in relating his fantasy to me so fully. I asked him whether he had any sense of why this fantasy, especially, might arouse him? He looked at me with a vacant expression, responding, "Well, it just does." I told him that other gay men in the interview sample had fantasies about the football (soccer) hero David Beckham or about any number of Hollywood heartthrobs, and I asked whether thoughts of any of these so-called "gay icons" stimulated him sexually in any way. Paris giggled, "I suppose I wouldn't throw Beckham out of bed, but to be truthful, I never think about that obvious sort of stuff when I'm masturbating; it would really leave me cold. In fact, I never think about hot guys I might see on the street or in the clubs. No, it's just the shaving fantasy, and the fantasy of this man wanking over me. I can't explain it, but that's the fantasy. If I tried wanking over Beckham, I think my prick would be limp."

An ordinary-looking man with a careworn face, Paris explained to me that as a nursing professional he participated in a variety of scientific studies because it pleased him to know that by donating blood, or testing experimental drugs, or talking to a behavioral researcher, he would be making some small contribution to the furtherance of human knowledge. He spoke with intelligence and sincerity, and he impressed me with his honesty. He then asked whether I wanted to know anything more, inquiring if he had already provided me with all the necessary information. I then chuckled, albeit silently and internally, and glanced at my watch—only ten minutes of the interview had elapsed, and I knew that we had barely begun. I explained that in order to understand his fantasy better, I would want to ask him some questions about his current life, about his childhood, and about his sexual biography. He rubbed his hands eagerly and said, "Ready when you are."

I asked Paris to describe his current life to me in as much detail as he possibly could, requesting that he do his best to paint a picture for me of his daily activities. Paris readily launched into a coherent narrative, offering a thoughtful depiction of his current life situation. Within minutes I learned that Paris lived in a small rent-controlled apartment, which he shared with two Siamese cats. Until recently, he had lived in a very large house in the countryside with "Angelo," his boyfriend of twenty-eight years; but sadly, only eighteen months previously, Angelo had unceremoniously dumped him, "trading" him in for a younger man—a seventeen-year-old male model. Angelo's rejection caused Paris great heartbreak; he quickly put on more than twenty-five pounds in the immediate aftermath of the breakup, gorging himself on cakes, pies, cookies, and other "comfort food" in a desperate attempt to compensate for his emotional depletion. His nursing work at the local hospital had proved a great source of respite from his domestic agonies. Paris explained that he had thrown himself into his job with increasing gusto, so much so that the head of nursing had recently offered him both a promotion and a substantial raise in salary. Paris also told me about his best friends, a hairdresser called "Blaise" and a fellow nurse called "Jackie," who had become something of a surrogate family. He spoke of his passion for his patients and for his hobbies, which included needlework and salsa dancing. All in all, Paris impressed me as a caring, intelligent, and morally upright person, soldiering on bravely and creatively after a traumatic breakup.

I then asked Paris to discuss his infancy and his childhood in as much detail as possible. He claimed that he had had a very normal, ordinary childhood, and that nothing remarkable had ever really happened. He explained that he loved his mother and his father very much, and that he remembered his growing-up years with great fondness. An only child, he did well at school, and he had lovely birthday parties; although he hated sports, he did excel in arts and crafts, and this compensated for his inability to catch a ball.

As a psychotherapist, I know full well that when people narrate their biographies, they often do so in a very idealized manner, smoothing out the rough edges of their histories, or even avoiding the problem areas completely; and though I believed Paris's account of his childhood, I also harbored a mild suspicion that he had neglected to tell me some of the more vulnerable and painful incidents in his life. After listening to Paris's recitation, I started to ask some probing questions. I inquired about the early lives of his parents, about his grandparents, about his early feeding—breast or bottle—and toilet training, and about a whole host of other areas of interest to the Freudian psychotherapist. Paris knew very little about his formative years, displaying what we refer to as the characteristic *infantile amnesia* for events taking place prior to the age of five or thereabouts. Although I listened to each interviewee with rapt attention, concentrating on every single detail of the narrative, I found myself becoming slightly drowsy with Paris. As a psychotherapist, one becomes drowsy for one of two reasons: Either one has had insufficient sleep the night before; or, more likely, the patient may be struggling to communicate something painful or traumatic, but he or she has not yet succeeded in finding the words for this experience, and in order to keep the hurtful memories at bay, the patient actually becomes *boring* in his or her interpersonal style—almost as if in a desperate attempt to make the psychotherapist fall asleep so that the painful experience cannot be shared.

On this occasion, I knew that I had enjoyed a good night's sleep before meeting Paris, and besides, I had had no symptoms of drowsiness earlier in the day, or during the recitation of Paris's masturbatory fantasy. The tiredness became apparent only when he had begun to talk about his childhood. I found myself aware of the rich, almost filmic, quality of his narration of the masturbatory fantasy compared to the rather bleak, undetailed, almost arid narration of his childhood. Psychotherapists will always be on the lookout for stylistic changes in our patients' speech patterns throughout the course of a therapeutic session. I began to formulate the hypothesis that something traumatic might well have happened to Paris in his childhood that could not easily be translated into words; and that as a result of this psychological blockage or repression, Paris had become anesthetized, numbed, unable to speak on the subject with his ordinary fluency. He had become boring not only as a means of avoiding talking about something, but as a way of calling my attention to this area of his history, in the secret hope that I might help him to explore this material further.

I have worked clinically for many years with men and women who have suffered physical or sexual abuse (and often both types) in childhood; and I have found, as I have already indicated, that patients with such a history will often respond in a vague, idealized way to inquiries about childhood memories: "Oh, my childhood was pretty normal, really," or "Standard stuff, you know, standard." Such descriptions have a defensive quality and reveal very little by way of formal information; they do, however, illuminate a great deal else. Through the rationalization, the patient recreates a tense emotional atmosphere in the consulting room. Why did the verbally dextrous Paris tell me so much about his masturbatory fantasy, so quickly, and yet so little about his childhood? Did he suddenly lose his linguistic abilities? That seems most unlikely. And why had I started to become somewhat bored? In order to unravel this conundrum, I would need to investigate further.

Sherlock Holmes Meets Sigmund Freud

Eager to discover the hidden origins of Paris's particular masturbatory fantasy, I asked him whether he could tell me something about his parents' marriage. I wondered: Did his mother and father have a happy marriage, and did Paris ever see his parents engaging in physical intimacies such as cuddling or kissing? Paris replied that he came from a strict family, and that he could not remember any caressing or canoodling in his family home. I commented that as an only child, Paris must have wondered why his parents had no other children, and I asked whether he knew the reason. He looked shocked, as though this thought had never crossed his mind: "I don't know, I guess *I* was so fantastic that they thought it would be redundant to have another child." My psychotherapeutic antennae bristled with suspicion, and I found myself hypothesizing that somehow the question of parental sexuality proved far too taboo a topic in Paris's family. My inquiry had prompted him to seize upon a rather grandiose and unlikely explanation for his parents' lack of physical contact—his theory that "*I* was so fantastic," and that therefore his parents would have had no need for any more intercourse.

I then moved on to the topic of "discipline." In my experience of interviewing patients over the years, I have found that if I ask whether any "abuse" took place during childhood, I will often be met with defensive denials and idealized responses: "Oh, no, none of that in our family." But I have discovered that if I use a less inflammatory word, such as "discipline," patients will more readily reveal stories of being beaten with belts or slippers, smacked on the face, and punished in all sorts of cruel ways. Clearly, the human mind finds it easier to tolerate the notion that our parents "disciplined" us than to acknowledge that they might have "abused" us.

After I gently inquired about "discipline," Paris became much more lively. He could certainly relate to this concept, and he told me, almost with glee, that his father used to "whack" him all the time, with both a belt and a slipper, because "I was a cheeky bugger, and I probably deserved it." Once again, I wondered why Paris called himself a "cheeky bugger," a phrase so resonant of homosexuality. Why had he not elected to call himself a "rascal," a "naughty boy," a "rebel," a "tearaway," or any number of other such monikers? What prompted him to construct a self-identity based on the notion of being a "cheeky bugger"?

Bit by bit, a more convincing picture began to emerge of Paris's family home. As the next hour unfolded, I realized that Paris's initial description of having had a pretty ordinary, normal, uneventful childhood could no longer be sustained. As our conversation progressed, he revealed that he had grown up in a much more desolate family environment than he had previously described, characterized by a lack of physical warmth between his parents and by frequent physical beatings at the hands of his father. Paris then confessed that he did wonder whether his mother might once have had an extramarital affair with a handsome next-door neighbor called "Roger," because her face always lit up whenever Roger and his wife, "Jessica," popped in for drinks.

As the clinical interview continued, I asked myself a number of inter-related questions about Paris's parents and about their marriage:

1. Why did the couple have only one child? Perhaps they had financial difficulties, or perhaps they had a wish to keep the world's population down; but then again, perhaps the sexual component of their marriage had begun to wither.
2. If the marriage had become increasingly loveless, as indicated by the lack of physical contact between mother and father, would either of Paris's parents have had an extramarital affair, either in a fully consummated way, or in a psychological manner (through fantasy, for example)? I certainly shared Paris's concern about the possibility of an affair, especially between his mother and the family's neighbor Roger.

3. And if Paris's mother did find herself sexually attracted to the next-door neighbor, did Paris's father also have an erotic interest in someone other than his spouse? And if so, *in whom*?

With these musings guiding my line of thought, I continued to investigate further aspects of Paris's early life. I wondered what sort of relationship Paris had nowadays with his parents, both octogenarians, still alive. He explained that he telephones his mother once each month just to check up on her health, but that his father never picks up the phone, and so Paris never speaks to him. Once again, my antennae began to twitch, and I inquired why Paris did not go for visits, and why he restricted himself to monthly telephone conversations with his mother. Did he not want to talk to his father as well? Paris replied, "My dad and I haven't been getting on so well. This is nothing new." I asked when he felt that his relationship with his father had begun to sour. "Oh," he responded, "it's always been that way. I'm used to it by now." I stared at Paris and told him that in view of the beatings that his father had inflicted upon him, it did not surprise me that he felt such bitterness. I then asked, "Did anything else ever happen to you as a child? Any other forms of cruelty of any kind?"

Paris shook his head resolutely, but then, after a long, reflective pause, lowered his head and closed his eyes. He then revealed that something else had happened during his childhood—a very unusual episode which had occurred only once. Paris recalled that at the age of nine years, he used to sleep on the top level of a bunk bed. On one particular summer evening, his mother had gone out, possibly to meet Roger, the neighbor; therefore, the father had full responsibility for Paris. Owing to the heat, Paris could not sleep, and so, dressed in his pajamas, he stepped off his bunk bed and padded into the living room, where he found his father dozing in front of the television. Paris woke his father, complaining that he could not fall asleep. Paris's father promptly lifted him up, carried him back into his room, and then, most unusually, climbed into the bunk as well, lying down next to his son in the cramped confines of the child's bed.

Paris thought this a bit unusual, but his dad explained that he would lie there until Paris fell asleep. Paris then started to moan, "But Dad, it's still so hot, I'm having trouble breathing," whereupon his father instructed him, "Well in that case, son, you'd better take off your pajama bottoms." This seemed a very strange instruction—should he not take his top off as well? But, unquestioningly, the nine-year-old boy removed his pajama trousers, thus exposing the lower half of his body. Then, squashed in a small bed with a very large man, Paris complained that he did not have enough room. His father tried to allay his discomfort by suggesting, "Oh, well, I'll take off my bottoms as well, then we'll have more room in the bed." He removed his trousers and his underpants, keeping his shirt on, his torso remaining thereby covered up.

As Paris continued to tell me this story, his eyes became quite moist, and I realized that he had probably never spoken about this episode from childhood to another living soul. I smiled gently at him, remaining quite silent, trying to offer some nonverbal communication to him that I appreciated his difficulty in relating this piece of childhood history.

"Then," said Paris, "something else happened." I nodded my head very slightly, conveying my willingness to hear more. "Well," Paris whispered, "he started to rub himself, you know . . . rub his cock . . . up against mine. It was all big and hard and hairy, and to be frank . . . quite scary. Next thing I know, he grabbed my hand and guided it to his cock, and then, well, after a while, with all the rubbing, he ejaculated all over my chest. He took my pajama bottoms, wiped up all the stuff, and then patted me on the head and told me to go to sleep. He got out of the bunk, grabbed his boxers and his trousers, and then he went back to the sitting room." At this point, Paris started to cry—not great floods of tears, but a small trickle. The atmosphere in the office became very charged, almost electrically intense, as I sat across from Paris, feeling very moved and very concerned.

"Gosh, I've never told anybody about that," he muttered, reaching for a tissue from the nearby box. He explained, "It's not that I didn't know that this happened. I do think about it from time to time, but only occasionally, and I haven't thought about it for years." After reaching for yet another tissue to mop up the increasing stream of tears, Paris looked at me and giggled, "Jeez, I hadn't thought I'd be talking about this today. When I came here, I thought I was just gonna tell you about my sexual fantasy and that that would be that. Instead, I'm having a whole bloody psychoanalysis today. It feels good, though. Maybe I needed to talk about this." I remained quiet, waiting to see what Paris most wanted to talk about at that point. He continued, looking at me with a professorial stare, "I know what you're thinking." "Oh?" I replied quizzically. "Yeah," he chimed, in quite a smug manner. "You're thinking that this incident with my father is what made me gay. Well, it isn't, 'cause I think I've been gay since I was at least six or seven. I've always known that I've fancied blokes, other boys at school, boys in pop bands, so I don't think this incident had any effect really."

Any mental health professional worth his or her salt will realize that it becomes both pointless and cruel to contradict a patient or client in the first interview. By doing so, one would confirm the patient's worst fears that the psychotherapist really will be an invasive, intrusive, omniscient wizard who can "read" the patient's mind like magic, claiming to know more about the patient than the patient knows about himself or herself. In truth, in spite of pronouncements from numerous colleagues in the fields of psychology and sexology who claim to know the real truth about the origins of homosexuality and heterosexuality, those of us in the psychotherapeutic field, by contrast, suspect that there can be many different types and degrees of sexual orientation, and that it seems unlikely that one's sexual orientation might be caused by a single gene or a single traumatic childhood experience. I have met many men in consultation who have had abusive experiences similar to the incident that occurred between Paris and his father, and yet many of them have become predominantly heterosexual in their adult lives.

Bearing all of this uncertainty in mind, I simply replied to Paris, "Well, I think it's very important that you've been able to tell me this story. It seems that it may be something that's been festering inside of you for quite some time, and I think your tears may represent some relief at having finally been able to share this story with someone." I continued, "I think that if we are really honest, we don't actually know what impact this incident has had upon you or upon the development of your sexual orientation. And I suspect that you too may be unsure what effect it may have had, and that might be the reason why you wanted to share this today with a psychotherapist. Perhaps in coming here you not only wanted to participate in this research project, but it may be that you also saw this as an opportunity to make contact with a therapist so that this story could be verbalized, perhaps for the first time."

Paris looked at me and confessed, "Yes, it is the first time. I never even told this to Angelo, and we were together for twenty-eight years." I asked Paris, "You're forty-nine years old, if I remember correctly?" "Yes, that's right," he replied. "And Angelo is how old?" I wondered. "Oh, let me see, he must be, yes, he would be sixty-six now. He's quite a bit older," said Paris, hanging his head, as though he had uttered something shameful. Anticipating his anxiety, I shared a thought with him: "You're wondering whether I think Angelo had been your father-substitute since he is so much older than you." "Well," Paris remarked, "that's how you shrink-types think, isn't it? But it's something that I've often wondered, and anyway, Angelo does seem to like his men on the young side."

I did not wish to bombard Paris with a barrage of psychoanalytical interpretations about the development of his sexual orientation or his sexual fantasies in the context of a single research-oriented interview. I knew that in all likelihood I would not see Paris again, and I did not wish to open up a whole set of psychological polemics that we would not be able to follow through in sufficient depth. But Paris had indeed anticipated my line of thinking. I did, in fact, wonder, quite seriously, whether his attraction to a much older man might have resulted from the erotic pleasure and fear generated by the physical closeness that he had experienced that night in his bunk bed. Throughout my career, I have encountered a small number of gay men who have sought considerably older male partners; similarly, I have met quite a large number of young women in my psychotherapeutic practice who have also sought much older male partners, and in a great many of these instances some sort of sexual abuse had taken place in childhood. Somehow, the attraction to the older partner serves as a reminder that sex can and does take place across the generational divide, and can also serve as an indication that one desperately hopes to find a new incarnation of an older person who might be more loving and more respectful. I must stress, of course, that I am speaking here about cases encountered exclusively in a clinical psychotherapeutic setting. I strongly suspect that Paris's attraction to Angelo may, perhaps, have represented in part an attempt to work through some of the complex feelings toward his sexually abusive father.

And what about Paris's sexual fantasy? Well, one need be neither a detective nor a psychologist to divine the strong interrelationship between Paris's detailed central masturbatory fantasy and his traumatic experience of sexual abuse in his bunk bed, which involved his father ejaculating upon him. In fact, the correspondences between the ingredients of the fantasy and the details of the traumatic scene become so strong that one would be hard pressed to offer a compelling alternative explanation about the specific content of Paris's fantasy.

To recapitulate, in Paris's favorite masturbatory fantasy, he finds himself in a bed, with his hands tied to the bedposts, and with his trousers removed. Curiously, he still keeps his shirt on, even though most sexual scenes end in complete nudity. Then, a strange man whose face cannot easily be identified enters, shaves Paris's pubic hair, ejaculates over Paris's body, and promptly departs.

Extraordinarily, virtually every detail from Paris's masturbatory fantasy can be traced back to an aspect of that primal night of sexual trauma from the age of nine. In his fantasy, Paris finds himself trapped on a bed with his trousers down, but still wearing his shirt. Obviously, this becomes an absolutely point-for-point repetition of the original abuse experience with his father. Further, in the fantasy, Paris cannot see the face of the man who restrains him, shaves him, and ejaculates upon him. This mirrors his own inability to see his real father's face in his darkened bedroom; additionally, the height differences between Paris's nine-year-old body and that of his tall father would have made it difficult for Paris to see anything other than the lower portion of his father's body while curled up next to his father in the cramped space. Also, the man in the fantasy reaches climax and spills his semen over Paris's body, just as the father had done. In real life, Paris's father had cajoled the boy into masturbating his large penis, whereas in the fantasy, Paris has his hands tied, and therefore cannot do that. He no doubt felt that his father had forced him to touch his father's penis, thereby stimulating a feeling that somehow Paris's hands had become tied. In the masturbatory fantasy, the childhood experience of having his hand clutched and restrained by his father becomes even more explicit, with rope to tie Paris's hands to the bedposts. As a nine-year-old boy, he had virtually no choice in the matter, and when his father had positioned Paris's hand on the grown man's genitals, the boy had to oblige. Of course, in the fantasy, Paris would simply not be able to masturbate the father/stranger, owing to the handcuffs on his wrists; thus in fantasy, Paris has fully protected himself from recreating the experience of being forced to masturbate an older man.

I did wonder about the important detail involving the application of shaving cream to Paris's pubic region, and the subsequent shaving of his pubic hair. Paris's father had not shaved his son on the evening in question; but then, a nine-year-old boy would not yet have become pubescent. Perhaps Paris has introduced this additional piece of fantasy material as a means of ensuring that in his fantasy, the stranger shaves him in order to transform Paris's hair-covered genitalia into something smoother, and hence more prepubescent. By analyzing this detail of the fantasy, we can better understand that sexual fantasies, though often exact repetitions of an earlier scene of trauma, sometimes become transformed, with new ingredients added for the primary purpose of better replicating the original scene. If Paris did not have his pubic hair removed, it would prove to be more difficult for him to imagine himself as a little boy being subjected to an unusual and unexpected scene of sexual contact. Thus, sometimes the fantasy will be transformed to replicate the original trauma in an exact fashion; at other times, the fantasy will become elaborated to increase the amount of pleasure or safety.

As I listened to Paris's story, and as I began to formulate some of these interpretive hypotheses within my own mind, I suddenly found myself staring at Paris's thick crop of wavy white hair. I began to wonder what color hair Paris would have had during his younger years, before it had turned white. Sometimes, in the course of clinical interviewing, the mind of the psychotherapist will wander down a seemingly unexpected path; but my colleagues and I take every detail very seriously, and we have discovered that when we do have a seemingly irrelevant thought, it may well bear fruit and provide us with further essential information. At this point, I took a calculated gamble, and I asked Paris quite innocently what color hair he had during his younger years. "Ginger," he replied, with a sour look on his face. "I had bright reddish, ginger hair, which I *hated*."

Personally, I have never quite understood why so many children—especially British children—with ginger hair become the objects of taunting on the school playground, and why comedians regularly regale their audiences with jokes about ginger-haired people. I suppose that, owing to the rarity of ginger hair, there may be some envy; furthermore, I know that we as human beings find it very difficult to tolerate difference, whether religious, political, sexual, or otherwise. With this in mind, I asked Paris whether he had difficulties at school as a result of having ginger hair, and he told me that indeed, the other boys would taunt him, calling him not only "poof" and "fairy," having demonstrated signs of effeminacy, but ridiculing him about his coloring as well, calling him "ginger faggot" and other cruel names. In younger years, Paris's schoolmates teased him about the ginger hair on his head, and later, during early adolescence, they laughed at his ginger pubic hair while in the showers after sports.

I felt grateful at this moment that I had trusted my intuition and asked a potentially irrelevant question. After learning of Paris's once ginger hair and of the cruel verbal abuse that he had suffered as a result, I understood more fully his unconscious reasons for including a scene of pubic depilation in his primary masturbatory sexual fantasy. By having the stranger eradicate the hair around his pubic region, Paris managed to accomplish two interrelated psychological tasks:

1. He succeeded in recreating his prepubescent body, devoid of pubic hair, as a means of both reliving the early scene of sexual abuse with his father and changing the father into an adult stranger, thereby minimizing the impact of the early intrafamilial molestation.
2. He allowed the stranger to shave him, thus removing the offending ginger pubic hair which had caused him to be taunted on the playground and later in the school showers.

Through an analysis of Paris's repetitive sexual fantasy, we can see a number of key principles in operation:

1. Sexual fantasies in adulthood often stem from earlier experiences.
2. Certain elements of the adult sexual fantasy may be direct repetitions of actual events in childhood.
3. Other elements of the adult sexual fantasy may be based on aspects of actual events in childhood, which we then *incorporate, disguise,* and *transform.*
4. Sexual fantasies allow us to change painful childhood experiences into pleasurable adult masturbatory or coital experiences.
5. Sexual fantasies depend upon wish-fulfillment, in that the fantasies allow us to reduce psychological distress through the act of eroticization.

I do not wish to imply at this point that every single adult sexual fantasy can be traced back to an originary sexual trauma, or that one single episode of sexual abuse will then become the sufficient basis for a later repetitive sexual fantasy. After all, Paris must have had other experiences in childhood that could have served as the basis for his primary sexual fantasy. But why did his unconscious mind choose this one to transform and repeat?

One must remember that an analysis of the sexual fantasy should never be reduced in a crude way to just one single moment of biography. There may well be many other people who experienced an act of enforced parental masturbation as children, but whose sexual fantasy life in adulthood contains not a trace of that experience. Some adults will repress these sorts of experiences entirely, whereas others will utilize quite different sorts of early events as the bases for their fantasies. And not all individuals will be affected in quite the same way by the same trauma. Some children will be more resilient by virtue of having greater parental or grandparental support. Furthermore, some of us will never have experienced gross abuse or molestation, and will have enjoyed safer treatment at the hands of our parents; therefore, our sexual fantasies may not be as overtly conflict-laden. We shall return to these points of difference in subsequent chapters.

Because Paris had both an abusive father and a neglectful mother, who was busy with her ostensible, if not probable, extramarital affair, I suspect that the impact of his early molestation by his father could not be diluted or contained in any way. He had no steady model of a parent who could soften the blow; therefore, his mind came to his rescue by helping him to process the early experience, making it the basis of something orgasmically pleasurable. His attraction to older men such as Angelo may have stemmed from his wish to find a better version of a father, with whom he could have sex in a more age-appropriate fashion.

Does Paris have a healthy sexual fantasy life? If a patient visited a psychotherapist and announced, "I masturbate about being shaved and then ejaculated upon while tied to a bed," how might the psychotherapist react? Should the therapist encourage such a fantasy? Call the local psychiatric hospital? Express concern? Adopt a "whatever-turns-you-on" policy? Or would we endeavor to understand the meaning of the fantasy, without reaching any rapid conclusions about its health or illness?

When a patient relates a private sexual fantasy to me in the course of a psychotherapeutic session, I try to remain as neutral as possible, neither encouraging nor discouraging the fantasy, *and* I refrain from adopting an attitude of "whatever-turns-you-on." Instead, I try to respond with an attitude of curiosity, interest, and what I could call "benign concern," allowing for the possibility that the fantasy may contain swathes of undiluted, unprocessed trauma, but always remembering that the fantasy produces pleasure as well. In general, I explore with the patient whether the fantasy might interfere with other aspects of psychological functioning in any way.

Before our interview ended, I asked Paris how he felt about his life in general. He told me that although he missed Angelo, he still had a reasonably good life, apart from the fact that at work he often felt that "my hands are tied," complaining about bosses who restrict his freedom and creativity. I dare say that anyone who has ever held a job of any sort will be able to relate to the experience of having one's hands tied at work. But for most of us this will be a metaphor, rather than the basis of nightly erotic stimulation. For Paris, climax could best be achieved by imagining his hands *tied,* quite literally. When he told me that he experiences his hands as being tied at work, I also wondered whether certain aspects of his private history, and of his private sexual history in particular, had managed to seep into his working life, and whether he did anything to contribute to complicated interactions at work that resulted in tied hands. Of course, these sorts of questions cannot be answered fully on the basis of a single five-hour research interview. Only by working psychotherapeutically over a long period of time would I be able to ascertain, with Paris, whether his fantasy represented something toxic and destructive in his mind that negatively colored other arenas of his waking life.

When one attempts to analyze a sexual fantasy, one needs to become a detective, using not only the psychoanalytical skills bequeathed to us by Sigmund Freud, but also the forensic skills of a Sherlock Holmes. Most of us workaday mental health professionals will not be blessed with the formidable interpretative powers of Vienna's greatest doctor, or with the acumen of fiction's finest detective, but both Freud and Holmes serve as good role models of curiosity as we wonder about the tiniest details of a puzzle, and about their possible significance.

A good psychotherapist, like a good detective, must also know when to share his or her findings with a patient. In conducting these very revealing interviews, I had to struggle at all times between the wish to share my preliminary hypotheses with the interviewees, and my sense of caution that if I did so, we might enter complicated terrain that we could not follow up on in a sufficiently helpful way. In the end, I did convey some of my thoughts and impressions to Paris, which he absorbed with some interest, and with some amusement, never having had contact with a psychotherapist previously, and not being familiar with the ways in which we think and conceptualize. Before the interview concluded, I asked him how he felt, and whether he would be willing for me to use his material, in disguised form, as part of my research. He told me that he felt fine, and that he had enjoyed having a good cry and appreciated the opportunity to "get it off my chest"—a very resonant image. As a man, he needed to put his story into words, to get it off his chest. As a boy, he needed, quite literally, to get his father's semen off his chest.

Paris told me that he would be happy to allow me to use his material in my writing and lecturing work if I thought that it could be of help to others. I explained that by exploring the possible links between early experiences and later fantasies, we could learn a great deal, particularly as a further cautionary note about the long-lasting effects of noxious events in infancy and childhood. We shook hands, and Paris left the office. I felt immense gratitude to this man for having allowed me to visit the inside of his mind and the inside of his biography, and I hope that if he ever reads this chapter he will feel both understood and treated with compassion.

Later that evening, after a long day of clinical interviewing, I went to the Royal Opera House to watch a performance of *La Traviata*. As the opera nears its climax, the hero, Alfredo Germont, sings a tender love duet with the heroine, Violetta Valéry, a courtesan dying of consumption. Although Alfredo knows that Violetta will not recover, and that she will not, in fact, last more than a few more minutes, he tries to comfort her, promising that he will take her away from her deathbed in Paris:

> *"Parigi, o, cara, noi lasceremo,*
> *la vita uniti trascorreremo,*
> *de'corsi affanni compenso avrai,*
> *la tua salute rifiorirà."*

> [*"From Paris, dear, we shall go away,*
> *to live our lives together.*
> *We shall make up for all our heartache,*
> *Your health will come back again.*]

As I listened to the strains of Giuseppe Verdi's music, I began to think about my interview earlier that day with the brave man who had survived a bleak childhood and had become a devoted nurse. I found myself wishing him well and hoping that his heartache could be reduced, and that he would one day find a loyal long-term partner. I felt a sense of parental protection toward him. But, unlike Alfredo, who tries to cure Violetta by taking her away from Paris, we as psychotherapists try instead to help patients *not* to take *flight,* but to live better within their own heads. At that moment, I thought, I shall call this man "Paris."

19   The Traumatic Roots of Sexual Fantasy

What beastly incidents our memories insist on cherishing!

—EUGENE O'NEILL, *Strange Interlude*

Bloodstream or Biography?

For many years, endocrinologists, pediatricians, psychologists, and psychiatrists have suggested that our sexual lives may contain few, if any, elements of choice, owing to the strong influence of genetic predisposition and of the hormonal levels in our mother's uterus during pregnancy. These researchers argue strenuously for a proto-biological theory of sexual orientation, and hence, of sexual fantasy. As a behavioral science researcher myself, I applaud all efforts, whether biological or psychoanalytical, to undertake primary research in order to shed light on important questions about human lives; however, I wish I could be quite as confident as the psychobiologists who insist that all sexual behavior can be explained by heritable factors or by intra-uterine factors.

While it may be impossible to experience full sexual arousal, and therefore sexual fantasy, without the necessary underlying biological preconditions, my research indicates that the detailed content of one's fantasy life develops not in the bloodstream, but in biography. As we have observed in the case of Paris, discussed in Chapter 18, fantasy may well emerge as a result of conflictual, traumatic, postuterine, real-life experiences that occur during our infancy and childhood years, which serve as a veritable lightning rod around which subsequent sexual fantasy can become organized.

I wish to propose that just as dreams, neurotic symptoms, and other behavioral manifestations stem from our formative, postpartum experiences, so too do our sexual fantasies. Of course, I do appreciate that our adult personalities result from a complex amalgamation of factors, which might include genetic, biochemical, neurophysiological, prenatal, and perinatal contributions as well as the more evident imprinting experiences from infancy and childhood. Certainly, one would be hard pressed to fantasize without a working brain. But in this era of biological psychiatry and pharmacotherapy, we run a risk of obliterating the role of the more traditional psychological explanations first adumbrated by Freud and his myriad colleagues over a century ago. Perhaps through a consideration of some case material, derived from my clinical psychodiagnostic interviews, we can begin to gain a fuller appreciation of some of the possible antecedents of fantasy content.

Graziella and the Glass Table

As "Graziella" waltzed into my consulting room, I burst into a broad, beaming smile. Although I do enjoy smiling quietly on first encountering a new patient or client, in part to alleviate the often-overwhelming anxieties most people feel when meeting with a psychotherapist, in this case my smile soon became a small giggle, owing to Graziella's own infectious laughter. As she walked down the corridor, she herself started to laugh, and then, in a full-fledged northern English accent, she exclaimed, "This is so-o-o daft, inn't it? Talking about me fantasies with a strange bloke? You must think I'm mental already." I composed myself and then introduced myself with a handshake and thanked Graziella for having made the long journey to London.

After I explained the purpose of our interview, the buoyant Graziella, like so many of the participants in the research study, revealed her life story in a no-holds-barred manner, answering all my questions with generosity. Although she had experienced a great deal of trauma and deprivation in her life, Graziella, now thirty-one years old, had survived, and she had managed to maintain a good sense of humor about her plight, for which I respect her greatly.

The only child of unwed teenage parents, Graziella had grown up in a very downtrodden, impoverished mining town. Her drunken, unemployed father had beat her mother quite regularly; but fortunately, due to a timely intervention from the local department of social services, Graziella's mother had managed to move to a women's shelter when Graziella was only one year old. The mother thereby avoided any further beatings from the tyrannical father. Unfortunately, however, Graziella's mother soon attracted a new partner who also became both physically and sexually abusive, slapping her in Graziella's presence, and on one occasion slamming her mother into a wall with brute force.

After relating these episodes to me, Graziella chuckled, "You've just got to 'ave a sense of humor about these things, don't ya? Otherwise it'd kill ya, you know what I'm saying?" I nodded in silent agreement, and as I did so, I began to realize that Graziella's humor-tinged philosophizing had probably become an essential characterological defense mechanism that helped her to soften the pain.

Although Graziella's father had clearly harmed her mother, I asked whether he had ever hit her, his own daughter. She resolutely denied that he had done so. I then explained that it would also be helpful to know whether her mother, out of sheer frustration, had ever hit her. Graziella immediately became quite serious, and for the first time she dropped her guard: "She never hit me, no, never, except for this one time, and I don't blame her really." I raised my eyebrows, expressing interest in further details, whereupon Graziella described the episode in full: "I must've been about three. I was at our council flat, and we had this glass coffee table in the sitting room, and I was coloring with some crayons. I guess I got a bit carried away and I started to color on the glass top—all over the fucking place. My mother cottoned on to what I was doing, and she leaned over from the back, and I guess she just lost it, but she smashed my face into the coffee table, and it shattered."

Both Graziella and I exhaled deeply, each of us affected by this story of early child abuse. I wondered what kind of physical damage her mother had inflicted upon her; for instance, if the coffee table had indeed shattered, might Graziella have needed stitches? Did she have any scarring? And worse still, did any of the shards of glass become lodged in her eyes? Graziella answered "yes" to all of these questions, explaining that she did, in fact, bleed all over the floor, and that she did require extensive stitching. She then hoisted herself up from the sofa, walked toward me, and showed me some very faint scars on her face that could be detected only at very close range. Fortunately, she did not become visually impaired in any way, and she could not remember whether her eyes had been washed out.

Graziella told me that she could not recall any of the details of her trip to the hospital. This, of course, did not surprise me. When young children experience really horrific traumas, such as having one's face smashed into a glass table, they will often, if not invariably, repress the event, as it becomes too painful to hold in conscious awareness. Professor Linda Meyer Williams, an American psychologist working at the Family Research Laboratory at the University of New Hampshire, published a landmark study in 1994 in which she demonstrated quite impressively that a substantial percentage of adults who as children had attended a hospital emergency room as a result of abuse-related injuries will have no conscious memory at all of the visits, even though Professor Williams could prove that they had received hospital treatment by examining their medical records. Clearly, trauma cannot always be held in our conscious minds; it often requires another route for expression.

After relating this grisly episode, in which she might have died, Graziella explained that "somehow," she had managed to grow up, and although she was "crap" at school, earning no qualifications at all, she did nevertheless manage to set up a very lucrative business, a specialist security firm providing protection for artists at rock concerts and other public events. Graziella informed me that she employs a team of "great big goons," broad-shouldered men weighing, on average, 250 pounds, who keep a firm eye on the door at various clubs and theaters, ensuring that no drunken troublemakers will infiltrate. Never having talked at length with a female security officer before, I became quite intrigued, and I wondered aloud how Graziella managed to thrive in a field that would ordinarily attract men.

In responding to my question, Graziella merely chortled with her characteristic humor. "I don't know, I guess men just see me comin', and they start to shake in their boots." I glanced at her diminutive frame and estimated that she must be no taller than 5'4" or perhaps 5'5"—she certainly did not look like the sort of woman who would make drunken lager louts quake. Clearly, something other than an imposing physical presence had catapulted Graziella into such an unusual and highly specific line of work, one which clearly suited her, and which she had developed with admirable success. But Graziella did not understand why she had devoted all of her adult energies to this type of employment, which involved safety and protection.

Graziella told me, again, with her good-humored style, that she had never married and had never really had a long-term boyfriend. Could she be lesbian, I wondered? But before I could inquire, Graziella anticipated my question. She explained, "In case you're wonderin', I only shag blokes. I love a nice, big piece of meat." I soon learned that Graziella had enjoyed maybe thirty different sexual encounters with thirty different men over the past decade, none of which had resulted in a lasting partnership. This confession hardly surprised me. I often meet women born to physically abusive fathers who will either find an abusive husband of their own, or, in Graziella-fashion, avoid an ongoing attachment to a man, living in perpetual fear that any marriage will invariably result in physical injury. These women develop a phobic response to heterosexual commitment, and many will experiment with lesbianism as an alternative.

After approximately four hours, I raised the question of sexual fantasy, and I asked Graziella whether at this point she would be comfortable reporting any fantasies that she uses, either during masturbation or during sex with a partner. She told me that often, in her fantasy life, she would imagine having sex with a beautiful woman. Graziella quickly underscored the fact that she has never, ever had a real-life sexual encounter with another female, but that during masturbation she does enjoy lesbianism. I then requested more details, whereupon Graziella explained that in her lesbian fantasy she always has sex with an anonymous woman. She can never see the other woman's face, but she knows that this woman must be twenty to twenty-five years of age, "at the most." Sometimes, in the middle of the fantasy, a man will appear, observing Graziella engaged in lesbian sex, and he will plead to join in. Graziella told me that she always refuses to turn her fantasy twosome into a threesome, and that she will "get off" from the thought that the man has to stand there on the sidelines, masturbating his "big erection," unable to touch either herself or her female lover.

I asked Graziella whether she enjoys any other sexual fantasies, and she replied, "Oh, yes, the one I just told you is really just one that I use for ordinary purposes. There is another, which doesn't have any men in it, that is probably the one that gives me the best orgasm, which really hits my G-spot." She proceeded to describe her most arousing and most frequently deployed masturbatory fantasy:

It's no big deal really, because not much happens, but I am sitting down on a settee, just like this one, and I am naked. Suddenly, a pair of arms—I know they're a woman's arms—comes around from behind, and starts to caress my tits. It feels unbelievable. I have no idea who this woman is, or what she looks like. I never see her face. She then starts to run her hands through my hair, and she pushes me over, and I am leaning down, and she then caresses my back and my shoulders. It feels amazing, very sensual, very erotic, not at all like male sex. [*Pause.*] And that's it. I come and come and come. [*Pause.*] I know there's not that much to it, but I just love the thought of this faceless woman massaging my back and breasts and all that. It really does it for me. [*Pause.*] So, do you think I'm a lezza?

I did not reply to Graziella's question as to whether she might be lesbian, simply because I do not know. According to her testimony, she has never had a lesbian experience in real life; by contrast, she has enjoyed frequent sexual encounters with men, whose large penises bring her pleasure. But, in fantasy, she derives orgastic satisfaction not from a man's penis, but from a woman's caresses. To compound matters even further, Graziella then explained that, although she relishes lesbian fantasies, she would never want to act them out, even if a beautiful, buxom blonde started to flirt with her. So, might she be a secret, unconscious lesbian who does not really know how much she craves a woman? Might she be bisexual? Might she be heterosexual with a creative penchant for variety? Might she be confused? Or might Graziella defy our traditional categories? I leave this an open question entirely.

Instead of trying to categorize Graziella, I asked her whether she and I could reflect upon the content of her sexual fantasies, and I wondered whether she had any theories that might explain why she preferred these particular fantasies as opposed to the many others which her mind might have created. Graziella's response did not surprise me. She simply shrugged her shoulders and sniggered, "I ain't got a bleedin' clue. It's just the way it goes. I told you I was 'mental,' didn't I?"

Graziella, like virtually every other person whom I have interviewed, seemed to have no conscious insight into the origins of her fantasies. I suspect that if she understood them, she might no longer cling to them with such force. But I have come to suspect that our fantasies represent an outpouring from our *unconscious* mind, and that because the fantasies contain *unconscious* content, we cannot, almost by definition, understand their content; and yet, we continue to immerse ourselves in these fantasies, with a certain quality of inexorability.

Although Graziella could not understand why she had chosen to masturbate to these particular images, I do have a theory, derived from my experience of her in the interview situation and from my knowledge of other individuals with similar experiences and similar characterological structures and personality styles.

As a little girl, Graziella suffered from a whole variety of deprivational experiences. She grew up in physical poverty, as well as emotional poverty, born to a violent, unloving father who beat her young mother. Owing to the dangerousness of her father, social services moved Graziella and her mother into a safehouse. Such events will predispose a young girl to develop a highly conflictual relationship with men, and I propose that Graziella both came to fear men and simultaneously to crave more contact with them, owing to their mysterious disappearance from her childhood. As an adult sexual woman, Graziella sought out men for sexual escapades, but in choosing thirty lovers over a ten-year period, she managed to discard them in rapid succession. Her incapacity to create a secure attachment to any one man belies her ambivalence, as she both craves men and fears them at the same time.

Although lesbianism can be a primary sexual tendency in its own right, I suspect that in Graziella's case, that of a woman who does enjoy sex with men, her lesbian fantasy propensities may have a defensive quality, protecting her from the dangers of the penis. Remember, Graziella has two fantasies that produce arousal:

1. A fantasy of exclusive lesbian sex with an anonymous woman gripping her from behind and massaging her breasts, neck, and shoulders.
2. A fantasy of lesbian sex with an anonymous woman, during which a man appears, but Graziella will not allow him to join in, and he must masturbate on the sidelines.

By fantasizing about exclusively lesbian sex, or about lesbian sex with a man relegated to the periphery, Graziella succeeds in sexualizing her wish to punish men and to eradicate them from her ambit. Many a heterosexual man would feel tormented if he found himself just inches away from two lesbians, only to be told that he can look but must not touch. From a psychoanalytical viewpoint, Graziella's two primary masturbatory fantasies allow her to express her underlying aggression to men.

But in the fantasy of Graziella making love to a woman while the man masturbates from a safe distance, I wonder whether she has allowed her unconscious mind to create a more idealized family constellation, with a maternal woman holding her, and a strong, erect male nearby, but not using his penis for destructive or abusive purposes. Although seemingly sexual on the surface, this particular fantasy may represent an attempt to recreate a family unit in which the parents wield their sexuality in a more benign and less abusive manner than in the real-life scenarios of Graziella's youth.

These fantasies pose still further questions. In particular, why does Graziella indulge in imagined lesbianism at all? If she harbors ambivalent feelings toward men, based in the main on her complicated relationship with her abusive father, then why does she not simply have a fantasy about being cruel, or about teasing or tormenting men? Why add lesbianism to the mix? Here we find ourselves grappling with the highly complex and overdetermined nature of sexual fantasies. Graziella not only suffered from having a dreadful masculine role model, but may well have had an even more disappointing relationship with her mother.

In my clinical experience with women whose fathers have raped them or perpetrated some other form of sexual or physical abuse, the women in question will inevitably loathe their fathers; but, quite surprisingly, they will often become even more venomous toward their mothers, for having failed to protect them in the first place. One of my female patients, vaginally penetrated by her father at a young age, understandably wished him dead, but she spoke at length of her even greater desire to tie her mother to a crucifix, *upside-down,* drive nails into her wrists and ankles, and leave her there until she bled to death.

Speaking clinically, I would imagine that Graziella has nursed a great deal of rage not only toward her absconding father but also toward her complicitous mother, who, in Graziella's mind, had partnered with a violent man, and had thereby prevented Graziella from having a stable father. The mother, by all accounts, did not nurture her daughter in the way a loving mother should, in part because she had to contend with her own traumas. I want to suggest that Graziella's lesbian fantasies represent not really a wish to adopt a full-time, conscious lesbian identity, but rather a desire to create a greater closeness to one woman in particular, namely, the neglectful, nonprotecting mother of her infancy and childhood.

Graziella experienced great danger throughout her childhood. During her first year of life, she would have observed her father beating her mother, and she would have heard screams and shouts. Although babies who witness and overhear domestic violence do not have the cognitive capabilities to make full sense of such cruel behavior, they nonetheless absorb an atmosphere of fear and terror, and they will invariably begin to howl as a response to the disturbing noises.

Graziella's mother had actually smashed her daughter's face into the glass table. Can it be any wonder that Graziella's fantasies might be described for the most part as highly tender and safe, a litany of satisfying caresses? I hypothesize that Graziella has created her masturbatory fantasies as a soothing refuge from the physical violence, the unpredictability, and the lack of physical and emotional security that she had to endure during her girlhood. Equally, it will hardly be surprising that in addition to scripting these masturbatory images in which dangerous men either disappear or become relegated to the side, Graziella has chosen a career as a security guard supremo, controlling a group of "goons," making the north of England a safer place.

Through my study of Graziella's sexual fantasies, I hope that we have gained a greater understanding of both the function of her fantasies (provision of safety, discharge of aggression toward men, and so forth) and their content (for instance, gratification of bisexual wishes, desire for closeness with a maternal woman). Furthermore, we must approach each fantasy rather like a giant jigsaw puzzle or mystery story. At the end of the analysis, every piece must fit in order that we may gain a clear picture of the contents of the mind of the fantasist.

I think I now understand why in her first fantasy Graziella indulges in lesbian sex with a woman and enjoys the taunting of an erect male masturbating a few feet away, safely out of reach. I think I also appreciate her need for lesbian affection in her fantasy, though not necessarily in her active sexual behavioral life. But I still remain puzzled by the curious detail in her second fantasy, namely, the fact that her lesbian partner approaches *from behind,* while Graziella remains seated on the settee, and the partner bends Graziella forward so that she can massage her neck and shoulders. This may seem an insignificant point, but I have found that through the analysis of these ostensibly trivial details, we can often obtain our best insights into the secret psychology of sexual fantasies and discern the private psychological fingerprints of an individual.

One must ask oneself, why does the lesbian sex unfold in such a way? Why does Graziella's partner not approach her from in *front,* veering perhaps toward Graziella's breasts or clitoris? Why does Graziella not make the first move? Why does she sit passively on the sofa waiting to be bent forward?

I propose that Graziella's masturbatory fantasy cannot be understood at all without a detailed knowledge of one of the most horrific traumas—if not *the* most horrific trauma—from her early childhood, namely, having her face smashed into the glass table. If you recall, the three-year-old child sat on her council flat sofa, coloring a picture with crayons; however, in her youthful enthusiasm, she started to draw all over the glass-topped table as well, evoking much wrath from her mother, who approached her from *behind* and rammed her face into the glass, causing bleeding, screaming, and a potential near-death emergency, necessitating an immediate visit to the hospital followed by stitches and scars. This violent incident must have occurred very unexpectedly and would have shattered not only the glass but Graziella's capacity to trust her mother.

Graziella's case mirrors that of Paris, described in Chapter 18, in that both of these individuals, like so many of the people whom I have interviewed, began to masturbate and hence derive sexual pleasure from a distorted version of their most scary childhood experiences. Paris successfully transformed sexual abuse by his father into a sexually gratifying experience with an anonymous male; Graziella also managed to transmogrify an episode of physical assault into a pleasurable fantasy. Both succeeded in rendering their lovers faceless, thus disguising the identity of the real perpetrator, namely, a parent.

By creating an anonymous woman who sneaks up behind her as she sits on the couch, and who then bends her head forward (into the table), Graziella has unwittingly succeeded in restaging her most frightening childhood memory; but in this situation, she manages to rechoreograph the trauma. Instead of smashing Graziella's face into the coffee table, the anonymous woman caresses Graziella's breasts from behind and strokes her neck, shoulders, and back, thus inducing pleasure. As a result, Graziella reaches a thundering orgasm, and she becomes satisfied.

Once again, we see the operation of a long-standing psychoanalytical observation, first espoused by Freud in 1920, and later developed by the American psychoanalyst Robert Stoller throughout the 1970s: As human beings, we will do all that we can to use our minds to minimize the impact of trauma. Freud did not focus at great length upon the use of masturbatory and coital sexual fantasies as a means of reducing the pain of trauma, but he did provide the first clue as to how modern psychotherapists and behavioral researchers might tackle this psychological problem.

It would be marvelous to think that we could experience the unavoidable traumas of the life cycle and yet feel no lasting effects. Unfortunately, this seems not to be the case. *One cannot be traumatized without experiencing a traumatic consequence.* The ancient Greeks certainly knew this when they first spoke about "trauma," which means, quite literally, "wound" or "injury." In other words, one cannot be wounded without some bloodshed, either physical or emotional; and sexual fantasy seems to be one of the many mechanisms that we use to help ourselves work through the impact of early physical, sexual, and emotional trauma.

Owing to the heightened emotional content of Graziella's early experiences, she has found it rather difficult to allow these thoughts to enter her conscious mind. Her masturbatory fantasies permit her a means of both engaging with the original trauma in distorted, sexualized, antisepticized form while avoiding having to dwell too long on the original realities. Thus, our sexual fantasies protect us and shield us from something potentially dreadful. Yet in doing so, they reinforce our wish to masturbate and hence allow us to avoid exploration of what lurks beneath. If Graziella could engage more consciously with her fantasies, she might become better able to appreciate her fears of both men and women, as well as her yearning for both men and women. As a result, she may, perhaps, be able to engage in more trusting, less paranoid adult relationships in her outside life.

The Strange Incident of the Expanding Penis

"Dahlia," a thirty-nine-year-old costume designer, spoke in a rather soft voice. A pretty, demure lady who dressed with great elegance, Dahlia moved with tremendous grace, almost gliding into the consulting room for her research interview. She ultimately surprised me, because in view of her refined appearance and manner, I suspected that she would not be the sort of woman who would volunteer to reveal her sexual fantasies to a man whom she had never met before. But in working on this project, I have learned that one must never prejudge an individual on the basis of stereotypical physical characteristics.

Dahlia explained that she had chosen to volunteer because she thought it "sounded interesting." She did not elaborate any further, but in spite of her apparent shyness, she seemed happy to persevere, and after I had explained the requirements of the interview and the content that we would be covering, she readily signed the informed consent agreement, allowing the interview to proceed.

Happily married, with a baby son, Dahlia worked as a costumier in a freelance capacity, and when she told me some of the films and theater shows for which she had created designs, I realized at once the extent of her competency and her professionalism. When I asked her how she had become interested in this line of work, she tittered, "Gosh, why do you even have to ask? What woman wouldn't dream of spending her day surrounded by clothes? I get paid money to buy, buy, buy clothes, and to dress gorgeous actors in clothes." She then mentioned the name of the dashing leading man who had starred in a historical film on which she had recently worked, jokingly boasting, "How many other married ladies get to see 'X' stripped down to his you-know-whats?"

By all accounts, Dahlia seemed to enjoy a trauma-free life. She spoke lovingly and glowingly of her "gorgeous" husband, "Robert," whom she had married four years earlier, and of her "magnificent" son, "Lester," who had fast become the center of her universe. Dahlia beamed at her good fortune at being able to earn a nice income from her work in the entertainment industry while meeting lots of famous and attractive people. She told me that she had a wide circle of friends from show business, and that she even found time to learn Italian and to practice the violin. All in all, Dahlia's life seemed quite perfect.

Her sexual history, in particular, struck me as ordinary and unremarkable. Since the age of sixteen, Dahlia had had four steady boyfriends, none of whom quite fitted the bill until she met Robert, a wealthy investment banker who absolutely doted on her. With each successive paragraph of her narration, Dahlia's life became ever more enviable, and I found myself wondering why such a seemingly healthy woman with a young baby, an enjoyable marriage, a busy career, a wide circle of friends, and money to burn would wish to sacrifice five hours plus traveling time—essentially an entire day—to speak to a psychotherapist about her private sexual fantasies. Still, we persevered.

When I asked Dahlia about her early years, she smiled, explaining, "On the whole, pretty good. Nice mum, nice dad, two brothers (one older, one younger), and two sisters (both younger). You know, the usual sibling jealousies and that sort of thing, the usual anger at mum and dad for not letting me stay out past my curfew. Nothing out of the ordinary." Once again, it all sounded very straightforward and very lovely—perhaps *too* lovely.

I probed and probed, asking about discipline, about any early bereavements, any punishments, any separations, any acts of cruelty, knowing that beneath the gleaming exterior of a polished biography, one can often discover a covert trauma. Dahlia responded to my questions in a nondefensive, good-spirited manner; but in spite of all my archaeological digging, I uncovered nothing of gross, or even of mild, concern. By this point in my research, based on the pilot computer data and on my psychodiagnostic interviews, I had already begun to find ample evidence that masturbatory and coital fantasies will stem from traumatic early experiences, but in Dahlia's case, I could find none. Perhaps I had overestimated the importance of my preliminary observations. Perhaps the trauma-laden fantasies of Paris and Graziella, described earlier, might be mere flukes or statistical artifacts. Perhaps I had attracted a very skewed research sample of traumatized people who needed to offload their fantasies in the presence of a trained mental health professional.

As we reached the fifth and final hour of our wide-ranging interview, I asked Dahlia whether she would be able to describe her most arousing sexual fantasy or fantasies to me, in as much detail as possible. Without missing a beat, Dahlia announced that, although she does not really need to masturbate all that often owing to her great sex life with Robert, she does utilize not one, not two, but *three* separate fantasies, which always induce a climax. She proceeded to describe each of these masturbatory fantasies in turn, stressing that she relied upon them only in solitude. When making love to Robert, she remained quite mentally faithful, thinking only of him.

Each of Dahlia's three fantasies can be described rather briefly:

1. In her first fantasy, Dahlia imagines a penis being inserted into her vagina. The penis expands and expands, not in length, but

in girth, and it becomes fatter and fatter, swelling to perhaps two feet in circumference. Amazingly, the walls of her vagina loosen accordingly, and somehow her genitals manage to accommodate this super-sized, gargantuan penis. Simply thinking about this "mega" penile appendage will cause Dahlia to achieve climax.

2. In her second fantasy, Dahlia drifts off into a state of reverie simply by picturing herself as pregnant. By closing her eyes and imagining herself with a baby in her womb, Dahlia reaches orgasm.

3. In her third and final fantasy, Dahlia imagines Robert, her wonderful husband, making love to an anonymous woman. Robert masturbates his penis and then plunges his organ into the awaiting vagina of the mystery woman, while Dahlia, sitting at the edge of the bed, masturbates by herself. This fantasy, in particular, proves quite helpful in stimulating a train of multiple orgasms.

After Dahlia completed her recitation of these three fantasies, a quiet voice inside my head piped up, and I heard myself wondering, "Is that it?" After more than a year of interviewing and collecting sexual fantasy data on all manner of convoluted and often extraordinarily graphic fantasies, Dahlia's seemed rather tame and straightforward: a large penis, pregnancy, and straight sex between her husband and another woman. I heard no tales of being chained to a bed, no stories of having a stranger shave her pubic hair, no one smashing her face into a glass table, and encountered no need for her to open up a security firm offering protection against danger. Perhaps Dahlia really did have a trauma-free childhood after all.

As I always do, I asked Dahlia whether she had any private hunches as to what her fantasies might mean, and once again, just like all the other interviewees, the otherwise verbally sophisticated Dahlia looked quizzical: "I haven't got a clue. These images just arouse me." I nodded understandingly and wondered to myself how the interview could progress from here, or how I might uncover any further meaning in her story.

As I have mentioned before, those of us who work as mental health professionals from time to time have private conversations in our heads while talking to our patients. Sometimes a seemingly bizarre thought

might pop into my mind that seems completely unrelated to the patient; for example, in the middle of a session, I once thought, "Ah, I
must remember to buy a pint of milk." Sometimes, a private thought
such as this might seem pretty straightforward—especially if, at that
particular moment, I had run out of milk and needed some more for
my office refrigerator so that I could make myself cups of coffee or tea
in between sessions. But these thoughts often seem to have a symbolic
nature; for instance, perhaps the idea of purchasing milk represents not
only a concrete reality but also some kind of communication from the
patient that he or she had once craved breast milk during infancy,
which never arrived. In fact, on this particular occasion, my thought
about buying a pint of milk did signify not only my own need to re-
stock the consulting-room fridge, but also, more tellingly, a covert message from the patient that her mother, who had recently visited, did not
take enough interest in her, and did not provide enough nurturance of
"emotional breast milk." The patient in question found herself struggling to put her anger into words, and my private musing during the
session about needing to acquire more milk proved a means of "picking up" on this aspect of the patient's anxiety and struggle. In other
words, at that moment she needed more maternal milk and could not
ask for it. After all, remember what had happened to Oliver Twist
when he pleaded for additional sustenance.

Mental health practitioners refer to such private thoughts as "coun-
tertransference" thoughts, a rather cumbersome term first introduced
by Freud during the early part of the twentieth century. We take coun-
tertransference thoughts very seriously because they will often provide
crucial clues.

In my meeting with Dahlia, I found myself having a private counter-
transference thought that I certainly did not articulate to her. I suddenly
found myself wondering, "What does Dahlia look like naked?" Although psychotherapists strive to preserve the consulting room as a
physically and sexually safe, nonerotic space, we will all, from time to
time, have a fleeting romantic or sexual thought about some of our patients. We never act on such thoughts—only an unscrupulous, unethical,
and mentally compromised person would be so unprofessional—but
they often contain useful information that might be helpful for our clinical work.

As Dahlia would be considered an attractive woman by anyone's standards, it might not be too surprising to learn that I had entertained such

a thought briefly, but as I do not think about every attractive patient in this way, I had to ask myself why I had *this* particular thought about *this* particular patient at *this* particular moment of the interview. Why, for example, did I not have this thought at the very beginning of the interview, when Dahlia first entered my office? I began to scrutinize my own mental processes and explore the potentially secret meaning of my question, wondering whether my unconscious mind had tried to help me out during a difficult clinical interview. And then, the penny dropped.

I explained to Dahlia that although she had already told me a very great deal about her infancy, her childhood, her adolescence, and her adult life, as well as her sexual behaviors and sexual fantasies, I still had one more question. I told her that I would find it useful to know more about her choice of career, that of costumier, which involves putting clothes on other people, and that this preoccupation had made me want to learn about how issues around being clothed and being naked manifested themselves in her family. For example, had she ever seen either of her parents naked? She replied that she could not remember any parental nudity. I then asked about her brothers and sisters—had she ever seen them naked? Dahlia explained that being so close in age to her younger sisters, the girls would invariably have had baths together, but apart from that she could not remember anything untoward. Finally, I inquired about her brothers. Dahlia told me that she had two brothers, one seven years her senior and the other four years her junior. Did she ever see her brothers naked? I asked, and did they ever observe her without any clothing?

At this point, the hitherto loquacious Dahlia suddenly paused and looked quite sullen. "Well, yes," she replied, "there was something." She continued, "I didn't know if this was really important before when you asked me about my childhood, but well, since you ask, well, yes, there was something that happened." Dahlia then proceeded to tell me that her elder brother, "Mickey," had experienced perinatal anoxia— lack of oxygen to the brain at the moment of birth—which caused some mild neurological damage, and as a result, Mickey suffered from nonspecific learning difficulties and speech impediments during his later life. When I had asked for information about Dahlia's siblings in the earlier part of the interview, she had skipped over these crucial pieces of biographical material.

Lowering her eyes and with a wistful look on her face, Dahlia proceeded to explain that Mickey could be rather problematic, and that because of his learning difficulties, he often found it hard to differentiate right from wrong. Shamefacedly, Dahlia then confessed that one morning, at the age of nine, she awoke in her bed with a jolt, having felt a hand on her vagina. She looked up and saw her brother Mickey, aged sixteen, stark naked, perched on the edge of her bed, with his right hand shoved under Dahlia's blanket, tickling her vulva, and with his left hand gripped around his very erect, postpubescent penis. Dahlia told me that she froze at that moment, confused by Mickey's behavior, slightly mesmerized by his giant penis, surrounded with black hair, and scared by the look of lust in his eyes. Eventually, Mickey stopped touching Dahlia and ran out of the bedroom.

This soon became a daily activity—Dahlia would awaken in the morning to find Mickey masturbating at the foot of her bed. He never penetrated her vagina with his finger or with his penis; instead, he would stimulate her outer genitalia while masturbating himself frantically. Dahlia could not remember whether he ever ejaculated in her bedroom, or whether, more likely, as she supposed, he would stimulate himself to a frenzy and then run into the nearby bathroom in order to "finish himself off."

Naturally, I asked how her parents or her remaining siblings had managed not to find out about this morning ritual. Dahlia explained that her father left the house every morning at six o'clock to go to work, and that her younger sisters and her younger brother, all early risers, would have already established themselves in the downstairs playroom, watching cartoons on television. Her mother would be cooking breakfast, ironing school uniforms, and performing any number of domestic chores, including vacuuming, in the downstairs kitchen, with the radio blaring in the background. In other words, in spite of his learning difficulties, Mickey would wait until their father had left the house, the younger siblings had become lost in their cartoons, and their mother had ensconced herself in a brouhaha of early-morning noise before entering the bedroom of his sleeping sister.

Dahlia admitted that these early-morning visits frightened her, but that she did not want to get Mickey into trouble because she loved him very much; therefore, she told no one. After about two years, these episodes ceased, probably at the time that Dahlia had begun to develop pubic hair herself and had begun to menstruate. After that point, she and Mickey became more distant, and today, he lives in sheltered accommodation, and she rarely visits him.

This new set of revelations did not surprise me; on the contrary, I now had a clearer sense of why this woman had volunteered to speak to a psychotherapist. Some of my interviewees agreed to participate in my study in part for the money, but Dahlia obviously did not need such a modest remuneration. Others, like Paris, seemed to have a genuine desire to assist the course of scientific research, but I had no sense that such an urge had contributed to Dahlia's motivation. I suspect that Dahlia had remembered her brother's masturbation all along, and though she made no *conscious* connection between her experiences as a little girl and her subsequent sexual fantasies, that some part of her mind was still preoccupied or indeed troubled by these thoughts, and for that reason she harbored a secret wish to find someone, ideally a professional, in whom she could confide, so that she might begin to explore this previously neglected chapter of her biography. Psychotherapists and other mental health professionals will be familiar with the phenomenon that I have described whereby a client, patient, or interviewee will talk at great length in very intimate ways while skirting around the most crucial areas of shame and vulnerability.

To her credit, Dahlia managed to muster the courage to talk about this early incident of sibling abuse; and with this new information in place, I could at last begin to make more sense of the jigsaw puzzle of her sexual fantasies. Now that we know that Dahlia's brother Mickey had manipulated her genitals and had masturbated in her presence (with Dahlia only nine, and Mickey a postpubescent sixteen), perhaps her three masturbatory fantasies might be better understood.

To recapitulate, in Dahlia's first fantasy she imagined a penis being inserted into her vagina, growing fatter and fatter. In her second fantasy, she would orgasm simply at the thought of being pregnant. And in her third fantasy, Dahlia would enjoy watching her husband, Robert, making love to some other woman, while she herself would nestle at the edge of the bed and then masturbate. What might be the potential connections between these three fantasies and Dahlia's experience of sibling molestation?

I wish to propose that when Mickey began to masturbate in front of Dahlia, he terrified her, in part because of the size of his penis. Dahlia has not seen Mickey's penis since her childhood, so we do not know whether he possesses an average-sized male member or an unusually large penis, but from the perspective of nine-year-old Dahlia, lying prone on her bed, the tumescent genitalia of her naked sixteen-year-old brother may well have seemed enormous. When Mickey started to touch Dahlia's vulva, she may also have developed a further fear, namely, that he would insert his fingers into her vagina, or worse, that he would insert his mammoth-looking penis inside her. Whatever knowledge she may or may not have possessed about sexual inter-course and procreation at the age of nine years, Dahlia did of course eventually learn the facts of life; and we often find that subsequently acquired adult knowledge creeps into the formation of our sexual fantasies, serving as an "overlay" on top of the original childhood scenario. Thus, when Dahlia created her first fantasy of being penetrated by a penis that grows inside her vagina, I suspect that she did so in order to master the traumatogenic fear of being penetrated by her sixteen-year-old brother's penis, which to her at the time may well have looked "two feet wide."

In the second fantasy, Dahlia imagines herself pregnant. Of course, it seems likely that literally billions of women worldwide have enjoyed a comparable fantasy, but few, I suspect, will have an orgasm simply from the thought of pregnancy. In Dahlia's case, I would argue that as a nine-year-old girl, she became so terrified of being impregnated by her older brother Mickey that thoughts of pregnancy began to preoccupy her. In her adult masturbation fantasy, she would dream of having become pregnant not by her brother, but by her loving husband, Robert, thereby experiencing pleasure in the knowledge that Mickey did not, after all, become the father of her child. Nevertheless, the fear remained that her slightly handicapped brother might have made her pregnant, something that she would dread, and yet, paradoxically, something that she might also crave at a more unconsciously conflicted level of mind. Psychotherapists and psychoanalysts have long observed that little girls choose their fathers and their brothers as their first honorary lovers and that they often pretend that the imaginary baby inside of them may be that of brother or father. By masturbating about being pregnant, especially knowing that her husband really did deposit his seed inside her, Dahlia can derive pleasure from taking control over her pregnancy. In other words, if anybody makes Dahlia pregnant, it will be Dahlia herself, through her fantasy, rather than her teenage brother through a rape.

Dahlia's third and final masturbatory fantasy—the one in which she has the opportunity to observe her beloved husband making love to another woman, while she herself sits at the end of the bed, pleasuring herself to the point of orgasm—may be the most perplexing. I would imagine that most women who discovered their husbands *in flagrante* with another woman would become enraged and reach either for the telephone number of a divorce lawyer or for a pistol. But Dahlia becomes quite sexually excited by this fantasy, so much so that she stimulates her own genitalia until she reaches climax. For many women, such a fantasy would defy all logic and common sense.

Nevertheless, when one considers Dahlia's childhood history, the fantasy becomes much more readily comprehensible. As a nine-year-old girl, Dahlia had to endure the anxiety, the fear, and the indignity of watching her brother masturbate himself while their mother remained downstairs, out of sight, vacuuming or listening to the radio. It would not be unreasonable to suppose that Dahlia would have wished for her mother to appear in her bedroom doorway, so that she could rescue her daughter from her teenage son. In this particular fantasy, Dahlia actually becomes the observer, rather than the participant. She has orchestrated her fantasy so that a safe man (her husband) makes love to another woman, while she enjoys the privileged position as onlooker at the edge of the bed. In choreographing her fantasy thus, Dahlia has managed to:

1. Identify with the aggressor.
2. Create a situation in which the sexual perpetrator will be observed by a grown-up.
3. Reverse the situation so that she avoids sex; another woman will be pounced upon instead.

By scripting such a fantasy, Dahlia has managed to turn something unpleasant into something highly arousing.

When one considers all three fantasies as a psychological triptych, one can readily understand the ways in which Dahlia's masturbatory fantasies represent different aspects of one primal trauma dating from the age of nine. In each of the fantasies, Dahlia becomes the powerful person in charge, no longer the victim that she experienced herself to be in childhood. Thus, her fantasy constellation permits her to conquer trauma, or, at least, to mitigate its toxic impact.

In view of this information, one can also readily appreciate the unconscious determination of Dahlia's choice of career. A competent, intelligent, and capable woman, Dahlia could easily have made a success of any number of different professions. Why did she particularly choose the career of costume designer, devoting her life to clothing women and men? Although the origins of our various career choices are usually multi-determined, we must remember that Dahlia became threatened and confused at the sight of her learning disabled brother appearing unexpectedly *naked,* sporting a large and menacing erection, on her bed, which caused her to feel unsafe and fearful of attack and impregnation. By devoting her adult professional life to the role of costumier, Dahlia can thus ensure that any naked men will not only be clothed, but also sufficiently clothed with layer upon layer of period garments—her specialty—to her full satisfaction. Like Paris and Graziella before her, Dahlia has proved to be a creative sexual fantasist, using her own private erotic musings to fulfill a wide variety of often unconscious psychological needs.

A Case of Fecal Exhibitionism

Some readers may find "Lucian's" sexual fantasy more graphic and visceral than the fantasies reported previously in this chapter. A twenty-four-year-old graduate student, Lucian lived with his girlfriend and three cats. He struck me as a well-groomed, well-presented, soft-spoken man with a kindly disposition, eager to cooperate with my research project. He reported nothing traumatic or out of the ordinary when relating the story of his life.

The eldest of three boys, and the only one to have pursued an academic career, Lucian attended an average, run-of-the-mill school, where, as a result of his intelligence and perseverance, he soon rose to become the valedictorian of his class. He told me that the other boys rather looked up to him for being so clever, but he also sensed that they secretly hated him, a typical envious response.

I inquired whether Lucian's schoolmates had ever attacked him in any way or teased him. He scrunched up his face and rolled his eyes upward, trying to access any repressed memories, but he could not, at first, remember anything untoward. Eventually, he paused, and he shrugged his shoulders, noting,

> There was one time that I felt got at by the other boys. I must've been about five or six, and I remember, I had to go to the loo [toilet]. I remember I had to have a pee only, but I used to get in-

timidated taking my penis out at the urinals—they smelled for one thing—so if I needed to use the loo, I would always go into one of the stalls and sit down. So I went to the toilet, got in the stall, pulled my pants down, and sat down, as you do. Suddenly, out of nowhere, three or four lads appeared in the school bathroom, and like monkeys, they pulled themselves up so that they were all peering over the top of the door of the toilet stall, and they could see me. They started laughing and mocking me, saying things like, "Lucian pees like a girl, Lucian pees like a girl. I can see your poo [feces]. I can see your poo. Look, Lucian's having a shit!" I remember that I tried to defend myself, telling the other boys that I was only pissing, but my voice was too soft, and they all kept laughing, and then they ran back to the classroom. Later that day, during the lunch period, they told all the other boys in the class that they had seen me taking a poo.

Child psychologists have long since known that boys of five or six years of age experience a heightened conflict around their genitals and private body functions. Old enough to know all about their penises, but too young to use them for overtly sexual purposes, boys of this age often feel quite genitally inadequate, and many will struggle as they try to assert a pseudo-masculine supremacy over other boys whom they perceive to be less tough, engaging in what the preeminent British child psychoanalyst Dr. Donald Winnicott once called the phase of "swank and swagger." Lucian, a clever and quiet chap, became an obvious target. Another child, upon being discovered in the toilet, might shrug off the jeering from his schoolmates and retaliate with a verbal retort or even with physical intimidation; but Lucian, a much more introverted child, became paralyzed, and although he tried to defend himself verbally, his voice could not be heard. Naturally, I wondered whether this episode would have had a scarring impact upon Lucian.

Lucian impressed me with his frankness. Not many twenty-four-year-old men would have had the courage to reveal such an intimate experience of bodily humiliation during their first encounter with a psychotherapist. Perhaps Lucian had a need to articulate something long pent-up inside his mind.

He talked with equal candor about his sex life with his girlfriend, "Genevieve," a fellow graduate student in the humanities. They had met as undergraduates, had become romantically and sexually entwined almost instantly, and had remained lovers for five years, sharing a flat and a life together. Lucian told me that he had a lovely sex life with Genevieve and that when he did have intercourse with her, he thought only about her—one of the very few men in my interview sample who remained so mentally faithful.

I then asked about masturbation. Lucian explained that because he shared his home with Genevieve, he had very little opportunity to masturbate, and that he much preferred to have "real sex"; but, from time to time, he did masturbate, often in the late mornings when he might be working from home on his doctoral dissertation and Genevieve had gone off to the library to do research. He told me that he sometimes purchased soft-core pornographic magazines such as *Penthouse*, and stimulated himself by looking at the pictures of the naked women.

I then asked Lucian whether he had other fantasies, or indeed, whether he had a favorite fantasy. He blushed ever so slightly, but then reported the following fantasy:

> Sometimes when I jerk myself off, I think about . . . well, you might find this pretty weird, pretty disgusting actually, but since you asked, well . . . [*Pause*] . . . [*Pause*] . . . I find it very arousing to think of men in a toilet, all in a row, having bowel movements. There might be three guys, all my age, mid-twenties, all in suits, in a loo, and for some reason they've left the doors open, so I can see all three of them. Their trousers and boxers are down around their ankles, and I can see them straining their faces, grunting, as they try to take a dump. As they push their shit out, they lift themselves up a bit on the seat, and I can see the turd coming out of their bums . . . [*Pause*] . . . and sometimes, if I'm really into the fantasy, I imagine that I go up to each of these three men in turn, and have a piss on their penises. And then I come.

After relating this fantasy to me in great detail, Lucian looked at me in order to gauge my reaction. Would I be disgusted or critical? In fact, I maintained a neutral expression on my face, as I always do, trying to avoid any judgments one way or another. I felt tempted to explain to Lucian that compared to some of the other fantasies that I have heard about directly, or have received in writing, his seemed relatively mild, but I refrained from doing so.

In view of Lucian's high intelligence, his verbal skills, and his willingness to access private parts of his mind with relative ease, I felt confident that Lucian would himself be able to make the connection between the experience that he had in the toilets of his elementary school and the subsequent masturbation fantasy, also set in a toilet, which had developed in the postpubescent period. The similarities seemed far too evident even to merit comment. Surely, a clever man such as Lucian would readily recognize the interconnectedness between his youthful experience of being laughed at for being caught with his trousers down, supposedly defecating, and the sexual fantasy of having three strange men exhibiting their feces while Lucian urinated on them, almost as if to prove his point: "You see, I told you I was only peeing, after all."

I asked Lucian directly whether he had any understanding of why he found this fantasy so arousing. To my great surprise, Lucian looked at me baffled, a blank expression on his face, and shrugged his shoulders. "I told you it was pretty weird, but I just get off on it. I was sort of hoping that you could tell me what it means." Perhaps this encounter more than any other has helped me to appreciate that our sexual fantasies become established in our minds as a means of dealing with some aspect of our mental life which has become *split off from consciousness*. In other words, something troubling, such as being discovered in the toilets in a shaming way, can be both remembered and also pushed to the periphery of consciousness. Psychotherapists refer to this process as "splitting." Lucian had not completely repressed the memory of the toilet trauma from the age of five or six; in fact, he remembered it in great detail. But because of the traumatic quality of that memory, he had pushed it to the very fringes of his mind, splitting off from ordinary consciousness. And yet, because the trauma needs to manifest itself somehow, he has cleverly managed to rescript the experience as the basis for his masturbatory fantasy. Although he really *did* know the origins of his sexual fantasy, he also managed simultaneously to *not* know, and he allowed the fantasy to serve as his memory of this humiliating encounter in the toilets.

To recapitulate, at the age of five or six, Lucian experienced a blush-making event, namely, several classmates invaded his privacy by peering over the door of the stalls and caught Lucian with his trousers down, "like a girl," and assumed he must be defecating. They later humiliated him verbally in front of his schoolmates. Although essentially heterosexual in his preferences, and able to function successfully with Genevieve, an adult woman, Lucian could not find a way to process the toilet trauma at the time, and so, it emerged years later, after puberty, in his private masturbatory fantasy. Lucian has cleverly, albeit unwittingly, deployed the mechanism of *reversal* in his fantasy. He has created a way in which he achieves sexual pleasure from the thought of three contemporaries, all males in their mid-twenties, caught with their trousers down, in a toilet, where the doors to the stalls just happen to be ajar. He masturbates and receives enjoyable sensations in his genitals as he watches these three men straining their facial muscles to defecate. Then, as the coup de grâce, Lucian eventually urinates on the men, justifying himself once and for all by showing everyone that he was not defecating, just peeing. Through his masturbatory fantasy, he has not only succeeded in exculpating himself from an accusation that links him with malodorous feces, but also extracted revenge against his childhood tormentors by covering them in urine.

Lucian's fantasy raises a number of provocative questions:

1. Could a fleeting childhood experience, of perhaps only sixty seconds' duration, have had such a compelling, determining effect on someone's subsequent adult masturbatory fantasy?
2. Why did the fantasy not emerge in Lucian's coital relationships with Genevieve?
3. How can Lucian remember the early experience, but not be able to make a conscious connection between the original trauma and the subsequent fantasy, both rather similar in content?
4. Presumably other young children will have had similar toilet experiences at similar ages. Why do they not use these scenes as fodder for their later masturbation activities?

We do not have obvious answers for these questions. I suspect that issues of modesty and bodily shame had already played a crucial part in Lucian's upbringing between the ages of zero and five years, and that he had already become quite sensitive about being seen naked by members of his family. Lucian could not necessarily remember these experiences, and therefore could not adequately describe them, but when I later asked him about any nudity in his home, he told me that to the best of his knowledge he never saw either his mother or his father naked, and that they always kept the door to their bedroom fully shut. To this day, although his body looks very trim and athletic, he becomes quite sheepish at the gym where he works out, always wrapping a towel around his waist before removing his underwear. It may be more traumatic for a young boy with anxieties about nudity, penis size, and other aspects of bodily exposure to be caught in the toilets; a hardier little boy may have found the act of discovery rather amusing or may have hit back in some way.

With my long-term psychotherapy patients, I always share my hypotheses about the possible meanings of their behaviors, symptoms, and fantasies at the appropriate moment. When a psychotherapist sees a patient regularly, one, two, three, four, or even five times each week, the clinician has many opportunities to discuss these matters in a slow and methodical manner. But I met each of the interviewees in my research project only once, albeit for five hours. I doubt that I would have received such frank replies from these men and women if they thought they would ever meet with me again. Knowing they would be seeing me once and once only allowed the interviewees to tell me their most intimate stories—rather like they would at a confessional. So, in the majority of instances, I refrained from sharing my psychoanalytical impressions with the interviewees, as we would not have had the time to discuss the implications properly.

But Lucian asked me directly, almost pleadingly, about my impressions of his masturbatory fantasy. In straightforward language, I told him that I could observe a great many parallels between his sexual fantasy and the episode that he had told me about many hours earlier in our interview, namely, the episode of being caught out in the stalls of his school lavatory. When I made this seemingly obvious connection, Lucian's jaw dropped. He looked utterly stunned and replied, "My god, you're right. And to think, I have been jerking off to this one for years . . . without realizing!"

20   The Fourteen Functions of Sexual Fantasy

Homo sum; humani nil a me alienum puto.
[I am a man, I count nothing human
foreign to me.]
> —TERENCE, *Heautontimorumenos*

So, just why do we fantasize, after all? With life becoming increasingly busy, do we not have better things to do? Freud argued that sexual fantasies result from experiences of frustration, and he regarded them as desperate attempts to gratify often forbidden wishes. This seems a good place to start; and without doubt, the wish-fulfillment hypothesis has served me well in my work with patients.

But I suspect that there may be other functions and other meanings to our sexual fantasies. As part of the computer-administered questionnaire that I sent to participants in the International Sexual Fantasy Research Project, I inquired about each respondent's own private theories regarding his or her sexual fantasies. Respondents noted that fantasies served the following purposes:

1. Fantasies help me to relieve boredom.
2. Fantasies cheer me up when I am depressed.
3. Fantasies allow me to perform acts that I cannot do in real life.
4. Fantasies permit me to have sex with people whom I would not or could not have sex with in real life.
5. Fantasies permit me to explore different sexual thoughts and activities.
6. My partner becomes more attractive to me in my fantasies.

7. Fantasies help me to become aroused with my partner or partners.
8. I cannot help myself. The fantasies just pop into my mind.
9. Fantasies are preferable to actual sexual experiences.
10. Fantasies make the outside world go away.

I find this list of self-descriptors very revealing. Clearly, for many of us, fantasy provides a chance to flee from the entrapments of our lives and minds and to explore new partners, positions, and activities that we cannot or dare not access in everyday life.

Helpful though this list may be, I wish to suggest that fantasizing may have other functions, which may not always be quite so consciously accessible. On the basis of my interview data, the quantitative computer-generated data, and my own clinical investigations over the decades, I have identified some fourteen different reasons why we may fantasize, many of which may be interrelated. I shall now enumerate these various fantasy functions, illustrating each with case material drawn from my psychodiagnostic research interviews.

1. Wish-Fulfillment

Following Freud's initial suggestion that fantasies stem from sexual frustrations and from an inability to achieve full gratification, the wish-fulfillment hypothesis has played a crucial role in psychoanalytical thought for over a century. The wishes requiring fulfillment may be either conscious or unconscious.

"Claudia," a forty-five-year-old woman, yearned to have sexual relations with her handsome brother-in-law, "Richie." Unable to violate the incest taboo, and unwilling to hurt her sister "Adeline," Claudia confined her passion for Richie to her private masturbatory ritual. Fantasizing about vaginal penetration by Richie's penis always induced a deeply satisfying orgasm, and Claudia would drift off to sleep fully content.

In similar vein, "Derek," an eighty-one-year-old physicist, one of the most elderly members of my research sample, explained that he would never fantasize about women when he masturbated. Rather, he would imagine checking his letterbox in the university laboratory and discovering a letter from the King of Sweden informing him that he had just won the Nobel Prize. A moderately successful scientist, but one who has never received great recognition from his peers, Derek had subli-mated virtually all his libido into his work, so that his research projects became his lovers. Since he would rather have success as a physicist than as a lover, he would regularly masturbate to the thought of receiving a letter from Stockholm. Many of us would not find a Swedish missive genitally arousing, but for Derek, this letter became the epitomization of his most erotically pleasing thought.

Virtually every sexual fantasy contains an element of wish-fulfillment. Without the gratification of the wish, we would not achieve climax. The wishes will invariably be forbidden, as with Claudia's wish for her brother-in-law, or they will be out of reach, as with Derek, who, in all likelihood, will never receive a Nobel Prize, much to his chagrin.

2. Self-Comfort and Self-Medication

Sexual fantasies provide respite from our daily troubles, and they af-ford instant physical release, as well as psychological release, when we find ourselves overwhelmed by anxiety, conflict, depression, or even fear of impending breakdown. Fantasies thus function as "over-the-counter" self-medicating palliatives, available at any time of day or night without a doctor's prescription.

"Daryl," a nineteen-year-old construction worker, came to see me for a research consultation after his very first girlfriend had walked out on him without any evident warning. Sent by his general medical prac-titioner, Daryl showed many signs of a moderate depression; in the re-ferral letter, the doctor wrote that in the wake of the breakup, he had learned that Daryl had begun to masturbate compulsively, so much so that he had torn some of the skin on the shaft of his penis. When I met Daryl, he told me that he now masturbated six or seven times a day, and that without his masturbatory indulgences, he thought he would go insane. He fantasized mostly about his ex-girlfriend, and he did not know how he could ever live without her.

"Boyd," by contrast, had lost his job. A twenty-eight-year-old assis-tant producer in a television company, Boyd had worked hard, but not hard enough to restore the failing profits of his employers. Fired, not for his incompetence, but because of job cuts across the board, Boyd plummeted into a spiral of depression as he spent four weeks at home, frantically applying for new posts, tensely awaiting interviews. In order to keep himself from smoking and drinking too much—a long-standing vulnerability—Boyd purchased some pornographic DVDs of bondage and domination and "beat off" furiously to the images on the screen. As Boyd explained to me, "After I jerked off, I would get sleepy, you know, just like a little baby, and then I'd nap. And when I'd wake up, I'd feel refreshed. I think those DVDs got me through my lay-off."

3. Trial Action

Fantasies afford us the opportunity to experiment with sexual thoughts that cause us conflict, and that we both hope and fear may one day be turned into action. In psychotherapy, we often speak of "trial action," a patient's first, fumbling steps toward the achievement of a certain maturational goal. For instance, a highly agoraphobic patient may be far too frightened to go to a party or to any social gathering. I can remember one agoraphobic patient who found any group of three or more people completely overwhelming. One day, this gentleman told me that he had struck up a conversation with an elderly lady on the bus—the very first time in his life that he had ever done so. The patient felt extremely proud, and it proved to be a key launching point for more social activity in the future.

"Florence," a thirty-nine-year-old virgin, found men so intimidating that in spite of her evident attractiveness, she would never accept any invitations from workmates for supper or even a trip to the movies. Florence also refrained from masturbation, as her puritanical parents considered any unnecessary touching of the genitals to be dirty. Her father, a cleric, often quoted medieval literature to her that denounced sex as unclean, since the man's penis discharges not only semen but also urine. Florence told me that she had sought counseling for her emotional inhibitions, and that as her treatment had progressed, her harsh, punitive internal world began to soften. One day she reported her very first act of "self-pleasuring," fantasizing about a young man in her office called "Ray." It took Florence more than a year to pluck up the courage to flirt with Ray, but eventually she did, and they dated for a while, having a number of reasonably satisfying sexual encounters. For Florence, her first masturbatory fantasy about Ray served as a form of trial action that allowed her to begin to conceptualize something previously taboo.

"Baxter," a fifty-six-year-old heterosexual man, yearned to try anal sex with his wife. She found the idea revolting, and she declared that she would never submit to such a form of penetration. Frustrated, Baxter soon incorporated images of anal intercourse with his wife in both his masturbatory activity and his coital relations with his spouse. When he penetrated his wife's vagina, he would sometimes pretend that he had actually inserted his penis into her rectum. Although he never did succeed in convincing his wife to try anal sex, his fantasies nevertheless represented a form of trial action as well.

4. Elaboration of Childhood Play

Long before we fantasize about overtly sexual matters in adult life, every individual has ample time to develop the capacity to fantasize. Developmental psychologists and child psychotherapists do not know exactly when fantasizing begins, but we suspect it starts rather early, possibly even during the third trimester of pregnancy, although this remains speculative. But certainly a newborn infant will fantasize about food in the form of breast milk, and a young toddler will fantasize about the day that he or she might be able to stand securely on two feet, just as mother and father do. By the time a child develops a more formal capacity for play, elements of fantasy become critical. For instance, imagine two children playing house. One may chirp, "Let's pretend I'm the mommy, and you're the daddy," or what have you. As we watch young children playing in an uninterrupted manner, we can easily become astonished by the creativity of the scenes that will sometimes unfold. I recently observed a four-year-old boy who pretended that he owned a shoe shop, and he stopped every single grown-up that he could find, offering to repair their shoes for only a dollar. All the grown-ups, eager to indulge this fantasy play, had to remove their shoes, as the lad pretended to be a cobbler, and he returned the shoes in pristine condition, whereupon he seemed happy to be given an imaginary one-dollar note.

As a little girl, "Brenda," now twenty-seven, used to fantasize about a very handsome cartoon prince from one of the animated films that she had enjoyed as a child. She and her slightly elder sister, "Carissa," would pretend that the prince had offered to marry them both, and they would dress up in their mother's long gowns and stage a "pretend" wedding. The fantasy of snagging the prince later became a key theme in Brenda's sexual fantasies, and as she grew older, her attentions turned from the Disney prince to none other than His Royal

Highness Prince William, grandson of the British monarch, thus finding a creative adult equivalent to a piece of early childhood fantasy play.

As a little boy, "Gene," the eldest of four siblings, would round up his younger brother and his baby sisters and dress them up in costumes, and then they would perform plays for their parents. Gene, now sixty-three, eventually became an actor. He ultimately wed a fellow member of the theatrical profession, and they have two children, both, unsurprisingly, in show business in one form or another. Gene told me that when he and his wife make love, he imagines that they have intercourse on a stage, in front of thousands and thousands of paying spectators, and that after he achieves orgasm, he receives a BAFTA award (the British equivalent of the Academy Award) for his performance. One can readily see the interconnection between his early pleasurable experiences of childhood play, when he was being lavished with parental attention, and the subsequent development of an enjoyable coital fantasy.

5. Establishment of Object Relationships

Psychoanalytical mental health workers often describe human relationships as "object" relationships. On the surface, this term seems deeply unfriendly, if not alienating. But it has remained in professional usage for many decades because, although we recognize that most people relate to other *people*, rather than to *objects*, we also recognize that people often treat others as objects, inflicting cruelty on them or relating to only a part of them. For example, a woman may complain, "My husband is only interested in my vagina." This sort of statement becomes indicative of an object relationship. However, the term can also be used to describe a more sophisticated and sensitive form of interrelating, and we might say of a cured, healthy patient that his or her object relationships have now become rich and rewarding.

We all struggle to maintain and to develop our object relationships in the world, and we have always known that sexual fantasies may function as a means of helping lonely or isolated people to establish object relatedness. Consider the following clinical vignettes drawn from my psychodiagnostic research interviews.

"Theodore," a fifty-three-year-old bank clerk from Colchester, had suffered from a long history of mental health problems, including a psychotic breakdown in his youth which had left him virtually friendless, and certainly bereft of a sexual partner. In his sexual fantasies, he would imagine himself at the center of a large cluster of women, all grabbing for his clothing simultaneously, ripping off each item in turn, and then pleasuring him to the point of climax. Although many people—many men, in particular—would also enjoy this same fantasy, for Theodore the fantasy performed an important psychological function. It permitted him to move from a posture of psychological retreatedness, wherein he had always found women terrifying, to one of psychological object-relatedness, wherein he would be able to engage with women, albeit in an interchangeable manner, with each woman equally replaceable by the next. Theodore's fantasy conveyed his strong wish, and his strong need, to seek contact from a multiplicity of sources, and for this reason he found the fantasy particularly enjoyable. It represented a small step toward the personal achievement of being able to interact with a number of people.

Another man who arrived for an interview with me, a sixty-nine-year-old retired stockbroker called "Wade," had a lot of friends, or, as he described the situation, "too many friends, in fact." Overwhelmed by the business of his life, Wade had "detoxified" his Filofax years earlier, and he told me that he had stopped returning telephone calls, e-mails, and letters from concerned friends, as he felt all his relationships to be meaningless. Within the space of several years, he transformed himself, unhealthily, from a socialite into a hermit. After marrying a new wife—his previous spouse having divorced him and fought him in a bitter custody battle for the children—Wade gradually began to become reequilibrated, and he started to socialize in small stages. At this point, he began to masturbate again, a practice which he had abandoned during his earlier period of depression, when absolutely nothing would arouse him. When he did masturbate, Wade thought about himself as a porn star or stripper performing for large crowds. The prospect of having sex or of removing his clothes in front of admirers not only made him feel younger, but also, as he explained, made him feel "more connected." Wade smirked and asked me, "Does this make me a sex maniac?" In this context I reassured him that I did not think he qualified as a sex maniac, but I wondered whether perhaps he had some anxieties about his sexual fantasies. He admitted that he did, but then confessed, quite poignantly, "but at least I'm having these fantasies. They make me feel in touch, whereas before, when I was in the slumps, I didn't like human beings very much at all." Clearly, both

Theodore and Wade, two men with difficulties in feeling "at home" with other people, used fantasies constructively to build bridges to the social world.

6. Transitional Objects and Phenomena

During the 1950s and 1960s, the English pediatrician and psychoanalyst Dr. Donald Winnicott wrote about how the helpless and dependent human infant progresses through the stages of the life cycle, gradually developing greater psychological independence. Although Winnicott identified many factors that facilitate healthy growth, especially sustained caretaking from loving parental figures, he also highlighted the importance of objects, sounds, or thoughts that assist the vulnerable baby in the crucial task of separating from his or her mother without feeling grossly abandoned in the process. Winnicott theorized about the vital role of blankets or soft toys such as teddy bears, which offer the child comfort in the form of symbolic mothering. He referred to these objects as "transitional objects," and he noted that although a teddy bear will never replace the love of a mother, the soft, breast-like quality of the teddy or the blanket provides transitional comfort that allows the infant to forge a relationship with that object, thus giving the overworked mother a few minutes of respite.

Not only does the baby need to have transitional objects to assist in the separation from mother's body, according to Winnicott, but the baby also benefits from other experiences. Hearing mother's voice calling out from a different room, for example, offers the baby a reassuring sense that mother has not disappeared, but does not have to be immediately available, either. Sometimes, knowing that the mother has "held" the baby in mind by *thinking* about the baby can be helpful in stimulating positive growth and development. Winnicott referred to these experiences as "transitional phenomena." Basically, these may be defined as sounds or thoughts that the baby experiences that give the baby an indication that mother, though not immediately present, has not become lost.

"Emmy" could readily be described as a "clingy" woman. She drove her poor husband, "Tobin," round the bend because she would never leave him alone. Tobin could never have five minutes of quiet in the marital home without Emmy intruding and starting up an animated conversation. One day, while cleaning out Tobin's clothes closet, Emmy found one of his pornographic magazines. Out of interest, she sat down and started to leaf through the photographs of naked women. Up until then, she did not believe that she had ever had a sexual fantasy, but now she surprised herself by becoming aroused, especially by a picture of a naked male model making love to a naked female model. She imagined herself as the female model, and she wondered what it would be like to cheat on Tobin. Eventually, she masturbated to the picture, and before long she had discovered a new hobby. Gradually, she became less clingy toward Tobin, who could not really understand quite why Emmy had begun to "chill out" so much. After all, his own behavior had not changed in the slightest. Unconsciously, Emmy used her fantasies as transitional phenomena to assist her in brokering a fuller psychological separation from the state of merger in which she had found herself in relation to Tobin. In this instance, both the wife and the husband appreciated the greater amount of psychological freedom and independence. Emmy has never told Tobin about the magazine, but in many ways she believes that the pornography has provided her with a private world all of her own.

For "Preston," a nineteen-year-old young man still living at home with his parents, sexual fantasies became important transitional phenomena because they helped him to separate psychologically from an overwhelmingly intrusive mother who, in particular, would often barge into his bedroom and discover him masturbating. Aware that he might be gay, but not fully certain of this, Preston told me that he would invariably masturbate to thoughts of handsome boys in his classes at his nearby college. In one of his recurrent fantasies, Preston imagined that he had "cruised" an attractive male on campus and brought him back to his parents' house for sex. As the fantasy continued, Preston took this man into his bedroom, and as they began to undress one another, he could hear his mother's footsteps heading toward his bedroom. With lightning speed, Preston raced to the door and locked it. As his mother began to bang repeatedly on the door, insisting on entry, Preston indulged in anal intercourse with this young man. Evidently, this fantasy proved exciting for Preston because it allowed him to enjoy the experience of locking his mother out for once, offering him the opportunity to explore his own sexuality in his own way. Of course, intrusive parents forge a deep impact upon the human mind, and their legacy cannot be dismissed so easily; therefore, whereas another young gay man may have had a fantasy set in the gym, in the forest, or at the swimming pool, Preston's fantasy takes place in his parents' home. And in the fantasy, he manages, for the first time, to lock the door, thus mastering his mother's potential physical and psychological intrusions.

7. Communication of Inner Conflict

Sometimes, sexual fantasies may have a primary function of communicating a deep, unanalyzed, unprocessed psychological conflict. Although the conflict may be understood consciously by the fantasist, more often than not it will be "split off" from consciousness, and thus unavailable to the fantasist for further thought.

"Garcia," a twenty-four-year-old newly qualified teacher, confessed his predominant sexual fantasy with a great deal of shame. He told me that he fantasizes about young boys in his class, especially boys of eleven or twelve years of age. He insisted that he would never, *ever* lay a hand on them. He knew all about the evils of pedophilia, and he had even attended lectures at college on the long-term, devastating consequences of child sexual abuse as part of his teacher training. He told me that I could rest assured that young boys in his class would always be safe. He confined his pedophilic tendencies to the inside of his mind. In spite of his fantasies—which, if enacted, would land him in prison— I found Garcia to be an intelligent and thoughtful person with a great deal of compassion. When I learned more about his history, which was filled with child abuse of various types, I began to hypothesize that his wish to have sexual contact with eleven-year-old boys lay not in a primary desire to harm them (although it would have that effect), but in a desperate attempt to love a boy as he had wanted to be loved at that age, the very age when his parents had sent him away to a boarding school overseas. Garcia used his masturbatory fantasy as a means of "leaking" distress and confusion. I referred him to a clinical colleague who has experience treating people with pedophilic fantasies and tendencies. I hope that Garcia will consult this colleague, learn to work through these impulses, and become less fearful of age-appropriate partners, whether female or, more likely in his case, male.

"Joelly," in contrast, explained to me that she enjoys fantasizing about having sex with an older man, specifically, a grey-haired man whom she might meet in a hotel bar while having a drink. This thirty-nine-year-old woman had never had a sexual experience of any kind with her father. In fact, Joelly's father treated her growing teenage body with dignity and respect. But she did have a very seductive mother who flirted with "anything that moved." Watching her mother "working the room," Joelly would often feel quite inadequate, and as she progressed through adolescence, she began to adopt more and more of her mother's kittenish, flirtatious mannerisms. By the time she reached college, Joelly had become so accomplished in the art of seduction that several of the male students called her a "prick-tease." It took her a while to discover that her fantasies of sex with older men, though not egregious in and of themselves, stemmed from her "oedipal" wish to steal her father from her mother. After a period in psychotherapy, Joelly's seductive behavior became more muted, and she would no longer bat her eyes at her girlfriends' partners quite so regularly.

8. Indulgence in Masochistic Punishment

Sometimes we can utilize our fantasies not as a source of sexual joy, but as a means of punishing ourselves for some crime that we have committed, either real or imaginary. Often, fantasies of punishing ourselves emerge after a great success rather than after a failure, a counterlogical clinical finding first identified by Freud, who argued that most of us cannot bear the guilt of becoming more successful than our parents, and that we sabotage ourselves whenever possible to alleviate these feelings.

"Jocelyn" had only recently received a promotion at work. As a result, this middle-aged corporate lawyer had received a huge bonus, a new office, and a Mercedes Benz. Clearly, she had arrived professionally. But all of this success took a great toll on her mind, and in her spare time, lounging in the privacy of her new office, she began to trawl the Internet for sadomasochistic pornography, occasionally masturbating in her chair when she believed that everyone had already gone home. Eventually, her boss discovered Jocelyn's secret Internet habit and reported her to the senior partner, causing Jocelyn to receive a formal reprimand, not to mention her huge shame and guilt for having "brought this on my own head." I suspect that the guilt at having achieved such success at work activated her sense of unconscious guilt, which she alleviated by sabotaging herself. After all, she could have easily used her home computer for Internet porn rather than her work computer.

"Lyndon" also used his fantasies to punish himself. A successful physician, with a growing reputation in his chosen specialty, Lyndon enjoyed visiting prostitutes who would flagellate him. He would pay extra to have the prostitutes engage in role-play with him, in which he would pretend to be a very ill patient. The prostitute would have to dress up as a nurse and perform all sorts of examinations of Lyndon's body. This would work him up into a frenzy, so much so that he had sexual intercourse "once or twice without a condom." Lyndon explained that he had explosive orgasms with these prostitutes, but that he would feel cheap and dirty afterwards. On two occasions he had contracted pubic lice from the sex workers he had visited, an awful and shaming punishment indeed for an intelligent physician working in the field of public health and hygiene.

9. Defenses Against Intimacy and Merger

Oftentimes, the prospect of intimacy becomes so terrifying for human beings that we do all within our power to erect potent barriers against ever forging a relationship. Sexual fantasy can become inextricably linked with a masturbatory addiction, so much so that the compulsive use of masturbatory fantasy functions as a means of keeping other human beings at a distance. I certainly do not wish to espouse the view that one must be in a sexual partnership as an adult in order to be psychologically healthy, but ideally, one must have the *capacity* to forge intimate relationships. Many widows and widowers, for example, will elect not to remarry after spousal bereavement, not because of their inability to sustain a relationship, but for various other reasons, including an understandable fidelity to their deceased partner. But for many, intimacy becomes not a sought-after desideratum, but rather a frightening obstacle.

I first met "Dora" as part of the Sexual Fantasy Research Project. Although she had once enjoyed a long-term relationship with a boyfriend, years ago, he had died overseas in the Gulf War. By the time I met her, she was thirty-eight years old and had remained single for more than fifteen years, never having accepted even an invitation for a dinner date with a prospective suitor. Dora had suffered from a major depression in the wake of her boyfriend's tragic death, but with the help of friends and family, she had recovered somewhat, enough, at any rate, to return to her job working in local government. Sadly, however, she never recaptured the zest and vitality she had once had. Initially, she had no libido at all, but after two or three years, she had found a local bookshop specializing in erotic literature for women. For the past decade or so she had relied exclusively upon her masturbatory fantasies, as stimulated by the erotic literature. Her favorite fantasies involved romantic scenes such as lounging on beaches or frolicking under waterfalls. The prospect of sex with a real, living man, as opposed to a fictional one, remained too threatening for this traumatized woman. After our interview, I referred Dora to a mental health agency in her part of the country in the hope that she might seek some psychotherapy or counseling.

I should mention that although I referred Dora and a small number of others for psychotherapeutic work after the interviews, I did so in fewer than 5 percent of cases. The vast majority of research interviewees managed the experience extremely well and provided no evidence of either needing or desiring further psychological support.

"Elwyn" also feared intimacy, though not as the direct result of a massive trauma, as in the case of the bereaved Dora. By contrast, Elwyn, who was forty years old, grew up in a household with a very fragile but aggressive single mother who would shout at Elwyn and his siblings with ferocity. If he arrived home ten minutes late from school, his mother would shout; if he forgot to wash his hands before supper, his mother would shout; and if he neglected to turn out the light in the bathroom, his mother would shout. After he left home to attend university far away, Elwyn began to have sex with women, but none of his relationships lasted more than two or three months. Eventually, he gave up trying, having had his heart broken on so many occasions. He turned instead to pornography as his erotic mainstay, utilizing a variety of different magazines, and he became proficient in the use of telephone chat lines, books, videos, and the Internet. In fact, he became, indisputably, a pornography addict. Interestingly, although he tried every single variant of pornography, he would never visit a prostitute, thus protecting himself against the pain of rejection from a directly available, living woman. When I inquired about his specific sexual fantasies, Elwyn told me that he particularly enjoyed masturbating to the thought of trussing up a woman like a turkey, and then "fucking her good and hard in the mouth, making her gag on my dick." I strongly suspect that this fantasy stems from a deep-seated wish to shut up his verbally intrusive mother by shoving something into her mouth.

10. Discharge of Aggression

As we already know, large numbers of sexual fantasies contain strong imagery of violence, whether overt or covert. Most (though not all) of us would view trussing up a partner like a turkey as an act of aggression, but how would we classify other forms of sexuality, such as "thrusting," "ramming," "bucking," and all the other potentially "rough" activities that may fall within the parameters of so-called "normal" sex?

"Cory," a twenty-year-old college student, enjoyed masturbating to thoughts of the pop star Kylie Minogue. He had posters of her on the wall of his dormitory room, and he became quickly aroused watching her DVDs. When he described his ultimate fantasy as "a night with Kylie," I encouraged him to provide more details, whereupon he explained, "I'd throw her on the bed, rip her clothes off, and shove my penis inside her. I'd give her a few good ones, and fuck her good and hard, with her head slamming into the headboard of the bed, making a lot of noise." If this fantasy became a reality, and if Kylie Minogue agreed to consensual sex with Cory, one could not accuse him of doing anything untoward or illegal. This would be an example of vigorous sexual intercourse. But, of course, the aggressive underbelly becomes very apparent, especially in Cory's choice of action verbs such as "throw," "rip," "shove," "fuck," and "slam." Although quite pleasant on the surface, Cory came from a broken, impecunious home, and it seemed clear from our conversation that he had experienced quite a lot about which he could be angry; unsurprisingly, he used his fantasy about the pop star in part as a means of discharging much pent-up aggression.

"Dexter," a forty-one-year-old groundsman at a local park, worked hard in the daytime, exerting himself physically, and thus felt entitled to party a great deal at night. He would frequent "hip" bars and nightclubs, chatting up all the beautiful women. Unfortunately for Dexter, he did not have a great "hit rate," and many of the women he approached would reject him flat out. If he did not succeed in picking up one of the "drunken dogs," he would return home by himself and "jerk off" while engaging in "dirty talk" with a woman on a telephone chat line. Dexter explained that he became most erotically charged when imagining himself "bitch-slapping" the woman on the other end of the phone. He would request that she pretend that he had slapped her on the face, entreating her to cry out, "Ow, that really hurt." This discharge of aggression would arouse Dexter, and ultimately he would climax. When I inquired about discipline in his early years, Dexter told me that his father had hit him "only once or twice," and that otherwise his parents had treated him lovingly. Unless Dexter had managed to repress additional episodes of violence, we must realize that although many sexual fantasies may be exact reenactments of earlier abuse, many others develop in more complicated, less easily understandable ways.

11. Avoidance of Painful Reality

Although all fantasies contain wishes, some of them might be described as "aspirational wishes" (e.g., "I really hope that one day, if I'm lucky, I might get to sleep with Scarlett Johansson"). These aspirational wishes may not necessarily be realistic, but they represent a striving for possible contact. After all, Miss Johansson has had relationships with partners, so at least a few people have succeeded in winning her affections. Many people harbor similar fantasies toward winning a lottery or a sweepstakes competition, theorizing that some people have won large pots of money, so, although the mathematical probability may be minuscule, one could still become a winner. But other wishes, however heartfelt, can never be achieved, and these often serve as cosmetic cover-ups that help us avoid deeply painful pieces of reality. I would refer to these wishes as "antidevelopmental wishes" (e.g., "One day, I will awaken to find that I am someone else, someone with irresistible appeal, maybe James Bond perhaps, and women will follow me down the street in large numbers"). These sorts of fantasies—imagining oneself as someone else—can prevent us from grappling with a middle-age paunch, a receding hairline, sagging breasts, crow's feet around the eyes, and all the other aspects of aging that remind us of eventual impending death.

"Lana," a pretty woman aged thirty-seven, desperately wanted to have a baby. However, owing to a tragic fall while mountaineering ten years previously, she had become completely paralyzed from the waist down, and her physician confirmed that she would never be able to have a baby. Unable to experience orgasm, or indeed any physical sensations in the lower half of her body, Lana still had her own version of sexual fantasies to which she referred as her "sexual dreams," in which a handsome mountain ranger would rescue her from her fall and make love to her, impregnating her; then, nine months later, he would help to deliver their beautiful, healthy, physically perfect baby. This struck me as a very understandable fantasy for someone in Lana's situation. In her waking hours, Lana felt so embarrassed and ashamed of her handicapped, disabled body that she rarely went out of the house; although she had, over the years, met a number of men in wheelchairs who had become partially paralyzed through crashes of one sort or another, she found them undesirable. She deeply craved an able-bodied male. Although her fantasy brought her temporary comfort, I wondered whether it had an anti-developmental quality rather than an aspirational one, and I referred Lana to a local counseling organization near her home in the hope that a sustained series of conversations with a sympathetic colleague would allow her to gain a greater acceptance of her physical capacities and realities.

"Lyn," another interviewee in the Sexual Fantasy Research Project, explained to me that she has only one fantasy. Whenever she masturbates, she imagines having tender, loving sexual intercourse with her late husband, "Gerald," who had died, sixteen years earlier, from cancer. Now seventy-one years of age, Lyn spoke about her depression and about her tendency to drink excessively at night. "I wish I could describe myself as the Merry Widow," she lamented, "but without Gerald, I just find myself marking time." Though one could hardly fault Lyn for fantasizing about the husband with whom she had forged a long marital life, one wonders whether the persistent fantasies may have militated against the likelihood of her meeting someone else for either a sexual relationship or satisfying companionship. Although younger readers may think of the age of seventy as a death sentence, older people regard seventy as merely the first wisp of old age. I know of many nonagenarians who enjoy healthy sexual relationships. One wonders whether Lyn might find a means of being among those in twenty years' time.

12. Evacuation of Sadistic Strivings

Although sexual fantasies permit some to discharge their aggressive urges, at times these impulses and tendencies may veer off the scale of ordinary human negativity and slide into the realm of murderous pathology. Sexual fantasies can serve as an outlet for the more sadistic aspects of human nature, and, further, may be a warning sign to police, forensic psychologists, and other concerned individuals about a person's degree of potential dangerousness. Unfortunately, we have very little data on the masturbatory fantasies of murderers; such information might help us to discriminate those members of the general public who have graphic murderous fantasies, unlikely to be expressed in real life, from those who actually progress to the perpetration of the most heinous crimes. We do know, for instance, from the prison diaries of the British multiple murderer Dennis Nilsen, a man who killed twelve young men at his home in Muswell Hill, North London, dismembering many of the corpses afterwards, that when he masturbated, he would often fantasize about dead bodies. If the law-enforcement agencies or the psychiatric sector had known about these masturbatory fantasies during Nilsen's earlier years, they might have identified him as a potentially "high-risk" patient and offered immediate psychological treatment.

I met "Whitney" during the early stages of my psychodiagnostic clinical interviews for this project. From the moment he walked in the door, he had a look of paranoid suspicion—darting eyes, furtive glances, and a face frozen in a stony stare—rather similar to the physiognomies of long-stay psychiatric patients with whom I had worked years earlier, only much more sinister. This fifty-six-year-old man cooperated fully with my questions and inquiries, and he had no hesitation whatsoever in telling me that his favorite sexual fantasies involved drawing blood from a woman's body. Once married, now divorced, Whitney explained that he had never actually caused a woman to bleed, and he did not regard himself as a dangerous person. But the sight of blood—in his fantasy, at least—aroused him considerably. I worked very hard to try to establish symbolic connections between early experiences in Whitney's childhood and his subsequent love of blood, but I must confess that I failed miserably. Whitney answered me in grunting monosyllabic monotones, and though he proved superficially helpful, his one-word answers made it difficult to develop a more full-fledged diagnostic conversation. Such an anemic interpersonal style will often be indicative of more deep-seated psychological turmoil. Often, with patients of this nature, one needs many more interviews over a more extended period of time to forge the connections that could establish the basis for dialogue. I found my interview with Whitney highly challenging, rather like pulling teeth, and I felt a great sense of relief when he left the room. I had no inkling that he had ever perpetrated bodily harm upon a woman, although I could not be certain; but I suspect that his fantasies permitted him to evacuate a murderous hatred, which, if left untapped, could indeed result in a violent criminal explosion.

I also met with "Chester," a twenty-nine-year-old taxi driver, who told me that he had beaten his young wife "many times" before she ran away, and that he felt deeply ashamed and regretful that he had lost control of his temper. When he fantasized, he often thought about being an evil, lecherous, Transylvanian count, not necessarily Dracula, but someone with a similar style. He would imagine capturing nubile maidens with extremely large breasts, keeping them imprisoned in his castle, and depriving them of food and water for days on end, until they became so faint that they would capitulate to his sexual advances. Stressing once again that he would never hurt a woman, Chester then explained that as the fantasy unfolded, he would imagine that he placed one of the weakened girls on the window ledge of a dungeon chamber, high in the top of the castle. Chester, as the "Count," would unsheathe his penis and then thrust it into the vagina of the weakened maiden with such strength that she toppled backward, out of the window, crashing to her death. At this point, Chester would bring himself to a terrific climax. I managed to obtain a fuller history from Chester than I had done from Whitney, and I discovered, very interestingly, that Chester's mother had died a violent death in a plane crash during his seventh year. On learning of this unusual and tragic piece of biography, I suddenly realized that his wish to thrust a maiden out of a high window and watch her plummet to death might well be related to the awful death that his own mother had experienced plummeting from a height of some 35,000 feet. By eroticizing the death of a maiden—enjoying her death in a sexual manner—he had managed, in symbolic form, to take charge of his own mother's deeply tragic demise.

13. Mastery of Trauma

A great many sexual fantasies involve the mastery of traumatic experiences. Chester, for example, the fantasied Transylvanian count, attempted through his particularly vivid fantasy to master the trauma of the heartbreaking death of his mother. His fantasy also served, incidentally, to vent his sadistic urges against women, some of which he had enacted through the battering of his wife. But for many of us, the mastery of trauma need not involve the release of unconscious sadism. The eroticization of trauma can simply be a creative solution to a painful life event.

"Bunny" surprised me by telling me that she never fantasized at all. I had of course known from the computer survey that a small proportion of women, in particular, claim never to have had sexual fantasies, but none of the women, or men for that matter, who came to London for an interview fitted into that category. After all, if one had no sexual fantasies, why on earth would one volunteer to speak to a psychotherapist for five hours about precisely that subject? I raised my eyebrows slightly to see if she would elaborate, and then Bunny confessed, "Well, all right, I do fantasize, I guess, but it's not a really juicy fantasy, like you must be used to hearing." She then explained to me that whenever she closed her eyes and masturbated, she would sees stars—literally— twinkling stars in the sky. The very thought of these stars makes this twenty-two-year-old hairdresser in training feel aroused. Sometimes the stars are yellow, sometimes red, sometimes orange. But the brightness and the gleam of the stars cause Bunny to become excited, and she will soon climax thinking about them. Apparently, she had only developed this fantasy during the past year. I soon learned that eighteen months previously, as she was walking home from work, two teenage boys had pounced on Bunny, pushed her to the ground, partially concussing her, and then ripped her skirt off and raped her, penetrating her vagina without condoms. Mercifully, she became neither pregnant nor infected with a sexually transmitted disease, but the act of physical, sexual, and psychological assault had caused her to become deeply anxious, depressed, and unable to function for at least six months. After she returned to work in her salon, she met a young male hairdresser called "Donovan" and embarked on a sexual relationship with him, which has proved to be a very good corrective experience. When Bunny has sex with Donovan, she thinks only about him. But when she masturbates, her mind generates pictures of the twinkling stars.

Somewhat perplexed at meeting a woman who found stars sexually stimulating, I asked for further clarification, but nothing that Bunny said made any great sense, and I became stumped. Then, I took a gamble, and, thinking about the colloquial expression "seeing stars," something people often say after receiving a blow to the head, I asked Bunny what thoughts had gone through her mind when the two rapists had pushed her down on the ground and started to rip her clothing before penetrating her. To my great surprise, Bunny replied in the most unselfconscious manner, "Oh, I saw stars, you know, like lights flashing right in front of my eyes. I think it must've been from hitting my head."

I suspect that, by focusing on the stars in her eyes at the moment of impact, Bunny had managed to keep her mind off the terrible rape happening right at that moment. I know from years of talking to survivors of child sexual abuse that when penetration begins, young victims often imagine themselves floating above themselves in a dissociated state, as though someone else was being raped by proxy. Bunny engaged in a similar psychological strategy, concentrating on the stars rather than on the rape itself, and this mental maneuver helped her to cope psychologically. Later, when she began to masturbate, stars and other colored lights became sources of sexual pleasure, thus assisting in the eroticization of the trauma and in its eventual mastery. Her loving and gentle boyfriend Donovan had also helped her greatly in mitigating the impact of the trauma.

Sixty-four-year-old lawyer "Clifford," in contrast, told me that he had stopped having sex with his wife some ten or fifteen years earlier, simply because it had become so very boring, and his wife would not acquiesce to any of his sexual requests, especially "dirty talk." In an effort to compensate for the lack of a sex life, Clifford had become "addicted" to masturbation, but even so, he could climax only when he imagined his fantasized female lover crying out, "Call me a dirty bitch, call me a fucking cunt. Tell me to lick your cock while you eat out my fucking cunt." He would then reply, "Yeah, bitch, I am gonna eat out your dirty cunt while you slurp on my cock." All of this "dirty talk," known in the clinical literature as "coprolalia," aroused Clifford tremendously and proved necessary in order to reach orgasm. Although many people find coprolalic activities arousing, for Clifford the ability to hear and speak "dirty talk" took on a particular meaning. In the course of obtaining biographical information about his early childhood, I learned that his punitive parents would take turns washing his mouth out with soap—quite literally—a barbaric form of "child discipline" quite popular in the 1940s and 1950s, the time of Clifford's childhood and adolescence. Whenever he uttered a dirty word, such as "damn" or "bugger," his parents would drag him kicking and screaming into the bathroom and actually jam a cake of soap into his mouth until he started spitting out bubbles. As a little child, he always thought that he would choke to death, and he became quite terrified. Although Clifford did not make the conscious connection between the soap incidents and his love of dirty talk, the link seems quite clear. By speaking in coarse language to his imaginary lover, and by entreating her to do the same, Clifford succeeded in triumphing over the cruelty of his parents, who would never let him utter even so much as a "darn" or a "drat." By indulging in coprolalic phrases, Clifford managed to engage in an act of defiance with orally triumphant overtones, as if to proclaim to his parents that the only object he will be eating will be a woman's vagina, certainly not a punitive bar of soap. Clifford, like Bunny, and like so many of the fantasists reported in this study, deploys fantasies as a means of dealing with early trauma, usually unprocessed trauma, in a creative and arousing manner.

14. Equilibration of the Self

Over the course of this research project, I have often wondered what human psychology would be like without the capacity to fantasize. I suspect that our minds would be exceedingly bleak. Although our fantasies may often be lurid, or troubling, or deranged by certain standards, I have come to view them as extensions of our *capacity for creativity*, the very imaginal creativity that assists novelists in developing convoluted plots, painters in conceiving new art works, composers in crafting new melodies and harmonies, and ordinary Joes and Janes in keeping a conversation aloft at a dinner party or in a bar. But not only do our fantasies keep us creatively fueled, they sometimes rescue us from complete breakdown and loss of a sense of self, performing a function that I conceptualize as the "equilibration of the self," putting us on a more even keel psychologically.

"Tyler," a highly competent, essentially sane man of thirty, works in an investment bank. Stressed beyond belief, with huge financial responsibilities, Tyler often feels "on the edge of breakdown." Of course, he used the word in its colloquial meaning rather than in its formal psychiatric sense. I had no evidence that Tyler could be at immediate risk of becoming schizophrenic, for example, but he did feel as though his mind might splinter into little shards at any second. When I discussed the role that sex and sexual fantasies played in Tyler's life, he responded, quite enlighteningly, "They keep me from going bonkers. If I couldn't fantasize and have a fiddle at the same time, I think my head would explode like one of those cartoon characters." During our interview, I found out that Tyler had very straightforward fantasies: intercourse with his girlfriend, intercourse with Britney Spears, a bit of bondage ("nothing too heavy"), and some sexual acts involving cherries and whipped cream. Certainly, by comparison with some of the other material contained in this book, Tyler would seem very tame on the scale of fantasies. But his capacity to fantasize provided him not only with wish-fulfillment, relief from stress, relief from depression, and so much else—in his case, it seemed to have as its primary function the ability to keep him sane.

"Caitlin," a middle-aged housewife, told me something rather similar. She explained that she would spend her days at home looking after the house, but that since her four children had all departed for university or had begun married lives of their own, her world had become quite empty. She discovered a Web site specializing in erotic stories and to her great surprise learned that at the "ripe old age of fifty-eight," she had become aroused by pornography, something in which she had not indulged previously. With her husband at the office and her children far away, Caitlin explained, she did not have much housework to do, and she had never had a paid job because of her previously extensive childcare commitments. So, she now spent her days reading, watching television, and exploring sexual fantasies on the Internet. She had learned, to her surprise, that lesbian stories of any description really turned her on, something she certainly had never previously explored, "in spite of having gone to a convent school." As a child, she had come to regard homosexuality as a sin, but as a grown-up, she had become more tolerant, and indeed, she found herself aroused by the thought of two women engaged in any sort of physical contact. As Caitlin explained, "Although I have a good life, it does get empty, very empty, and without the Web site, I'd feel that someone had taken a part of my self away. Yes, I think that's right. It feels like part of my body. Without it, I don't know how I'd get through the day."

21   The Mysterious Boxing Gloves, Or, Can Fantasies Be Trauma-Free?

Out of my own great woe
I make little songs.

—Elizabeth Barrett Browning,
"From Heine"

Tom Cruise's Stick Shift and Michelle Pfeiffer's Smile

Do all fantasies originate from bodily trauma, sexual trauma, early abuse, or humiliation? After examining the case histories presented in the preceding chapters, one might be justified in concluding that everyone I interviewed has suffered physical cruelty, sexual abuse, or bodily humiliation of some sort, whether that be Paris's father ejaculating on his son, Graziella's collision with the glass-topped table, Dahlia's encounters with her learning disabled brother Mickey, or Lucian's embarrassment at his schoolmates taunting him in the toilet stall. Surely, not everybody has endured such cruelties during childhood, and even if they have, could it really be the case that these episodes will be sufficient causative factors in determining the nature of our erotic fantasies?

A thirty-four-year-old jazz singer, "Marissa," told me that she has one abiding sexual fantasy, and it involves the Hollywood actor Tom Cruise. Ever since she first saw him dancing in his underpants in a 1980s romantic teen film called *Risky Business*, she has remained erotically faithful to him. No other man excites her as much, not even her kindly boyfriend, "Flynn," her steady partner for the past eight years. Although Marissa enjoys sex with Flynn, she always engages in an intra-marital affair, fantasizing about Tom Cruise during lovemaking with her boyfriend.

Marissa struck me as a charming, warm-hearted, soft-spoken young woman who seemed to lead a reasonably healthy life. And although she did "cheat" on Flynn by fantasizing about Tom Cruise, she explained that her lust for Tom would never really interfere with her affections for Flynn, whom she hoped one day to marry. Similarly, in recounting her childhood history, Marissa spoke of having grown up in a loving household with two doting and nurturant parents.

The fantasy of sex with Tom Cruise seemed innocent, almost child-like. After all, Marissa had not chosen a ruffian such as Steve McQueen, or Vin Diesel, but, rather, a boyish-looking film star who appealed, initially, to teenage girls. When I asked Marissa to elaborate upon the fantasy, however, I learned that her imaginary lovemaking with the actor had adopted a somewhat racy quality. She explained that in her favorite fantasy, Tom Cruise whizzes down a motorway in a sleek red sports car, and when he notices her trying to hitch a ride, he stops and opens the door. She immediately enters his car, and, overwhelmed by his handsome face, she straddles him, and they begin to kiss. Tom closes the door to the car, pulls on the stick shift, and zooms off at an electric speed. He clutches the stick shift once again, increasing his speed, with Marissa still astride him, her thighs parted wide. Eventually, Tom penetrates Marissa without a condom, and as the car reaches a dizzying 130 miles per hour on the motorway, he ejaculates inside her.

All in all, this seems like a rather straightforward erotic fantasy, and I would imagine that many other Tom Cruise devotees would also become aroused by it. Perhaps one need explore no further: a good-looking film star, a fancy sports car, a stick shift—what more could a woman want? And with no evident traumas in her early biography, I wondered whether I had finally stumbled upon a normal, trauma-free sexual fantasy.

Still, a dogged interviewer to the last, I continued to explore why this particular fantasy excited Marissa so much. If she loved Tom Cruise with such passion, why did she not fantasize about having sex with him in her own bed, or in a reenactment of a scene from one of his films, *Top Gun* perhaps, or even in a threesome with her boyfriend?

Why did her repetitive fantasy always take place in a *sports car,* whooshing down the motorway, and in a *red* sports car to boot? I attempted to engage Marissa in a dialogue about the specific details of her sexual fantasy, but she offered no help. Lacking in deep conversational skills, Marissa felt that by recounting her fantasy, she had already earned her fee in full, and she seemed unclear as to why I felt that I needed to know more about the color of Tom's sports car, exclaiming, "It doesn't really matter. Red's just a great color."

Since Marissa had already charmed me as a delightful young woman, and since her attraction to Tom Cruise seemed reasonably wholesome, I began to believe that we would have nothing else to talk about. Perhaps some people simply do fancy film stars because they find them sexy—end of story.

As we neared the conclusion of our interview, I asked Marissa whether there might be anything else that she would like to tell me, any other information that I might find useful. I wondered whether I had neglected to ask her about any important areas of her life, even though I had spent nearly five hours with her, covering what I thought to be every imaginable twist and turn in her biography. Marissa coughed, and in a lowered voice, volunteered, "I don't know if you need to know this, but in addition to my sister 'Colleen' and my baby brother 'Pip,' I also had another brother, but he died more than twenty years ago. I thought that maybe you'd want to know about that."

My jaw dropped, both literally and metaphorically, at the sudden discovery that Marissa had had another brother. I wondered why I had not heard about this brother before, whereupon Marissa replied, "Well, you asked me if I *have* any brothers and sisters, so I just told you about Colleen and Pip, they're my brother and sister. 'Barney' isn't my brother anymore, well he is, but he isn't, if you know what I mean. I mean, he's dead, so I don't think of him as my brother, well, I do, but I don't. Oh, you know." Marissa continued to trip over her words, unsure as to whether she should still classify Barney as a brother.

Naturally, I became concerned about this loss, and I wondered whether she would be able to tell me how and when Barney had died. Marissa's eyes began to moisten as she explained that shortly after her eleventh birthday, when her older brother, then eighteen years of age, had just passed his driving test, he had taken the car out for a spin with his girlfriend on the motorway near the family home. Tragically, Barney had somehow lost control of the car and crashed head-on into an enormous long-haul truck at a high speed, dying instantly. Barney's girlfriend survived, but she could remember nothing of the moments leading up to the crash. Marissa told me how much everyone had loved Barney, and how his sudden death had devastated the entire family, but they had all decided that they must "move on," and so they resolved not to dwell on his memory. Although Marissa's parents did not forbid them from mentioning Barney, the children quickly realized that it would be best to avoid the subject, something which Marissa also had done in her lengthy interview with me.

Although she had spoken only of her sister Colleen and of her younger brother Pip during the earlier portion of the interview, I suspect that my final question authorized Marissa to share the painful story of Barney's accident and his ultimate death. She had never met a mental health professional before, and had perhaps, unconsciously, hoped that by volunteering to speak to me about her masturbatory and coital fantasies, she might also have an opportunity to talk about her much missed brother.

I asked Marissa whether she would be able to tell me something about Barney. She leaped at the chance to describe her deceased brother as handsome, funny, and sexy, a good disco dancer and a young man with much promise. Her description of Barney sounded rather like the encomia that one might read about Tom Cruise in a film magazine. Although I do not know whether Cruise has a reputation for being an accomplished dancer, Marissa had earlier explained that she first fell in love with him after she had seen him dancing in his underwear in the film *Risky Business*. Could Marissa's fantasy of Tom Cruise be in any way an attempt to reincarnate her dead brother Barney? Somehow, it felt inappropriate at that moment to share my newly developing thoughts with Marissa about the origin of her sexual fantasy, especially in view of the fact that she had just begun to cry over the memory of her brother. I therefore kept my thoughts to myself and listened to Marissa as she told me more about Barney, who did, indeed, sound like a kindly and loving young man whose death no doubt traumatized the family.

After another twenty minutes, Marissa composed herself and announced that she would feel comfortable finishing the interview and the psychological tests. She did so, and I thanked her for her contribution to my research project and for her courage in being able to talk about a deeply important event in her life, one which had remained a semi-secret for such a long time. Marissa told me that she felt much better for having reminisced about Barney in this way, and that she wished me well with the project.

After she left my office, my thoughts began to race. Marissa had seemingly offered me a crucial missing piece of the psychological jigsaw puzzle presented by her fantasy. Could the sexual fantasy about Tom Cruise be an unconscious transformation of the horrible scene of Barney's death? I began to sketch out the argument in my mind.

Knowing that Marissa had just turned thirty-four, and having read a newspaper report announcing Tom Cruise's fortieth birthday a year or two previously, I quickly established that the age difference between Marissa and Barney would be almost exactly the same as that between Marissa and Tom. Although an attractive man, fancied by countless moviegoers around the world, I wondered whether Marissa had *opportunistically* fallen for Tom Cruise, an almost exact chronological peer to her brother Barney, thereby enlisting Cruise as a leading man in her private psychological screenplay. By latching on to an attractive man who resembled her brother in so many ways, Marissa had managed to use the actor as a means of bringing her brother back to life in symbolic form.

The argument becomes even stronger when we ask ourselves why Marissa chose to make love to Tom Cruise in a sports car, driving fast on the motorway, rather than in any of a number of other, more practical locations. Perhaps by setting her fantasy in a fast car with a stick-shift control, she manages to use Tom Cruise to restage her brother's last car journey; but this time, the car does not crash. Instead, Marissa has engaged the imaginary services of a top-flight, *Top Gun*, action-man racing driver—the star of a spate of *Mission Impossible* films—to take the wheel. With Tom in the driver's seat, the car and all of its passengers will be safe; no one will die, even though Marissa straddles Tom in the process, causing him to ejaculate inside of her.

One can imagine a girl of eleven being rather enamored of her cool, handsome older brother who has just learned to drive; and one can speculate that a girl of that age might just, in fact, be a bit jealous of Barney's girlfriend as well, wishing that she, too, could go for a spin in her brother's new car. In this fantasy, then, Marissa accomplishes several psychological tasks simultaneously. Not only does she make love to the handsome Hollywood hero, but by doing so in a sports car, she also succeeds in taking the girlfriend's place (a symbolic substitute for taking her mother's place in her father's affections); furthermore, and perhaps most crucially, by masturbating to a fantasy of sitting in a speeding sports car that does not crash, Marissa manages, albeit briefly, to undo the lingering horror of her brother's death. Additionally, by having brother-substitute Tom insert himself into her body, Marissa, in a way, succeeds in always having her brother *inside* of her, if not genitally, then certainly psychologically, internalizing his cherished memory.

The fantasy of speeding with the aptly named Tom *Cruise* up a highway, without dying, no doubt brings great pleasure to Marissa, whose brother, sadly, did not survive his last journey in a sports car. Every time Marissa masturbates to this particular fantasy, and every time she invokes this fantasy during lovemaking with her boyfriend, Flynn, she manages to bring her brother back to life in unconscious symbolic form. She thus uses erotic thoughts to assist her in the mastery of trauma. Once again, we see the operation of the basic unconscious mechanism of mastering trauma through eroticization, rendering the terrifying and unprocessable into something sexy and manageable.

I neglected to ask Marissa whether she remembered the color of her brother's car. Perhaps he drove a red car, but equally, it might have been blue, or white, or any other color. Indeed, after Barney crashed into the truck, the car would have become spattered with his blood. I wonder whether Marissa has placed Tom Cruise in a red sports car in an act of mental defiance, since, in a sense, she has turned her brother's red blood into a shiny coat of sexy red paint. In Freudian analysis, every detail contains meaning, and though we can never guarantee that we have made an accurate interpretation, we must endeavor to make sense of the details.

At first, Marissa's sexual fantasy of a road trip with Tom Cruise perplexed me. It seemed innocent enough, the sort of fantasy that other Tom Cruise enthusiasts might readily enjoy. But her older brother's death in a dreadful traffic collision sheds new light on the fantasy and its meaning. Suddenly, the idea of making love to a handsome older man while speeding down the highway makes infinitely greater sense, especially when one considers that this time, the driver survives.

From a methodological point of view, the analysis of Marissa's fantasy reveals that no matter how much biographical data one collects about a person or about their erotic desires, one often cannot provide a complete understanding of the fantasy until the critical piece of information becomes available. Understanding a sexual fantasy thus resembles cracking the Da Vinci code; though many may have tried to solve the riddle, the ultimate solution depends upon obtaining at least one more critical piece of data that may not become apparent until the final chapter of the investigation. In the wake of Marissa's fantasy, and others of similar ilk, I now find myself musing over whether *every* sexual fantasy might well contain a *secret key* awaiting discovery through psychological analysis.

But how might we make sense of the fantasies of people who suffered no abuse, no humiliation, and no bereavement? Can one not simply have an uncomplicated, trauma-free fantasy that cannot be deciphered in such a Sherlockian manner?

During the course of my interviewing, I spoke to a young man called "Del," a twenty-three-year-old British psychology graduate who seemed highly suspicious of my interview study. In a truly bombastic manner, Del demanded to know what sort of psychology I practiced. I told him that I work within a broad psychoanalytical tradition, and that the writings of Sigmund Freud have proved very useful to me as a psychotherapist. Arching his eyebrows in disbelief, Del assured me that Freudians have become outdated, and that his lecturers at college had dismissed Freud as an unscientific manufacturer of psychological myths. As I attempted to explain that more mental health professionals in Great Britain practice within a Freudian framework than any other, Del interrupted me, interjecting, "I'll bet you're just trying to show that our sexual fantasies are all about our mothers, aren't you?" I attempted to reassure this feisty and provocative young man by explaining that, although I did study and train within the Freudian school, I also strive to preserve an open mind and endeavor to refrain from prejudging the data. I explained that if I already knew the origins of sexual fantasies, I would not be undertaking such an exhaustive study of the subject. This comment seemed to reassure him, and he allowed me to continue with the interview.

When we reached the final hour of our conversation, I asked Del whether he would be able to speak to me about his most arousing sexual fantasy. He grinned, as if conjuring up the fantasy in his mind at that very moment, and replied, "Sex with Michelle Pfeiffer." When I attempted to gain more information about the precise nature or circumstances of the fantasy, Del simply laughed, exclaiming, "I just told you. Sex with Michelle Pfeiffer. That's it, just plain sex with her. She's got such an amazing smile. It gets me all excited." Naively, I asked why Del enjoyed this particular fantasy above all others. He looked at me with complete incredulity, wondering why any researcher would even need to ask such an obvious question. "She's hot . . . scorching, in fact," he replied, rolling his eyes to the top of his head. In spite of all my subsequent efforts to probe, Del refused to engage in further conversation; in fact, I rather suspect that he enjoyed watching me squirm, as he seemed absolutely determined to prove that no Freudian analysis would be necessary to understand his self-explanatory lust for Michelle Pfeiffer.

By this point Del had become increasingly obstreperous, and I decided that it would be best to move on to the administration of the standardized pencil-and-paper tests, which constituted the final portion of the interview. Del seemed to take pity on me, and perhaps repenting somewhat for his hitherto disputatious manner, he smiled. "If you're wondering whether Michelle Pfeiffer looks like my mother, you're on the wrong track. My mum's a lovely woman, but she's short and dumpy with tiny tits. She's nothing like Michelle Pfeiffer." I refrained from responding to Del's comment, but I did wonder why he had decided to slip this extra piece of information into the mix.

Does Del's favorite sexual fantasy about intercourse with the glamorous Michelle Pfeiffer have a hidden and archaic meaning? Does his mother actually resemble Michelle Pfeiffer? Or does Del simply fancy Michelle Pfeiffer because "She's hot . . . scorching, in fact," with a lovely smile, and therefore no further explanation will be required?

With many of the interviewees in my research study, I had made good progress in unearthing the secret, hidden, invariably traumatic roots of their sexual fantasies. But with Del, and with a small handful of other interview participants, I became baffled. Either these few interviewees had experienced no pertinent traumas, or, if they had, I could not find them. Del clearly wanted me to believe that he had had an extremely normal childhood and that nothing untoward would be uncovered from his storehouse of memories. He also wanted me to appreciate that he has a short, dumpy, and small-chested mother, and that therefore any attempt on my part to conceptualize Michelle Pfeiffer as a symbolic equivalent of his mother would be much misguided. Still, I did wonder why Del needed to describe his mother's physical appearance.

I then realized that although his mother may be short and dumpy with small breasts, and that no Hollywood casting director could possibly confuse her with Michelle Pfeiffer, one might wonder what she would have looked like to Del during the earliest weeks and months of his infancy. To a breastfeeding baby, even a short mother of 5'2" would look like a giant; and lactating breasts, providing the infant with a steady stream of milk, would no doubt be a focal point for the baby's attention. We also know from a growing number of research studies conducted by developmental psychologists that when a mother smiles at an infant, the infant will usually smile back with a look of joy and delight at being recognized and appreciated. Perhaps pleasure first develops in the nursing relationship between the young mother and her newborn baby. Perhaps Del's lust for Michelle Pfeiffer represents both an adult male's attraction to a beautiful, sexy film actress, and also a little boy's love for a nurturant mother, who, at the time of his birth, looked not short, dumpy, and flat-chested, but, rather, very voluptuous, with an enveloping smile. Perhaps Del's protestation that Michelle Pfeiffer and his mother have *nothing* in common in fact shows that somewhere in the recesses of his mind, there may actually be a psychological connection between his mother—the woman who once pressed him up against her body—and Michelle Pfeiffer—the woman against whom he would like to press his body now that he has become a biologically mature male.

For many years I worked in a medical school attached to a large teaching hospital where I taught psychology to young physicians-in-training. During my nine years on the staff, I learned a great deal about the art of diagnosis, and I soon came to appreciate that with emergency-room patients, the diagnosis is usually self-evident. Blood gushing from a lacerated wrist, for example, indicates a probable suicide attempt. In other cases, the cause might be more obscure, but once the test results come back, the correct diagnosis becomes more apparent. Persistent coughing could be the result of a transient respiratory infection, or it could indicate something more sinister, and only a chest X-ray can clinch the diagnosis. In a small number of cases, however, neither the presenting symptom, nor the clinical interview, nor the history-taking, nor the associated tests may afford the doctors a clear diagnosis. Trainee physicians occasionally walk away stumped, deciding to monitor the patient for further developments or to call in a more senior physician to render an opinion.

Psychotherapeutic diagnosis, rather like medical diagnosis, can often be reasonably straightforward, but it can also, at times, be more complicated. On some occasions, one can never know the complete story. A good psychotherapist must be able to tolerate the lack of a solution. In thinking about Del, I realized that I had no convincing answer as to the meaning of his fantasy, but, rather, a number of working hypotheses.

In his case, one might eventually come to discover that:

1. Del's fantasy developed because of a traumatic, real-life experience involving a Michelle Pfeiffer look-alike.

2. Del's fantasy of Michelle Pfeiffer represents a symbolic transformation of a real-life experience with a loving maternal figure; and in Del's effort to avoid an incestuous attachment, he transferred his affection for the mother onto an idealized mother-substitute—Michelle Pfeiffer.

3. Del's fantasy contains no traumatic or even historical antecedents. He fantasizes about Michelle Pfeiffer simply because he enjoys masturbating over beautiful women.

4. Del's fantasy results from some other source as yet unidentified by modern clinical psychotherapy or psychoanalysis, or demonstrates some alternative intellectual paradigm such as evolutionary psychology (which might trumpet, for example, the virtues of Michelle Pfeiffer's child-bearing hips).

Del's fantasy also serves as a reminder of the importance of modesty in the collection of data and in its analysis and interpretation. Perhaps only a set of extended clinical interviews would permit us to find the secret key to Del's interest in Miss Pfeiffer—or perhaps not.

The Return of Jared

I began this study with a discussion of "Jared," an economically privileged young businessman who seemed to have everything except peace of mind. In spite of his stunning girlfriend, his lucrative career, his flashy possessions, and his sparkling social life, Jared struggled sexually with his obsessive, repetitive fantasy of watching young women attack one another with boxing gloves, and he masturbated to a German DVD that depicted such scenes in graphic detail. When I introduced Jared as a character in this narrative, I did so in order to illustrate the private nature of sexual fantasies, their range, and their potential impact upon romantic partnerships. But I did not at that point offer any biographical information about Jared's childhood or any information about factors that may have contributed to the development of his masturbatory penchant.

I began the book with Jared's account because, on the surface, he appears to be highly "normal," hugely successful, and socially sophisticated, the sort of person that women might want to date and men might want to emulate. However, beneath the polished exterior, Jared harbored a secret that tormented him.

How did his sexual fantasy originate? When I asked Jared why the boxing *fräuleins* aroused him so much, he looked at me with a blank expression, unable to offer a coherent explanation of his own masturbatory behavior. In this respect, Jared did not differ from most of the other research interviewees.

In spite of his verbal dexterity, Jared's vocabulary proved surprisingly sparse when reciting his family history. I learned that he had grown up in a distinctly underprivileged region, the only son of two warring parents. Jared also had a sister, "Linette," some five years his senior. He described his parents as "extremely" young; his mother was only twenty-two years old at the time of his birth, his father twenty-four. Frequently unemployed as a result of his alcoholic binges, Jared's father found it very difficult to support his family, and when he did obtain work, typically in a factory, he would often be sacked after a few weeks or months. His mother proved a more reliable provider, working at the check-out counter at a local supermarket. Although she brought home a regular wage, she had very little time to spend with Jared, and the young boy grew up in a household of emotional deprivation, cared for intermittently by his sister Linette and by a succession of neighbors. This bleak, quasi-Dickensian background lurked beneath the glamorous big city lifestyle that Jared had eventually created for himself.

Fortunately, Jared had suffered no physical or sexual abuse, and he experienced no bereavements. He felt quite bodily safe. Sadly, however, he also felt neglected and abandoned from an emotional point of view, and owing to his father's drunkenness and his mother's long working hours, Jared became a proficient fantasist from a very early age, always making up stories and plays, frequently drifting off into a dream-world of his own devising.

At the age of ten, when Jared returned home from school one after-noon, he heard a great deal of shouting coming from his parents' bed-room upstairs. As he mounted the staircase, the noise became louder, and he could hear the sound of slapping and punching. He called out to his mother, who screamed at him to go into his room and shut the door. Jared obeyed his mother's orders, although he kept his ear close to the door. Eventually, the screams intensified, and soon Jared heard loud noises on the staircase and the sound of slamming doors downstairs.

Timidly, the young boy emerged from his bedroom and found his mother crouched at the bottom of the stairs, her face black and blue, clutching her rib cage in evident pain. She explained that Jared's father had just run out of the house, and that he would not be returning, ever. In fact, after this episode, Jared never saw his father again. Clearly, Jared's parents had struggled with long-standing marital difficulties and a history of domestic violence that they had endeavored to keep well hidden from the children. But, fueled by the father's drinking be-havior, a row had escalated involving the infliction of many savage blows, and after landing his last punch, Jared's father had pushed his wife down the stairs, causing her rib to break. Jared does not remem-ber crying—only feeling a sense of bewilderment—but he did recall his mother whispering to him, "With your father gone, love, you are now the man of the house."

This painful episode had changed the very landscape of Jared's child-hood, and I became very moved listening to his recitation of events. With no male role model nearby, Jared worried at one point that he might become a sissy, and so, to harden himself, he began to spend time with a rough crowd at his school. By the age of fourteen, he and his schoolmates had discovered pornographic magazines, and they would regularly indulge in group masturbation sessions in the base-ment of a friend's house, passing the magazines back and forth and be-coming excited by the photographs of the beautiful naked women. Soon, he and his friends also began smoking marijuana and commit-ting petty crimes such as shoplifting. As Jared recalled, "God, I could've become a criminal, I don't know why I didn't."

Fortunately, one of his teachers recognized Jared's strong academic aptitude and took him under his wing, coaching him on his college en-trance examinations. Jared eventually earned a place at a prestigious university, and after completing his bachelor's degree, he took his

M.B.A., eventually catapulting himself into a job as an investment banker. By the age of twenty-nine, Jared had become quite rich. Although his newfound academic and professional achievements brought him pleasure, they also masked the pain of Jared's fragmented family situation.

Jared did not recall when the boxing fantasies had begun, but he did explain that he had had them for a long time, well before he had purchased the German film. Finding the DVD, *Boxen-Frauen,* proved fortuitous; the film had made Jared feel that others shared his "twisted" masturbatory fantasy, a fantasy that had provoked much shame and guilt.

I asked Jared whether he had ever boxed as a child, or whether he had ever worn boxing gloves for any reason. To my surprise, he told me that he had never seen a pair of boxing gloves in his life, apart from in the German DVD. We both looked at one another, rather stumped, wondering why the boxing gloves had taken on such an erotic appeal. I had certainly encountered many research participants and patients who had developed a fetishistic preoccupation with an item of clothing—for example, a piece of fabric, a blanket, a rubber boot, or a pair of panties—but in virtually every case we could establish a real-life connection between the fetish object and an earlier childhood experience involving a similar object. In Jared's case, we could find no overt link.

In my discussion with Jared, I wondered about the significance of the lesbian overtones to the fantasy: two beautiful buxom women dressed in scanty costumes taking swipes at one another. I wondered whether he enjoyed other types of lesbian pornography. He told me quite candidly that he had seen a fair number of lesbian videos at stag nights and "boys' nights" out, and although he could appreciate the stunning, big-bosomed women in the films, the lesbianism per se did not cause him to become erect. In order to achieve arousal, he needed to think simultaneously about both the boxing gloves and the boxers. Fantasizing about boxing gloves alone would leave him limp, as would fantasizing merely about any two women with bare hands, devoid of the gloves.

I had pursued the theme of lesbianism with Jared because many colleagues and I have discovered that men's sexual fantasies about lesbians, often regarded as definitive proof of one's heterosexual male credentials, may be nothing of the sort. In fact, as I have already indicated, psychoanalytical studies have revealed that men who have experienced a great deal of maternal deprivation often need to fantasize about *four* breasts, rather than *two*. We regard this tendency as a means of compensating for mother's absence (either physical or emotional) during the first year of life. Jared, of course, would qualify as someone who experienced a certain amount of emotional deprivation, owing to his mother's long working hours; hence my interest in considering his attraction to lesbianism.

As our interview progressed, I became more fully acquainted with the contours of Jared's biography, both past and present. Of the many pieces of data that he shared, the violent interchange between his parents, I concluded, might well have been the most traumatic single episode from his developmental years. I asked Jared whether his father had ever hit his sister, Linette. He replied that to the best of his knowledge, he never had; he saved his physical abusiveness for his wife. Jared seemed curious as to why I had asked the question. I then perplexed him further by inquiring as to the hair color of his mother and his sister. He told me that his mother had blonde hair, and his sister had chestnut hair.

I explained to Jared that I had an idea, and wondered whether the two women in the fantasy, one blonde and one brunette, might represent his mother and his older sister. I pointed out that in view of the physical abuse which had occurred in the household, and in view of the fact that his mother had asked him to become the man of the house at the tender age of ten, Jared might have felt frightened. Assuming such a responsibility could seem daunting when he would not have had either the physical or the emotional capability of undertaking such a role. I told him that I suspected he would have felt that he needed some assistance; perhaps by clothing symbolic versions of his mother and his sister in boxing gloves, he could, in his mind, arm them, so that if his father, or any other threatening man, ever appeared in their lives, they would be able to protect themselves.

Jared looked at me quizzically, replying, "That doesn't make a lot of sense to me. I know you're the psychotherapist and all that, but it just doesn't ring true." Patients often initially reject their psychotherapists' hypotheses. Sometimes they do so because the speculations make no sense, and in fact the psychotherapist's initial guesses may be quite wrong; on other occasions, the psychotherapist may have actually put his or her finger on an uncomfortable truth, which the patient may need more time to take on board. I have frequently had patients say to me, "You know that remark that you made to me last year about my mother, which I thought was crazy—well, I think you're right, but it's taken me this long to admit it."

Jared's dismissal of my suggested interpretation, therefore, did not distress me. I offer all of my observations to patients in the spirit of opening a dialogue; I float ideas for us to think about together, and regard any idea that I may have as a tentative speculation. In this way, I am more like Dr. Watson than Sherlock Holmes. Of Arthur Conan Doyle's immortal characters, Watson comports himself with the greater modesty, unafraid to ask silly questions or to get it wrong, whereas Holmes always knows the right answer and seems never to make a mistake.

I explained to Jared that perhaps my observation made no sense at all, but that it might be an idea that we could hold in mind together when thinking about the possible meaning of his sexual fantasy. Jared seemed to appreciate this comment, and he agreed to think about it further.

I have not seen Jared since our interview, and I suspect I may not ever see him again. I do not know whether he has in fact thought more about the possible meaning of his masturbatory behavior, whether he wants to, whether he needs to, whether his fantasies have continued to cause him distress, whether his fantasies have changed, or whether he has found some way to incorporate them less conflictually into his lovemaking with his partner Lucy. Although tempted to undertake an extensive series of follow-up interviews, I have not done so as of the time of writing this book, owing to increased commitments in my clinical work. Therefore, I do not know whether Jared has come to recognize some validity in my hypothesis or if he regards my interpretation as nonsense.

As I indicated earlier in this chapter, sometimes one finds a very convincing key that unlocks the door to a fantasy, sometimes one draws a blank, and sometimes one locates a number of keys, one of which might just open the door to an individual's secret fantasy world. In the preceding chapters, I have presented a wide range of case histories in order to demonstrate that a psychotherapist can sometimes help an individual to identify underlying traumas that may contribute to the development of a certain sexual fantasy. But in spite of the skill and experience of any particular psychotherapist, he or she may also draw a blank, or provide, at best, a *working hypothesis* as to the meaning of a fantasy, which must be tested and retested as new biographical information emerges.

On the basis of the cases that I have studied thus far, both from my psychotherapeutic practice and from my clinical psychodiagnostic interview data, I can conclude that approximately 90 percent of masturbatory fantasies contain elements of obviously traumatic incidents which became eroticized. The contents of such fantasies most often coincide with the contents of an evidently traumatic biographical episode from the prepubescent period. In the remaining cases, I could not reliably establish a connection between a gross prepubescent trauma and a subsequent adult sexual fantasy. However, psychotherapists know from clinical work with clients and patients that many traumas remain repressed in the unconscious mind and therefore cannot be readily accessed in the course of only one interview, however long. Therefore, on the basis of the data available to me, I can reasonably conclude that *trauma functions as a key ingredient in the genesis of adult sexual fantasies.* I have of course encountered sexual fantasies that seem devoid of traumatic content, but in each of these cases, one can establish at least a reasonable link between the fantasy content and early infantile experiences of a pleasurable nature.

Am I Biased? Scientific Research as a Communal Activity

Having now practiced as a psychotherapist for many years, I have developed an increasingly strong interest in two particular topics, namely, the impact of infantile and childhood experiences on the development of the adult personality, and the impact of traumatic experiences (whether prepubescent or postpubescent) on the development of the adult personality. Having listened to numerous private narratives of emotional turmoil, I have come to the conclusion—a conclusion shared by hundreds of thousands of clinical and research colleagues around the world—that early childhood experiences, especially those of a traumatic nature, exert the largest influence on later life experiences. This idea may not appeal to everyone. Many people do not wish to acknowledge the impact of early abuse, or of early abandonment, because of the pain involved; but these experiences appear and reappear in my work with patients on a daily basis, so much so that one cannot practice psychotherapy without recognizing the formative role of these early impressions.

Critics propose that the vision of psychotherapists, especially Freudian psychotherapists, has become clouded because we meet only with people who have had a difficult, turbulent, or traumatic childhood. Healthy people with happy childhoods never come to a psychotherapist in the first place, these critics say, because they have no need for treatment. Of course, this may well be true. However, I have worked not only in psychiatric hospitals and community mental health centers with extremely abused and psychologically unwell men and women; I have also worked in private practice, a setting which attracts, on the whole, much healthier people, most of whom, if not all, have nevertheless suffered in some way, and whose early suffering has impacted their current characterological styles.

I certainly concede that my patients and interviewees may not be representative of the British and American populations at large, but they cannot be described categorically as unrepresentative either. As the interviewees originally came to me from a database of randomly selected members of the *noninstitutionalized* population, I suspect that they can be regarded as more "normal" than not.

Any social scientist undertaking research work must, however, confront at least two key methodological problems, namely, the possibility of a sampling bias, and the possibility of an interviewer bias. A sampling bias occurs when one attempts to draw broad conclusions on the basis of an unrepresentative group of people. For instance, if we wanted to test the hypothesis that all women enjoy drinking beer, we would, in all likelihood, obtain different results from different groups of women. I could administer a drinking preferences questionnaire to ten women in a nearby bar, for example, or I could give my questionnaire to ten women in a convent. Each group may offer very different responses. With this in mind, one could readily suppose that my case histories—most of which contain a great deal of early trauma—may be unrepresentative of the population at large. It may be the case, for example, that only a traumatized person would volunteer to participate in an interview study about sexual fantasies in the first place.

I can neither prove nor disprove that my interviewees may be more traumatized than the average person in Great Britain or the United States today. One might argue, by way of contrast, that only a person with a great deal of ego-strength and ego-integrity (in other words, someone blessed with a great deal of mental health, or someone sufficiently comfortable in his or her own skin) would have the courage and the capability to speak freely about sexual fantasies. Perhaps the interviewees in my research sample may even be much healthier than the average person. In truth, I do not know. Certainly, I found them all to be solid people, no more and no less so than those I meet in my day-to-day travels. To the best of my knowledge, not a single interviewee had ever spent time in a psychiatric institution, and fewer than 5 percent had ever had counseling of any kind. None had experienced intensive psychotherapy or psychoanalysis. I only know that I have painstakingly accumulated a large set of data, much of which contains painful clinical evidence of early traumatic experiences, and much of which seems to reflect the impact of these experiences on the development of the individuals concerned.

In order to counter the possibility of a sampling bias, I of course supplemented the interview data with formal questionnaire data from 17,170 Britons (13,553 completed primary responses and 3,617 completed pilot responses) as well as formal questionnaire data from 3,433 Americans—a truly representative sample drawn from the YouGov panel. The data from the questionnaires confirmed that large numbers of Britons and Americans have suffered from memorable trauma at one or more points during their lives.

As for interviewer bias, I endeavored to conduct as comprehensive an interview with each of my research subjects as I possibly could, covering all aspects of their lives, ranging from their favorite hobbies to their favorite fantasies. Although I did not ask directly, "Have you ever had a trauma?" I always conducted the interviews in a psychotherapeutic style, using a great deal of silence to allow the interviewee to engage in the process of "free association," in which people tend to speak uninhibitedly, without restriction or censorship. And because I spent many hours with each interviewee, a certain amount of trust developed between the participants and myself, thus allowing for a fuller disclosure of the most private areas of biography.

I have certainly foregrounded the possible role of trauma in the genesis of sexual fantasy, in part because this theme appeared with such surprising frequency in the material, but also because few investigators of sexual fantasies have previously appreciated the potential role of trauma. Most of us regard ourselves as the supreme architects of our sexual lives, choosing our partners, our fantasies, and our pornography.

But the data I have collected suggest that we may have less conscious control over our fantasies and sexual predilections than we would wish to believe. This is a topic of immediate relevance to psychological professionals and members of the general public alike, not merely an academic question without implications for our everyday lives.

In spite of the very large sample size, I have conducted this research in the hope that it will represent not a definitive exploration of the subject, but rather a contribution to a growing body of knowledge about sexual fantasy. Scientific research generally proceeds in tiny steps, with each new worker building upon the findings of colleagues from previous generations. In this way, scientific investigation becomes not the preserve of any one single author, but a communal activity, wherein each of us pools his or her data in the hope that eventually a truer, fuller picture will emerge. Alfred Kinsey cracked open the field of sexological research, and Nancy Friday initiated a public discourse around sexual fantasy in particular. I hope that I have used the best of their methodologies, as well as the best aspects of Freudian psychoanalysis and contemporary trauma theory, to create a more comprehensive and integrated approach to the developmental origins of sexual fantasy.

PART FOUR

Sexual Fantasies and the Outside World

Does it really matter what these affectionate people do—so long as they don't do it in the streets and frighten the horses!

—Mrs. Patrick Campbell

22   Do Fantasies Ruin Relationships?

*"Twelve years doesn't mean you're
a happy couple. It just means you're
a long couple."*

         —NEIL SIMON, *The Odd Couple*

Guilt and the Intra-Marital Affair

Think back to your wedding day, or to the moment when you first met your lover. In view of the excitement experienced by so many of us when we finally consummated our relationship with our intended, why would anyone ever want to cheat, or even fantasize about some*one* or some*thing* else?

Let us consider the case of "Diego," a forty-one-year-old electrician who has only ever slept with one woman—his lawfully wedded wife. A staunch Catholic, he first met "Carmella" twenty years previously, at a church in a little village just south of Carmella's ancestral home. Diego found himself very attracted to the young, raven-haired Spanish maiden, and after having received permission from her father, Diego proposed marriage.

During their first several years together, Diego and Carmella enjoyed intercourse two or three times per week, but after the birth of "Cristoforo," the first of five children, sex between them became increasingly infrequent. Ultimately, after the arrival of "Luisa," their youngest, the marriage became completely devoid of sex. As the years progressed, Carmella had put on more than fifty pounds in weight, and Diego lost his desire, revolted by the sight of his "fat, fat, fat *mujer* [woman] with the saggy tits." On the rare occasion when Diego would develop an erection in bed, he had only to take one look at Carmella and he would become immediately detumescent—in other words, he would become limp.

In order to gratify his still prominent sexual urges, Diego found himself becoming increasingly addicted to masturbation. As an electrician, he spent most of his days traveling in a large van from worksite to worksite. He began to park it far away from his house, and crouching beneath a tattered blanket in the back of the van, he would manipulate himself to climax. Diego would fantasize about a nice *muchacha* [young girl] he had seen on the street, or access pornographic pictures on his cell phone. He cherished these private masturbation sessions; as he reported to me in his interview, "It takes all the stress away. I feel cleansed, like a big weight is off my shoulders . . . and my balls."

Having extolled the virtues of masturbating in his van, Diego then looked crestfallen, confessing to me, "Well, it's true, I do feel like a big weight has been taken from me, especially from my balls, but at the same time, another weight has come on. I feel bad about Carmella. I would never cheat, but it feels like I am cheating all the time. She would die if she knew how dirty her husband is." Diego asked me, as a marital psychotherapist, whether most men fantasize about someone other than their wives. I reassured him that an extremely large percentage of men engage in what I have called the *intra-marital affair*. However, as I suspected, this knowledge brought him little comfort, and he sighed, lamenting, "Then we will all roast together." A committed Catholic, Diego feared that such a "horrible" crime in this life (in other words, mental infidelity) would surely be punished in the afterlife.

Before he left my office, Diego looked at me with a pained expression on his face. Obviously, his guilt had reached such epic proportions that he had begun to suffer greatly. He threw his hands up, saying, "I know Carmella has got fat and ugly, but she is my wife. She is the mother of my children. Why do I do it? Why do I cheat?"

Diego's explanation for his intra-marital affair—that he simply had to begin masturbating about the *muchachas* because Carmella had become fat—seems far too simple. We might identify this train of thought as the "Diego Theory," or the "Commonsense Theory," of the affair. It goes hand in hand with the theory that fantasy arises because making love with the same woman or the same man can become tedious. As one of my interviewees, "Missy," explained, "*Brief Encounter* is a fantastic film, my favorite in fact, but I couldn't watch it every night, could I?" One can readily appreciate the temptation to expand one's erotic repertoire, however, and to go beyond familiar postures and tried-and-true roles.

But as we already know, the roots of sexual fantasizing often, if not always, lie very deep indeed; therefore, in order to understand the impact of fantasies on both marital and nonmarital partnerships, we must delve further. Sometimes we engage in intra-marital affairs in order to bring variety into our lives, or simply to have some fun and play; but often, the intra-marital affair serves as a reenactment of childhood trauma, a flight from a painful external or internal reality, or even a protection against the fear of being engulfed by the emotional and physical demands of our partner.

The Case of the Internet Pornography Addict

What impact do sexual fantasies have upon our intimate relationships? Do fantasies enhance our pleasure with our partners, or do they jeopardize our marriages? Perhaps we can provide a fuller answer to these questions by exploring a clinical case.

Since the late 1990s, I have worked with an increasing number of marital couples or long-term partners who have presented for couple psychotherapy because the woman has discovered the man engaged in the constant use of the Internet in order to examine pornography. This type of addiction has become an area of growing concern in recent years. In fact, Internet pornography and its compulsive (and at times perverse) use have become such troubling and preoccupying issues that my colleagues and I in the Society of Couple Psychoanalytic Psychotherapists in Great Britain devoted no fewer than three separate conferences and study days to this topic in 2005–2006 alone.

Consider the case of "Mr. and Mrs. Jaccoby," an attractive, well-educated, affable couple, ages thirty-six and thirty-five, respectively, who arrived at my office in deep distress. After nearly a decade of reasonably happy sexual activity, Mr. and Mrs. Jaccoby had stopped making love entirely after the birth of twin girls. Each partner rationalized the lack of sex, convincing themselves that the demands of raising two newborn babies left them little time for intimate physical contact, and that when they did have five minutes to spare, after the twins had fallen asleep, they themselves needed to catch up on sleep as well. Neither Mr. Jaccoby nor Mrs. Jaccoby seemed overtly concerned, reasoning that they would resume their lovemaking after the twins had become more independent and would no longer wake them up in the middle of the night.

One day, Mrs. Jaccoby plucked up the courage to ask Mr. Jaccoby whether he had resumed masturbating, a reasonable question in view of the fact that the couple had had no sexual intercourse for almost a year. Mr. Jaccoby denied masturbating, explaining that the twins exhausted him. Mrs. Jaccoby admitted that she had not had time for masturbation either. Apparently, Mr. and Mrs. Jaccoby believed each other completely, because, as Mrs. Jaccoby noted, "Our relationship has always been based on complete honesty and trust."

But one evening, Mrs. Jaccoby went to bed early, at 9:00 P.M., with a sore throat, and Mr. Jaccoby offered to look after the little ones. At 1:00 A.M., Mrs. Jaccoby awoke in bed and to her surprise discovered that she could not find her husband. She put on her robe and bedroom slippers and padded around the house trying to find him. To her dismay and shock, she located her husband in his study, asleep in front of his computer, with his trousers down, quite literally, around his ankles, and a crumpled tissue in his hand. Mrs. Jaccoby looked at the screen and began to retch, suddenly realizing that her husband must have masturbated himself to sleep watching deeply sadistic pornography, in which one could pay to watch women inserting large and dangerous objects into their vaginas.

Mrs. Jaccoby went ballistic and started screaming at her husband, who awoke abruptly, utterly shamed and humiliated. The evidence of Mr. Jaccoby's private masturbatory ritual could not be denied, since his wife had caught him red-handed. She immediately threatened divorce, infuriated and disturbed that not only had her husband wasted their hard-earned savings to pay for "vicious pornography," but that he had also lied to her, cheated on her, and, most disturbingly, revealed his long-standing sadistic fantasies, all at once. How could she ever make love to Mr. Jaccoby again, knowing that he derived orgasmic pleasure from the sight of women masturbating themselves with various potentially lethal instruments?

When they entered my consulting room, the situation looked grim. Mrs. Jaccoby spoke in an entrenched manner, rather like a hard-boiled prosecuting attorney who had prepared an airtight case against the ne'er-do-well defendant, and who had every intention of convicting him for several concurrent life sentences. "I can't possibly continue in this marriage," she shouted, "because in one fell swoop I've discovered that my husband is a cheat, a liar, and a sex maniac, *and* a psychopath." Her screams reached such an intensity that I began to worry whether my colleague in the adjoining office would soon be tapping on my door, asking us to keep the noise down.

Mr. Jaccoby desperately tried to defend himself. Terrified that his wife would seek custody of the twins, as well as a divorce, he offered to submit to any form of rehabilitation in order to save the marriage, even reaching into his wallet, extracting his credit cards, and handing them to Mrs. Jaccoby, in the hope that she would become the jailer and prevent him from using them to access the sadistic Internet Web sites.

Mrs. Jaccoby threw the credit cards on my consulting room floor in a contemptuous manner, and to my amazement, cried, "Maybe we can stop you logging on to the Internet, but these pictures are already in your head. The only way I'd take you back is if you had a lobotomy!" In many respects, Mrs. Jaccoby had focused with lightning precision on the core anxiety at that moment. She seemed less troubled by Mr. Jaccoby's use of the Internet pornography site than she did by the dawning recognition that these pictures might now be stored in his mind forever, that he might conjure them up during any future lovemaking sessions, or that he might even have relied upon these images to excite himself during past erotic encounters. Mrs. Jaccoby had become so incredibly distressed because she had discovered that her husband had cheated on her not extramaritally, but intra-maritally.

Like many men in his situation, Mr. Jaccoby began to explain that the women on the Web site meant nothing to him at all. He did not even know their names. Surely, he pleaded, "You should cut me some slack. I mean, it's not as though I've shagged your sister." This proved a most unfortunate defense, and Mrs. Jaccoby, already in a persecuted and tormented state of mind, retorted, "Oh, so now you want to screw my sister? I'm calling a lawyer today." Once again, Mr. Jaccoby parried, "But all men look at pornography, it's no big deal. I just do it every now and again." Unfortunately, Mrs. Jaccoby seemed unconvinced.

At this point, I became dreadfully worried that the situation had already escalated out of control and that it would not be possible to restore tranquillity and joy to this marriage. But Mr. and Mrs. Jaccoby *had* agreed to come for help, which I always regard as a good sign. I

wondered whether the despondency that I felt mirrored some depressed part within each member of the couple that could not readily
be expressed.

To their credit, the Jaccobys agreed to embark upon a course of intensive couple psychotherapy, which lasted for nearly three years. Mrs.
Jaccoby managed to express her rage at Mr. Jaccoby for his Internet
"crimes," and Mr. Jaccoby allowed her to do so without becoming immediately defensive—not an easy task for a man in the firing line, already overwhelmed by his own shame and guilt. We spent a great deal
of time exploring why Mr. Jaccoby had become aroused by the thought
of women harming themselves vaginally, and whether his arousal from
these images actually represented a displacement of his own wish to
harm significant female figures in his own history.

Before long, a litany of episodes of cruelty emerged as Mr. Jaccoby
spoke of how his mother had beat him throughout his childhood as a
matter of course, and how, until he reached the age of thirteen or fourteen, she would often administer painful and humiliating enemas into
his anus. We wondered whether the wish to stick hard objects inside a
woman's genitals might be an unconscious attempt to reverse the pain
of having had objects inserted inside his rectum. This interpretation
made a great deal of sense to Mr. Jaccoby, and he wept, which rekin-
dled some tenderness and compassion in Mrs. Jaccoby for the man she
had once happily wed, and with whom she had produced two beautiful
babies.

We also devoted considerable attention to the impact of the birth of
the twins on the couple's sex life. Delivering two large babies, each
over six pounds, had, according to Mrs. Jaccoby, "fairly ripped me in
two," and she had experienced many obstetric complications during
the birth, including the fear that one of the twins might be strangulated
by the umbilical cord, a not uncommon occurrence. The arrival of the
twins, resulting from an unplanned pregnancy, brought much joy into
the Jaccoby household, but also much misery. The unexpected birth of
not one, but two, hungry mouths proved a great drain on the couple's
physical, emotional, and financial resources.

To my surprise, during one session Mr. Jaccoby blurted out, "When
I saw those babies coming out of your vagina, I just wanted to push
them back inside." Mrs. Jaccoby looked startled, as did I, and we wondered what this meant on a deeper level. Did Mr. Jaccoby's excitation
by the sadistic pornography, which had peaked shortly after the birth

of the twins, have any connection with this wish? Mr. Jaccoby spoke more fully at this point about his resentment toward his daughters, and then he talked about his hatred toward his younger sister and brother. He had not kept in contact with either of them, even though they all lived fairly close to one another. We wondered whether the thought of women inserting large objects into their vaginas aroused him because this provided him with a means not only of attacking his hated mother and reversing the trauma of the enemas, but also of preventing the mother from producing any more rivals. Often a fantasy will serve a multiplicity of functions.

This observation seemed to make a great deal of sense to both Mr. Jaccoby and Mrs. Jaccoby; and over the following months, Mr. Jaccoby reported that his temptation to log on to the Internet became "less and less powerful with each passing day." Gradually, the shouting that had characterized the early sessions with this couple became transformed into more thoughtful speech and mutual interchange. As our work progressed, we all found it much more manageable to think with one another about the meanings of Mr. Jaccoby's Internet pornography symptom and about the nature of the Jaccobys' marriage.

One would be mistaken to suppose that couple psychotherapy becomes an arena in which we examine only half of the relationship, however. Although Mrs. Jaccoby began treatment hoping that I would be able to "cure" Mr. Jaccoby, as "only *he*" had committed anything untoward, it soon became clear that both members of the couple had contributed powerfully to the creation of the emotional atmosphere within the household. Mrs. Jaccoby, the child of divorced parents, did not realize how much venom she had stored up inside her owing to a spate of injuries she had suffered during her life, especially during her earliest years. Her father had cheated on her mother, leaving the latter quite depressed, and, on more than one occasion, suicidal. As a little girl, Mrs. Jaccoby once had to wrest a bottle of tablets from her mother's hands to prevent her from taking an overdose. Indeed, she listened to many lectures from her spurned mother about "the evils of men" and how they became slaves to their penises.

Together, we explored the impact of these childhood events on Mrs. Jaccoby's subsequent development and on her choice of a marital partner. Mr. Jaccoby sympathized with his wife as she allowed herself to become more vulnerable in his presence, and she felt touched and delighted that he could offer her emotional support and kindness, something that had rather disappeared on both sides since the birth of the babies. We examined the ways in which Mrs. Jaccoby would use her husband as a punching bag, verbally assaulting him even when he had done "nothing wrong," in part as a means of avenging her mother and punishing her father.

With so many skeletons tumbling out of the closet, the leaden atmosphere which had once permeated my consulting room at last began to lift, and to my great delight, after nine months of therapeutic sessions, the Jaccobys announced that they had resumed their sex life. Although it had seemed strange at first, they soon found it "as easy as riding a bicycle." I did wonder whether Mr. Jaccoby had relied upon any sadistic fantasies to arouse himself, and whether Mrs. Jaccoby had wondered about this as well, but when I worked with the Jaccobys I had not yet undertaken my research on sexual fantasies, and I did not rush to ask them about their fantasy life. Inquiring about a couple's sexual fantasies with three people present in the room can be very exposing and should be done only after very careful consideration and with great clinical diplomacy; otherwise one or both members of the couple might feel rather invaded.

I now know from my research that people can have different sexual fantasies during intercourse than during masturbation. Often, the more primitive and sadistic fantasies burst into the mind during the privacy of solo masturbation, whereas during intercourse one might be more inclined to think about one's partner. However, as we have already established, the line between coital and masturbatory fantasies may not be quite so clear, and I have now encountered hundreds of cases whereby one member of the couple can become aroused *only* by drawing upon private, often shame-laden masturbatory fantasies.

As the psychotherapeutic treatment with the Jaccobys unfolded, the mistrust, the hurt, and the devastation began to recede, and our sessions took on a more ordinary quality, allowing us to think about the impact of the birth of the girls, and how the couple could struggle to transform themselves from a *twosome* into a *foursome*. We also talked about the frustrations that both were experiencing in their daily lives. Mr. Jaccoby found his job frustrating and lacking in creativity, whereas Mrs. Jaccoby found full-time motherhood a burden and longed to return to an office setting—ordinary anxieties that preoccupy every young couple with children.

After nearly three years, the couple ended their psychotherapeutic work by mutual agreement. Mr. Jaccoby had stopped using the Internet for pornography, although he confessed that he did still have sexual fantasies about other women. He claimed, however, that he no longer became aroused by the thought of women roughly inserting sharp objects into their vaginas, much to Mrs. Jaccoby's great relief. He explained that he did become aroused by the thought of watching a woman use a vibrator on herself, and that he and Mrs. Jaccoby had managed to incorporate vibrators into their erotic repertoire, arguably a healthier sublimation of his long-standing symptom. Lovemaking had resumed, and both Mr. and Mrs. Jaccoby had applied for new jobs. The couple asked to shake my hand, and they departed with warm smiles of gratitude on their faces, satisfied that we had all worked very hard to reequilibrate, and then strengthen, this once endangered marriage.

One year later, I received a Christmas card from the Jaccobys announcing that Mrs. Jaccoby had become pregnant again. Six months later, a photograph arrived in the mail of the twin girls, now five years old, both holding their beautiful new baby brother. Naturally, I wrote to congratulate the Jaccobys. The birth of a baby does not always signify an achievement. As my former teacher and colleague, the London-based psychiatrist Dr. Estela Welldon, has noted in her landmark book *Mother, Madonna, Whore: The Idealization and Denigration of Motherhood*, published in 1988, the birth of a baby can signify the beginning of a cycle of abuse; therefore, one should never assume that the arrival of a child indicates health and happiness. But in the case of the Jaccobys, the birth of a new baby revealed, I suspect, that both had mastered many of their earlier anxieties, especially, for Mr. Jaccoby, his hatred of his younger siblings. Because of his hard work in our sessions, he could now both tolerate, and indeed welcome, a new infant in the family.

Of course, not all stories end quite as tidily as the tale of the Jaccobys. Over the years, my colleagues and I have encountered innumerable marriages wrecked by intra-marital affairs and extramarital affairs alike. I have certainly worked with a number of couples who harbor, in particular, completely incompatible sexual fantasies, and whose relationships have ended disastrously. I can remember one case of a man who fantasized about large-busted women, and whose wife *also* fantasized about large-busted women. For a time, they even shared the husband's pornographic magazines, but eventually the husband became understandably jealous of his wife's growing interest in lesbianism, and the relationship terminated. I can also recall another couple in which the male partner confessed one evening that he liked to fantasize about naked men, and the female partner admitted that she preferred fantasizing about naked women. This couple eventually separated, after which he found a boyfriend and she found a girlfriend. However, the story did not end there. A year later, the young man in question left his boyfriend to resume sexual relationships with women, and the young woman left her girlfriend to embark upon a satisfying sexual encounter with another man. It seems that when we consider the subject of sexual fantasy and its role in the context of a relationship, there may well be no hard and fast rules.

Can a Festering Sexual Secret Enhance a Marriage?

In the course of practicing psychotherapy and conducting research interviews, I have also stumbled upon marriages that seem to survive precisely *because* one or both partners maintain a secret sexual fantasy. The following case will help us to explore the vexing question of whether a sexual secret—either a fantasy or an enactment—may ever have potential value within a relationship.

"Malvina," a fifty-six-year-old woman, entered my office wearing a tweed suit and a string of pearls. She rather resembled a character from a 1930s or 1940s film or novel; in fact, she looked exactly like a cross between an Agatha Christie suspect and a P. G. Wodehouse extra. I wondered whether she would be able to manage talking about her sexual fantasies; I also wondered whether I would feel comfortable discussing sexual fantasies with such a prim-looking lady.

Surprisingly, talking about sex proved completely unproblematic for Malvina. She launched into the interviewing process with gusto, explaining that she shared her home with "Avery," her husband of thirty-eight years, with whom she had produced five healthy children, all now grown. Her husband worked as a medical doctor in the village where they lived, and Malvina told me that owing to Avery's job, they knew everybody, and they liked everybody. It all seemed quite idyllic.

Although Malvina and her husband had had a reasonably satisfactory, if somewhat unadventurous, sex life during their long marriage, she told me that her attraction to him had completely disappeared over the past five years. Malvina did not know why this had happened, but she explained that she had simply begun to find her husband's body disgusting. Her waning sexual interest in her husband had coincided with her discovery of sadomasochism. At a village fair, Malvina had met "Kurt," a local music teacher some ten years her junior. Although Malvina had known Kurt for a very long time, "something sparked" between the two of them on this particular occasion, and to her surprise, she found herself visiting Kurt's house later that evening. A single man of long-standing, Kurt explained to Malvina that he maintained a "dungeon" room in his house, replete with restraining devices, whips, chains, cuffs, and slings. At first Malvina expressed shock, as she had only ever had very conservative sex with Avery, but, as she explained, "something inside me began to quiver, and I felt a real tingle of excitement down below."

Before long, Kurt had enticed Malvina to undress, and he strapped her to an extraordinary contraption that resembled an operating table in a surgical theater. Naked and cuffed, Malvina lay there in "terrified anticipation" as Kurt attached a toothed clamp to each of her increasingly erect nipples. He fixed the clamps to an elaborate rope-and-pulley system, and then he began to tug. As Kurt pulled, gently at first, and then more vigorously, and the clamps pierced her nipples, Malvina experienced an excruciating combination of pain and pleasure intermixed. Eventually, she climaxed without having her genitals touched at all—the first time that she had ever reached orgasm in this fashion.

This sadomasochistic sexual activity soon became such a preoccupation for Malvina that she would arrange to meet Kurt every day of the week at lunchtime for a session lasting at least ninety minutes. If, for some reason, she had to miss an encounter with Kurt, she felt deprived and depleted. Malvina explained that Kurt had opened up an entirely new world for her that she never knew existed, but one which felt "so right."

In addition to her sadomasochistic activities with Kurt, Malvina began to collect sadomasochistic pornography, which she stored in a carrier bag and kept hidden in a locked suitcase in her attic. She had downloaded some of this pornography directly from the Internet, and she had purchased the remainder—a combination of magazines and story books—on furtive trips to larger cities such as Exeter and Birmingham. When Malvina could not meet with Kurt, she would masturbate to the sadomasochistic pornography, enjoying sexual fantasies about women being tortured.

Malvina's situation raises a number of compelling questions. Most particularly, one cannot help but wonder how a demure, middle-aged, provincial housewife and mother of five, who had done little more sexually than practice the missionary position with her staid and sober husband, could suddenly become a proficient practitioner of sadomasochism, integrating a daily, ninety-minute session of steamy sex into her domestic life. When I posed this question to Malvina, she chortled, emitting a full-throated laugh. "Yes, it is rather amusing, isn't it? I mean, just a short while ago, I was almost virginal, since Avery and I hadn't done it in ages, and now, I'm like the new Cynthia Payne." Malvina then noted that until she met Kurt, she knew practically nothing about sadomasochism, and she found the thought of sexual pain "disgusting." Her views had changed dramatically; as she noted, "I've done a full 180-degree turnabout. Have you seen this sort of thing before?"

Although I did not dwell on the sexual histories of others in the course of my interview with Malvina, I have indeed observed this phenomenon previously. Sometimes, people with long-standing erotic preferences suddenly awaken one day to find they have become receptive to something completely unexpected. A patient with whom I worked years ago, a gentleman in his early sixties, abruptly announced to his wife one day that he wished to leave her to pursue a gay lifestyle. He had never so much as kissed another man before, but over the course of a few years, he had begun to experience a growing number of sexual fantasies and dreams about other men, and he knew that he could no longer deny this increasing body of evidence. As he told me, "It was like a volcano suddenly erupting in my mind, without any warning, just like the explosion on Krakatoa."

I have since encountered this phenomenon in a number of individuals. Borrowing from my former male patient's description of his experience, I have come to think of this as the "Krakatoa Complex," a reference to the volcano that erupted on a remote Indonesian island in the summer of 1883. Although most adult men and women seem to have relatively stable sexual identities, which become fixed in early childhood and do not vary greatly across the life cycle, others will experience the unexpected, changing their sexual repertoire or sexual orientation seemingly overnight. Surprisingly, sexologists and psychologists have devoted very little attention to this group of individuals. I hope that Malvina's story may stimulate further research into this phenomenon. Of course, sexual orientation does not actually alter overnight—Malvina and others would have had unconscious fantasy structures already developed in their minds predisposing them to particular sexual patterns and preferences—but to many of those who have experienced the Krakatoa Complex, it certainly feels as though the volcano has exploded without warning. Each can identify the critical juncture when his or her sexual preferences seemed to change in an instant, in an unmistakable fashion.

When I inquired whether Malvina's husband had become at all suspicious, she denied this furiously. As a busy general medical practitioner, he devoted long hours to his surgery, and thus she had the whole day free to herself. As long as she prepared his supper, which she always managed to do, Avery seemed content. I wondered whether Malvina had any wish to leave Avery and move in with the music teacher Kurt. "Oh no," she winced, "I only want to have sex with Kurt; otherwise, we have nothing in common. But Avery and I are spouses. We are soul mates. We just don't have sex, that's all."

In my work as a couple psychotherapist, I have discovered that when one member of a partnership embarks on an extramarital affair, the other one will often be shocked when the secret finally becomes revealed. The shock often lasts for only a short period, however, for once the secret is exposed, the injured party will suddenly realize, "Oh, yes, now I know why you didn't come home until 3:00 A.M. that night, and why you forgot my birthday, and why you had to rush away from our son's graduation ceremony so quickly." Suddenly, the cuckolded party recognizes that he or she had access to a wealth of clues already, which, for whatever reasons, could not previously be acknowledged.

Malvina told me that she had every intention of maintaining her secret trysts with Kurt for the foreseeable future; in fact, she doubted that her marriage to Avery would survive, in spite of their thirty-eight-year relationship and their five grown children, if she had to live without her sadomasochistic sessions. According to Malvina, her daily rendezvous had saved her marriage. Certainly, she put forward a very convincing case for keeping one's sexual fantasies and extramarital sexual enactments secret. Nevertheless, after Malvina left my office, I felt distinctly uncomfortable. In all my years of training and practice as a psychotherapist, I have never seen any good come from harboring secrets. In fact, I have always observed the opposite—people driven mad by secrets in the family.

To be frank, I remain undecided in my thoughts about Malvina's situation. Certainly, I would not be alone in feeling a sense of outrage should I ever find myself in Avery's position and discover my wife's infidelities. And yet, Malvina had created an arrangement that, at least from a conscious point of view, seemed to bring her much satisfaction; therefore, in spite of my clinical propensity to root out secrets and minimize the potential destructiveness of predominantly sadomasochistic relationships, I have endeavored to keep an open mind. She is not the first spouse to have led a "double life," nor will she be the last.

In this chapter, I have discussed the cases of Diego, racked by guilt over his intra-marital fantasies, of Mr. and Mrs. Jaccoby, who survived their marital battle against Internet pornography with the aid of psychotherapy, and of Malvina, who continues to practice extramarital sadomasochism and to utilize sadomasochistic fantasies without the conscious knowledge of her husband. I have chosen these three situations—three out of many possible scenarios—to illustrate the great range of ways in which sexual fantasies can function within a marital relationship or long-term partnership. No two couples will use sexual fantasies in the same way, and for better or worse, we as clinicians have no blueprints for what constitutes the perfect marriage, and certainly no roadmaps for what constitutes the healthiest way to deploy one's sexual fantasies.

Some of my colleagues have at times suggested to me that in a truly healthy marriage, one would not need sexual fantasies at all. As one psychoanalyst reasoned, "Only a really troubled person would need to rely on fantasies. If the quality of the marriage is stable, it would be sufficient to fantasize about your husband or your wife. Only an infantile person will need fantasies." At one level, I understand this classic position. But when I quoted my research data to this skeptical psychoanalyst—data suggesting that more than 90 percent of adults fantasize quite regularly, and that nearly 90 percent of men and nearly 60 percent of women use pornography—my colleague stumbled over his words, quite shocked by these figures.

Researching this topic in relation to partnerships and marriages has made me appreciate that every couple constructs its own sexual vocabulary and sexual climate. For some people, an unspoken arrangement such as the one that developed between Malvina and Avery would be untenable, but for others, this situation might well suit. For all we know, Avery, the family physician, may have a lover on the side as well, and therefore might be pleased to discover that Malvina has Kurt. As a psychotherapist, I would argue simply that a healthy marriage usually requires extreme honesty; however, we as mental health professionals enter dangerous territory if we attempt either to prescribe or to proscribe particular behaviors to our patients. Our primary task will always remain that of being responsive to those individuals who visit us, seeking help for aspects of their lives, overt or covert, secret or shared, sexual or otherwise, which cause them grief or despair.

I do not fully understand why Malvina came to see me. Perhaps she did feel guilty about her situation and unconsciously wanted a clinical consultation to find out whether I regarded her sexual life as perverse. Perhaps she wanted to boast. Perhaps she needed some extra cash and a return ticket to London so that she could purchase some more sadomasochistic pornography or visit a sadomasochist club. I do not pretend to know.

Should We Share Our Fantasies . . . or Act Them Out?

In recent years, I have delivered numerous lectures on the subject of sexual fantasy to clinical colleagues at various psychological organizations throughout Great Britain. During the discussion period following these talks, my colleagues invariably ask a number of illuminating questions and share their own views and experiences in a helpful manner. Although colleagues have posed many different questions about the subject, one question stands out as the most frequently asked, namely, "In your professional opinion, do you think couples should share their fantasies with one another, and should they ever act them out?"

At the risk of being disappointing, I can only say that I wish I knew the answer to this vexing question. I know of many cases where couples have shared their sexual fantasies with helpful consequences, but the consequences can also be disastrous. Similarly, I know of cases where partners have enacted various scenarios successfully, and with pleasure, and other cases where such attempts have ended in tears. I shall illustrate these different possibilities with a few brief vignettes.

One evening, while lying in bed, "Kara," a forty-one-year-old schoolteacher, asked her husband of many years, "Salvatore," a thirty-nine-year-old poet, what he thought about when he masturbated. Kara had asked Salvatore this question before—many times, in fact—and he had always replied, "You, darling. I always think about you." This untruthful answer seemed to satisfy Kara's narcissism, but recently she had discovered a pornographic magazine rolled up in Salvatore's jacket pocket, and she could no longer believe that he did not fantasize about anyone else. Eventually, Salvatore admitted that he did masturbate while thinking about other women, and he explained that he especially enjoyed the thought of ejaculating on women's faces. Kara recoiled and told Salvatore that she would not allow him to do so, as she regarded that as a form of degradation, but that she did not mind if he masturbated to such thoughts. In fact, since Kara knew that she now had one or more female porn-star rivals, she rather enjoyed the thought that Salvatore would be ejaculating over them and keeping her pure.

Another couple, twenty-three-year-old taxi driver "Yuri" and twenty-four-year-old trainee chef "Celine," also found themselves discussing their sexual fantasies. After Yuri revealed his fantasies of a threesome with two bisexual women, he pressed Celine for hers, and for the first time, she told him that she often thought about being penetrated "savagely" by a well-endowed Afro-Caribbean man during her lovemaking sessions with Yuri. Knowing of Yuri's vast sexual experience, Celine assumed that he would be rather open-minded about her fantasy; but, in fact, he became enraged at the thought of an Afro-Caribbean man performing sexual acts on his girlfriend. His face turned red, and he fumed with jealousy and stormed out of the flat, seeking refuge in a friend's spare bedroom. When Yuri returned home the next day, Celine began to cry, "Why can't I fantasize about just *one* imaginary black man? After all, you're fantasizing about *two* people." Yuri replied that her description of the black man's big penis made him feel inadequate, whereas he had protected her by pointedly refraining from describing the breast size of the two bisexual women in his fantasy. He then retaliated further by mocking Celine, telling her that his fantasy women had much larger breasts than she did. A fight soon developed, with both Yuri and Celine insulting each other in an increasingly infantile manner. Afterwards they agreed that they would never discuss their sexual fantasies again.

"Riley," an unemployed man, and "Lissa," a successful optician, both twenty-nine, had married two years previously and had enjoyed a reasonably satisfying sex life. One evening, Lissa bashfully hinted that she had a new idea to spice up their sex life. Riley's pupils widened with anticipation. Lissa explained that she often fantasized about dressing up in a skimpy black cocktail frock, with black fishnet stockings and "fuck-me" shoes, and then perching herself on a barstool in a very fancy hotel. She explained that Riley would enter the bar thirty minutes later, after she had had a few drinks, and begin to flirt with her, as though he had never met her before. In Lissa's fantasy, Riley would have to find a way to take her upstairs for a steamy sex session. Riley listened attentively to Lissa's fantasy and then berated her for never having told him this before. He jumped at the chance to enact it, and the following weekend he booked a room at an expensive hotel. As planned, he "picked up" his own wife, pretending to be seducing a stranger. Both Lissa and Riley agreed that they had never had such exciting sex, and they have since repeated this scenario in a number of other hotels.

"Mark," a forty-one-year-old journalist, and "Marge," a thirty-one-year-old social worker in a shelter for battered women, had a rather strained sex life for many years, plagued by Mark's frequent bouts of depression and erectile dysfunction. One day, Mark told Marge that "for years" he had fantasized about performing anal sex with her. He had always enjoyed a powerful erection during private masturbatory sessions while thinking about anal penetration with Marge, and he hoped that they might try it. She resisted this suggestion for many months, disliking the very idea of anal sex. As a social worker, Marge had had many female clients whose male partners had sodomized them, and in each case, the women had felt grossly violated. Eventually, after much coaxing from Mark, who was still struggling with intermittent impotence, Marge relented, and she allowed him to penetrate her rectally. This proved a huge mistake from Marge's point of view. She experienced severe physical pain, and after Mark withdrew his penis, she became anally incontinent; unable to stop herself, she defecated on the bed sheets. This prompted Mark to retch, and both became deeply distressed. This episode of attempted anal intercourse caused an enormous rift in their relationship, and a year later they instituted divorce proceedings.

Sharing or enacting fantasies can prove a great boon to a partnership, as in the case of Riley and Lissa, or can be taken in stride, as with Kara and Salvatore. But sharing or enacting fantasies can also damage a relationship or reveal the vulnerabilities and wounds that may already be present, as in the cases of Yuri and Celine, and Mark and Marge. Clearly, psychotherapists cannot offer guidelines on how fantasies should be managed; each couple must negotiate this for themselves. But one should proceed with thoughtfulness. It cannot be accidental that the vast majority of American and British men and women have never shared their truest, most private sexual fantasies with their partners.

Throughout this chapter, I have attempted to explore the impact of sexual fantasies on marriages and long-term partnerships, examining not only how fantasies promote guilt or pleasure, but also how they may provoke relationship crises or contribute to the maintenance of marital secrets. I have also examined the thorny questions of whether one should ever share one's fantasies or enact them with one's partner or partners. In any case, the use of fantasies can either diminish or increase in intensity depending upon the state of a marriage or relationship at any given point in time. An interviewee called "Phoebe" told me that after she and her husband survived the first "tricky" months of lovemaking, becoming used to each other's naked bodies, all of her long-standing sexual fantasies seemed to "melt away." She had come to love her partner's body so much that her old fantasies became redundant. "Tamara," yet another interviewee, had exactly the opposite experience. She did not fantasize until she discovered that her husband had begun to cheat on her. Although still married to her husband, she now finds it impossible to have sex with him *unless* she fantasizes about someone else. Fantasies can often remain static throughout the life cycle, but for many individuals, fantasy displays a certain amount of fluidity, often becoming a barometer of both marital satisfaction and marital longevity.

23 Normality and Perversion in the Bedroom and the Boardroom

A mind all logic is like a knife all blade.
It makes the hand bleed that uses it.
—RABINDRANATH TAGORE, *Stray Birds*

Is Your Fantasy Perverse?

Whatever the origins of our sexual fantasies, whether trauma-based or not, and whatever the impact on our relationships, whether deleterious or not, many people yearn to know, "Is my fantasy healthy, or is it a sign of perversion?" In fact, the fear of being thought to be sexually "deranged," "odd," "unusual," "sick," or "perverse" by one's partner, or indeed by oneself, constitutes perhaps the greatest obstacle preventing people from discussing their fantasies in a more candid manner.

But before we proceed any further, we must define what actually constitutes a "perversion." For many decades, mental health professionals and members of the general public alike have bandied that term about in a free-wheeling manner, often exacerbating the sense of shame and guilt people have about their sexual thoughts, feelings, and practices. But ideas about what constitutes a perversion have changed over time. Throughout much of the twentieth century, for example, psychoanalysts described anyone who engaged in homosexual activity as suffering from a perversion, whereas nowadays, a much more tolerant, understanding view of homosexuality predominates in the field. Mental health practitioners no longer automatically regard gay and lesbian people as perverse. We recognize instead that gay and lesbian people, just like heterosexual people, can be either extremely healthy or extremely troubled, with most people, regardless of sexual orientation, falling somewhere in between.

Although we no longer view divergent sexual orientations as perversions—a hangover from the nineteenth century—we do retain the use of the term "perversion." We use it, however, in a very specific, carefully defined manner. The late Robert Stoller, a leading American psychiatrist and psychoanalyst, offered the most widely respected description of perversion, defining it, quite straightforwardly, as the erotic form of hatred. In other words, a perversion could be characterized as any act in which one derives orgasmic pleasure from harming someone else or even oneself. Pedophilia, for example, rape, or any form of incest would all constitute clinical perversions because a victim suffers harm as a result of the perpetrator's search for a combination of sexual and aggressive gratification.

In Great Britain, Dr. Estela Welldon, one of the world's leading psychiatrists and a specialist in forensic psychotherapy—the branch of the mental health field devoted to the diagnosis, treatment, and prevention of sexual perversion and violence—has offered an even richer and fuller definition of perversion that I have found extremely useful in my work. In a careful explication of the concept, based on her long experience of treating dangerous patients by psychoanalytical means, Welldon noted that a true perversion is characterized by no fewer than twelve interrelated qualities:

1. The person engaged in a perversion seems to have no choice in the matter. The perversion is experienced as a compulsion. In other words, if the patient practices pedophilia, for example, he or she will claim to have no option, reporting that no amount of threat or legal injunction can prevent him or her from engaging in the perverse activity.
2. The individual practicing the perversion treats the other as an *object*, rather than as a *person*. In psychoanalytical vocabulary, we regard this as an instance of relating to someone as a "part-object" rather than as a "whole-object." In other words, the victim is merely an orifice to the perverse person.

3. The person afflicted by perversion will have no concern for the person upon whom the perversion is practiced. Protests such as "Oh, but I really love this child" are little more than rationalizations.

4. The perversion is practiced compulsively and repetitively.

5. The perversion is often hidden, or encapsulated, and thereby practiced in secret.

6. The person engaged in perverse activity usually regards his or her actions as bizarre or inexplicable, and therefore is unable to understand the origins of the perverse enactments.

7. The sexual perversions are used to release pent-up sexual anxieties, not to create intimacy with another person.

8. The perversions are enacted in order to express hatred rather than love.

9. In most cases of perversion, the perpetrator violates the bodily boundaries of the victim.

10. The perverse practitioner engages in deceit.

11. The perverse individual is generally unable to mourn the early losses that might have contributed to the development of the perversion in the first place.

12. The perverse activity serves as a manic defense against an underlying depressive state.

In my work, I tend to use the term "perversion" very infrequently, restricting it, for the most part, to pedophiles, rapists, and others who derive sexual pleasure from harming others or, in extreme cases, themselves. Forensic psychotherapists generally differentiate between those who *fantasize* about something perverse (in other words, someone who masturbates about rape, for example) and those who actually *enact* perverse behaviors by violating the bodily safety of another person. An actual rape cannot be considered as anything other than perverse. A rape fantasy becomes more difficult to classify. I have certainly thought that in many cases those who become aroused by rape fantasies may well be channeling their aggression into the fantasy, thus making it less likely that they will engage in an enactment of rape.

The Internet has challenged our thinking in this area. For years, forensic mental health professionals classified only actual bodily enactments as perversions, but nowadays one can masturbate to deeply violent images broadcast on the Internet in a compulsive, repetitive manner. Such activity may qualify as a sexual perversion.

I would regard a sexual fantasy as perverse if it fulfilled two essential criteria:

1. The fantasy requires sustained perpetration of sadism toward oneself or one's "love-object."
2. The fantasy becomes so all engrossing that it prevents one from forging an intimate relationship with another person and interferes with successful functioning in other areas of one's life.

Consider the story of "Julius," a man in his late seventies who had begun masturbating at the age of fifteen, and who had continued to do so at least twice each day for the next sixty-plus years. Julius has had one central masturbatory fantasy throughout his life, of which he never tires. He masturbates to the thought of tying up a particular girl who rejected him in adolescence and penetrating her so roughly that she begins to bleed vaginally. In his fantasy, he then slaps her across the face with his penis, bruising her cheeks, and he climaxes as he calls her a "fucking whore" and a "fucking bitch." Julius has dated women intermittently over the past half century, but he has never succeeded in forming an ongoing partnership with a woman. In fact, his masturbatory fantasy has remained his most steady companion. I would regard Julius's fantasy as perverse—not as a means of judging him, but rather in a purely descriptive sense—owing to the sustained, fixed, unalterable nature of the fantasy and its highly sadistic content. Many men have aggressive fantasies about women, but the vast majority also manage to make love to their female partners in tender and sensitive ways, thereby offering evidence of a more adaptable, creative erotic life. But in Julius's case, the fantasies became so compelling that they may well have prevented him from becoming more intimate.

In thinking about perversion, it may be important to remember that some people regard their own fantasies as perverse even when no expert would, in part because of a deeply internalized sense of shame about sexual matters. One twenty-year-old, "Loretta," whom I interviewed, blushed when I asked about her fantasies, worrying that I would be disgusted by the scenario, which she regarded as "very perverse." I braced myself for a story of unmitigated cruelty, but in fact Loretta told me that she fantasized about making love to her married lecturer at the university. I waited for more details, but she supplied none. I asked in a calm voice, "Is there anything else that you wish to tell me about your fantasy?" Loretta replied, "No, that's it. Isn't that awful? I'm trying to get over it, but he's just so cute." To her mind, fantasizing about a married man, and an older one to boot, constituted a great psychological crime, a true perversion. I wonder whether Loretta would still regard her sexual fantasy as perverse after she had read the extraordinary range of fantasies contained in this collection, which seems to include examples of nearly everything that human beings could possibly imagine.

Can Fantasies Destroy Our Lives?

As we know, our fantasies can provide us with an enormous amount of daytime or nighttime pleasure, functioning, in part, as our very own private cinema, where we choose the film, the actors, the lighting, the sets, the costumes, and the props, as well as the script. But for many individuals, especially those with trauma-filled histories, choice becomes an impossible luxury; instead, the script will, in most if not all instances, be preselected. For those who have endured marked traumas, sexual fantasies may exert a detrimental effect on their minds and relationships. Additionally, fantasies can influence one's working life, damaging opportunities for professional achievement.

Earlier, I described at length the case of Paris, the middle-aged male nurse who enjoyed masturbating to the fantasy of having his hands tied to a bedpost while an anonymous man shaved his pubic region and then ejaculated over him. We traced this fantasy to Paris's childhood experience of sharing a bed with his father, who ejaculated over his son. After Paris reached maturity, he embarked upon a long relationship with Angelo, a much older man who treated him rather cruelly. One might argue that Paris's earlier trauma with his father, and its subsequent reinforcement through constant masturbation, predisposed him to seek a father-like partner who would abuse him in various ways. The connection between Paris's early trauma, his sexual fantasy, and his unconscious choice of a partner seems quite clear.

You may also recall that when Paris began telling me about his job as a hospital-based nurse, he reported, "my hands are tied." Listening to him, I wondered whether his sense of frustration at work could be related to his fantasy of actually having his hands tied to the bed, or to the early childhood experience of feeling as though his father had tied his hands, as the father had virtually smothered Paris when he lay next to him in the bunk bed on that fateful night. My conversation with Paris forced me to ask myself whether sexual fantasies in fact infiltrate our places of work—spilling over into the boardroom, if you like, as well as the bedroom—thus affecting our careers.

Within minutes of meeting "Herman," another interviewee, I learned that he ran a large computer software design company, employing twenty-five staff members and boasting an annual turnover of more than $15 million. Herman's business credentials impressed me, and I wondered how he had found the time to leave his office to spend five hours in an interview with me. When one factored in the requisite traveling time, nearly two hours each way, Herman would not, I suspect, have managed to spend any time at all at his office that day. He explained that, although he had made a great success of his current company, he had only recently recovered from a terrible series of financial blows. *Three* previous computer companies he had founded had all failed within eighteen months of start-up. Herman jokingly stated, "I must have a curse or something."

Herman had not only buried three companies but had also buried three wives, metaphorically speaking. His first marriage ended after only six weeks when he discovered that his wife had begun to have sex with his brother. His second marriage terminated after a year when he learned that his wife preferred women. And this third marriage ended due to "sexual incompatibility." Herman explained that his third wife had had a very high sex drive; he simply could not keep pace with her voraciousness in the bedroom. At only forty-one years of age, Herman had already married and divorced three times, surrendering a small fortune to each of his ex-wives, and had experienced three business failures. He certainly did seem to be suffering from an unfortunate series of events. He chose to think of himself as simply "unlucky."

As one might expect, Herman had had a very strained childhood. He described his alcoholic mother as distant and unpredictable, reporting that she often resorted to slapping him and his younger brother. Herman cataloged a series of relentless physical blows to his face and buttocks, administered on a regular basis during his mother's drunken rages. Indeed, he frequently found himself quite baffled. "I never knew what my crime was," he said. "The blows just came without any warning, and without any provocation on my part." His father seemed a passive and ineffectual figure who tolerated his wife's alcoholism and never protected his sons from her physical assaults. When Herman's mother became particularly drunk, she would storm into his bedroom, seize his possessions, "whatever she could find," and begin to rip them to shreds, whether items of clothing, schoolbooks and papers, or other personal effects. In the world of Herman's childhood, everything would eventually be attacked, and often destroyed.

At the age of thirteen, Herman fell madly in love with "Faye," a pretty young girl from his class at school—his first teenage romance. One day, after lessons, he brought her home, and they went upstairs to his bedroom to do their homework together. The mother became outraged when she discovered that Herman had taken a girl into his room and then had the temerity to close the bedroom door. She burst into his room, drunk, and began to taunt Faye with grossly inappropriate sexual comments. Herman particularly remembered his mother sneering, "You don't want to go out with my son. He's got such a little prick. It's pathetic." Understandably, Herman felt utterly mortified. Such a brutish encounter with Herman's mother must have terrified the young Faye, and she refused to speak to him after this episode.

College proved a great respite for him because at last he could leave the toxic environment of his family home. Although relieved to be away, Herman encountered great difficulties academically. A smart lad, no doubt, Herman somehow managed to sabotage his work. He failed to complete assigned essays and even slept through at least two crucial exams. I suspect that Herman could easily have obtained an honor's degree, but in fact he left the university three years later with mediocre results, just scraping through, in fact. Somehow, a pattern of self-destructiveness had already taken root in Herman's character structure.

Apart from his brief teenage tryst with Faye, Herman had no other girlfriends throughout his school years or at college, contenting himself instead with masturbation. In his favorite masturbatory fantasy, Herman would imagine himself standing before an audience of middle-aged women who would berate him for being a "loser." To punish him, these women would pull his trousers and underwear down and then spank him on the buttocks. Afterward, they would taunt him over the small size of his penis, calling him names, especially "Needle Dick." In real life, Herman told me, he has a perfectly normal-sized penis, but in his fantasy he imagines his penis to be two or three inches smaller. Although many would regard his sexual fantasy as deeply painful and poignant, Herman would reach a highly pleasurable climax at the thought of this scenario.

At the present time, Herman has managed to reequilibrate himself financially by establishing a new and highly lucrative business, but he confided a private fear to me: "What if it all comes crashing down around my ankles, just like all my other businesses?" When Herman articulated his anxiety about his business collapsing around his *ankles,* I could not help but wonder about the correspondence between his choice of vocabulary and the content of his sexual fantasy. Would some tyrannical mother pull down the company's trousers, only to discover a tiny "Needle Dick," all based on show and not on substance? It seemed clear to me that Herman's early childhood experiences had contributed to his fantasy life, and that, in turn, the masturbatory rehearsal of his punishment fantasy had become the coloring force not only in his marital relationships but also in his business dealings. I did, in fact, fear for the future of his current business enterprise.

In my meetings with the interviewees for the Sexual Fantasy Research Project, I remained highly aware of the primary nature of my task: to conduct an interview. I had to resist the temptation to embark upon psychotherapeutic work with some of the more emotionally complicated participants in the interview sample. But I never lost sight of my ethical responsibility as a psychotherapist to attempt to be helpful, if at all possible. I solved my dilemma by remaining an interviewer, first and foremost, completing each interview experience as thoroughly as possible, but, at appropriate junctures, I would also offer expressions of psychotherapeutic concern. During my conversation with Herman, I addressed his fear about the possibility of sabotaging his fourth company.

I told Herman that I very much appreciated his anxieties about the future welfare of his computer company, and that I could certainly begin to see a pattern emerging between his early life, his fantasies, and the destruction of his marriages and his previous businesses, and I thought that he, too, could detect this increasingly evident trend. Herman agreed with my observation. I explained that, in my experience, early childhood tendencies and structures often shape our mental lives in an insidious way, quite unconsciously, and I wondered whether he might find it of value to talk to one of my colleagues. Herman giggled and told me that he had no interest in psychology. I reminded him gently that he had in fact volunteered to speak to a mental health professional, and that he had dedicated an entire working day for this very purpose. I suggested that perhaps part of him recognized something potentially destructive in his personality and wanted some assistance. Once again, he dismissed my comments.

At the end of the interview, I thanked Herman for his generous participation, and I reaffirmed that he would be most welcome to contact me at any point in the future, if he ever felt the need for a referral. I explained that I had a very trusted colleague who worked near Herman's home. Herman lifted his eyebrows in an expression of interest, but then he shook my hand and departed, and I did not hear from him again. His failure to pursue psychological help may well be yet another expression of his internalized struggle with self-destruction, as though a part of him has become identified with the mother who enters his room and tears his possessions in two.

Perhaps Herman has by now sought other means of support, perhaps not. Over the years, my colleagues and I have encountered innumerable Hermans—earnest, well-meaning people who, in spite of their endowments and abilities, seem hell-bent on self-sabotage. I wish to suggest that the central masturbatory fantasy may offer us a clue as to those who may be most at risk for these behaviors; and further, I want to underscore that psychotherapy has often proved itself a very valuable method of treatment for those still gripped by deep-seated self-destructive propensities.

The Woman Who Lived in a Toilet

"Despina," a twenty-nine-year-old mother of three, told me that she had agreed to come for her interview because, plainly and simply, she needed the cash. A cleaner in a railway station, Despina earned very little money, and with Christmas approaching, she thought it would be helpful to participate in the interview study. She then paused and added, "Well, also, I do have an interest in psychology. I really like to know what makes people tick." Despina batted her eyes at me in what struck me as a rather flirtatious manner, and she purred, "Besides, I've never met a psych . . . a psycho . . . a. . . ." She stumbled over the word, stuttering, and finally managed to get it right.

As soon as Despina began to recite her history, I immediately understood why she had begun to flirt. When Despina was eight, her twelve-year-old brother had sexually abused her by inserting his fingers into her vagina and anus at regular intervals. When she was nine, her father had begun to abuse her as well, forcing her to perform fellatio on him. When she was ten, a teenage boy who lived nearby raped her on several occasions. And when she turned twelve, her brother, then sixteen, also began raping her, with his penis, both vaginally and anally. Additionally, Despina explained, her mother had kept a stick in her handbag at all times, a big, thick stick, rather like a policeman's truncheon. If she ever "misbehaved," her mother would thwack her on the backs of her hands and on the backs of her thighs with a minimum of three strokes. Listening to Despina's account of her childhood experiences touched me greatly. With so much sexual and physical abuse, it did not surprise me that she would sexualize her adult relationships with men and use flirtation as a characterological defense against an anticipated attack.

Despina reminded me of my very first female psychotherapy patient, a woman with a similar history, whose parents used to beat her senseless. Although more than twenty years have passed since I worked with that particular patient, I shall never forget her very first words to me in our initial session. She looked at me with terror and asked, "So, when are you going to hit me?" Dumbfounded, I asked why on earth she thought I would hit her. This woman simply stared at me, and she said in a totally deadpan manner, "If you don't hit me, well, then, you'll be the first man in my life who hasn't." As a young trainee, I experienced a rude awakening. I certainly never imagined at that point in my career that a woman could possibly be abused by every single important man in her life: father, brothers, uncles, teachers, and even the local priest.

During my interview with Despina, I found myself modulating my voice, speaking in soft tones, anxious to assuage her fear that I, too, would be an abuser. Having learned that she had endured many horrific experiences as a young girl, I asked her how she had managed to survive so much abuse. Despina fluttered her eyes once again and replied, "Lots of drugs, lots of drink, lots of sex." In retrospect, I should have known the answer, for when one has endured such repeated and persistent sexual and physical abuse, one has very few alternatives, madness being the most likely outcome in many cases, but also substance abuse and other forms of addiction—anything, in fact, which numbs the mind from pain.

Unsurprisingly, in view of such a marked history of abuse, Despina had found it impossible to concentrate on her lessons at school. She giggled, "I'm thick as two short planks. Not a brain cell in my head." She had left school at age fifteen, without a single qualification, and within a year had married "Corbin," the father of her children. As one might expect, Corbin also beat Despina on a regular basis. Once, he pulled out four large clumps of hair from her head, causing her scalp to bleed. A heavy drinker, Corbin would rape Despina whenever he wished. As she explained, all three of her children could be described as the unplanned products of marital rape. I had heard many dreadful histories during the course of my interviewing work for this research project, but Despina's may well have qualified as the most bleak and heart-wrenching. Her life seemed unrelentingly grim in every respect.

I asked her whether she had any joy in her life at all, and she explained, "Well, I like a good laugh, I do. And when I can afford it, I go to a local club, which sometimes has a ladies' night, and we watch the male strippers." When I inquired what, in particular, she liked about the male strippers, her face turned steely, and she exclaimed, "Well, it's only fair that we girls get to see the men on display for a change." Of course, it occurred to me that as a much-abused child, Despina's body would have been on display on far too many occasions; therefore, it made great sense from a psychological point of view that she would want to extract some revenge by watching the male dancers remove their clothing.

Despina then looked at me rather shamefacedly, announcing, "Mind you, I did get into big trouble with Corbin the other week. I wanted to go out to see some strippers with the girls, and I told him that he would have to look after the children. He blew his top because *he* wanted to go to the pub that night." I asked what had happened, whereupon Despina replied, "Well, Corbin just stared me down, and said, 'Little Shit, I'll fucking slap the shit out of you if you go out with the girls,' and so I didn't." Incredulous, I inquired, "Why did Corbin call you 'Little Shit'?" Despina laughed, "Oh, everyone calls me that. It's my nickname. Ever since I was a child. Everyone calls me 'Little Shit.'" I must have looked horrified, unable to maintain my normal neutral expression. Despina reassured me, "It's okay, I don't mind. I rather like it. People mean it in an affectionate way."

To my ears, "Little Shit" sounded quite horrible—a brutal, denigratory nickname that would humiliate most people. But instead of pursuing further discussion about Despina's nickname at this point, I asked for additional information about her job, knowing only that she worked as a cleaner at the railway station. When I wondered what precisely this entailed, Despina explained that she has full responsibility for the toilets, noting, "It's disgusting work, but someone's gotta do it. I sometimes think I spend my whole life with my head in the toilet bowl, cleaning up other people's piss and shit." I wondered whether Despina had ever thought about finding other employment, especially as she had already worked in this job for eight years. She looked at me in a pitiful manner and intoned, "Well, dear, what else would you like me to do? Maybe I could become a psychologist. I think I'd be a good one." Responding to her comment concretely, I asked if she had ever considered completing her education, whereupon she choked, "What me, back at college? The only way I'll see the inside of a college is if they hire me to clean."

Despina could not remember who had first called her "Little Shit"; perhaps her mother had done so, perhaps her father. At any rate, the nickname had taken root quite early, and it had stuck ever since. Somehow, her very identity became associated with excrement. She had been raped, beaten, assaulted, impregnated, and lived much of her life in a toilet, surrounded by the remnants of the urine and feces of thousands and thousands of strangers. If ever one could put forward a case for the childhood determinants of adult career choice, Despina would surely be the star witness.

As the final hour of the interview approached, we began to speak about Despina's sexual fantasies. At first, she blushed, concerned about my reaction. I remained silent, allowing her further space to collect her thoughts and speak. "Well," she whispered, "it's all about my family. My brother and my father." I nodded in silent encouragement. After a short pause, she braced herself and began to speak again: "They are both raping me at the same time, one in my fanny [vagina], the other up my bum [ass]. Then they come inside me, and when they finish, they pull out, and they make me suck their pricks. My father's prick tastes all right, 'cause he's been in my fanny, but my brother's prick is disgusting, covered with my shit. But he makes me lick it, and I've got to clean it up. He says, 'Make it shine, "Little Shit."' And then I come."

At this point, Despina began to sob. Her flirtatious, tough-nut exterior had melted away, and suddenly I could see traces of the little abused girl seated on the sofa in front of me. She confessed that she had never told a single soul about the contents of her sexual fantasy before, and that hearing it spoken out loud made her feel quite sick. She expressed the worry that she might be a "complete perv." I told her that in view of her history of abuse and of being taunted with a nickname such as "Little Shit," it made great sense to me that she should collect all of those painful childhood ingredients, combine them tidily into the same fantasy story, and then eroticize them by bringing herself to orgasm. "So I make sense, do I?" she cried. "Yes, you do," I replied.

I learned that Despina had begun to masturbate to this fantasy at the age of eighteen or nineteen, and that although she had utilized a range of other fantasies over the years, including lesbianism, this scene with her brother and father proved to be the most arousing. Despina's story, rather like Herman's, demonstrates yet again the impact of early cruelty on later development. As the cruelty becomes sexualized and reinforced in one's mind during fantasy, it contributes, in my estimation, to self-destructive patterns of behavior during one's adult life that affect one's relationships and career path. I wonder whether Despina's parents knew that when they first called their daughter "Little Shit," they may well have consigned her to a lifetime of cleaning out latrines, with her head, quite literally, "in the toilet bowl."

24   Sanctum Sanctorum, Or, Probing the Unprobable

It is a very ungentlemanly thing to read a private cigarette case.

—OSCAR WILDE,
The Importance of Being Earnest

Penetrating Questions Revisited

In Chapter 1, I posed twenty-two questions about sexual fantasies. Although I have addressed most of these questions in some detail throughout these pages, I shall now attempt to provide some concise answers.

Question 1: What is a sexual fantasy?   A sexual fantasy may be defined as an image, a thought, or a fully elaborated drama that passes through one's mind principally during sexual activity, either coital or masturbatory, often resulting in orgasm. Sexual fantasies must be distinguished from sexual daydreams or fleeting sexual thoughts. Sexual fantasies may be very simple or highly complex, may be tender or sadistic, and may cause the fantasist psychological pleasure or psychological pain. In general, people keep their sexual fantasies hidden from their partners and even from their psychotherapists or other confidants.

Question 2: What constitutes a "normal" sexual fantasy?   Having now studied more than 23,000 American and British fantasies, I cannot identify a so-called "normal" fantasy. It would be a gross oversimplification to describe as normal *only* those fantasies involving loving, genital intercourse with one's long-term partner or spouse. I certainly interviewed many happily married people who nursed very aggressive fantasies, often about their beloved spouses. On the basis of the data, I must conclude that the minds of American and British citizens contain much diversity and complexity, and therefore, speaking about a "normal" fantasy may well be meaningless.

Question 3: Why do we have sexual fantasies in the first place?   We do not know how and why sexual fantasies first developed. Evolutionary psychologists have suggested that sexual fantasies contribute to the facilitation of sexual arousal, which in turn facilitates procreation. Thus sexual fantasies may play an important, previously unrecognized role in the continued propagation of the human species. Freudian psychotherapists and psychoanalysts have speculated that our fantasies may have developed as both a means of gratifying wishes and of conquering intrusive memories of early traumatic experiences.

Question 4: What purpose or purposes do our sexual fantasies serve?   In Chapter 20, I enumerated fourteen separate reasons why people might fantasize, ranging from wish-fulfillment and mastery of trauma to self-medication against pain or the elaboration of childhood play. For many, fantasies remain an unending source of fun and enjoyment; for others, they remain a constant reminder of early injuries. For a large percentage of individuals, fantasies provide pleasure and pain simultaneously. Sexual fantasies no doubt serve a multiplicity of interrelated functions.

Question 5: Does everybody have sexual fantasies?   According to psychoanalytical clinicians, everyone has *unconscious* fantasy structures—in other words, subterranean tendencies toward certain preferences or predictable ways of acting (whether sadistically, masochistically, depressively, and so forth). In most adults, these unconscious fantasy structures find representation in conscious sexual fantasies that occur during masturbation or during intercourse with a partner. According to my research findings, at least 90 percent of all adults experience daydreams, which may or may not be of a sexual nature. As for sexual fantasies, the data reveal that approximately 96 percent of adult males have sexual fantasies and approximately 90 percent of adult females do so. It should be noted that these might well be conservative figures, as I have met many individuals over the years who profess, on first questioning, to have no sexual fantasies at all, but later on, often during the course of psychotherapy, will admit to fantasizing about sexual scenarios.

Question 6: Should we be worried if we have no *fantasies at all?*   A separate study would be required to assess the personality characteristics of the nonfantasizers. At the present time, psychotherapists cannot reliably differentiate those who fantasize from those who do not. On the basis of my clinical experience I would hypothesize that many of those who claim to have no sexual fantasies may well be struggling with strong feelings of shame and guilt around sexual matters, and might be utilizing the defense mechanism of repression as a means of banishing all sexual thoughts from the mind.

Question 7: Should we ever share our fantasies with our partners?   As I have already indicated, I cannot provide a definitive answer to this most complex of questions. I have reported cases where partners seem to have benefited from having discussed their sexual fantasies with one another; but, similarly, I have also encountered some couples who have experienced great distress upon learning of one another's truest fantasies. Some couples have claimed that risking self-disclosure about such intimate matters promotes further emotional trust and union. Much will depend, of course, on the preexisting strength of the couple's attachment to one another. Above all, one must proceed with thoughtfulness before deciding whether to share one's most private sexual fantasies.

Question 8: Should we ever share our fantasies with our friends?   Often, it might feel rather less exposing and more manageable to share fantasies with friends than with partners. I know of many men, for example, who would not hesitate to talk about extramarital affairs or rape fantasies with their buddies at a Friday-night poker game, but who would never dream of discussing such fantasies with their female partners for fear of causing outrage or offense. Similarly, I have interviewed a number of women who have shared their fantasies—particularly those involving men with extremely large genitals—with their girlfriends, but who would not impart this to their husbands or boyfriends for fear of promoting feelings of inadequacy. Although entrusting one's fantasies to a friend may be an act of great faith, and may serve to enrich the friendship, one must remember that friendships can, and often do, sour. Promises of confidentiality can be broken along with the friendship, and the fear of this occurring can cause great anxiety.

Question 9: Would it be wise to act out our sexual fantasies with our lovers?   Acting out fantasies requires a great deal of compassion, creativity, and trust on the part of both partners; I have seen a number of marriages founder when such role-plays have gone awry. Certainly, psychotherapists would recommend much consideration before enacting a sexual fantasy scenario, bearing in mind that a fantasy and a reality might be experienced rather differently. One must also be prepared for some surprises. I recently interviewed a woman who indulged her husband's wish to spank her and call her a "bitch." When the husband described the potential scenario, the wife became excited and offered her consent. But when the couple actually brought this fantasy to life, the wife felt "cheapened" and "revolted," and she deeply regretted her decision. For many, the fantasy will be exciting precisely because it will never be enacted.

Question 10: Can our fantasies ever be damaging or dangerous?   In some instances, sadistic fantasies can serve as stepping stones to sadistic actions. My colleagues and I in the forensic mental health field certainly know of many cases of patients whose criminal career began in their own minds. Once, years ago, I had the opportunity to interview a psychotic serial killer in a maximum-security setting. I learned that before his incarceration, this man could make love to his wife only if he fantasized about clutching a switchblade knife. Some years previously, he had embarked on a killing spree, using a knife as his weapon, causing much carnage.

Of course, not all examples will be this dramatic, but in many instances, fantasies can nevertheless reinforce self-destructive patterns of behavior and thought and cause real damage to oneself or others.

Question 11: If we fantasize about "ordinary" sex, does this mean that we must be boring?   I am deeply struck by the number of people I have met who feared that they might have "boring" fantasies, especially those that involved making love to their boyfriends and girlfriends or to their husbands and wives. As yet, I can find no formal, documentable correlation between richness of fantasy life and richness of external life (as measured by conversational fluency, academic achievement, and a host of other variables). Clinically speaking, however, I did find quite a number of the interviewees who shared rather simple, nonelaborate sexual fantasies to be also rather simple and nonelaborate in their general demeanor; subsequent research may perhaps establish a link between the richness of one's fantasy content and the richness of one's social, professional, or domestic life. As yet, I can offer no definite pronouncement on this matter.

Question 12: If we have very outlandish fantasies, does this mean that we must be mentally unbalanced?   Those individuals who presented with very elaborate and complex fantasies seemed to come from every walk of life. Among the clinical interviewees whose fantasies could be described as "outlandish," I detected no traces of formal mental illness. In fact, the most psychologically troubled participant in the interview cohort had, in fact, the least complex and least intricate fantasies of all the many research participants.

Question 13: If we fantasize about our partners during sex or during masturbation, does that mean that we have a good relationship?   Men and women who provide evidence of having a high fidelity quotient—in other words, those who do fantasize about their spouses or regular partners as a matter of course—often, though not invariably, have a very good, strong relationship. However, I know of many securely attached marriages in which neither partner fantasizes about the other, thereby offering evidence of a low fidelity quotient. Similarly, I know of couples with a high fidelity quotient who also engage in multiple extramarital affairs, and who report very bitter and strained marriages.

Question 14: If we fantasize about someone other than our partners during sex or masturbation, does that mean that our relationship might be in trouble?   If we find ourselves in the grip of an intra-marital affair, this does not necessarily prove that our relationship must be in trouble; however, the intra-marital affair may sometimes be a harbinger of subsequent marital difficulties. By fantasizing about someone other than our regular partner, our unconscious mind generates an opportunity for us to examine our relationship—to inquire privately and honestly whether there may be difficulties that have propelled us into the arms of a fantasized lover. We may conclude our self-examination delighted by the knowledge that our relationship remains intact, and that our intra-marital affair represents no more than a playful indulgence.

Question 15: If we fantasize about something "illegal," does this mean that we may be at risk for acting it out?   Fortunately, fantasy often exerts a strong containing function for the human mind; as a result, we manage to encapsulate some of the more aggressive and destructive aspects of our personalities into the fantasy content itself. I have talked to many doctors, priests, social workers, nurses, and other members of the "caring professions" who have had very violent fantasies that they have never enacted and, most likely, never will enact. If, however, the fantasy becomes perverse—in other words, unmitigatedly sadistic, or repeated compulsively and unceasingly—then a somewhat higher risk for ultimate enactment may be present. Mercifully, even those with compelling perverse fantasies—for example, those involving pedophilia—often refrain from ever harming anyone in real life. If one finds oneself struggling with "illegal" fantasies about cruelty and torture, this may indicate a severe difficulty with aggression owing to earlier childhood trauma; in such instances, it might be prudent to consult a qualified mental health professional, especially if one has worries about the likelihood of an eventual enactment.

Question 16: Do our fantasies represent just a bit of private fun, or do they have more profound implications for how we lead our lives?   In Chapter 23 on the so-called "bedroom-boardroom" phenomenon, I advanced the hypothesis that our fantasies may determine not only how we approach our intimate relationships, but also how we approach our working lives. I suspect that the bedroom spills into the boardroom more dangerously in those individuals with unprocessed and untreated histories of trauma than with those who have not suffered trauma, but this may not invariably be the case. For many, the fantasy remains safely encapsulated or integrated in the mind so that it can function with a reasonable degree of nonconflictualness.

Question 17: How can we explain the range of fantasies experienced by human beings? In other words, why do some people prefer to be kissed and cradled while others enjoy the infliction of often agonizing physical pain?   I have two answers to this particular question. In large measure, the content and the structure of our fantasies will depend on the nature of our infantile and childhood experiences. Those individuals who have experienced a great deal of childhood trauma will be more prone to regular fantasies of sadism. However, some individuals with horrifically abusive histories have rather tender fantasies, but only because, in my estimation, they enact their abusiveness in real-life, destructive activities. I have, however, met many people with relatively stable histories who nevertheless have quite lurid fantasies, and here one must allow for the possibility that aggressively tinged fantasies can result not only from primary trauma, but also from human creativity and from the capacity to allow oneself to regress to a more primitive mental state without becoming fixated at an infantile level of functioning. In other words, most aggressive and destructive fantasies stem from early abuse, but in some cases such fantasies might actually represent a *developmental achievement,* that is, the capacity to expand one's mind to encompass all variety of human experience, without actually acting out such experiences.

Question 18: Can we ever change our fantasies?   For the most part, my clinical data indicate that fantasy structures remain reasonably constant throughout adult life; however, changes in the emotional state of one's intimate relationship can either fuel or quell particular fantasy constellations. One of my patients, a law-abiding male, had very aggressive masturbatory fantasies about raping women; yet, these fantasies became prominent only when he fought with his wife. During periods of marital contentment, the patient seemed to have much less need to masturbate to his rape fantasies. One should also mention, perhaps, the "Krakatoa Complex," discussed in Chapter 22, a phenomenon whereby some external or internal event will serve as a trigger to open up a whole new world of fantasy possibilities that previously have lain dormant, often for many years. As yet, we have too few case reports in the clinical psychotherapeutic literature about structural changes in the nature of masturbatory and coital fantasies to draw any substantial conclusions. Most case reports of long psychoanalytical treatments do not chronicle or explore the changes in the patients' sexual fantasy content or frequency over time, because up to this point most mental health professionals have refrained from investigating this area in a sustained manner.

Question 19: How often do we lie about our sexual fantasies?   In retrospect, I wish I had included a question of this nature as part of my computer-administered survey for the Sexual Fantasy Research Project. I do not know the answer to this question, although, on the basis of my clinical work, I suspect that human beings lie quite regularly about their fantasies. In an extremely large number of cases, both in my psychodiagnostic interviewing and in my psychotherapeutic practice with patients, I remain impressed by the number of times that men and women have prefaced their discussion of sexual fantasies with the qualifying phrase, "I've never told this to anyone before," or "I can't believe I'm telling you this." Certainly, I have noted a difference between "true fantasies" and "barroom fantasies." As I mentioned previously, a man in a bar sharing a fantasy with his friends may well be telling the truth when he reports a wish to have sex with Britney Spears, but in most instances his report of the fantasy will stop at this point, omitting the more revealing details of what he wishes to do *to* Britney Spears, or *with* Britney Spears, or vice versa. Sexual fantasy remains a relatively taboo area of discourse, and because of the ignorance, shame, and secrecy surrounding the topic, many people lie about the content of their fantasies, unsure of what response a more honest revelation would elicit.

Question 20: Do our sexual fantasies differ from our daydreams or our nighttime dreams?   Sexual fantasies differ from daydreams and from nighttime dreams in that most sexual fantasies involve explicitly sexual material and culminate in an orgasm, whereas most daydreams and nighttime dreams will not be overtly sexual and do not result in climax. Of course, the line between daytime and nighttime cognition and between conscious and unconscious cognition can readily become blurred. Teenage boys, for example, sometimes experience an ejaculation or "wet dream" at night more powerfully than one during waking coitus or masturbation. A more extensive, comparative analysis of the differences between these varying states of mind would be a most welcome contribution to psychological studies.

Question 21: Is there a difference between the fantasies that we have during sex with a partner and the fantasies that we indulge in during private masturbation?   One striking difference does exist between coital fantasies in the presence of a partner and masturbatory fantasies in the absence of a partner—principally, the fidelity quotient. In other words, we will be much more likely to fantasize about our partners during intercourse than during masturbation. The complexity of a fantasy may also depend upon the duration of the lovemaking session. Those who have quick intercourse may not have sufficient time for a detailed fantasy to unfold, whereas those who devote a longer, more luxurious period of time to masturbation may be surprised at what might emerge. Likewise, prolonged intercourse may produce more intricate fantasies, and quick masturbation may not require much fantasy stimulation at all.

Question 22: Do we control our fantasies, or do our fantasies control us?   In many ways, this could be described as the $64,000 question, the subject of much contention and controversy in psychological and sexological circles. As a psychotherapist, I have met many people over the years whose fantasies have troubled them because of religious prohibitions, parental prohibitions, repetitions of early sexual abuse, or any combination thereof, and who have desperately attempted to erase these fantasies from their minds; but in virtually every case, the fantasies continue to erupt into consciousness, Krakatoa-style, and cannot readily be avoided. Certainly, highly traumatized individuals have very little conscious control over their fantasies. But I have also met people who claim that they have some degree of control over their fantasies. One of my patients told me that he could fantasize about "anything and everything," for example, and described himself as an "erotic sculptor." As he remarked, "Give me a topic, and I can turn it into a fantasy, just like a sculptor takes a piece of clay and can turn it into anything." Undoubtedly, some people have more control over the direction of their fantasies than others. On the whole, I have found that most people do not seem to be the ultimate architects of their own sexual fantasy lives. As a young gay male patient once reported, "If I could be straight, I would. Life would be so much easier, and my parents would be cooler about everything. But I can't. I just can't fantasize about women. So that's that." One should allow for the possibility that, while some individuals may be able to sculpt their erotic lives, for many the erotic propensities will sculpt them.

The Ten Key Dimensions of Sexual Fantasy

Having now surveyed the panoply of sexual fantasies, I have become extremely impressed with the fact that, as human beings, we have much in common; at the same time, I have become impressed by the extraordinary diversity among humans in their attitudes and thoughts about sexuality. I am fascinated by the fact that two women from different counties could have exactly the same detailed and elaborate fantasy about Mel Gibson, or that two men from completely different backgrounds could imagine the exact same rape scenario, down to the last detail. Perhaps these people had all watched the same pornographic film at some point, which had triggered their ideas for the fantasies, but perhaps not.

Having immersed myself in the sexual fantasy data, I have identified ten dimensions that characterize all sexual fantasies and that indicate the range and scope of fantasy life. A brief description of each of these dimensions follows.

Dimension 1: Tenderness—Sadism.   All fantasies can be rated on a
  continuous scale from extremely tender to extremely sadistic.

Tenderness and sadism refer to the way our partner or partners treat our body, and the way we treat the body or bodies of our partner or partners. Each one of us can locate our own preferred fantasy or fantasies somewhere along this continuum.

Dimension 2: Activity—Passivity.   In each key sexual fantasy, we will find ourselves either actively performing and orchestrating the scenario (whether through forcing, cajoling, insisting, pressuring, or requesting) or becoming the passive recipient of someone else's staging.

Dimension 3: Simplicity—Complexity.   Some sexual fantasies are very simple in content and style, whereas others are intricate and complex. The complex ones are based on a detailed narrative and sometimes involve a whole cast of characters.

Dimension 4: Relatedness—Retreatedness.   In every sexual fantasy, each person will position himself or herself in relation to his or her fellow human beings. In some fantasies, an individual may be very engaged and related with his or her partner or partners, but in others the fantasist will be retreated, perhaps fearful of contact with other human beings. A fantasy involving sex with a named person will be much more indicative of a related posture, whereas a fantasy involving sex with a dead person, an animal, or an object will reveal a retreated posture.

Dimension 5: Fluidity—Rigidity.   This dimension describes the relative fixity of our fantasies. Do we have the capacity to explore different fantasy scenarios and different partners, which is indicative of fluidity, or does the fantasy adopt a more classically perverse structure and never vary throughout the course of adulthood, which is indicative of rigidity?

Dimension 6: Object Constancy—Object Diversity.   Each of us differs in the degree of mental fidelity we display in relation to our partners. A person with a high degree of object constancy will fantasize predominantly about his or her regular partner, whereas an individual with a high degree of object diversity will be much more eclectic, substituting love-objects quite liberally, and often quite quickly.

Dimension 7: Consciousness—Unconsciousness.   This dimension refers to the degree to which one has become able to allow fantasy material to emerge into consciousness. Clinicians often speak of "unconscious sadists," in other words, individuals who act very savagely toward others interpersonally, but who would actually regard themselves as gentle pussycats. Mental health professionals often express concern about those people who cannot tolerate their own "shadow" side, as that aspect of their character will be "split off and become incapable of integration into their personality structure."

Dimension 8: Expansivity—Restrictedness.   Though similar to the Simplicity—Complexity dimension, Expansivity—Restrictedness refers to the capacity to tolerate a particular fantasy for a more protracted period. Some people are aware of their fantasies and may entertain them briefly, but then attempt to push them out of their minds. We refer to those individuals as restricted. By contrast, an expansive person demonstrates the capacity to entertain different fantasy constellations and to explore them and play with them without engaging in self-censorship.

Dimension 9: Ego-Syntonicity—Ego-Dystonicity.   Often our fantasies bring us great pleasure and sit comfortably in our minds in a relatively conflict-free manner. We would classify such fantasies as ego-syntonic. By contrast, many people suffer great shame and guilt and become highly distressed by their sexual fantasies. We would classify those fantasies as ego-dystonic.

Dimension 10: High-Arousal Intensity—Low-Arousal Intensity. Years ago, I met a man who told me, "I've never had a *bad* orgasm." This may well be true. But when one speaks to people about the differing intensities of arousal that result from particular fantasies, one discovers that all fantasies can be rated on a continuum ranging from "most arousing" to "least arousing." High-arousal intensity refers to fantasies that produce an explosive

orgasm, whereas low-arousal intensity refers to those culminating
in a pleasant and mildly satisfying orgasm.

I have identified these ten dimensions in order to help organize the
wealth of descriptive data about sexual fantasies and as an aid to other
psychological and sexological researchers. The categories listed above
may help future investigators to draw useful conclusions. For example,
if we had access to people's sexual fantasies, and discovered that everyone with a high "sadism" rating, combined with a high "activity" rating
and a high "ego-syntonicity" rating (in other words, someone who felt
comfortable with his or her sadism), ultimately progressed to a life of
sexual crime, then we might eventually be able to use this sort of information about sexual fantasies in a diagnostic-predictive manner. The
British murderer Dennis Nilsen, mentioned in Chapter 20, would probably have scored quite high on all three of these dimensions. If more research had already been done on sexual fantasies, and if authorities had
known about Nilsen's sexual fantasies before he acted them out, he
could have been identified as a high-risk person worthy of careful
scrutiny or even requiring prophylactic mental health treatment.

In the meanwhile, each of us can rate ourselves along these ten dimensions. I suspect we would find a huge difference between the sex
lives of those who have high ratings on tenderness, relatedness, object
constancy, consciousness, and expansivity, on the one hand, and those
with high ratings on sadism, retreatedness, object diversity, uncon-
ciousness, and restrictedness, on the other. Perhaps one day, dating
agencies and matrimonial services may be better able to match potential partners by utilizing confidential knowledge about clients' sexual
fantasies. Such factors may prove to be much more pertinent to com-
patibility than whether one enjoys films, eating out, and country walks.

Sherlock Holmes or Dr. Watson? What Kind of Sexologist Are You?

Studying human sexuality requires a combination of tolerance, fortitude, a sense of humor, and what I have come to regard as a strong
"psychological digestive tract." In analyzing so many sexual fantasies
and experiences, I have had to absorb a great deal of abuse-related material, much of it quite graphic and highly disturbing. And just when I

thought that I had heard every possible story about human sexuality that one could ever imagine, another one suddenly appeared. As I began to write this concluding section, a colleague told me one especially unusual story, which defies ready classification.

"Parker," a forty-nine-year-old gay man, would invite men back to his home for casual sex. Upon entering the apartment, each man would be assaulted by loud chirping noises and would then notice that Parker kept ten or twenty birdcages in his sitting room, each containing four or five small parakeets. Parker would retire briefly to his bedroom and return to the living room stark naked, with the exception of a pair of Texan-style leather cowboy boots. After instructing his guest to undress, Parker would perform anal sex on him. As Parker neared climax, he would stamp his boots loudly on the floor, and his guest would hear a loud crunching sound. After both men had reached orgasm, Parker would remove his boots and turn them upside down, whereupon two crushed parakeets would tumble onto the floor, often eliciting a reaction of revulsion and fear in the other man. Not having interviewed Parker, I know nothing about his background or his fantasy life, but I have included his story as yet one more instance of the extraordinary and often shocking vagaries of human sexual arousal.

In discussing my research with mental health colleagues and with friends, acquaintances, and associates from other academic disciplines, I have been truly staggered by the range of response to some of the findings. Many colleagues have reacted with genuine open-minded curiosity, amazed by the diversity in the data, whereas others have become overnight moralists, casting aspersions on many of the fantasies contained in this collection and dismissing them as "sick," "twisted," and "certifiable." I was struck by how quickly everyone, regardless of his or her training, turned into a full-time professional sexologist, offering "expert" opinions about every aspect of my research.

During the early stages of the interviewing, I derived a small amount of clinical and intellectual satisfaction from having managed to establish some connections between traumas and subsequent adult sexual fantasies. For a brief period of time, I felt rather like Sherlock Holmes, the agile sleuth who would always crack the secret code and apprehend the culprit. But as the research progressed, I became increasingly less Holmes-like. I now model myself much more on his modest sidekick, Dr. Watson, particularly as I have become infinitely more aware of the complexities of the data. Many questions arising from this project remain obscure or even unanswered. For instance, in my zeal to discover the contents of the hidden sexual fantasies of the British, I have not fully engaged with one of my great mentors, the pediatrician, child psychiatrist, and psychoanalyst Dr. Donald Winnicott, who wrote intelligently on the potential importance of what he termed the "incommunicado." Speaking about the process of free association, wherein the psychotherapist encourages the patient to articulate whatever ideas or images enter his or her mind without restriction, Winnicott wondered whether each of us might actually possess a special private piece of our mind—the incommunicado—which should *remain* private and never be shared. Winnicott worried that if the analyst knew every single one of the patient's secrets and dreams, the patient might feel too raw, too exposed. Other clinicians, by contrast, would endorse the notion that only by revealing *everything* will the patient feel truly understood.

In collecting research data from my interviewees, I always started from the assumption that it would be helpful to know as much about their sexual fantasies as possible. Likewise, in my psychotherapeutic work with patients, I have always believed that if private arenas of guilt and shame can be verbalized, their impact may be lessened. I still advocate the importance of talking about private experience with a trusted confidant or professional, but I do wonder whether we have underestimated Winnicott's valorization of the incommunicado. Perhaps we all do need to have some arena of absolute privacy or secrecy in order to feel more fully in control of our mind. This polemic remains very much an open question for me at the present time.

I have also become aware that although many people find the subject of sexual fantasy of great fascination—sometimes clinically interesting, sometimes academically interesting, sometimes culturally interesting, and sometimes of interest as a source of titillation—I have also met a small but vociferous contingent who find the whole subject distasteful, maintaining in no uncertain terms that anyone who fantasizes, especially about someone other than one's partner, must be in serious need of professional help. Of course, the data reveal that sexual fantasies, even ostensibly racy ones, are completely normative. But one still encounters a strong antisexual element in our culture among those who would prefer to eradicate all mention of this important though often hidden aspect of human psychology.

Final Fantasies

In the interests of inclusiveness, I want to offer a further set of responses: some representative views from those who replied to my computer-administered questionnaire in a rather different way. Unlike the many thousands of participants who revealed their fantasies about their sisters-in-law, their next-door neighbors, their teenage daughters, their bosses at work, or some Hollywood celebrities, the following individuals claimed either that they had no fantasies, or that, if they did, they would certainly not share them with me. Furthermore, some respondents could not easily decide upon a fantasy, and others, albeit a small minority, seemed to be pulling my leg, although I cannot be absolutely certain. Herewith I provide a smattering of responses from the potential leg-pullers, the equivocators, and the non-on-your-lifers.

JASPER

Me and my partner, me in monkey suit, her greased up with batter and a large traffic cone on her head.

BELLA

Making jam.

ROTH

I would like someone to paint my house.

BYRON

Other than Britney Spears dressed in crotchless knickers and fluffy bunny slippers slapping me black and blue with a large haddock, nothing really springs to mind!

The Equivocators.

BERND

Sorry, I don't have a special favorite. It varies with circumstances and company.

LORCAN

Can't remember.

ELLEN

Not in the mood, so can't think of one.

ZOFIA

I am not sure what my most sexually arousing sexual fantasy is.

FRITZ

Not sure.

CONSUELO

I try not to encourage myself to have fantasies that could or should happen out of respect for my husband.

ENOCH

My wife would kill me if I answered this question.

DON

Hmmm, can't really put them into words.

Not on Your Life.

ALOYSIUS

No.

JADE

No way! That is private information . . . only to be shared with my spouse.

BEULAH

Never have them—sex is the most painful and uncomfortable situation for me. Sex = Nightmare.

FABIAN

Don't have them.

DEIRDRE

This is not a fantasy but I need to comment as to why there is no comment or answer to your inquiry. I believe the greatest asset in sexuality is that it can remain and I believe is intended to be Private. I am not and have never been ashamed of my sexuality BUT I also have learned that when put in proper perspective, time and place as well as content, human sexuality is not as big a deal as others try to make it. Warped ideas, idealisms, and preconceived notions of the concept of it being bigger than life is a false emotion. Finding Christ brings not only peace to sexuality, it also controls unwanton desires.

JOSEFINA

I don't have fantasies. My time with my mate is all I need to be satisfied!!!!

FRIEDA

I don't think the world is full of people who have sexual fantasies. Some of us have reasons for not doing so. My husband and I both have chronic medical conditions and are on multiple medications. We are not intimate but we are both happy with each other and that we have someone who understands our physical limitations. I find the questions rather humorous because I couldn't fathom us behaving such as the described fantasies. I am not mocking this study, just wanted to point out that it is difficult to relate when your life centers daily around your basic survival.

TRINNY

Sorry, don't know.

QUINBY

You're joking.

SELWYN

I see fantasies as just a stop-gap. To simply be with someone I love is far superior.

CELESTE

My fingers will not let me type such words right now. I do not feel comfortable with that—if I write or tell you, they will not be MY fantasies anymore.

URBANO

No fantasies, not turned on.

NOLA

Look, I can't do this. How can a normal human being be doing this? It is not good. I don't do it at all.

OTIS

Sorry, this is a bit too much for me.

VESNA

Sorry, you are about ten years too late.

ALDO

I bet you would you dirty buggers.

CRISPIN

Will this be published? ·

ETTORE

Don't fantasize as now in the twilight zone of life.

GYORGY

What is the point of fantasy? It's like dreaming about being rich, and about as useful.

JACKIE

As stated previously I would only confide my sexual fantasies with someone I trust completely, and that does not include you.

I hope that this study contributes in some small way to the facilitation of a dialogue around sexual fantasies—a dialogue that can move beyond both titillation and condemnation to assist in creating greater understanding of human psychology and human sexuality. At least 90 percent of all human adults have sexual fantasies, possibly more than 90 percent, in fact, as do an indeterminate number of adolescents and even children. I hope that mental health professionals will become more sensitive to the need to work more extensively with sexual fantasies during the course of psychological treatments. I also earnestly hope that a study of this nature will allow people—mental health professionals and members of the general public alike—to become less castigatory of sexual thoughts that may not correspond with their own. Although we live in a post–sexual revolution era, we still struggle with the legacy of many centuries of sexual prudery and inhibition, and as a result, millions of people still lead very unsatisfying sex lives. This can be remedied, and a study of the vicissitudes of sexual fantasy could play an important part in the healing process by helping us to conquer early traumas and by reducing the amount of shame and guilt so prevalent within our culture.

Throughout this book I have emphasized the role of abuse and trauma. I have done so because the data have led me to conclude that early aversive experiences may well play a crucial role in the genesis of sexual fantasies and behaviors as well as in the formation of behaviors in other areas of our lives. Although we know only too well the impact that early infant and child abuse can have on the development of depression, anxiety disorders, eating problems, and a host of other psychological conditions, I do not think we have fully appreciated the extent to which abuse can penetrate into what many of us wish to regard as the private sanctuary of our fantasy life. I have learned that the effects of abuse may prevail longer and penetrate deeper than even many mental health professionals and traumatologists may have imagined.

Although I stand by my findings, as they have emerged directly from careful research and from the firsthand testimony of thousands of American and British fantasists, I also hope that this research will stimulate further investigation by my colleagues from many disciplines. If we can pool our knowledge, perhaps we can make a more solid contribution to the eradication of psychological suffering, especially as it manifests itself in the sexual arena. Finally, I hope that by sharing my psychological style of thinking, I will have taken some small step in helping to demystify how psychotherapists approach their work; I trust that if anyone struggling with emotional difficulties has wondered what a psychotherapist might sound like, how a psychotherapist might think, and how a psychotherapist might function, then this account of my work will be of some value.

I wish to leave the penultimate word to "Moira," a forty-eighty-year-old woman who participated in this project. In many respects, Moira's words capture what I have tried to convey in the preceding chapters. This generous woman shared her thoughts and experiences with great candor, responding, at one point: "I think sexual fantasies are really your imagination kind of helping you along towards a better quality orgasm, actually." In reflecting on her fantasy, Moira worried, "I . . . I can't get my head round it, and I would dearly, dearly love to know if . . . am I the only one?"

> There's that one particular fantasy that's kind of locked in the deep, dark recesses of my mind, erm, and . . . it's to do with something . . . just that happened once in my life, um, and it only ever did happen once, but it was obviously enough to kind of spark or give birth to this particular fantasy. I was with my sisters in a cinema, and this . . . man was sitting next to me, and he started very, very subtly to kind of . . . touch my . . . touch me—I was ten years old at the time—and, um, he didn't . . . kind of . . . he was just kind of exploring in a . . . quite a subtle way, and I knew that what he was doing was wrong, um, it didn't feel right, but at the time I was kind of too embarrassed to kind of say anything. Anyway, that's the only time it'd happened, and it was all forgotten about until years and years later, when I suppose I, sort of, first started to experience, you know, orgasms. And then I thought . . . and then something happened, I don't know what exactly, but . . . something in my mind happened and . . . to enable me to reach satisfaction, um, I would use, um, what happened, and I kind of created a fantasy around that. For years, it kind of tormented me, you know, and it made me feel so guilty, and it was kind of like a layered cake. Yes, it made me feel guilty, and yes, I achieved orgasm through my guilt. You know . . . why?

For years, this sexual fantasy had perplexed Moira and tormented her, and yet it brought her sexual pleasure as well, a combination of factors that converge to create what I have called the masturbatory paradox. Fortunately, as Moira has aged, she has found acceptance from a number of different sources in her life, so much so that she now has the capacity to share her experiences in a nonsensationalist and thoughtful manner in the hope that others will benefit. She offered a final comment about her long-standing troublesome fantasy: "I'm nearly fifty years old, I'm a mature woman, and . . . and I think there's no shame anymore. I think, that's it, let it . . . let it out."

Fantasies cause pain, but for many they remain and will continue to remain a source of playfulness, of creativity, of fun. I conclude with perhaps my two very favorite fantasies from a collection of approximately 24,000. I have chosen one from a woman called "Miriam" and one from a man called "Reuben."

MIRIAM

WHEN MY PARTNER MANAGES TO LAST FOR MORE THAN TWO MINUTES.

REUBEN

My favorite sexual fantasy?

Wife turning into a 6-pack and pizza after sex.

Appendix: Sexual Fantasy Questionnaire

The following questionnaire contains detailed and explicit questions about sexual fantasies and sexual behavior. Some of the questions are extremely intimate and personal. Your responses will not be analyzed individually, but combined with those of others who are taking part in this survey. They will contribute to a research project about the nature of human sexual fantasies, which will provide us with a better understanding of human sexuality. All of your answers will be treated with the utmost confidentiality, and your identity cannot be traced in any way by the people commissioning this research or any other third party. We guarantee, and are bound by a professional code of conduct to ensure, that only your answers to the questions will be used by the researchers, and that your name, address, and your private e-mail address will never be revealed or used in relation to this study.

Everybody who takes part in this project will have their account credited with $1 and be entered into a number of ADDITIONAL PRIZE DRAWS with $50 CASH PRIZES.

This questionnaire is divided up into sections and at the beginning of each section you will be given the choice either to answer the questions in that section or to skip that section and move on. For every section you complete, you will be entered into a PRIZE DRAW to win one of FIVE $50 CASH PRIZES.

We realize that some of the questions in this poll are of a very personal nature. It is very important that you think carefully about the questions, and that you answer each question as honestly as you possibly can. If there are any questions that you would prefer not to answer, then you need not do so; however, it would be extremely helpful to the research project if you could answer as many of the questions as possible.

> **Are you happy to continue with the questionnaire?**
> ○ Yes
> ○ No

> **Which of the following age groups do you fall into?**
> ○ I am under 18
> ○ I am 18 or over

All those *Thank you very much for agreeing to take part in this question-*
who are *naire on sexual fantasies. Unfortunately, because of the nature of*
under 18 *the questions in this poll, we are bound to insist that respondents are 18 years of age or over.*

We hope you will continue to take part in YouGovAmerica surveys in the future.

All those *Thank you very much for agreeing to complete the following ques-*
aged 18 *tionnaire on sexual fantasies. This data will help to inform a re-*
or over *search project about the nature of human sexual fantasies, and will be invaluable to researchers in the field of human sexuality.*

Before you begin to complete this questionnaire, please read the following definitions of terms, which may be useful.

What do we mean by the term 'SEX'?

By "sex," we mean any kind of intimate bodily contact between two or more people. This includes: contact between the penis and the vagina, contact between the penis and the anus (or the bottom), contact between the penis and the mouth, contact between the vagina and the mouth, or contact between the anus (or the bottom) and the mouth. For the purposes of this survey, "sex" does NOT refer to mouth-to-mouth kissing or cuddling.

What do we mean by the term 'SEXUAL FANTASY'?

By "sexual fantasy," we mean any private thought that crosses your mind during masturbation, or during sexual activity with a partner. People can also have

sexual fantasies while watching or reading pornography or other kinds of liter-
ature. A sexual fantasy does NOT refer to a dream which occurs at night whilst
asleep. Some people have referred to sexual fantasies as "waking dreams" –
they tend to occur whilst awake, and they often lead to sexual arousal.

Section 1: Background Information

This section is about your personal circumstances and general sexual experi-
ence. Everybody who completes this section will be entered into a PRIZE
DRAW to win one of 5 additional $50 CASH PRIZES.

**If you would prefer to skip these questions and move onto the
next section then please tick the appropriate box.**
- ○ I am happy to continue and be entered into the PRIZE DRAW
- ○ I would like to skip these questions and move onto the next section

All who **What is your current relationship status?**
agree to
- ○ I am married, and I live with my spouse
continue
- ○ I have a regular sex partner, to whom I am not married, but
with this   with whom I live
section
- ○ I have a regular sex partner, to whom I am not married, and
    with whom I do not live
- ○ I have more than one regular sex partner
- ○ I do not have a regular sex partner
- ○ Other

All **On the grid below, please indicate how many, if any, children you
have in the following age groups living at home with you.**

	1	2	3	4	5	6	7+
Under 1 year of age	○	○	○	○	○	○	○
Between 1 and 3 years of age	○	○	○	○	○	○	○
Between 4 and 6 years of age	○	○	○	○	○	○	○

continued on next page

	1	2	3	4	5	6	7+
Between 7 and 9 years of age	○	○	○	○	○	○	○
Between 10 and 12 years of age	○	○	○	○	○	○	○
Between 13 and 17 years of age	○	○	○	○	○	○	○
Grown up children – 18 years of age and older	○	○	○	○	○	○	○
None	○	○	○	○	○	○	○

If you are in a relationship, please state how long you have been in that relationship [Please type in the number to the nearest year(s). If you have been in a relationship less than one year, please just type 1 (not 'one'). If you are not in a relationship, please type N/A and if you would prefer not to answer, please type PNTA]

Please think again about the previously given definition of 'SEX' as any kind of intimate bodily contact between two or more people except mouth-to-mouth kissing or cuddling.

Now please tell us, on average, how often you have sexual relations?
- ○ I have never had sex
- ○ I have had sex in the past, but I do not have sex now
- ○ I have sex less than once a year
- ○ I have sex approximately once a year
- ○ I have sex once every few months
- ○ I have sex once a month
- ○ I have sex once a fortnight
- ○ I have sex once a week
- ○ I have sex two times a week
- ○ I have sex three times a week
- ○ I have sex four or five times a week
- ○ I have sex every day
- ○ I have sex more than once a day
- ○ Prefer not to answer

All except
those who
say they
have never
had sex

How many WOMEN have you had sexual contact with in your life? (By sexual contact we mean oral sex, vaginal sex, anal sex, or any combination of these) [Please type in numbers e.g. 1, 2, 500. If you do not know, please give as best an estimate as you can. If you would prefer not to answer, please just type in PNTA]

And how many MEN have you had sexual contact with in your life? [Again, please type in numbers e.g. 1, 2, 500. If you do not know, please give as best an estimate as you can. If you would prefer not to answer, please just type in PNTA]

People start to have sexual relations at different ages. How old were you when you had your first sexual encounter? [Please type in numbers e.g. 16, 21, 35. If you cannot remember, please give as best an estimate as you can. If you would prefer not to answer, please just type in PNTA]

All How satisfied are you with your sexual life?
    ○ I am extremely satisfied with my sexual life
    ○ My sexual life is quite satisfactory
    ○ My sexual life is reasonable
    ○ My sexual life is mediocre
    ○ My sexual life is quite unsatisfactory
    ○ My sexual life is entirely unsatisfactory
    ○ Prefer not to answer

All except
those who
say they
have
never had
sex

Of the times when you do have sex, how often, on average, do you have an orgasm, or climax ("come")?
    ○ Every time
    ○ More than half the time
    ○ About half of the time
    ○ Less than half the time
    ○ Never
    ○ Prefer not to answer

Section 2: Sexual Fantasies I

This section is about your experiences of sexual fantasies. Everybody who completes this section will be entered into an ADDITIONAL PRIZE DRAW to win one of five $50 CASH PRIZES.

All   If you would prefer to skip these questions and move onto the next section then please tick the appropriate box.

○ I am happy to continue and be entered into the PRIZE DRAW
○ I would like to skip these questions and move onto the next section

A sexual thought might be a fleeting image that pops into your mind, or, it might be a long 'daydream'. Please estimate the number of sexual thoughts that you have per day. [Please make a rough estimate and type the number using the number keys on your keyboard e.g. 1, 20, 200. If you do not know, please give as best an estimate as you can. If you would prefer not to answer, please just type PNTA]

How often do you fantasize ABOUT YOUR PARTNER whilst having sex WITH YOUR PARTNER? [If you DO fantasize during sex with your partner but NOT about your partner, please select that option. If you do not have a partner, please select that option]

○ Every single time
○ Very often
○ Quite often
○ Not very often
○ I do fantasize during sex with my partner but never about my partner
○ I don't have a partner
○ I don't fantasize
○ Prefer not to answer

How often do you fantasize ABOUT SOMEONE ELSE other than your partner whilst having sex WITH YOUR PARTNER? [If you DO fantasize during sex with your partner but ONLY about your partner, please select that option. If you do not have a partner, please select that option]

- ○ Every single time
- ○ Very often
- ○ Quite often
- ○ Not very often
- ○ I do fantasize when having sex with my partner but only about my partner
- ○ I don't have a partner
- ○ I don't fantasize
- ○ Prefer not to answer

How often do you fantasize ABOUT YOUR PARTNER whilst MASTURBATING? [If you DO fantasize whilst masturbating but NOT about your partner, please select that option. If you do not masturbate or do not have a partner, please select the appropriate options]

- ○ Every single time
- ○ Very often
- ○ Quite often
- ○ Not very often
- ○ I do fantasize whilst masturbating but not about my partner
- ○ Prefer not to answer
- ○ I don't have a partner
- ○ I don't fantasize
- ○ I don't masturbate
- ○ Prefer not to answer

How often do you fantasize ABOUT SOMEONE ELSE (other than your partner) whilst MASTURBATING? [If you DO fantasize whilst masturbating but ONLY about your partner, please select that option. If you do not masturbate or do not have a partner, please select the appropriate options]

- ○ Every single time
- ○ Very often
- ○ Quite often
- ○ Not very often
- ○ I do fantasize whilst masturbating but only about my partner

○ Prefer not to answer
○ I don't have a partner
○ I don't fantasize
○ I don't masturbate
○ Prefer not to answer

Please state which, if any, of the following describe your reasons for having a sexual fantasy. [Please tick all those that apply]

○ Fantasies help me to relieve boredom
○ Fantasies cheer me up when I am depressed
○ Fantasies allow me to perform acts that I cannot do in real life
○ Fantasies permit me to have sex with people who I would not or could not have sex with in real life
○ Fantasies permit me to explore different sexual thoughts and activities
○ My partner becomes more attractive to me in my fantasies
○ Fantasies help me to become aroused with my partner or partners
○ I cannot help myself. The fantasies just pop into my mind
○ Fantasies are preferable to actual sexual experiences
○ Fantasies make the outside world go away
○ Not applicable / I never fantasize
○ Other
○ Prefer not to answer

Which of the following BEST describes how you really feel about your most private sexual fantasies?

○ I am totally relaxed with my sexual fantasies, and I feel comfortable talking to anyone about them
○ I enjoy my sexual fantasies and I would discuss them with trusted people
○ I enjoy my fantasies, but I do not talk about them with anyone
○ My fantasies make me slightly uncomfortable
○ My fantasies cause me some concern
○ My fantasies cause me guilt or shame
○ My fantasies horrify or torment me
○ Not applicable / I never fantasize at all
○ Other
○ Prefer not to answer

All who feel uncomfortable In the previous question, you said that your sexual fantasies make you feel slightly uncomfortable. Why is this? Please tell us in as much detail as you can, what it is about your fantasy, or fantasies, that make you feel uncomfortable?

Section 3: Sexual Fantasies II

This section continues to explore the content of your sexual fantasies. Please note that the questions contain some very explicit fantasies. Everybody who completes this section will be entered into an ADDITIONAL PRIZE DRAW to win one of five additional $50 CASH PRIZES.

All If you would prefer to skip these questions and move onto the next section then please tick the appropriate box.
- ○ I am happy to continue and be entered into the PRIZE DRAW
- ○ I would like to skip these questions and move onto the next section

All who agree to continue with this section About which, if any, of the following have you ever had a sexual FANTASY or FANTASIES? [Please tick all those that apply]
- ○ Sex with my regular partner
- ○ Sex with someone of the same sex as myself
- ○ Sex with the partner of someone I know
- ○ Sex with the partner of someone I don't know
- ○ Sex with someone with an ethnic background different to mine / interracial partner(s)
- ○ Sex with a friend
- ○ Sex with a friend's partner
- ○ Sex with a work colleague
- ○ Sex with a boss at work
- ○ Sex with a stranger
- ○ Sex with a man and a woman at the same time
- ○ Sex with two or more men
- ○ Sex with two or more women
- ○ A threesome
- ○ An orgy
- ○ Watching a man and a woman having sex
- ○ Watching two or more men having sex
- ○ Watching two or more women having sex

○ Being watched during sex
○ Displaying one's breasts in public
○ Displaying one's genitals in public
○ Swinging or partner-swapping
○ Stripping off in public
○ Spying or peeping on someone undressing
○ Undressing in front of someone else
○ Watching pornographic films
○ Reading pornography
○ Being in a pornographic film
○ Being filmed during sex
○ In my fantasies, I assume the identity of someone other than myself
○ I have never fantasized about any of the above
○ Prefer not to answer

About which, if any, of the following have you ever had a sexual FANTASY or FANTASIES? [Please tick all those that apply]

○ Playing a dominant or aggressive role during sex
○ Playing a submissive or passive role during sex
○ Being violent towards someone else
○ Having violence practiced on you by someone else
○ Forcing someone to strip
○ Being forced to strip
○ Forcing someone to masturbate
○ Being forced to masturbate
○ Spanking someone else
○ Being spanked
○ Using a whip or paddle or cane or slipper or strap
○ Blindfolding someone else
○ Being blindfolded by someone else
○ Tying someone up
○ Being tied up by someone
○ Using handcuffs or bondage restraints or collars on someone else
○ Having someone else use handcuffs or bondage restraints or collars on you
○ Gagging someone else
○ Being gagged by someone else
○ I have never fantasized about any of the above
○ Prefer not to answer

And about which, if any, of the following have you ever had a sexual FANTASY or FANTASIES? [Please tick all those that apply]

○ Wearing clothes of the opposite sex

○ Wearing clothes of the same sex

○ Sex with a transvestite (that is someone who dresses as the opposite sex)

○ Sex with a transsexual (that is someone who has had a sex change operation)

○ Spitting on someone

○ Being spat on by someone

○ Urinating ('peeing') on someone

○ Being urinated ('peed') on by someone

○ Defecating ('taking a crap') on someone

○ Being defecated ('crapped on') on by someone

○ Sex with a teenager aged 16 years or older

○ Sex with a teenager under 16 years of age

○ Sex with a child

○ Sex with an infant

○ Sex with a brother

○ Sex with a sister

○ Sex with mother

○ Sex with father

○ Sex with a brother-in-law

○ Sex with a sister-in-law

○ Sex with mother-in-law

○ Sex with father-in-law

○ Sex with other blood relative

○ Sex with other relative (not a blood relative)

○ I have never fantasized about any of the above

○ Prefer not to answer

And about which, if any, of the following have you ever had a sexual FANTASY or FANTASIES? [Please tick all those that apply]

○ Necrophilia (sex with a dead person)

○ Vibrator (or other electric device)

○ Dildo (or artificial penis or other similar sex aid toy)

○ Strap-on penis

○ Nipple clamps

○ 'Butt' plugs

○ Underwear

○ Food items

○ Body shaving

○ Body hair

○ Autoerotic asphyxiation (restricting your breathing through strangulation)

- ○ Sex with animals
- ○ Fetishism
- ○ Fat or obese people
- ○ Infantilism (e.g. being dressed in nappies / being fed by a bottle)
- ○ Humiliating someone else
- ○ Being humiliated by someone else
- ○ Being raped
- ○ Raping someone else
- ○ Talking dirty
- ○ Role-playing
- ○ Body odors
- ○ Body fluids
- ○ Kissing
- ○ Romantic scenes
- ○ I have never fantasized about any of the above
- ○ Prefer not to answer

All   Have you ever had a sexual fantasy involving a celebrity / well-known personality? If so, please type in their name(s) below and as much detail of the content of the fantasy as you are willing to give. If not, please leave blank or type PNTA.

Section 4: Sexual Fantasies III

This section has just one question which asks you to describe your most sexually arousing sexual fantasy. Please remember, that all of your answers will be treated with the utmost confidentiality, and your identity cannot be traced in any way by the people commissioning this research or any other third party. We guarantee, and are bound by a professional code of conduct to ensure that only your answers to the questions will be used by the researchers, and that your name, address, and your private e-mail address will never be revealed or used in relation to this study.

Everybody who completes this section will be entered into an ADDITIONAL PRIZE DRAW to win one of five additional $50 CASH PRIZES.

All   If you would prefer to skip this question and move onto the next section then please tick the appropriate box.

    ○ I am happy to continue and be entered into the PRIZE DRAW

    ○ I would like to skip this question and move onto the next section

All
who are
happy to
continue
   In the space provided below, please write your most sexually arousing sexual fantasy. That is, please write out, in as much detail as you feel comfortable giving, the fantasy which turns you on more than any other. Your answers will contribute to a research project about the nature of human sexual fantasies, which will provide us with a better understanding of human sexuality, so it would be helpful if you could be as detailed as possible.

Section 5: Other Sexual Experiences

This section is about other kinds of sexual experiences you might have. Everybody who completes this section will be entered into an ADDITIONAL PRIZE DRAW to win one of five additional $50 CASH PRIZES.

All   If you would prefer to skip these questions and move onto the next section then please tick the appropriate box.

    ○ I am happy to continue and be entered into the PRIZE DRAW

    ○ I would like to skip these questions and move onto the next section

All
who are
happy to
continue
   How often, on average, do you MASTURBATE on your own? That is, how often do you masturbate without your partner or someone else watching you?

    ○ I have never masturbated

    ○ I have masturbated in the past, but I do not do so now

    ○ I do masturbate but I never masturbate on my own

    ○ I masturbate on my own less than once a year

    ○ I masturbate on my own approximately once a year

    ○ I masturbate on my own once every few months

    ○ I masturbate on my own once a month

    ○ I masturbate on my own once a fortnight

    ○ I masturbate on my own once a week

    ○ I masturbate on my own two to three times a week

    ○ I masturbate on my own four to five times a week

○ I masturbate on my own once a day
○ I masturbate on my own twice a day
○ I masturbate on my own three or more times a day
○ Prefer not to answer

How frequently, if ever, have you had sex with a male or female prostitute or other sex worker?

○ Never
○ Once
○ Twice
○ 3 to 5 times
○ 6 to 10 times
○ 11 to 20 times
○ 21 to 30 times
○ 31 to 50 times
○ 51 to 100 times
○ 101 to 200 times
○ Over 200 times
○ Prefer not to answer

And have you ever been paid to have sex?

○ Never
○ Once
○ Twice
○ 3 to 5 times
○ 6 to 10 times
○ 11 to 20 times
○ 21 to 30 times
○ 31 to 50 times
○ 51 to 100 times
○ 101 to 200 times
○ Over 200 times
○ Prefer not to answer

Which of the following kinds of pornography do you use or have you ever used? [Please tick all those that apply]

○ I do not / have not ever use(d) pornography
○ Videos / DVDs
○ Soft core magazines
○ Hard core magazines

○ Erotic literature / stories
○ Still images from the Internet
○ Moving images from the Internet
○ Sound only – e.g.: 'phone lines
○ Live peep shows / strip clubs
○ Lap dancing / table dancing
○ Other
○ Prefer not to answer

Please indicate how often, if at all, you use the Internet for each of the following purposes.

	Never	Monthly	Weekly	Several times a week	Daily	More than once per day	Prefer not to answer
Chat rooms (of a sexual nature)	○	○	○	○	○	○	○
On-line dating	○	○	○	○	○	○	○
Soft core pornographic pictures / still images	○	○	○	○	○	○	○
Hard core pornographic pictures / still images	○	○	○	○	○	○	○
Soft core pornographic films or film clips	○	○	○	○	○	○	○
Hard core pornographic films or film clips	○	○	○	○	○	○	○
Soft core pornographic stories	○	○	○	○	○	○	○
Hard core pornographic stories	○	○	○	○	○	○	○
Webcam activity (of a sexual nature)	○	○	○	○	○	○	○
To arrange a sexual 'hook-up'	○	○	○	○	○	○	○

Section 6: Emotional and Sexual Health

This section is about your emotional well-being and sexual health. Some of the questions cover very sensitive issues. Everybody who completes this section will be entered into an ADDITIONAL PRIZE DRAW to win one of five $50 CASH PRIZES.

All   **If you would prefer to skip these questions and move onto the next section then please tick the appropriate box.**

- ○ I am happy to continue and be entered into the PRIZE DRAW
- ○ I would like to skip these questions and move onto the next section

All
who are
happy to
continue

Over the past two weeks how often have you been feeling down, depressed, or hopeless?

- ○ Not at all
- ○ Some days
- ○ More than half of the days
- ○ Every day
- ○ Prefer not to answer

Over the past two weeks how often have you had little interest or pleasure in doing things (i.e. stopped getting pleasure from things that you used to enjoy)?

- ○ I have not experienced this feeling at all
- ○ I have experienced this feeling on some days
- ○ I have experienced this feeling on more than half of the days
- ○ I have experienced this feeling every day over the past two weeks
- ○ Prefer not to answer

Over the past two months, have you drunk or used drugs more than you meant to?

- ○ Yes
- ○ No
- ○ Prefer not to answer

Over the past two months, have you ever felt the need to cut down on your drinking or drug use (non-prescription drugs)?

○ Yes

○ No

○ Prefer not to answer

How often do you daydream? Please note, daydreams need NOT BE of a sexual nature.

○ Never

○ Occasionally

○ Once a day

○ Twice a day

○ 3 or 4 times a day

○ 5 or 6 times a day

○ 7 or 8 times a day

○ 9 or 10 times a day

○ Between 11 and 15 times a day

○ Between 16 and 20 times a day

○ More than 20 times a day

○ Don't know

All   Are you currently taking any prescription medication or medications for any health-related condition?

○ Yes

○ No

○ Prefer not to answer

All those who are taking prescription medication or medications for any health-related condition   Which, if any, of the following are you currently taking? [Please tick all that apply]

○ Viagra

○ Hormone Replacement Therapy

○ Antidepressants

○ Tranquillizers

○ Cialis (for erectile dysfunction)

○ Levitra (for erectile dysfunction)

○ Other medications (please specify below)

○ Prefer not to answer

If you are taking any prescription medication or medication for any health-related condition not listed above, please use this space to list the medication(s) you are taking and explain what you are taking this for.

All   Many people living in the United States will contract a sexually transmitted infection (S.T.I.), sometimes known as an S.T.D., though not everybody will be diagnosed. Have you ever been told by a health care professional that you have a sexually transmitted infection?

    ○ Yes – I have been told
    ○ No – I have not been told
    ○ Prefer not to answer

All those who have or have had a S.T.I.   Which, if any, of the following infections do you / did you have? [Please tick all that apply]

    ○ Chlamydia
    ○ Gonorrhea
    ○ Syphilis
    ○ Genital herpes
    ○ Genital warts (H.P.V.)
    ○ Hepatitis B
    ○ Hepatitis C
    ○ HIV
    ○ Other
    ○ Prefer not to answer

The following few questions are about your past. They are of a very sensitive nature but please try to be as honest as you feel comfortable being.

All   At any point in your lifetime, have you ever been subject to any kind of PHYSICAL abuse? Please include anything that you have experienced, whether or not you have told anybody or reported it.

    ○ Yes – when I was under 16 years of age
    ○ Yes – when I was 16 years of age or over
    ○ No – never
    ○ Don't know
    ○ Prefer not to answer

If yes **Please tell us at what age you were first subjected to this PHYSI-CAL abuse.**
- ○ Aged 5 or under
- ○ Aged 6 to 9
- ○ Aged 10 to 12
- ○ Aged 13 to 15
- ○ Don't know
- ○ Prefer not to answer

At any point in your lifetime, have you ever been subject to any kind of SEXUAL abuse? Please include anything that you have experienced, whether or not you have told anybody or reported it.
- ○ Yes – when I was under 16 years of age
- ○ Yes – when I was 16 years of age or over
- ○ No – never
- ○ Don't know
- ○ Prefer not to answer

If yes **Please tell us at what age you were first subjected to this SEXUAL abuse.**
- ○ Aged 5 or under
- ○ Aged 6 to 9
- ○ Aged 10 to 12
- ○ Aged 13 to 15
- ○ Don't know
- ○ Prefer not to answer

At any point in your lifetime, have you ever been subject to any kind of EMOTIONAL abuse? Please include anything that you have experienced, whether or not you have told anybody or reported it.
- ○ Yes – when I was under 16 years of age
- ○ Yes – when I was 16 years of age or over
- ○ No – never
- ○ Don't know
- ○ Prefer not to answer

If yes Please tell us at what age you were first subjected to this EMO-
TIONAL abuse.

- ○ Aged 5 or under
- ○ Aged 6 to 9
- ○ Aged 10 to 12
- ○ Aged 13 to 15
- ○ Don't know
- ○ Prefer not to answer

All And has anybody ever forced or convinced you to have sex when
you actually did not want to? [Please tick all those that apply]

- ○ Yes – when I was under 16 years of age
- ○ Yes – when I was 16 years of age or over
- ○ No – never
- ○ Don't know
- ○ Prefer not to answer

If you Please tell us at what age you were first forced or convinced to
were have sex when you actually did not want to.
under 16

- ○ Aged 5 or under
- ○ Aged 6 to 9
- ○ Aged 10 to 12
- ○ Aged 13 to 15
- ○ Don't know
- ○ Prefer not to answer

All Which, if any, of the following have you had professional contact
with for whatever reason? [Please tick all those that apply]

- ○ Psychologist
- ○ Psychotherapist
- ○ Counselor
- ○ Psychiatrist
- ○ Psychoanalyst
- ○ Psychiatric nurse
- ○ Occupational therapist
- ○ Art therapist
- ○ Music therapist
- ○ Drama therapist
- ○ Play therapist

○ Marriage counselor
○ Family therapist
○ MFT (marital and family therapist)
○ Marital psychotherapist
○ Group analyst
○ Group therapist
○ Social worker
○ Other (please specify below)
○ None of these
○ Prefer not to answer

All If you have had professional contact with another health worker, not listed above, please specify here.

Section 7: More Backround Information

This FINAL section is very short and asks some general questions about you.

Some people have sexual contact with men, some people with women, and some people have contact with members of both sexes. In terms of your sexual identity, do you consider yourself to be...?
○ Straight (Heterosexual)
○ Gay (Homosexual)
○ Bisexual
○ Don't know
○ Prefer not to answer

Many people think about having sex with someone other than their regular partner, and many people have actually had sex with someone other than their regular partner. Which of the following have you ever experienced? [Please tick all that apply]
○ I have fantasized about other people during my relationship with a regular partner
○ I have kissed another person during my relationship with a regular partner
○ I have fondled another person during my relationship with a regular partner

○ I have had oral sex with another person during my relationship with a regular partner

○ I have had vaginal sex with another person during my relationship with a regular partner

○ I have had anal sex with another person during my relationship with a regular partner

○ None of these / I do not have a partner

○ Prefer not to answer

How would you describe your parental upbringing?

○ Extremely strict

○ Quite strict

○ Strict

○ Not very strict

○ Permissive

○ Quite permissive

○ Prefer not to answer

On a scale of 0 to 10, where 0 means 'not very important' and 10 means 'very important', how important a part of your life do you consider religion to be?

○ 0 – not very important

○ 1

○ 2

○ 3

○ 4

○ 5

○ 6

○ 7

○ 8

○ 9

○ 10 – very important

○ Don't know

And what is your religion?

○ Protestant

○ Catholic

○ Mormon

○ Orthodox

○ Jewish
○ Muslim
○ Other (please specify here)
○ I don't have a religion
○ Don't know

If you consider yourself to be a member of another religion, not listed above, please specify here.

Generally speaking, do you think of yourself as a...?

    ○ Republican
    ○ Democrat
    ○ Independent
    ○ Other
    ○ No preference

And finally, on a scale of 0 to 10, where 0 means 'not very strong' and 10 means 'very strong', how strong are your political views?

    ○ 0 – not very strong
    ○ 1
    ○ 2
    ○ 3
    ○ 4
    ○ 5
    ○ 6
    ○ 7
    ○ 8
    ○ 9
    ○ 10 – very strong
    ○ Don't know

Acknowledgments

I could not have written this book without the sincere cooperation of more than 23,000 anonymous American and British men and women, all of whom not only contributed their time but also shared the private contents of their minds with unusual frankness, for which I extend my deepest thanks and most heartfelt appreciation. I particularly wish to convey my gratitude to that brave subset of research participants who traveled to London from all over Great Britain to speak to me for lengthy and exacting face-to-face psychodiagnostic assessment interviews. These meetings, combined with my own clinical work, have become the veritable backbone of my thinking and of my research formulations, and I trust that the many interviewees who participated in the Sexual Fantasy Research Project will be satisfied that I have not only preserved their identities but that I have used their material in a respectful manner, in the interests of psychological research.

This book owes its genesis entirely to a very practical suggestion from my dear friend and colleague Oliver Rathbone, managing director of Karnac Books of London, who has published my clinical and academic books over many years. At a crucial lunch meeting, I told Oliver that I wished to devote my next book to a further exploration of the works of Sigmund Freud. Oliver nearly fell asleep in his soup, but ever eager to haul me into the twenty-first century, he suggested instead a book on the psychology of sexual fantasies, derived from my work as a marital psychotherapist specializing in the sexual difficulties of couples. Not only did he provide me with an unexpectedly rich research and writing opportunity, but also, in true gentlemanly fashion, he even had the graciousness to encourage me to take the manuscript to another publisher.

Without the invaluable guidance, good humor, bonhomie, and occasional wickedness of Patrick Walsh, indisputably the best, the most dedicated, and the funniest of literary agents, this data would have accumulated dust in my office. With the skill of a consummate psychotherapist, Patrick managed to tolerate my inhibitions, anxieties, and pleas of overwork, and even to take time away from his own Christmas holiday to help me shape my data into a coherent proposal. I could not have completed this book without his sustained encouragement and confidence and without the cheerful support of his unusually helpful colleagues at Conville and Walsh, notably Sam North, who first introduced me to Patrick, as well as Susan Armstrong, Robert Dinsdale, Ed Jaspers, and Jake Smith-Bosanquet.

In New York, the delightful and wise Emma Parry of Fletcher and Parry treated me to a most enjoyable tour of literary Manhattan, for which I thank her greatly, and introduced me to Jo Ann Miller, the peerless editor of psychology books at Basic Books, who has provided untold encouragement and advice on the shaping and molding of this manuscript. Nearly half of all the best American psychoanalytical books that I have read owe their existence to Jo Ann—the deaconess of psychology publishing—and I remain extremely honored to have had the opportunity to learn from her. I also extend my grateful thanks to the hospitable team at Basic Books, including Tim Brazier, Jodi Marchowsky, Kay Mariea, Niki Papadopoulous, and John Sherer.

At Penguin Books, the youthful and visionary Helen Conford steered this project from its earliest incubation to its final publication with consummate skill and intelligence. With terrific patience, Helen has proved to be the best of midwives. Aided and abetted by a talented team of colleagues, especially Bela Cunha, Sarah Coward, and Richard Duguid, I thank everyone at Penguin Books for the confidence they have had in the project.

I also owe an enormous debt to the literally dozens of people who offered invaluable aid in realizing the Sexual Fantasy Research Project. I wish to convey my deepest appreciation to Nadhim Zahawi, joint chief executive officer, and to the entire team at YouGov pollsters for their assistance with the design of the various research survey questionnaires and for supplying me with access to their randomized panels of American and British men and women. A true gentleman and a staunch ally, Nadhim extended numerous courtesies, providing me not only with much-needed support and counsel but also with a wonderful staff team, headed by the indefatigable Sarah Jordan and the clear-headed Panos Manolopoulos. The even-tempered and quick-witted Joe Twyman, special projects director at YouGov, proved to be the very best of statistical consultants, responding to a multitude of questions with laudable patience. Julia Rogers, operations director, proved extremely helpful with the coordination of the American data, and Stephan Shakespeare, chief innovation officer, has always remained a loyal source of encouragement.

Funding for this increasingly behemoth project came in the welcome form of development money from Channel Five Broadcasting in the United Kingdom. The eternally congenial Dan Chambers, emeritus director of programmes, provided the necessary financial support to administer the bulk of my work and offered me an opportunity to create a timely television documentary on the subject of sexual fantasies, which proved invaluable as a means of clarifying my thinking on this complex subject. Both Dan and his partner, Rebecca Cotton, have played a crucial role, supporting this project from gestation to completion. At Tiger Aspect Productions, the television production company that sponsored *Britain's Sexual Fantasies,* Dunja Noack distinguished herself as the very best of executive producers, nurturing the project with extraordinary devotion, perfectionism, warmth, and jollity. Justine Kershaw and Peter Grimsdale supervised the program as channel commissioners. I also wish to extend heartfelt thanks to the many other members of the production team, from whom I learned a great deal, especially Fred Casella, producer-director, as well as Antonia Davies, Elaine Foster, Donal McCusker, Jenny Spearing, and my research assistants, Guro Elstad and Christian Young. I extend warm thanks as well to Sara Ramsden, former controller of Sky One Television, for having engaged me as a consultant to her own six-part documentary film on sexual fantasies.

I owe a huge debt of personal and professional gratitude to Michael Iacovou and his colleagues at M. S. Iacovou and Company for their ongoing assistance in sorting out various complicated contractual matters with all due professionalism and cordiality.

My teachers, colleagues, friends, and students in the mental health and psychotherapy field—too numerous to thank as keenly as I would wish—have served as the mainstay of my professional life. I have had the privilege of learning so much from so many that to single out a few would seem unfair. However, I do wish to extend my thanks first and foremost to my cherished colleague and mentor Margot Sunderland, director of the Centre for Child Mental Health in London, who has provided me with an intellectual home for many years now, and whose generosity and graciousness remain unequaled in the psychotherapy community. Sir Richard Bowlby, president of the Centre for Child Mental Health, and Xenia, Lady Bowlby, have supported my work unstintingly over the years, and they have taught me a great deal about attachment theory, for which I remain grateful. Graeme Blench, codirector of the Centre for Child Mental Health, distinguishes himself as a model of cheer and compassion. I also thank the delightful office staff at the centre, especially Ruth Bonner, the highly capable administrator.

I happily acknowledge the generous support that I have received from the Winnicott Clinic of Psychotherapy and from its emeritus director, the Right Honourable Leo Abse, as well as from its incumbent director, Eric Koops, and from the trustees, especially Lord Jones, Christine Miqueu-Baz, and Cesare Sacerdoti. Through a timely Senior Research Fellowship, the Winnicott Clinic of Psychotherapy allowed me to take a much-needed sabbatical from the labors of ongoing teaching.

My comrades at the Tavistock Centre for Couple Relationships, formerly the Tavistock Marital Studies Institute, have taught me most of what I know about the psychology of intimate relationships. Dr. Christopher Clulow, the emeritus director and Senior Fellow, has treated me with great collegiality over the years, and I have learned much from his passionate commitment to the amelioration of troubled marriages. Susanna Abse, the new director, and her many staff colleagues, both clinical and administrative, have helped me more than they will have realized.

Professor Ann Kurth, a leading light in the field of sexual health and sexual epidemiology, has served as my principal research consultant, guiding me through the complexities of large-scale survey research and supervising every stage of the work with tremendous intelligence and passion. Dr. Avi Shmueli, a polymathic colleague whose skills straddle many clinical disciplines, from psychoanalysis to clinical neuropsychology, offered expert consultation over psychological testing and interviewing. He took valuable time from his own seminal research on attachment theory and couple relationships and on the psychology of the divorcing couple to offer assistance whenever I needed some.

Dr. Valerie Sinason, psychoanalyst and child psychotherapist and a dear friend of long standing, not only read the manuscript in its entirety but also supported my work and facilitated my growth over many decades, generously sharing her own crucial discoveries about the impact of extreme forms of child abuse. Dr. Estela Welldon, the international dean of forensic psychotherapists, became my first and most influential teacher in the forensic field. I cannot fully express how much of her clinical thinking and wisdom I have internalized over the years. Professor Susie Orbach and Dr. Joseph Schwartz have made so many contributions to the development of my psychoanalytical understanding that I often do not know which ideas originated in my consulting room and which derived from fruitful conversations—often heated ones—at the dining-room table.

Pauline Hodson, whom I had the honor of succeeding as chair of the Society of Couple Psychoanalytic Psychotherapists, offered crucial emotional and intellectual support during a period of "research exhaustion." Lloyd deMause, director of the Institute for Psychohistory and president of the International Psychohistorical Association, one of our most fearless researchers in the field of child sexual abuse, has taught me an unparalleled amount about child maltreatment and its causes and prevention since our first meeting in 1981, publishing my fledgling efforts in this field, for which I thank him tremendously. The sagacious and intellectually bountiful David Leevers read the manuscript in its entirety and made a bevy of extremely judicious comments. In addition, my good friend Margaret Bluman of Penguin Books served as an invaluable source of encouragement throughout the writing process.

Other professional colleagues who have made useful contributions to my thinking around the subject of sexual fantasy, sexual psychopathology, traumatology, and related clinical topics include Dr. Stella Acquarone, the late Mrs. Enid Balint, Dr. Bernard Barnett, Margaret Baron, Professor David Beisel, Professor Rudolph Binion, Dr. Thaddeus Birchard, Dr. Sandra Bloom, Professor George Bonanno, Professor Robert Bor, the late Dr. John Bowlby, Dr. Abrahão Brafman, the late Professor Margaret Brenman-Gibson, Christel Buss-Twachtmann, Donald Campbell, Judy Cooper, the late Dr. Murray Cox, Lynne Cudmore, Katy Dearnley, Zack Eleftheriadou, Dr. Susanna Isaacs Elmhirst, Dr. Laura Etchegoyen, the late Professor Reuben Fine, the late Lucy Freeman, Professor Jesse Geller, Professor Sander Gilman, the late Dr. Mervin Glasser, Dr. Lawrence Goldie, the late Professor Melvin Goldstein, Professor Jean Goodwin, Professor Dr. med. Michael Günter, Dr. Elif Gürisik, Professor Melinda Guttmann, Dr. David Hewison, Stevie

Holland, Professor Sheila Hollins, Dr. Earl Hopper, Oliver Howell, Oliver James, Dr. Cynthia Janus, Dr. Samuel Janus, Dr. Dorothy Judd, the late Dr. Melvin Kalfus, Pearl King, Professor Robert Langs, the late Dr. Margaret Little, the late Professor Ronald Mack, Dr. Joyce McDougall, Jeannie Milligan, the late Marion Milner, Professor Juliet Mitchell, Mary Morgan, Elspeth Morley, Dr. Robert Morley, Dr. Michael Moskowitz, Anna Motz, the late Professor William Niederland, Viveka Nyberg, Felicia Olney, the late Professor Mortimer Ostow, Professor Dr. med. Uwe Henrik Peters, Jennifer Riddell, the late Dr. Ismond Rosen, Joanna Rosenthall, Professor Peter Rudnytsky, Jane Ryan, the late Dr. Charles Rycroft, Dr. Allan Schore, the late Professor Flora Rheta Schreiber, Dr. Sonu Shamdasani, Professor Jerome Singer, Professor David Livingstone Smith, the late Professor Robert Stoller, Professor Herbert Strean, Helen Tarsh, Professor Bessel van der Kolk, Susan Vas Dias, Christopher Vincent, Dr. Hisako Watanabe, Kate White, Rachel Wingfield, and Dr. Sarah Wynick.

Former students and clinical supervisees with whom I worked closely during the writing of this book have also made a great contribution to my thinking, and in particular, I thank Rosemary Campher, Barry Christie, Valentine Davies, Derek Draper, Stefano Ferraiolo, Graeme Galton, Gillian Gordon, Lynn Greenwood, Tom Higgins, Joan Kingsley, Christine Miqueu-Baz, David O'Driscoll, Jane Wynn Owen, Gwendolyn Parkin, Adah Sachs, Camilla Sim, Betsy Spanbock, and Lili Tarkow-Reinisch—all extremely gifted clinicians in their own right.

I owe further thanks—for courtesies large and small—to Nadia Abisch, Yvonne Anderson, Craig Barbour, Peter Bazalgette, Marcel Berlins, Joe Callaghan, Debbie Catchpole, Robert Crozier, Tess Cuming, Jane Dony, Ben Dowell, Katie Ellis, Lisa Forrell, Elizabeth Hadland, Joanna Hall, Wendy Halsall, Sebastian Harcombe, Nicky Hughes, Venetia Kay, Reverend Beric Livingstone, Dr. Ben Maxwell, Dr. Caroline Maxwell, George Maxwell, Isobel Maxwell, John Noel, Lisa Perrin, Penny Potsides, Reverend John Priestley, Dr. Jonathan Riddell, Anthony Royle, Jonathan Sacerdoti, Paula Stone, Brandon Storey, Dan Welldon, and Matthew Williams.

Dr. Brendan MacCarthy, president emeritus of the British Psycho-Analytical Society, director emeritus of the Child Guidance Training Centre at the Tavistock Clinic and of the London Clinic of Psycho-Analysis, and my very favorite of psychoanalysts, died on December 22, 2005, just days before I had completed the first draft of this book.

Brendan knew all about this project on sexual fantasies, and he offered much sage advice throughout the research and writing period. His own groundbreaking work on the sexual abuse of very young children and his work on the treatment of incest survivors have made it possible for contemporary psychoanalytical clinicians to function more effectively in the "farther edges" of the field of trauma. A man of unique strength and gentleness, of fortitude and benignity, of rigor and flexibility, of warmth and toleration, of humor and gravitas, he remains my role model of compassion and inspiration, both professionally and personally, and it saddens me that he died before his time.

Finally, I thank Kim, who makes every day a concert, and the family for their constant love, and for so much more—*tacent, satis laudant.*

Brett Kahr
Centre for Child Mental Health
London
England
September 1, 2007

ANNOUNCEMENT:
The Sexual Fantasy Research Project

Brett Kahr will be conducting ongoing clinical and empirical research about the nature of our sexual fantasies. He would be pleased to hear from adults, aged eighteen years or older, not only those who reside in the United States of America, but anywhere in the world. If you wish to participate in this anonymous, confidential project, please contact:

www.sexualfantasyproject.com

Index